Owen Morgan

The Light of Britannia

The Mysteries of Ancient British Druidism Unveiled - The Original Source of Phallic

Worship

Owen Morgan

The Light of Britannia
The Mysteries of Ancient British Druidism Unveiled - The Original Source of Phallic Worship

ISBN/EAN: 9783337252854

Printed in Europe, USA, Canada, Australia, Japan

Cover: Foto ©ninafisch / pixelio.de

More available books at **www.hansebooks.com**

MORIEN

THE

LIGHT

OF

BRITANNIA.

THE

MYSTERIES OF ANCIENT BRITISH DRUIDISM UNVEILED:

THE ORIGINAL SOURCE OF PHALLIC WORSHIP.

AND THE

SECRETS OF THE COURT OF KING ARTHUR REVEALED:

THE CREED OF THE STONE AGE RESTORED.

AND THE

HOLY GRAEL DISCOVERED IN WALES.

BY

OWEN MORGAN, BB.D.

(MORIEN).

THE **W** WORD.

DEDICATION.

WE dedicate the following pages to the sacred memory of those of our ancestors, who, a vast multitude of aged and young Druids and Druidesses, were massacred in A.D. 61, on the Mona side of the Menai Straits, by the Roman legions under the command of General Paulinus Suetonius. The Roman general was accompanied by young Agricola, who afterwards became Governor of that part of the Britannic Dominion which the Romans succeeded in conquering, and, subsequently, was the father-in-law of Cornelius Tacitus, the brilliant Roman historian. The description of the said massacre, written by Tacitus, was, no doubt, imparted by Agricola to his eloquent son-in-law, and it is, therefore, we believe, the testimony of an eye-witness of the awful event! The slaughter of the British priests and priestesses, all of whom were non-combatants, was, however, speedily avenged, for the British nation uprose in arms and slew scores of thousands of the Romans, and, commanded by Queen Victoria I. (Buddug—Boadicea), marched, with fire in their eyes, towards Mona. At New Market, Flintshire, the British and Roman armies met in deadly conflict. According to Tacitus, who erroneously describes the scene of battle as near London, the Britons were eventually defeated in the battle. That Queen Victoria I. perished seems certain, for her grave is still shown near the said New Market, in the midst of many a heap of bones of warriors slain.

The following is the description by Tacitus of the slaughter of the Druids on the Menai shore :—" He " (General Paulinus Suetonius) " resolved to subdue the Isle of Mona " (Anglesey), " a place inhabited by a warlike people, and a common refuge for all discontented Britons. In order to facilitate his approach to a difficult and deceitful shore, he ordered a number of flat-bottomed boats to be constructed. In these he wafted over the infantry, while the cavalry, partly by fording over the shallows, and partly by swimming their horses, advanced to gain a footing in the island."

Tacitus seems to have mixed together two episodes in the invasion, and made both appear as one. The Romans must have arrived in the Menai Straits by sea, doubtless from Blackpool, Lancashire, a distance of 60 miles as the crow flies, or from the coast of Devonshire, and sailing by St. David's Head, Pembrokeshire, reached the coast of Caernarfon, a distance of about 170 miles. The Romans appear to have crossed the Menai at Pont-Din-Orwych, the ordinary ferry from time immemorial, and thus is described what the Romans beheld on the shore of Anglesey:— "On the opposite shore," states the Roman son-in-law of Agricola, "stood the Britons, close embodied, and prepared for action. Women were seen rushing through the ranks in wild disorder, their apparel funereal, their hair loose to the wind, in their hands flaming torches, and their whole appearance resembling the frantic rage of the Furies!

"The Druids were ranged in order, with hands uplifted, invoking the gods, and pouring forth horrible imprecations.

"The novelty of the sight struck the Romans with awe and terror. They stood in stupid amazement, as if their limbs were benumbed, rivetted to the spot, a mark for the enemy.

"The exhortations of the general diffused new vigour through the ranks, and the men by mutual reproaches inflamed each other to deeds of valour.

"They felt the disgrace of yielding to a troop of *women* and a band of *fanatic priests*; they advanced their standards and rushed on to the attack with impetuous fury.

"The Britons perished in the flames which they themselves had kindled."

The torches carried by the Druidesses, and the other flames referred to, indicate the atrocious barbarity perpetrated by the Romans upon "a troop of women" and "fanatic priests," was done at night. As if providentially left to mark the spot, a short time ago a Roman coin bearing the figures of Romulus and Remus, sons of Mars, or the devil, being suckled by a she-wolf, was discovered in a garden on the said side of the Menai, near a vast cemetery of bones, where the massacre is supposed to have taken place.

Doubtless all non-combatants—and all Druidic priests, like our present clergy, were emphatically so—together with the infirm and the aged of both sexes, had retired to the refuge of Mona, and were there butchered as described by Tacitus.

Their ancient religious lore will be found in the following pages.

THE  ECHO.

SYNOPSIS.

CHAPTER IV.

Mound graves of the Druids—what they signified—coffin called Ark in Welsh—why—Druidic Ecclesiastical Year—why the church is called the "Bride of the Lamb"—Arthur, the Sun as Arddâr or Gardener—Arth, Welsh for Bear—speculation as to why the Northern Constellation came to be named "Bear."

pp. 34–39.

CHAPTER V.

The year 4619, B.C.—Tebah, or Cow—Tebeth, the tenth month of the Sacred year of the Jews—Tebah, the name of the Ark of Noah—Aaron entering the Holy of Holies, signifying the same thing as Noah entering the Ark—the name Noah and the Welsh Naw, or Nine, identical—Ark of the Covenant called Arôn, identical with Arawn and Aaron—Bovine Enclosure of the Druids—the Sacred Cow: its four udders the four "rivers" of Eden—Bull Apis, of Egypt—two he-goats of the Day of Atonement—Sacred Cow of India—Light of Revelation went from the West and not from the East—Indian records to that effect—seas around Britain regarded anciently as sacred—Britain referred to as the Holy Island—the Beaver sacred to the Sun—the Taurine symbols of King Solomon's temple—Britain's Bulls of Many Hills; the signification of the name—Three Bulls and Three Cows of Druidism—the substitution of human Triads—their names—Egyptian Neith and Nêdd (Neath) identical—the symbol of the Triune Word of Druidism \|/—Mount Meru, Mynydd-y-Marrw and Mount Moriah, identical symbols—Divine soul of the Sun—illustration—Adam identical with the Druidic Tegid, Taliesin and Arthur—Eve, or Iva, identical with Mary, Miriam, Venus Genetrix, and Myrrah—the Hebrew and Phœnician Patriarchs identical with the Sun in Nine of the Constellations—Cromleâch, what it signifies.

pp. 40–59.

CHAPTER VI.

Three Sacred Apples of the Druids—the Apple sacred to the Sun—popular Apple Rites still observed by Celtic Nations—their signification—Cider a Sacramental drink among the Druids—Cakes and Ale and the Eucharist—the Juice of the Apple, with other ingredients added, named Lamb's Wool—why—Cauldron of Avagddu—Britain named "The Island of Apples," or *Insula Pomorum*—identity of "Holy Greal" with "Cread," or, round earth above the rational horizon, symbolised by a Sacred Round Dish—"Avalon," a fraud founded on truth—the whole of Britain the real Island of Apples—Britain a symbol of the whole earth, and each Druidic Circle a symbol of Britain—the Boiling of the Cauldron of Ceridwen signifying the fermentation of the earth in spring—the roasted apple, and the Old Sun's Death at the winter solstice—Homer's description of the round shield of Achilles—Round Towers of Ireland and the Maypole—the "Crowned Babe" of the Druids—God's melodious vociferation echoed back by Cêd, and the "voice" becoming incarnate in the Sun's luminous body—Melody of Memnon and its signification—Arthur's Court—Ireland and the Hades of the Druids—Annual Death of the Old Sun on the Tropic of Capricornus, at noon, every Dec. 20th in his ark, Cêd, 40 hours—Renewed, as a "Crowned Babe," on the morning of each Dec. 22nd—dramatically represented as in a stone kist in a tumulus—the tumulus a symbol of the Earth as the matrix of Cêd, and Mount of the Dead and the Garden of the Sun in springtime.

pp. 60–81.

CHAPTER VII.

CHAPTER VIII.

CHAPTER IX.

CHAPTER X.

CHAPTER XI.

CHAPTER XII.

CHAPTER XIII.

CHAPTER XIV.

TO THE READER.

IN sending forth the following pages to the public, it is necessary to say a few words in reference to one feature of the work, which, in a corrupt form, is well-known to the learned throughout the world, namely, Phallic worship. That is the name given to the worship, by the ancients, of the generating functions of the Sun and Nature. In that worship the worshippers employed certain symbols, which were formerly regarded as most holy. In course of many centuries, the nations lost sight of the original pious meanings attached to the said symbols, which eventually became associated with the orgies and lewd revelries of the Bacchanalia, which were carried on at night. The earnest-minded and pious religious philosophers of old attempted to stem the torrent of iniquity by instituting a system called the Lesser and Greater Mysteries, and to carefully ascertain, before admitting anyone to a knowledge of them, that he was qualified, morally and intellectually, to be entrusted with that knowledge. There cannot be much doubt the successors of those religious philosophers are the present order of brotherhood called Freemasons, which stands at the head of the fraternities of the civilised world. For the first time in the history of what may be called modern nations, as distinguished from the older nations which combated the Roman Empire in all its majesty, the Phallic Worship's incorrupted source is revealed in the following work.

Writing of the Phallica, whose original emblems were the acorn and cup of the Oak, the Rev. J. Lempriere, D.D., states: "It never conveyed, among the ancients, any impure or lascivious reflection." He states, also, "the people held it in the greatest veneration. It was looked upon as an emblem of fecundity."

Justin Martyr alludes to these things as follows: "For I myself when I discovered the evil disguise which was thrown around the divine doctrines of Christians by the evil demons, to deter others from them, laughed, both at the authors of these falsehoods and their disguise and the popular opinion: and I confess that I both prayed and strove with all my might to be found a Christian. Not because the doctrines of Plato are entirely different from those of Christ, but because they are not in *all* respects like them; no more, in fact, are those of others—the Stoics, for example, and poets and prose writers. For each, seeing through a *part* of the SEMINAL DIVINE WORD, that which was *kindred* to those, discoursed rightly.   *   *   We worship and love, next to God, the Word."   *   *   "All writers, through the engrafted *Seed of the Word* which was planted in them, were able to see the truth darkly, for the *seed and imitation of a thing which is given*, which is given according to capability, is one thing, and the *thing itself* of which the communication and imitation are given according to His grace, is another."—Justin Martyr's *Apology to the Emperor Antoninus Pius*, p. 68, s. 13.

So, according to this early Christian Father, the doctrine of the Seminal Logos of the Gentile world was an "imitation" of the incarnation of the Word in the Lord Jesus Christ, and Divine grace is an essence from the Word engrafting or fertilising dormant souls, considered as spiritual seeds.   Therefore, the Phallica, which was really the doctrine of the Seminal Word, symbolically rendered, was typical of the said incarnation.

The doctrine will be found dealt with, at large, in the following pages.

FIAT JUSTITIA, RUAT COELUM.

Ashgrove.
   Treforest.
      Glamorgan.

CHAPTER I.

THE student of religious beliefs finds that pious philosophers of the past, in their solemn inquiries into the mysteries of Time and Eternity, and the relation of the Creator and the created to each other, perceived two principal agents at work, engaged in perpetuating the things at first created in the visible world around them. Those two agents are the male and female attributes, which the said philosophers regarded as having emanated from the dual nature—masculine and feminine principles—in the Creator himself, who is invisible and incomprehensible to the human finite intelligence. The said pious philosophers of old adopted, as symbols of the said two attributes of the Creator, the acorn and the cup of oak, hence we discover that in the earliest epochs of recorded time, mankind assembled in oak groves for the purpose of tendering humble worship to the Almighty. By the acorn the worshippers symbolized the masculine attribute, and by the cup the feminine attribute, of the Creator's dual forces as manifested in the operations of the Sun and Nature. Both attributes themselves were invisible, and most mysterious and sacred, and all the worshippers could do was to employ, to indicate the two principles, the instruments used by them to carry on their Divine operations. In the earliest ages of the world, so far as we are acquainted with their history, the acorn was used to symbolize the expression of the Creator's fatherhood, and the cup the motherhood of Cêd, otherwise *Anian*, that is to say, the expression of the Anima of Nature's Mother. To the Creator himself the Druids gave the name Cêli (Concealing), and to His Consort the name

A

Cêd (Aid). Very early in the history of mankind, a certain
kind of idolatry of an obscene character, indeed, to our
mode of thinking, revolting nature, named Phallic
worship, identical with what is called Linga and Yoni
worship, arose among the nations from the above mode of
regarding the operations of the Creator's creating attributes,
the said attributes being regarded as emanations of
Omnipotence as active and passive from himself, and therefore the Creator and Cêd, his consort, father and mother of
the Sun and Nature, were a spiritual hermaphrodite, or
bi-sexual—both one—hence one of the Orphic hymns
refers to the Creator as--

"Jove is both male and an immortal maid."

Adam's Eve was extracted from himself. In the Bible both
the Phallic and Linga and Yoni worship are referred to by the
names "whoredom" and "harlotry." The Prophet Jeremiah
refers to those kinds of worship, or idolatry, by the words
"The Lord said also to me in the days of Josiah, the King,
'Hast thou seen that which back-sliding Israel hath done?
'She' (Israel as a nation) 'is gone up on every high mountain, and under every green tree, and there hath played the
harlot."[1] There is a deeper meaning than is generally
understood in the following observation of the Prophet
Ezekiel, "My Holy Name shall the House of Israel no
more defile, neither they nor their kings, by their whoredom
nor by the carcases of their kings in their high places.[2]
They have even defiled my Holy Name (W) by their abominations they have committed. * * Now, let them put
away their whoredom and carcases (emblems of the Phallica)
of their kings far away from me, and I will dwell in the
midst of them forever." In the Old Testament, the
expression "Name" and "Word" of God are synonymous
in meaning, and the name Jehovah signifies both to the

[1] Jeremiah III., 6. [2] Ezekiel XLIII., 7, &c.

Hebrews, for Jehovah is the Name Symbol of the Logos or the Word, the creating expression of Divine Will. But in the idolatry of the Phallus, Priapus, &c., which was represented in Britain by the May Pole, Obelisk, &c., the creating Word of God (Logos) was set forth by means of the Phallus, known also as Linga, and in Welsh by the name Said (Stem), and, originally, by the acorn. What was intended to be conveyed symbolically by each of the said masculine emblems was the fertilising force of the sun, transmitted by means of its rays, collectively considered, imparting to the seed germs in Venus the life in the earth's loam, in spring considered as her ovary, animated by the principle of germination or conception. Employing the Linga or Priapic emblem instead of the whole Word (\|/) to symbolise the creating expression of the Divine Mind, is what is meant by the prophets by the expression "defiling" the "Holy Name," in the idolatrous High Places of Palestine, which, until the introduction of the said emblems into them, were regarded as sacred to the worship of God's attributes through the Son or Sun and Cêd, through Nature, in their respective triune (\|/) manifestations in the course of the whole year.

The Shechinah and the Ark of the Covenant, in the Holy of Holies, symbolised the same masculine and feminine principles transmitted from the Creator and Cêd, as did the Acorn and Cup in the earliest open-air temples of God, whether in oak groves or in stone circles on the summit of mountains. The triune Shem, or Word, Jehovah, visited the patriarch Abraham in the Oak Grove of Mamre (Memra, Chaldean for Word of God), and he addressed the three, called "men" in our version, collectively as one Adonai or Lord. The Shechinah resting on the middle of the Mercy Seat, or the Seat of Reconciliation, states Calmet, was flanked, on each side, by a winged

bull, named Cherub. The Shechinah and the two
winged bulls implied precisely the same thing as the three
"men," but one Adonai, who visited Abraham under the
oaks, namely, the triune Name Jehovah, or the Word of
God. But, while the Shechinah symbolised the fatherhood
of the Creator transmitted through the sun, and the Ark
the motherhood of Cêd transmitted through the earth, the
two winged Cherubim, or Bulls, one on each side, would symbolise, in correct Druidism, the Creator's perfecting, and
defending from the destroyer, attributes. In other words,
the three emblems symbolised the sun's triplet emanations
in spring (the middle emblem the sun on March 21st); in
summer (June 21st); and in winter (December 20th); and
which three emanations the Druid poets personified by the
names Alawn (Father Hermes), Plennydd (Sun longest day),
and Gwron (Hero). Cêd's Anima, as expressed through the
earth in spring, the earth being then, in spring-time, in the
Zodiacal sign Virgo, or the autumnal Equinox point, was
symbolised by the Ark of the Covenant as the Consort of the
Shechinah, or the Creator's essence of fatherhood transmitted
through the sun into the earth in spring. It must be borne
in mind it was not the material earth that was meant by the
Ark, but the passive or feminine principle of the Creator
below and animating the material creation, which principle
was supposed to exhale through the earth's substance, and
compared to Sea Foam (the exhalation being called Venus,)
until it came into contact with the active principle of the
Creator, as father, passing to the seeds of the earth, through
the agency of the material sun, with propagating results;
the Manna in the Golden pot, and the Rod of Aaron, which
budded inside the Ark, typifying the said results.

That King David understood what the Ark symbolised
is evident enough by the following circumstances :—The

sacred penman describes the ceremony observed when the Hebrew nation conveyed the Ark of the Covenant from the house of Obed-Edom into the city of Jerusalem, and he describes the behaviour of King David on the said occasion. exhibiting his *membrum virilis* (translated "uncovered himself," and in the margin "the nakedness of his flesh"). "And David danced before the Lord with all his might, and David was girded with a linen ephod. And as the Ark of the Lord came into the city of David, Michal, Saul's daughter, looked through a window and saw King David leaping and dancing before the Lord, and she despised him in her heart." Later on, David returned to bless his household, and when he appeared to the offended Queen, the royal lady remonstrated with him in reference to what she regarded as his reprehensible conduct, earlier in the day, in the open streets of Jerusalem in the procession. With indignant scorn she said to him "How glorious was the King of Israel to-day, who *uncovered himself* to-day in the eyes of the handmaids of his servants" —his officers—"as one of the vain fellows *shamelessly* uncovereth himself." He wore the ephod, or sacred tunic, as a priest, and we are not to understand he threw it off. No doubt the royal palace had been, since the scene was witnessed by the "handmaids," the spectacle of quiet hilarity, as the blushing maidens whispered laughingly to each other what their royal master had been seen doing that day in front of the Ark in the open street of the Holy City—conduct peculiarly galling to a refined and cultured wife. But David had performed what he had done as a solemn religious ceremony, and was, in his turn now, much offended by the scorn and withering sarcasm of his offended queen. David answers her reproachfully with the words "It was before the Lord!"—in the foreground, apparently, with his face towards the Ark, his back being towards the

East point of the heavens, the opening leading to the Ark being in the direction of the East, and that was " before " the Lord, the Sun's virility, and David. wearing the ephod, was the Lord's representative on that occasion— David is the Druidic Dovydd, which signifies Tamer of the Elements, which, until the sun rises in spring in the east, are supposed to be in conflict with each other. " It was before the Lord," said he, and adding most ungenerously " The Lord who chose me before thy father (Saul) and before all his house, * * therefore I will play before the Lord, and I will yet be *more vile*"—apparently echoing the most galling word Michal had used—" and I will yet be more 'vile' than thus, and I will be base in mine own sight; and of the handmaids of my servants, whom thou hast spoken of, of them *I shall be had in honour*." The last observation was deliberately intended to hurt the feelings of the royal lady his wife. The narrative goes on to state Queen Michal had no issue to the day of her death. Why ? Because she had despised David's *membrum virilis* in its representative capacity, on the occasion in question. But Josephus (p. 152) states that Michal had had five children already by her real husband, from whom King David had stolen her away. This fact is mentioned to prove she was not barren naturally, but through a curse. David had dwelt long in Philistia, and he afterwards evinced so much respect for Baal, the sun god of that country, as to name one of his sons, Beelidah, after him. Queen Michal, prior to the foregoing described affair, had saved David's life when her father, King Saul, sought to kill him. She had dropped him from a window, and had afterwards placed an idol (Teraphim, which Dr. Inman states must have been handy) in his bed, and had reported that David was there ill. King David's " leaping and dancing" had nothing of a "vile" nature in them themselves, but exhibiting his *membrum virilis* was vile in the eyes of virtuous Michal, and one's sympathies are entirely with her. She thought her husband was publicly behaving lewdly in the open streets, in the presence of the assembled nation, in the principal city of Palestine; but the truth is, David thought he represented the "Husband" (Ishi—Hosea ii., 16) or Phallus, pertaining to the Ark, on the occasion, and he had performed by leaping and dancing and exposing the "nakedness of his flesh" a Phallic rite, a knowledge of which, as it appears, he had acquired in Philistia, and supposed it pertained also to the worship of Jehovah as well as to Baal. He was not far wrong, and his act is justified in the Bible by the curse which fell on poor Michal! It is clear the antics of King David on the occasion astounded the royal daughter of the late King Saul, which indicates that Phallic rites were then new to the nation of the Hebrews, or, at least, to the Queen. Voltaire referred jocularly to the Ark as "the box," but the reader of the foregoing will now understand that it was not a mere *box* but the vulva of Venus, wife of the sun, daughter of Cêd (Der Ketos), Consort of the Most High Celi, parents of both the sun and the infant earth, named Calen (chaotic lump) by the Druids, and developing to be Morwyn (Venus) when arrived at her conceiving period, or spring.

In the foregoing we have referred to the three personified masculine Triad, being the three principal emanations of Celi through the sun. We have now to refer to a feminine Triad from Cêd, through the earth, as emanations from the great mother Cêd (Cetus, otherwise Der Ketos), Consort of Celi. The sun, from December 22nd to March 21st, is, in Druidism, regarded as an infant, and is named Hu Gadarn (Hesus the Mighty); and, during the same period, the infant earth, his sister, is named, as already stated,

Calen. Then, by a process of miraculous transformation, both the sun and the earth acquire each a change compared to the change which takes place in both of the human sexes when they reach the state of puberty. Then, in the course of the succeeding rest of the year, we have the masculine emanations personified as three (\|/), as already described. Corresponding with them are the feminine triads, being three emanations of Latona, who, in Druidism, is named Cêd (Aid), who is identical with the Latin Cetus and the Greek Ketos, or Whale or Dolphin, the "Aid" and the mother of both the sun and Calen on December 22nd, as will be explained in the future pages. At the vernal equinox, March 21st, the earth is Mor-'wyn (The Holy Maid of the Sea Foam); at the summer solstice, June 21st, the earth is Blodwen (Holy Flora) ; at the autumnal equinox, September 23rd, the earth is Tynghedwen (Holy Fortune)[1], referring to the ripened crops. Tynghedwen has joined with her another feminine character called Dyrraith (Barren), identical with the Greek Beroe, and referring to the condition of the earth during the rest of the solar year, so that the third of the female triad is Tynghedwen-Dyrraith, considered as one female character with two attributes. The dual attribute of Dyrraith is barrenness, and furiousness in defence of her offspring—the offspring of Tynghedwen (Fortune) and Dyrraith, who is often called a greyhound bitch —hence, occasionally, a Cromlech is called Llech y Vil-Ast (Stone of the Greyhound Bitch). That name refers to the natural instinct implanted by the great Goddess Mother Cêd in all mothers, whether human or animal, to defend their offspring at the risk of their own lives, an instinct the Druids evidently regarded as being most sacred. Now, while the Hebrews by the Shechinah and the two winged bulls referred to the triune nature of the Name Jehovah,

---

[1] Drawn from Holy Fortune is the literal meaning of Tynghedwen.

the Consort Ark was a Unit, unless the variety of the coverings of the Holy of Holies implied two additional female characters, which we think they did. We must here bring another scriptural narrative to illustrate this :— " And the Philistines took the Ark of God, and brought it from Ebenezer to Ashdod. When the Philistines took the Ark of God they brought it into the temple of Dagon." *Dag* is Hebrew for fish, and the idol Dagon was a young man in the act of emerging from the mouth of the fish. "And when they of Ashdod arose early on the morrow, behold Dagon was fallen on his face to the earth before the Ark of the Lord. And they took Dagon and set him in his place again. And when they arose early on the morrow morning, behold Dagon was fallen upon his face to the ground, before the Ark of the Lord, and the head of Dagon and both the palms of his hands were cut off on the threshold, only the stump of Dagon was left of him." In the margin is given " the fishy part "—Dagon's upper part coming out of the fish (out of Cetus or Der Ketos) was a symbol of the infant sun. It appears the writer of the above narrative sought to convey that during each night Dagon had amorously sought the Ark, and that on the second attempt upon the virtue of the Arkite Goddess of Israel, he was nearly annihilated by her husband (Ishi), the God of Israel, but not the Almighty Celi of Druidism; and that Dagon, in endeavouring to come out for a purpose had received the *coup de grace*, and tumbled out of the " fishy part," which is said to be left " empty" (Rik in Hebrew). It appears from the above that the Ark symbolised Venus, while the outer covering, which was of the skin of the whale (Ketos), symbolised Cêd, the mother of Venus and the rest, Flora, and Tynghedwen-Dyrraith. The Phallic nature of the narrative is further shown by what follows :—" The hand of the Lord," we

are informed, "was heavy upon them of Ashdod, and He
destroyed and smote them with "Emerods." Now, Calmet,
in reference to the word "Ophelim" in the original, which in
the authorised version is translated "Emerods," states,
"Interpreters are not agreed as to the signification of the
word Ophelim." On turning to Dr. Inman's *Ancient Faiths*
(Vol. I., p. 18), we find that Omphalos signifies Navel, and
that by dividing the word Omphalos we find that Om signifies
maternity, and Phallos paternity, hence the name Phallus for
the Linga or Priapus. We, therefore, conclude that the
terrible disease which afflicted the Philistines was not due to
"Emerods," but to the disease of the *membrum virilis*. In
the original Hebrew the word "Ophelim" occurs in Deut.
xxxviii., 27, and the particular effects of the disease are
described in the following significant passage :—"And thou
(the sufferer) shalt *grope* at noon day," and the consequent
result of the malady is shown by the words :—"And thou
shalt betroth a wife, and another shall lie with her,"
clearly implying the "Ophelim" would make him incapable
to perform the marital obligation, owing to the diseased
condition of his *membrum virilis*.

The poor Philistines decided to send back to the Jews
their Ark, stealing which, and especially the insulting
conduct of Dagon, had brought such sufferings upon them.
Like honest people, they decided upon making what
amends they could for the mistake which they had
committed through ignorance, on behalf of Dagon and
themselves, by forwarding with the Ark a "trespass-
offering." That meant an offering to the Lord for a sin
committed through ignorance.[1] " And he shall make
amends for the harm he hath done in the holy thing, and
shall add the *fifth* part thereto, and give it unto the priest,

[1] Lev. v., 16—19.

and the priest shall make an atonement for him with the Ram and the trespass-offering; and it shall be forgiven him."

The Philistines, however ignorant of other things, seem to have known the demands of the law of Moses in such offences as they had committed, for we are told distinctly that the number of articles forwarded with the Ark were *five* golden "Ophelims," and five golden mice. Unquestionably the *five* golden "Ophelims"—the same name given to the disease as to the *membrum virilis*—were on behalf of Dagon, who, as implied by the offering, had offended through ignorance. Golden mice were, according to Selden, votive offerings in the East, for lustration and cleansing, and five were offered now on behalf of the five Cities of Philistia.[1]

The Ark of the Covenant was placed by the Philistines in a cart, drawn by *two* milch cows, which had, at the time, young calves. A cow is called Tebah in Syriac and in the Egyptian language, from which the name of the City of "Thebes" is so called, and it implies the City of the Sacred Cow. During the period the sun rose in spring in the zodiacal constellation of the Bull (from 4,619 B.C. to 2,504 B.C.), the Egyptians had a Sacred Bull, called Apis, as representing the sun at that season of the year. The earth's power of conception at the same period would be symbolised by a Sacred Cow, afterwards symbolised by Venus. The Druidic Twba, from which the English Tub is derived, seems to have been given mistakenly to the Arkite Cow of Egypt, or *vice versa.* Druids, in very remote times, symbolised Cêd, Venus's mother, floating in the sea of Annwn (chaos) by the figure of a bare pole, or naked, ship, or tub. When the Sacred Cow—the Ashtaroth of the Zidonians—was adopted to symbolise the Arkite earth,

---

[1] Eadie's Bible Note to Lev. v., 5.

the old appellation of Mother stuck to the Sacred Cow. It should be understood the great Mother Cêd's three emanations were understood by the female trinity of the Druids, and the three graces of Greece. We know that Homer, 3,000 years ago, in describing Ulysses visiting the British Island, met there a priest whom Homer describes as a " Mighty Theban."[1]   The *two* Cows, accompanying the Ark, " took the straight way to the House of the Sun, that is Beth-Shemesh, lowing—' bellowing the want they felt '—as they went along, and turned not aside to the right hand or to the left ; and the Lords of the Philistines went after them to the border of Beth-Shemesh."

The Ark and the two Cows—white ones, no doubt—now turned to the field of Joshua, identical with Hu Gadarn or Hesus the Mighty of the Druids, otherwise Taliesin, Tegid, &c., and stood there, where there was a great stone (Obelisk or Phallus symbol ?).   The name of the great stone was "Abel," which, in Druidism, signifies Son of the Sun, or of Hu Cylch y Ceugant, which implies the Son of the Almighty Celi, of the Circle of Infinitude.   But "Abel," in the Shemitic pedigree is Dis or Typhon, as will be shown presently. "And the Levites took down the Ark of the Lord, and the coffer that was with it, wherein the jewels of gold were, and put them on the great stone."   To adorn it probably like adorning a May Pole.   " And the men of Beth-Shemesh "—who were Jews—" looked into the Ark "— when in contact with the Obelisk—" and they, to the number of fifty thousand and seventy, were killed by the Lord ! " We agree with Dr. Chalmers, it was no wonder the people of Beth-Shemesh were anxious to get rid of the Ark !   It " killed," or caused suffering, everywhere except among its favourites, the Levitical priesthood !

---

[1] *The Odyssey.* Book IV.

Now, the inference is the following: the Philistines, it is implied, knew the Ark was the consort of the God of the Jews, whose virility the Shechinah symbolised, and by sending the *two* white cows with the Ark, they sent *two* female consorts for the *two* winged Bulls, one on each side of the Shechinah, on the lid of the Mercy Seat. They themselves represented Baal (Sun) as a Bull, and his consort by the Cow Ashtaroth, who was, afterwards, like Isis II., of Egypt, humanised; but the horns were left on the head of each, as subsequently the ram's horns were left on the head of Jupiter Amon, who was originally Aries or Ram. The narrative goes on to state the priests sacrificed the two cows on the spot: they would have no other goddess than the Ark. They stuck to the Virgin Venus and her surrounding symbols.

BLODWEN   MORWYN   TYNGHEDWEN
(Flora)   (Venus)   (Ceres)

CHAPTER II.

THE British Druids compared the annual journey
of the sun to the duration of human life. He
is "born" at the winter solstice, and begins
his career as a child, called Hu Gadarn (Hesus the Mighty),
on December 22nd. At the vernal equinox (March 21st)
he reaches maturity, and is then married to Mor'wyn, the
Earth; described poetically as the Holy Maiden of the Sea
Foam, or Venus, otherwise Aphrodite. The result of their
union is the seed germs of the earth's ovary receiving from
him (the sun), the fertilising influence, and they instantly
begin to germinate. The process of development continues,
under the fostering care of the influence of the Father, by
the agency of the sun, and of Cêd, through the agency of
Venus, Holy Maiden of the Sea Foam. The personified sun

drops his original title of Hu Gadarn (Hesus the Mighty), and assumes the new title of Tegid, on his marriage day, March 21st. Tegid signifies All Beautiful, and the title is so retained until the summer solstice (June 21st), when he is in the full effulgence of his strength, and his wife is now in her bloom, and is called Blodwen (Holy Flora). Between the summer solstice and the autumnal equinox (Sept. 23rd), he begins to decay, and comes to be called, Tegid Voel, or Bald-All-Beautiful, in reference to the sun's rays beginning to diminish in strength and quantity, the rays being compared to hair, and the sun's disc to a head. His wife now (September) gives birth to her offspring, meaning the "fruits of the Earth." She is named Holy Fortune, or Tyng-hedwen-Dyrraith, and is endowed with the characteristics already described. The sun now enters upon the period of old age and decrepitude. He is now called by divers names or titles, namely, Dyvnwawl Moelmud (Sombre Light, Bald and Dumb) ; Arawn (slow, or to wait) ; Said-Wrn (Saturn). This name signifies Said (Linga or Phallus), and Gwrn (Urn)—a matrix symbol. Gwrn, or Urn, was the vessel in which, in ancient times, the ashes of the Druidic dead were deposited, and the name Said-Wrn (Saturn) implies that the virile power of the personified sun has disappeared, and that his *membrum virilis* is now dead, or unable to reanimate the seeds in the Urn, and its former force is itself now exhausted in the earth, considered as an Urn. Another title of the sun, in his full strength, is Arthur, or Arddir (gardener or husbandman), and he is the husbandman of the Earth—the Garden. What has caused an immense amount of confusion, is the practice of the Druids, when the Druidic system of religion was familiarly known in all its details, to, sometimes, give the names Hu Gadarn, Arthur, Tegid, Taliesin, Tegid Voel, &c., indiscriminately to the personified Sun in *every* stage of his annual progress, instead of limiting each title to the particular season to which it legitimately belongs. All titles of the sun, except Hu Gadarn, are comprehended in the great Triad, or the Druidic Trimurti, called Plennydd, Alawn, and Gwron, explained in Chapter IV. The same remark applies also to the variety of titles given by the Druids to the earth during the year. Thus, the three Queens of Arthur (the sun), are described Morgwen la Fai (the earth in spring) ; the second is said to be the Queen of North Wales (the earth in summer) ; the third, the Queen of Desert Places (the earth in winter). Again, the three fair ladies of Arthur's Court are said to be, Lady Dywin (incorrectly spelt " Dywir ") ; Lady Enid ; and Lady Tegau Eurvron. The " Court " is the sacred circle, called the " Round Table," but really the Gorsedd, or great stone circle of Druidism. " Gorsedd " signifies Great Throne.

Lady Enid (Soul) is identical with the Holy Maiden of the Sea Foam (Venus). She is said to be the daughter of the Niwl (the mist). An old Welsh adage states :—

> " Niwl y Gwanwyn Gwasarn Gwin (old spelling " Gwynt).
> (Mist in spring is the source of wine).

Three other adages are translated as follow : —

> Mist in Summer is the source of heat,
> Mist in Autumn is the source of rain,
> Mist in Winter is the source of snow.

Gwenwyver corresponds with Flora. The name is a compound of three words : Gwen (Holy), 'Wy (Water), and Mêr, mutated to Vêr (Essence). The whole compound signifies Holy—Water—Essence, meaning the sap of the earth streaming up in vegetation and trees under the influence of the heat left in the atmosphere at night, after the disappearance of the day sun, and called the nocturnal sun (Bacchus). The first shows Enid is the daughter of warm

Humidity, identical with Neptune,[1] who, correctly, is the second person of the Latin Trinity, who is also named Oceanus. Niwl (mist) is the joint influence of the Eternal Father Celi, and the Eternal Mother Cêd. The passive exhalation arises from Cêd through the earth; the masculine or active principle passes from Celi through the sun, which imparts the fertilising influence to humidity, which communicates it to the seed germs, causing them to fructify and develop.

Dywyn (to make fair), signifies the earth's surface in summer, and corresponds with both Flora and Juno. Tegau Eurvron signifies the earth's surface at harvest-time (Ceres). Tegau signifies to beautify. Eurvron signifies Golden Breasted, and implies the golden ripened fruits of the earth. Her symbols are a variegated-dyed mantle, a golden goblet, and a knife. Her beautiful mantle signifies the charming dyes of the earth's produce; her golden goblet, the liquor-producing fruits of the earth; her knife, the cutting operations of harvest-time. It must be borne in mind the journey of the sun up the ecliptic, from December 22nd to June 21st—from the Tropic of Capri to the Tropic of Cancer—was divided into *Seven* stations, with three principal stations which embraced the seven, hence the north point of the heavens, where the sun ends his journey upwards, is called Septentrio—seven in three—in Latin. The sun in seven stages is the seven gods of the Phœnicians. The sun in three principal stations, viz., at the vernal equinox, summer solstice, and the winter solstice, is personified in each, and is named in reference to the three stages, by the Druids, Alawn, Plennydd, and Gwron (beginning at the vernal equinox): Hermes

---

[1] Jupiter is the Sun on March 21st; Neptune, Sun on June 21st; and Pluto is the Sun on December 20th.

(Harmony). Causitor, and Hero (Arthur, St. George, &c.).
Lady Enid, or Venus (Earth, on March 21st), was represented by the Pythian priestess of the Delphic oracle, as
we shall explain farther on. The said seven personifications
of the sun's seven emanations are, as already stated, the
seven gods of the Cabiri (Phœnicia), who are said to be the
sons of Samin, or Heaven, meaning the Most High Celi
of Druidism. The earth's anima is also divided into *seven*
corresponding feminine emanations, called the Seven
Atlantides, comprehended in *three* principal feminine consorts, already named and referred to under several poetical
figures. The masculine triad is symbolised by the sign /I\ (on
the forehead it was worn thus : ᵜ, as the Jews do still the
letter Shin ש on the Phylactery), the female by \I/. The
masculine emanations, considered collectively, are referred
to as Tan, which is a corruption of the Druidic Tâd
(Father), and whose three emanations are Creator,
Decorator, and Heroism. The sign is now represented thus :

The loop implies the Vulva of the supreme Mother, Cêd
(Cetus). It is a symbol of Egypt and among other Eastern
nations, and which, states St. Jerome on Ezekiel ix. 4–6,
is the sign of the cross. Baring-Gould states that Gesenius
in his Hebrew Lexicon states, "Tau" is the signum
cruciforme (sign of the cross). It was the "mark" placed
by a man robed in white, like a Druid, on the foreheads
of the men who sighed and cried for all the abominations
that were done in the midst of Jerusalem. It was also the
sacred protective "mark of Cain" (Nôd in Welsh, and it was

to the land of Nod Cain went). It is also shown as a tripod or three props, as the Adlais ("Atlas") or reverberation of Celi's Word, under every cromlech, holding it up, that is to say, the top slab—symbol of the flat earth. It was anciently believed the earth was flat-bottomed, but rising conically out of the water, and held up underneath by the reverberation of the Word, or commanding utterance, of God, symbolised by the three props, thus /I\. This is the idea symbolised by the sign, and referred to in the Epistle to the Hebrews as follows : " Who being the brightness of His Glory, and the express image—or reflection—of His person, and *upholding* all things by the Word of His power: " and by St. John by the words, "And he was clothed with a vesture dipped in blood; and his Name is the Word of God," Rev. xix., 13; and by St. Peter, who states, " For this they are ignorant of, that by the Word of God the heavens were of old, and the earth standing " (by the Word of God) " out of the water and in the water," II. Peter, ii., 5. It is seen here St. Peter himself was not infallible.

We proceed now to describe the negative principles of the Kingdom of God according to Druidism. There are three evil masculines, opposed to the three good emanations, symbolised by the sign \I/, or, as reverberating and holding up the earth, shown thus /I\. The evil ones are personified also, and named Avagddu, Cythraul, and Atrais, which signify Darkness, Pulveriser, and Soddener. These three, like the Three Goddesses of good principles, have three consorts, viz:—Annhras, Malen, and Mallt, or Graceless, Grinder, and Soddener. Now, the three Marys in the Gospel are the consorts of the Triune Word or Logos, but like the corrupt Oriental trinities generally, the third is a devil, and Mary—Mary Magdalen—is a she-devil with *seven* devils in her! These are the seven evil emanations opposed to the

seven stations of the sun, and seven daughters of Atlas (Adlais)
(the earth's seven corresponding emanations), when, step by
step, he passes during the year through the seven planetary spheres.   But the physical fertilising influence on the
seeds of the earth, was not the only good the sun exercised on
earth.   It was supposed that when he was " renewed " or re-
born a babe from Cêd on December 22nd, myriads of lives,
apart from physical or natural bodily existence, emanated at
the same time from Cêd, the universal mother.   The sun was
their leader from Gwenydva, a district of Annwn, or Hades,
their birthplace, and those lives, transmitted from the sun,
evolved through the animal creation up to the human.   Their
mechanical or physical animation was the contribution of
Cêd, the universal mother ; but, intellectually, the " lives "
would be inert without the additional Awen, " inspiration," or
the reasoning faculty, imparted to them direct from God,
through the sun.   In the system of Nature, the Druids
regarded the space traversed by the sun from the first day of
the solar new year (December 22nd) to the equinoctial line,
or the vernal equinox (March 21st), as the kingdom of God's
system of lives, occupied also, the Druidic philosophers
thought, by evil influences, until chased away by the march-
ing up of the sun's Divinity.   Man, they believed, occupies
during the present life the middle line of that system
(the equinoctial line of the moral world).   He is entrusted
with free will, and is a free agent; can do good or evil as he
pleases, hence his moral responsibility.   The space from
the equinoctial line of the moral system *downwards* to
where the old sun *disappears* on December 20th, is, in
the moral world, occupied by the " lives " of the animal
kingdom in their tribes or divers species, in the moral
system of nature.   They cannot innovate, or change, or
improve their condition, but are bound by the rules of an
unerring fate or law, which is called instinct, and Greddv

by the Druids. But the nearer certain species of animals are to the "line of liberty" occupied in that system by man, the more evidence of intelligence they manifest. This animal space is called, in Druidism, Cylchau yr Abred, or, in classic writings, the Circles of Transmigration, or of Metempsychosis. "Cylchau yr Abred" signifies, the Circles of the Father-Son (Ab) of all things that run (Rhêd).

The bottom rung of the circles is down south in Annwn (Hades) ; and its top rung on the equinoctial line of liberty (east to west), occupied by mankind, where, for the first time, a created being has been entrusted with capacity enough to light and control fire. The Druids saw that the Creator made nothing in vain, and that nothing, except forms, were annihilated in the physical world. They believed therefore that human lives are of eternal duration, constantly in honour or dishonour ; and eventually, through Celi and Cêd's infinite mercy, to enter into everlasting honour and happiness. But what of the lives of animals ? They theorised and supposed that animal lives were human lives in process of gradual development, developing, transmigrating, and eventually to attain to the line of liberty. It should be borne in mind, the lives and not the bodies of animals they considered. The circles of transmigration were the "Hell" of the Druids ; and a man who had polluted his soul by evil deeds and evil thoughts, during his existence as a free agent, was relegated to that depth in the circles of transmigration to which he himself had qualified himself during his state of free will, which was deemed a state of probation. One of the maxims of the Druids was "Nid cir i Annwn ond unwaith" (there is but one visit to Annwn, or Hades). The meaning is, that no man, whatever his conduct had been during life, would be so devoid of goodness, as to have qualified himself to occupy a position lower than that occupied in the system of nature by the lowest animal in that system.

On the northern side of the equinoctial line on which human existence is stationed in this life, is the Gwynvyd, or Heaven, of the Druids. When the sun has ascended northwards of the celestial equinoctial line in spring, he gradually increases in glory, power, and majesty, and the earth under his influence blooms, and scatters fragrance, and is a veritable garden of the Lord ! The earth is then "a land flowing with milk and honey." It is then the Adonidis Hortus (the garden of Adonis or the Sun) of Phœnician worshippers. The prophet Isaiah (xiv., 13), refers to the north in these words :—"Thou hast said in thine heart, I will ascend into heaven; I will exalt my Throne above the stars of God; I will sit also upon the mount of the congregation, *in the sides of the north;* I will ascend above the heights of the clouds; I will be like the Most High." Dr. Delitzsch translates the above differently; instead of "Mount of the Congregation" he renders it "the Mount of the Assembly of Gods," and "in the corner of the north" instead of "sides" of the Authorised Version. He then states " the reference cannot be to Mount Zion, which was neither a northern point of the earth, nor was it situated on the north of Jerusalem," and he adds that "the passage in Psalm xlviii., 3, has no bearing on this passage at all." " The prophet," the learned writer states, " makes the King of Babylon speak according to the general notion of his people * * * who placed it (Heaven) on the summit of the northern mountains, which were lost in the clouds; just as the Hindoos place it on the fabulous mountains of Kailàsa, which lie towards the north beyond the Himalayas." Of course, the inference as to what Isaiah *meant* by the expression "corner of the north" and "the Mount of the Assembly of Gods," is Dr.

Delitzsch's own. What we assert is, that the Druids believed the entrance to Gwynva or Gwynvyd, their names for the Abode of the Blessed, was in the northern heavens, at, apparently, the point attained by the sun at the summer solstice, or in the Tropic of Cancer; and the reader of the foregoing passages will have understood their reasons for that belief. Arthur seems to have been associated in the minds of the Druids with the exercise of the sun's greatest force in dispelling darkness and its destructive agents in the physical world during his journey up the ecliptic. In the Welsh language, the apparent circle traversed by the constellation Ursa Major around the polar star, is named the Round Table of Arthur in the heavens, and the Druidic name of Ursa Major is "Arthur's Plough," which conveys the notion of a farm or garden in the heavens. The stars are referred to by the Druids, as Arthur's heifers—the Lyre is called Arthur's Harp. It will have appeared to the reader the Druids supposed the godly enter heaven in the northern sky, and that the first entrance into life is from the southern point. Faber, correcting Pope's translation of a passage in Homer's *Odyssey*, lib. xiii., v. 102, renders the passage thus :—

"Sacred the *South* by which mankind descend :
But the gods enter at the northern end."

The cave of nymphs, to which the passage directly refers, is clearly intended to symbolise the old ideas respecting the future, after the termination of each earthly existence, of reward and punishment, and that by "gods," the godlike is meant. The godly enter heaven northward ; the ungodly are relegated back to the circles of Metempsychosis in the southern direction, from the moral equinoctial line, or the line of liberty of human existence, on earth. That was the Druidic theory.

CHAPTER III.

IT should be borne in mind by the reader that the Druids, in their enquiries after the Divine nature, while tracing it by the light of nature, passed beyond the boundary of the material world. They supposed, as already mentioned, the Divine nature consisted of two principles, the active and the passive, and that those principles were intellectual, omnipotent, and eternal. Beyond them no mind could go, hence to the Almighty the Druids gave the name Celi, or Keli (Concealing), and to the passive principle the name Cêd (Aid). In course of time, it appears, the Druids gave the name Cêd to that constellation (Cetus) in which the sun, between 8,000 and 10,000 years ago, appeared in the south at the winter solstice, or on December 20th, in exact Druidism. The Latins called a whale, Cetus; and the Greeks named it Der Ketos; and the world, corrupting Druidism, came to suppose a whale to be the mother of the sun, because the Druids had taught that Cêd was the Consort of the Celi Almighty. How other nations came to confound Cêd with a whale, with Cetus and Ketos, or dolphin, we know not. It is evident the Druids believed in the eternity of matter in an atomic condition, and also in the eternity of water; and that the passive, that is, the feminine, principle of the Divine nature pervaded both from eternity. Theorising as to the origin of the universe, they, like St. Paul, believed, " the invisible things of Him, from the beginning of the world, are clearly seen, being understood by the things that are made; even His eternal power ;" the Druidic Philosopher took in his hand the lamp of Nature, and sought to explore the mysteries of the eternal Celi and Cêd, by its light. He imagined a period before creation began, when darkness and silence pervaded illimitable space, and when only the Celi, Cêd, and the atomic elements and water existed. Employing the figure of the relation of husband and wife to each other, to the Celi and Cêd to each other, the Druidic Philosopher theorised, that, at some inconceivable distant period, the active principle of Celi concentrated its energy in the passive principle of Cêd, and as the result of contact, as in electricity, a ball of dazzling brilliancy, called the Sun (Son) of God, bounded into space, from the nature of Cêd, and illuminated the awful gloom. Immediately after, under the sun's influence, the atomic elements began to evolve into solidity, and to it, as plastic chaos, the Druids gave the name Calen. To this day a formless mass of anything, such as a lump of butter, soap, etc., is called " Calen " in the Welsh language.

The moment after the active work of the creation of the universe had commenced by the Celi and Cêd, the Celi was named Iòn (Leader Lord) ; his spirit in the sun was called Iona (Dove) ; and Cêd (Aid)'s emanation pervading matter was named Anian (Anima Mundi). Cêd was supposed to be black, and as the consort of the Celi, but . afterwards mother of the Sun, she was called y Vorwyn Ddu (the Black Virgin), mother of Venus. She was called also Latona, or Moon—Lloer in Welsh. Latona is simply another name for the great mother-goddess Cêd, the Cetus of Latins, and the Ketos of the Greeks. The moon, six days old, is meant, resembling in shape a boat, which was used as one of the symbols of Cêd, because it was supposed she pervaded the waters of eternity before the

sun and earth were "born" of her. This is the reason
why the moon came to be called the Queen of Heaven,
Consort of Almighty Celi.   The sun itself was represented
as the son of Celi and Cêd; but the High Priest of the
Sun on earth, the Archdruid, was the symbol of the
incarnating power of the sun and earth in spring, and
the Druidic "Church" was Morwyn or Mary, the incarnated "Sister-Spouse" of the Archdruid, called Gwyddon
or Odin.   All seeds in the concrete were the gift of Cêd,
but their fructification was performed in the spring time of
the year.   It seems, as said before, exceedingly probable
that the Latin name for seed, *Satus* (Cetus), is due to this
most ancient idea that all seeds came from Cêd, the Consort
of the Most High God, whom the Greeks called Der Ketos.

In the description of the sanctuary of the Hebrews, which,
owing to its vast importance in dealing with the origin of
religious beliefs, we shall examine at some length, there
appears to be a very curious mixing of figures or symbols.
We have there goat's hair and ram's skin brought into
curious juxtaposition.   At the winter solstice the sun is
in the sign of the Goat (Capri); at the vernal equinox
the sun is in the sign of the Ram.   It appears as if the
Jews symbolised the earth at the vernal equinox, or spring,
by the emblem of a goat, and the sun, at the same time, by
the emblem of a Ram or Aries, which was the symbol of
Jupiter Amon (In Hidden Father).   The ancients, when
the sun was in the sign of the Goat (December 22nd,)
would naturally symbolise the earth's Anima by the figure
of a she-goat, and the Hebrews by the goat's hair of the
membrum virginalis of the Eastern (March 21st) entrance
into the Holy of Holies, seem to have dragged the goat's
hair symbol from its proper place, at the winter solstice,
and used it to symbolise the appendages of the *membrum*

virginalis of Venus, or the earth's conceiving power in the springtime, instead, and thereby making the She-Goat to be the consort of the Ram (Aries)!

The Druids held that the passive principle of the first feminine cause, personified as Cêd, operated through her conceiving attribute, personified as Venus Geneterix, and influenced the material earth from below the earth. Cêd bears the same relation to Venus as the Almighty does to Apollo (the sun). One is regarded as agent of the great Mother, and the other of the great Father. Cêd's influence from below was supposed to be exercised by exhalations— the breathings, as it were, of the great Mother. God's influence, from above, through the sun, was supposed to be exercised by the agency of warm dew or humidity. This agent of the Father was personified by the Druids and named Nevydd Nâv Neivion. Nevydd (Heavenly), Nâv (Constructor), Neivion (Volatile or buoyant), Iôn (Leader Lord). The name, therefore, signifies: Iôn, Heavenly-Constructor-by-the-Agency-of-Humidity. As a poetical personification, Nevydd Nâv Neivion is identical with Neptune, otherwise Oceanus, the second person of the Latin trinity, and implies the sun as the transmitting cause, as warmth in dew, on June 21st.

The Cave and the Pythoness seated on the tripod astride the Cave, at Delphi, symbolised both the navel and Cêd's conceiving power, personified as Venus Geneterix. Both Apollo and Jupiter are names of the sun in spring, but the name Apollo refers to the sun as the Son of the Creator, who is referred to by the Druids as the higher Sun of the Circle of Infinitude, above the Zodiacal sun; and Jupiter is the expression of the Creator's inner and hidden creating fatherhood or Pater. The sun, in his old

age at the winter solstice, described as Saturn, is often confounded with the Almighty, and Saturn, in consequence.
is said to be the father of Jupiter, Neptune and Pluto. The
Cave at Delphi, underneath the tripod, symbolised the matrix
of Cêd, herself influencing her daughter, Venus, seated on
the tripod. The Priapian or middle staff of the tripod caused
conception ; the umbilicus. or navel, from the mother to the
child or seed, continued the nourishing work until the birth.
The Greek poem *Eumolpia* states the navel symbol at
Delphi was sacred to the earth (Venus) and to Neptune.
That signifies the warm humidity at night caused by the
sun's heat in summer, nourishes, in combination with the
feminine principle, the growing seeds of the earth, as the
navel attached to the mother transmits by her own agency
nourishment to the growing babe in her womb. Therefore, the root of each seedling is compared to an umbilicus,
or navel, and it and the matrix of the seedling are agents
of Venus Genetrix.

Now, the round surface of the earth above the rational
horizon is the belly of Cêd, and she is the Druidic circular
"church." Her centre surface to the womb is the navel
and vulva symbols of the goddess Venus Genetrix, or the
conceiving and nourishing powers of the earth personified.
In the Welsh language the navel is called Bogel. It is
compounded of Bo(d), existence, and Cêl (mutated to Gêl),
concealed—concealed existence—referring to the concealed
living seedling of the earth, and the living child in the
womb of the mother. The centre of a wheel is likewise called
Bogel, or navel, in that language. The form of the word
"Navel" leads us to believe it is a Welsh word, and that
it is a compound of Nâv (God constructor) and El (Haul,
or Sun), and not derived from the Sanscrit *Nabhi* as
scholars suppose. Celi and Cêd are one, and co-operate

in the work of creation. Another figure under which the centre of the Druidic circle went was garden; the garden of the sun—the garden which the Lord himself planted. Venus, as the personified conceiving surface of the earth, is called the garden of Adonis; and the Roman Catholic Church, borrowing the figure, and substituting the Virgin Mary for Venus, describes the Virgin Mary as a garden; as a Mystical Rose: and as the Ark of the Covenant: and confounding her with Cêd describes her as the Mother of God (sun of the new year—December 25th in Julius Cæsar's Calendar), and with the crescent moon, six days old, as a symbol of Cêd under the figure of a boat, describes her as the Queen of Heaven. Thus the Virgin Mary is confounded with both Cêd and with her daughter, Morwyn or Venus Marina, otherwise Venus Geneterix.

The great Druidic temple of Avebury (Ab and Rhi: God the Father—sun and Son) is a vast circle, with a very lofty bank sloping back all round the circle. At the base of the bank inside is a deep trench for holding water. Running round the outer edge of the vast arena, enclosed by the deep and broad trench, were one hundred great stones placed endways in the earth, and fixed at regular intervals from each other. This vast enclosure symbolised the round earth above the rational horizon, and the hundred stones and the circular fosse full of water symbolised the sea, and illimitable space around and beyond it. The centre of the enclosure was a symbol of the earth as the garden of Arthur (the sun), otherwise Adam (Ad Hama is Persian for the sun), Noah, &c., the gardener of the Creator. Thebes, the celebrated Egyptian city, was a similar symbol of Venus as a garden, but instead of Venus it was said to be sacred to the holy Tebah, which, it will be remembered in the Egyptian language, signifies cow. Afterwards, the cow was substituted by a second Isis, the first being Isis the great mother, precisely as Cêd is the mother of Venus. Most writers confound the two Isises—mother and daughter —with each other. We remind the reader that the en- closed garden commenced to be sacred to the cow about 4619 B.C., when the sun in spring commenced rising in the sign of the Bull of the Zodiac, and the sun, therefore, came to be regarded as a bull himself. No doubt the "hundred gates" of the City of Thebes were really one hundred stons like those at Avebury, encircling the "city," otherwise, the Garden of the Sun, the Gardener of the Almighty Celi and of Cêd.

"The voice of God," states the Druidic adage, "is heard in the voice of Anian," which is another title to Venus. We are told the Pythonic priestess sitting on the tripod which was astride the Cave at Delphi, delivered oracular utterances while under the influence of the exhalation rising from the cave. This implied the exhalation came from Cêd, the mother of Venus, whom (Venus) the priestess symbolised, and that it met the masculine principle of the Deity coming through the sun on the threshold of her own person, and that, as the active and passive principles, they asserted themselves intellectually in her matrix, and the fraudulent priest listened with his ear to her navel, pretending to hear "the voice of God" in the matrix of the wife of Apollo (the sun), represented by the priestess seated on the tripod astride the Cave, which symbolised the entrance into the vulva of Cêd (Cetus), herself the wife of Iôn, the two being the parents of both Venus and Apollo, or of the conceiving function of the earth, and the masculine principle symbolised by the middle Pryapian rod and the two others, or tripod, in contact with the person

of Venus's representative. It will be seen it was Apollo,
as regent, and not his father, the Most High, that was
pretended to whisper in the body of the young Pythoness
on the tripod at Delphi. Still, he was the Word of the
Creator himself, and while the Pythoness was Venus incarnate, the priest who heard the Word was the Word
incarnate, and interpreted to mortals the Divine utterances of Apollo heard in Venus incarnate. In a similar
manner the Hebrew High Priest was supposed to receive
from the Oracle, in the sanctuary, the oracular utterances
of Jehovah, which was the Word of God, and not the
Almighty Himself. Whether the Almighty did thus in
ancient times speak to mortals the reader will judge for
himself.

It is said of the Cave in the Temple of Apollo at
Delphi that it was on the middle of the whole earth. The
same thing was said of the Ark of the Covenant in the
Temple at Jerusalem. All the ancient churches of
Christendom are built east and west, and all the worshippers turn their faces towards the east when repeating
the Creed; towards the point of the heavens from where, in
spring, the sun transmits into the earth his fertilising
influence as the consort of Venus (Gwen-y-Môr, otherwise Mor'wyn). The Priest and the Church are now
incarnate son and daughter of Apollo and Venus, and
the priest interprets what both the Church invisible and
the visible are saying. Indeed, the message comes to the
priest through the visible Church, the Bath-Kol, or the
daughter's voice, as the Divine words came to the Delphic
priest through the agency of Venus, and to the Hebrew
High Priest through the agency of the Ark of the
Covenant.

To each of the ancient churches there is a door facing the south, where, on December 20th, the great mother Cêd (Cetus, otherwise Der Ketos) was supposed to be stationed in the sea to receive the old sun's Divinity into her own body to shield his Divinity, represented as a flying white dove, from the Power of Darkness, which was said to have shattered the old sun's body in the heavens at noon on December 20th. And the old sun received each year a new body in his mother, and he reappeared after forty hours, rejuvenated, as explained elsewhere. Inside, beyond the southern porch of the church is the baptismal font, which is the matrix symbol of Cêd, the personified invisible church. There the spiritual regeneration, by water and the Spirit, takes place in baptism, precisely as the old sun was supposed to be regenerated from Cêd, in the sea, on the morning of December 22nd, by the spirit of Celi, or the Creator, co-operating with his consort Cêd in the water. Outside, and directly opposite to the porch, is a cross on the top of a pyramid. On the top of the cross, called Tau, is a loop. Both cross and loop are plentiful on most ancient Egyptian monuments. That loop is the symbol of the open vulva of Cêd, prepared to receive the sun in his escape from the cross of his murderous enemy in the heavens, and through which he returns "renewed." The porch, and the cross on the pyramid opposite to it, are the said cross with the loop called Tau, and are to be understood as one figure. The middle part of a church is called the nave. Pollux states the belly of a ship is called Ketos (Cêd or Cetus) in Greek[1] Nave is from Navis, a ship or Ark, and implies also navel. The central mast is the navel, and it communicates with the

---

[1] Dr. Potter's *Archæologia Græca*. Vol. ii., p. 128.

hold, emblem of Cêd (Ketos). Cêd (earth) as a belly was represented roaming in the sea, and so does a ship with her navel in her centre. It is evident the Druids sometimes represented Cêd lying with her head westward ; her belly, the round earth, above the rational horizon ; her navel personified as Venus Geneterix (she that produces or causes—a mother). Her feet were represented, open like a triangle, towards the sun rising at the summer solstice and winter solstice respectively ; the apex of the fork would be on the equinoctial line, opposite the virile sun in spring rising due east.

C

CHAPTER IV.

IN the language spoken by the Druids, namely, the Welsh, a grave is called *Beddrôd*, which signifies, literally, circular grave. The English *Bed* seems to be derived from the first word in the Welsh compound. In Welsh, coffin is still called *Arch* (ark), and no doubt it was originally given to the stone kist (which also is Welsh), in which, anciently, the Druids placed the remains of the dead low down in the centre of the *Beddrôd*. The primitive meaning of the word *Arch* (Ark) in Welsh, is command, order, or bidding ; it is also used in the sense of request or supplication ; " Archav *arch* im' *Nav* y Dewin doethaf," (I'll supplicate a request to the Divine Constructor, the wisest diviner). It will appear, from the above, the Druids applied the name Arch to a kist or coffin to imply that death was the result of the will or command of the Creator. The word, too, came to be employed to describe supplication, from the suppliant condition of the dying. The round tumulus is the ancient *Beddrôd* form of a Druidic grave. Each circular tumulus is the symbol of the round earth above the rational horizon, and that symbolised, as already stated, the female protuberance—the cavity in which the navel (Venus) communicates with the child in the womb of Côd. It seems that, in the ancient world, the matrix of the personified mother of Nature was regarded in two ways. Those who buried the dead with their feet towards the south— the most ancient mode of burial, as the contents of stone kists indicate—regarded the grave as the matrix of Côd (Aid), the mother of all ; those who buried the dead with the feet towards the east, regarded the interior of the circular grave as the matrix of Venus Geneterix, or Morewyn, sometimes named Gwen-y-Mor (the Holy One of the Sea, signifying the exhalation of the earth), and that the resurrection would be in the springtime. We believe it is perfectly evident that the Druids favoured the former idea. And those who observed the old custom of burying in the *Nave*, &c., of churches, followed the example of those who entertained the former idea when burying with feet directed south. One of the old Bards compares Owen Glyndwr to a son of Côd, and, therefore, brother of the sun and earth :

> " Ar *drydedd*, Cymmyredd Côd,
> I Wynedd wiw a aned."

> And the third, beloved by Côd,
> To North Wales was given.

Côd in modern Welsh signifies gift ; and a tribute is called Teyrn-Gôd, signifying a gift to the king.

It appears to have been a disputed question among the Ancient Druids as to from what direction the life would return into the body at the resurrection of the dead. Those who buried their dead with the feet directed southward believed life would return from Annwn with the. or in the, sun. Others, who buried with the feet towards the east, believed that life would return from Gwynva (Heaven, spring) to be reunited with the body on earth. In Welsh a tumulus is called Tomen ; Tom (soil) and En (principle of life). We find the same idea in the Welsh Gwrn (Urn) in which, anciently, the Druids deposited the burnt ashes of the dead. Gwrn is an abbreviated form of Gwr-en, which signifies the Source of Life of Man, clearly a reference to the reanimation of the dust in the Urn. The same hope of a reunion with the body after death is implied by

c 2

Tomen, the round mound, called also Barrow, in which
the Druids buried the dead.   We have many references
to Tomen as the sepulchre of the dead, as—

> "A gasglo domen, a gaiff un câr cywir"

(He who will gather a tumulus will have one faithful friend)

meaning the grave.

> "Tomen Elwyddan nis gwlych gwlaw—
> Mae yma Odyn o danaw:
> Dyn wnai Gynon ei gwynaw."

The Tumulus of Elwyddan is not drenched with rain,
For there is a kiln under it.

The word " Odyn," which we have translated " kiln," seems
to be used as a figure for Cêd, as the original source of the
perpetual exhalation of the earth as a life-giving principle.

The Druid's ecclesiastical year commences at midnight on March 20-21. That is the time of the vernal
equinox, and the sun was then—at the period with which
we are dealing—in the sign of the Ram (Aries)—it is
now in the Fishes,—hence the Ram-Sun, as the Father's
agent in the heavens, between the invisible Creator or
Father and the earth (Venus), and operating on the
seeds in her, the sun was, himself, often called Father
by some nations, whereas he was but the transmitter of
the impregnating essence.   Hence the sun in spring was
mistakenly called Iu Pater (Jupiter) that is Iu Father.
He is represented with the horns of a ram on his
head, in reference to his being then in the sign of
the Ram of the Zodiac.   At the same time of the year he
is called Father Hermes, or Father of Harmony, by some
nations, in reference to the equal day and night and the
comity existing at that period of the year between the rival
forces of creation and destruction ; in other words, between
summer and winter, or, the Divinity in the sun, and the

Devil existing in the darkness. It was regarded as the period of a drawn battle between Arthur (Sun) and Avagddu (Pluto). Nennius and Geoffrey have substituted for Avagddu the "Saxons." Arthur, being the Druidic title of the sun, is represented as fighting the "Saxons" in twelve battles, instead of saying that he annually fights the Power of Darkness through the twelve signs of the Zodiac. When the sun was in the Zodiacal Ram sign, March 21, the earth was opposite in the autumnal equinox in the west, and the earth then was called Virgin (Venus), being in the sign Virgo of the Zodiac, that name having been given to the constellation because the earth was in the west of the heavens when the sun rose in spring in the eastern heavens in the sign of the Ram. These figures or emblems have been borrowed to set forth Christ and His Church, and they are described as the Ram, or "Lamb," and the "Bride," "the Bride of the Lamb." In ancient days, as we have already said, when the sun rose in spring in the sign of the Bull, the earth was symbolised by a Sacred Cow. To be consistent the "Bride" of the Ram should have been a "Sheep"—and the Church is actually called Ewe, but spelt "yew," the Greeks, &c., having humanised In Pater and humanised Aphrodite (Venus), they alluded to ram-horned Jupiter as the Consort of the "Bride," or Venus, represented as a lovely woman.

In the following we give the signs of the Zodiac as they were about the beginning of the Christian era in their relation to the sun and the earth. On March 21 the sun was in the sign of the Ram and the earth in the sign of the Virgin; on June 21 the sun was in the sign of Cancer and the earth in the sign of the Goat; on September 23 the sun was in the sign of the Virgin and

the earth in the sign of the Ram; on December 22, the
sun was in the sign of the Goat and the earth in the sign
of Cancer. At the season of September the earth casts
forth her ripened fruits, and what is not gathered returns to
her ovary, by which the Druids meant the soil, or the
earth's loam. That season was sacred to the Virgin or
earth. It appears the Druids paid more attention to the
four seasons than to the twelve signs of the seasons and
their constellations. No doubt they had a Zodiac of their
own and that the names of their Zodiacal signs exist now
among the various names or titles of God in the Welsh
language, for those names are names of the Deity's various
emanations which come to the earth through the sun. The
vernal equinox the Druids named Eilir (second generation);
the summer solstice Hevin–Hâvhin–(sunny temperature) ;
autumnal equinox (Elved) —Hel Med(i)—(gathering fruit
or harvest); winter solstice (Arthan) (Arthur's season ?).
Arthan is puzzling. It seems to be made up of Arth (Bear)
and man (place). We know Arthur, or Arddir, signifies gardener or husbandman. But Arth is Welsh for Bear. The
characteristic of Arthur (sun) at the winter solstice, or from
November 20th to December 20th (Druidic Mythology), is
Valour in Fighting the Power of Darkness. He is the sun
as Archer, armed with a bow and arrow, engaging the enemy.
It seems as if the Druids had given the name to the sun before
they came to the northern latitudes, and that in reference to
Arthur's fighting and terrible qualities, displayed towards
the close of the solar year when face to face with his
enemy, the Druids afterwards gave his name to the bear,
which no doubt was often seen in Britain in remote times.
Volney states the name Typhon signifies a bear, and
that it also signifies, in Arabic, Deluge or Anarchy. But
the Orientals, at some very remote period, in personifying
the characteristics of the sun at the winter solstice, gave him

the devil character, and called him Typhon, or devil, which is the third person of the Egyptian and other trinities. In Druidism, the sun is called Arthur as one of his names throughout the year. Strange that the sun's personified third emanation at the winter solstice, discredited as Typhon, a destroyer, in Egypt, should signify the sun's said emanation and also bear in that country, while in Britain the sun's personified third emanation should imply, not etymologically, but poetically, both heroism as a divine attribute, and bear. It is a striking proof that the Egyptians borrowed of the Druids, and afterwards wrongly interpreted the character of Arthur at the winter solstice.

In concluding this chapter, we say the circular " church " of the Druids was sacred to Cêd and her three daughter goddesses, and to the Creator and his three son gods— Alawn, Plennydd and Gwron, or as usually given, Plennydd, Alawn and Gwron.

CHAPTER V

N the year 4,619 B.C., according to M. Dupuis's Calculation of the Precession of the Equinoxes, the sun began to rise on March 21st in the Zodiacal sign of the Bull, and continued to do so until 2,505 B.C., when he entered the first point of the sign of the Ram at the said March 21st. We will now return to the further consideration of the circumstances of the Hebrew Ark of the Covenant among the Philistines.

In Chapter II., we have shewn the Druids represented the emanations of the great mother, Cêd, by three maidens, called Morwyn, Flora, and Tynghedwen—Dyrraith. We are told the Ark of Israel was sent back, accompanied by *two cows*. The Goddess Ashtaroth, or Easter, was, at this very time, represented by a sacred cow by the Philistines, and by most, if not by all, ancient nations. It is well known the Cherubim, one on each side of the Shechinah, or the Divine Light, were two winged bulls. The Ark matched the Shechinah, and the two cows matched the two winged bulls, one on each end of the Mercy Seat. In the Hebrew calendar, the tenth month of the sacred year is named Tebeth, which, no doubt, is the same as the name Tebah, or Cow. The said tenth month corresponds with our December (Old Style). It will be seen, when we come to consider Noah's Ark, which is also called Tebah, or Cow, that this fact is of enormous importance. The Ark of the Covenant is called Arôn, or Arawn, one of the Druidic titles of the sun at the winter solstice, or to be exact, on December 20th. Aaron entered the Holy of

Holies to the Ark, &c., near the autumnal equinox. It is important for the reader to bear in mind the autumnal equinox marked the ending and the beginning of the civil year of the Jews, and the vernal equinox the ending and beginning of their sacred year, and that they had dragged the solar rites of the end and beginning of the solar year to the end and beginning of their civil year, with some incidents relating to the solar year, to the end and the beginning also of their sacred year.

Aaron entering into the Holy of Holies and the presence of the Ark of the Covenant, signified the same thing as Noah going into his ark, Tebah. The name Noah signifies the Druidic Naw, or Nine, sometimes No; and as Naw, or the sun in the ninth sign of the Zodiac, he entered Tebah, the ark, the beginning of the tenth sign of the Zodiac (the sign of the goat), but in Hebrew the tenth month. Note, the hair of a goat is the embellishment of the eastern outlet of the Holy of Holies, and bear in mind the dislocation of emblems by the Hebrews to which we have already alluded. On the other hand, if we count from the birth of the sun, which the Druids give on December 22nd, we find that September 22nd is exactly nine months from the former date. Aaron entered the Holy of Holies and to the presence of the Ark on the ninth month of the solar year (September), and Noah entered the Ark on the ninth month of the sacred or Zodiacal year (end of November). The only difference is that Aaron bears the name of Arawn (Arôn), old sun, and Noah is named by the number of the Zodiacal sign in which he (the sun) appears at the time, beginning with Aries on March 21st. In the Egyptian language, Athor is another name for cow, and it became synonymous with prayer, in the same sense as a "church" has become to be designated "house of prayer." To further prove that the Jews dragged the rites of the end and the beginning of the solar year to the end and beginning of their civil year, we beg to point out that the scapegoat and the other goat, which they slew near the autumnal equinox, are, apparently, the sun symbol of the he-goat (Capri) of the Zodiac, and the earth symbol as a she-goat—the two implying the sun and earth at the winter solstice. We shall return to this fascinating branch of our subject later on ; we now return to the bulls and cows symbol.

Now, the Druidic Circle is named Buarth Beirdd, which signifies Bovine Enclosure of Bards. We find in Druidic Mythology reference to a white bull (Tarw Elgan) and a white cow (Buwch Laethwen). The white bull signifies the sun in the spring in the sign of the Bull—4619 B.C. to 2505 B.C. In the first place, the whole earth was the Buarth Beirdd, or the Bovine Bardic Enclosure ; secondly, the Druidic Circle or " Church," the emblem of that circular enclosure. One of the figures employed to describe the character of the enclosure as representing the circle enclosing the earth within it, was the Garden of the Lord, that which He Himself had planted, as is said of the Garden of Eden. The white or sacred cow in the centre of the emblematical circular garden or "church" of the Druids, was the symbol of the earth's fertile essence, derived from Cêd through the earth from beneath. Instead of the cow, Venus (Morwyn or Maid) was afterwards substituted to symbolise the said fertile essence of Cêd operating on the material earth in the spring. The Almighty Celi transmitted his masculine emanations through the sun ; his Consort, Cêd transmitted her emanations through the earth's substance, and both Celi and Cêd, by their respective agents, made the surface of the earth fruitful. When the earth's fertility was sym-

bolised by a white cow, the sun was symbolised by a white
bull. The white cow in the middle of the garden was the
symbolical quintessence of the garden, as representing the
fecundity of the whole earth. Paradise is a Persian name
signifying enclosed garden. The four "rivers" of Paradise
or Eden are the streaming four udders of the sacred white
cow, as the garden symbol of the round earth and its
essence. This is the garden of Arthur, otherwise St.
George; the garden of Phœbus; the garden of Ida; the
Adonidis Hortus; the garden of Taliesin, or the sun in
spring under many appellations; and the Garden of Eden.
It was in a garden near the Place of a Skull, close to
Jerusalem, the Sun of Righteousness was laid in a stone
Cist, or Kist, grave. The Early Church held that the
"Skull" referred to was the Skull of Adam. By Adam
was meant the old sun and represented as a skull (round)
dying on December 20th in every year.

The Egyptians assert that the sacred bull Apis, symbolising the sun in the Egyptian "church," had no earthly
father, but that a ray of light—like the Shechinah, and the
Eye of Light of Druidism—came down from heaven upon
the sacred cow, his mother, and that that was followed by
the birth of the bull Apis.[1] This is poetical language,
describing Apis's "priestly" character, and has no reference
to the bull's body.

As we have already pointed out, the Druids personified
the sun's emanations at three distinct stages of the solar
year, namely, March 21st, June 21st, and December 20th,
and they symbolised the three stages by the strokes \|/,
usually shown in the form /|\, and it was called the Name
of God, or, in Hebrew, Shem Iao (Name Jehovah).

---

[1] *Ancient Faiths*, vol. iii., p. 201.

Payne Knight states, "In most of the Greek and Roman statues of the bull that we have seen, whether in the character of Menevis or Apis, of both of which many are extant, of a small size in bronze, there is a hole upon the head between the horns." [1]—When the figure for the middle hole was inserted the three symbols would appear thus \\/. The middle stroke would be the Linga, implying the sun's virile power in spring. The two side strokes are referred to by the chief Bard, Taliesin, in his Càd Godden, as "The Royal Knees," [2] the Said or Linga being between them.

In the Hindoo Puranas, there are mentioned three notable islands, lying in the west of the world. One of them is called the White Island. In Welsh poetry, Britain is very frequently referred to as the White Island. Until the Latin Church came to influence the ecclesiastical words of the Welsh language, the Welsh word for holy was Gwyn (white, masculine) and Gwen (white, feminine). Therefore, White Island signifies really Holy Island, and was not given to Britain in reference to its white cliffs.

In the *Asiatic Researches*, in the article on "The Sacred Isles of the West," is given an allegory discovered in the Hindoo Puranas, describing the introduction of knowledge into the world. The gods (priests), we are told, churned the sea by using the Isle of Man as a churn staff. In the Sanscrit, Mandara is the name given to the "churn staff," and is supposed to signify the Isle of Man. That island is certainly named Monœda, by Ptolemy, and Manand, according to Col. Vallancey, by the Irish Senachies. In Welsh, the Isle of Man is called Mônwy (Cow of the Water), to distinguish it from Môn (Cow), the Welsh

[1] *Symbolical Language*, p. 9, sec. 32.
[2] *Rites and Myths of the British Druids*, p. 100.

name for Anglesea. To this day, according to a popular Welsh proverb, "Môn (Cow) is the mother of the Welsh people" (Cymry).

"After churning the sea," the allegory goes on to state, "for five years, froth appeared. After three years more, Varuni, or Suara, appeared with her intoxicating liquors" (inspirations).

"The cow, Camadhenú, or Surábhi, appeared after another year's labours."

According to the Brahmàn-da-Purana, the cow was worshipped by the gods. The name "gods" in Druidism had a two-fold meaning: (1) The Divine emanations; (2) Those priests of Druidism selected to represent those emanations in the Druidic church; hence Greek writers state the Druids regarded their priests as "gods."

The gods (priests) kept the cow, Camad-henú [1] The White Island (the home of the white or holy cow) is said, in the legend, to be surrounded by a sea of milk. That signifies the "milk" had flowed from the four udders of the sacred cow, or church, of the Druids. That, we believe, signifies that streams of religious knowledge and wisdom had flowed to the four points of the earth from the Druidic circular temple, figuratively referred to as a white or holy cow and its four udders.

The Brahmins acknowledge that the light of revelation came to them from the West, and that the Vedas (gods) reside in the White Island (Britain) in human shape.[2] Their shades are still seen by fancy's eye, flitting about the Gorsedd of the National Eisteddfod of Wales!

---

[1] *As. Res.*, xi., pp. 133 and 135.   [2] *Ibid*, p. 69.

"Even the chalk with which the Hindoos mark their foreheads" (thus \I/) "must come from the White Island. Accordingly, Vishnoo" (Alawn or Hermes) "and several other holy men," one being a priest representing Alawn or Hermes, &c., "brought numerous lumps of it at different times" (to India).[1] "All the Avatars (incarnations of Vishnoo), ten in number, came originally from the White Island."

"There are," they state, "many manifestations and forms of Bhagavan, O Muni; but the form which resides in the White Island" (the Archdruid) "is the primitive one."[2] "The White Island is the holy land of the Hindoos." Not only is it called the White Island, but actually also Locure in the Puranas, and "Lloegr" is the universal name of England in the Welsh language to this day, and signifies Lloer, or arkite moon. Faber, in his work on the Mysteries of the Cabiri, makes the following observations:—"A cow seems to have been adopted as perhaps the most usual emblem of the Ark," —correctly, shrine of the Ark)—"and a serpent as that of the sun, while Noah himself was sometimes worshipped under the form of a bull, and sometimes, in consequence of his union with the sun, is hieroglyphically described as a serpent with the head of a bull."[3]

"Theba, in the Syrian dialect, signifies a cow," and he further states, that Thebes, the capital of Boetia, owed its name to the circumstance of Cadmus being led by an animal of that species to the place where the city was afterwards built. The meaning, however, of Theba in Hebrew is Ark. That fact proves conclusively that the name, as applied to an "Ark," came to be adopted by the Hebrews at a period *after* the cow was being used by the Egyptians

[1] As. Res., xi., p. 70.   [2] Ibid, p. 92.   [3] Orac. Vet. Opsop., p. 6.

to, speaking generally, symbolise the various sacred functions of Nature. Lucan informs us that the priests of Heliopolis assured him that Astarte and Europa—one the consort of Baal and the other the consort of Jupiter (a sheep it ought to have been, for he was a ram) were both cows — were the same person; accordingly, as Europa was represented to have been carried away by a bull, so Astarte (Ashtaroth, Easter, &c.,) was represented with cow's horns.[1]

Both the Isle of Man and the Isle of Anglesea were other shrines of Venus, each of the said islands being sacred to the Holy White Cow. To revert to the Taurine symbol : "By this bull god, made of brass," says Borlase, "the Cimbri (Kymry, or the Welsh) swore to observe the articles of capitulation granted to the Romans, who defended the Adige against them. After their defeat Catulus ordered this bull to be carried to his own house, there to remain as the most glorious monument of his victory."[2]

This god ranked with Jupiter, Esus, and Vulcan, being called Tarvos Trigaranus (y Tarw Trigorn—the Three-Horned Bull), and supposed, therefore, as it appears, to symbolise the same idea as the trinity before-mentioned did.

It is interesting at this point to observe what King Jeroboam did.[3] He made *two* golden bulls, and placed one in Dan and the other at Bethel—the two extremities of the kingdom, with the Shechinah and Ark in the temple at Jerusalem *between* the two, in the territory of Judah and Benjamin, and not, as is generally understood, in the town of Dan, at the foot of Mount Libanus in the north, but, as

---

[1] *Cabiri*, by Faber, pp. 177, 178, & 181.
[2] *Mys. of The Cabiri*, Vol. I., p. 21.
[3] I. Kings, xii., 26, 27, 28.

we believe, in the territory of Dan on the south-west of
Jerusalem, while Bethel was to the north of that city.—
Vide Calmet's Bib. Dic., plate cxcviii. The great object
of the Jewish hierarchy was to centralise at the temple the
national worship of the Jews. We reiterate, it is known the
two cherubs, one on each side of the Ark of the Covenant,
were winged bulls. The twelve oxen under Solomon's Molten
Sea indicate the Taurine character of the temple symbols.—
1 Kings vi., 25. Did King Jeroboam attempt to decentralise
the national worship, and make the whole of the kingdom
the symbol of "the garden of the Lord," with its centre in
the temple? And did his two golden bulls, one at each
extremity of his kingdom, imply the widening of the
sanctuary? The attempt evidently resulted in a violent
rupture between Jeroboam and the hierarchy, or priesthood,
whose overbearing influence he appears to have attempted
to curtail. It should be noticed also, that Aaron refers to
the golden calf as "gods," which implies something in it
indicative of plurality, doubtless three horns or three heads
to the golden calf.

In Druidic Mythology, an Avanc, or Beaver, is said to
have been drawn to land by Ychain Banawg Hu Gadarn
(Hesus the Mighty)—"Ychain Banawg" signify, literally,
Oxen of Many Hills. What drawing the Avanc or
Beaver to land is will be explained in connection with
the wonderful allegory relating to the death and birth
of the sun, but we simply add here the sun disap-
pearing every evening into the western seas was compared to the Beaver, which also is amphibious. His
hind legs are web-footed, and he also enters into his
home in the waters, as the Druids supposed the sun did
every night when he descended into the Western Ocean.
"Ychain" signify Oxen, and "Banawg" a Multiplicity of

Mountains or Hills; from Ban (Hill), Banau, plural, (Hills). "Awg" in Welsh signifies *full of*, or *many*, as Drain*awg* (hedgehog), many thorns; Brwyn*awg* (full of rushes). "Awg," which is often confounded with "Og," is an affix to primitive nouns. "Og" is an affix denoting speed, as Heb*og* (hawk), Ysgyvarn*og* (a hare), Llwyn*og* (a fox). Treban*awg* signifies a Home among *many* Hills or Mountains. Ban is often, in Wales, a name for a high hill, as Ban Brycheiniog and Banau (plural) Brycheiniog (the Breconshire Beacons). Then the four stations of the sun, in Druidic language, are referred to as follows: The vernal equinox is called Al*ban* Eilir; the summer solstice, Al*ban* Hevin; the autumnal equinox, Al*ban* Elved; the winter solstice, Al*ban* Arthan. Then certain stations of the moon are named Banau (Bans) of the moon.

"Ychain Banawg," therefore, manifestly, signifies Oxen of Many Hills. Hu Gadarn is the infant sun; and when the said oxen are referred to as the oxen of the infant Son named Hu Gadarn, it is clear that oxen of the sun is implied, and that the ceremony took place on each December 22nd.

Any circular stone temple of the Druids is named Buarth y Beirdd — Cattle Pen of the Bards: not "Oxpen" of the Bards; for *Bu* (e sound to the u) signifies the same thing as the Latin *Bovis*, and implies the cattle genus. For "oxen" we are to understand bulls. Bulls being too dangerous to meddle with, and to be used in the religious symbolical rites of Druid bards, the more easily managed oxen came to be used instead, as substitutes for bulls. Thus evidently there were *three* cows and three bulls employed as symbols by the Druids, in their cattle pen or circle. In reference to the sacred oxen, styled as

D

being of, or belonging to, "many hills," the expression, we think, refers to the "many hills" upon which stood the many Druidic sanctuaries to which the sacred oxen belonged.

We are plainly told by Dionysius that "the rites of Bacchus * * were duly celebrated in Britain."[1] "Hence arose that veneration for the bull, the constant symbol of the Deity of the Ark." But Faber did not realise that the Ark itself was the symbol of Isis the First (Cêd), and that the shrine on the deck of the Ark was the symbol of her daughter, Isis the Second, who is called also Venus, Gwen-y-Môr, otherwise Morwyn, in Druid language. That shrine, under the figure of a Cow (Theba), was the consort of the Bull, otherwise the Taurine Sun. Another name for Venus among the Druids was Brydwen (Britannia), and the Island of Britain, surrounded by the sea, was regarded as her shrine, carried on the surface of the ocean by Cêd, the Consort of Celi, symbolised as an Ark.

The Druids used three bulls to match the three cows in their religious system, as they did three apples to symbolise the sun at the three stages in his annual course, as seen above the horizon. They are referred to in the Welsh Triads as three regal bulls or sovereigns of Britain.[2] Three consort cows are also mentioned in the Triad.[3] There are, moreover, three demon bulls referred to, which, to scientifically set forth the system, would necessitate three demon cows, which, no doubt, there were, and the latter bulls and cows would be black.

The first-named three bulls and three cows—the third cow *spotted* to indicate her dual character, like Tynghedwen-Dyrraith—of the sun and nature, are also frequently referred

[1] *Dionys. Periey. Ver.* 565.
W. *Arch iol.*, vol. ii., pp. 4, 13, 76.   [3] *Ibid*, vol. ii., p. 22.

to as three demi-gods and demi-goddesses.[1] Demi-gods: Plennydd, Alawn, and Gwron. Demi-goddesses: Mor'wyn (Virgin), Blodwen (Flora), Tynghedwen-Dyrraith (Barren). Tynghedwen (Fortune) is in two words: Tyn (a pull) and Cêd (great goddess mother)—a pull from the goddess mother. These, we repeat, are the mythological three sister-spouses of Arthur; Morwen la Fai, Queen of the east of Wales (sun, her husband, then rising due east in spring), the second sister-spouse is said to be the Queen of North Wales (sun then rising north-east at the summer solstice), and the third sister-spouse of Arthur is said to be the Queen of desert places (the sun, her husband, being then at the winter solstice, unable to fertilise her seeds, she being regarded as the garden—the earth—of Arthur as a husbandman, therefore she is now said to be barren). The three demi-goddesses are poetical personifications of the earth at the three stages of the year, corresponding with the three poetical personifications of the sun at his three stages. The fore-going makes

---

[1] The Egyptian goddess Neith is the Druidic Nêdd (dd as th in the). Nêdd in Welsh signifies—that which works into foam; also, a whirl or turn; the character being given to the Great Mother because it was supposed she had intervolved creation into visible existence. Nyddu is the Welsh for the verb—to spin, to turn; Naddu (e sound to u.) is the Welsh for—to work or to cut into form. The Egyptian Neith is represented as wearing a collar of Nine beads. The Nine beads probably imply that she creates natural lives and vegetation from Capricornus (Dec. 22nd,) to Virgo (Sept. 23rd), the produce of the earth by the agency of Venus or Nature, otherwise Virgo, the situation of the earth, in Druidism, when the sun is in Aries (March 21st). "Neith is the Mother of Nature" and of the sun, as Isis I. (Cêd). "She is the Nerfe of the Etruscans—half fish and half woman." Here mythologists of the present day are in error; when the human and fish combinations are shown it is the young sun emerging from the mouth of the fish at his new birth (Dec. 22nd,) is meant. She is Naus (Ark) the Great Mother of all gods" and goddesses. Thus we find Nêdd or Neith is identical with Isis I., the mother of Isis II., who in her turn is the sister-spouse of Horus who develops into Osiris. She is also Athene (Divine Wisdom), after whom Athens is named. A town in South Wales is called after her ("Neith") namely Neath —in Welsh, Nêdd. Another town in the same district is called Môn (Cow),

it pretty clear that the "oxen" of Many Hills were *three*
in number. It may be asked if the shrine which contained
the Beaver symbolised the same mythological idea as
Cêd (Cetus—whale) did, namely, the old sun's mother,
otherwise Latona, or Spirit of Chaos, whence he (the sun)
had originally come, and if the three oxen of Many Hills
symbolised the sun at three of its stages, as it appears
rising over the horizon on March 21st, June 21st, and
December 20th, or the beginning of the vernal equinox,
the summer solstice, and the winter solstice, illustrated
thus \\/, how came it that it is said *three* oxen, representing one Taurus of the Zodiac, are said to have
drawn the shrine of the Beaver (Avanc) out of the lake?
We answer the three oxen, the three apples, &c., were
symbols of the three principal emanations of the One
Creator, as creating, perfecting, and defending attributes
in spring, summer, and at the shortest day respectively,
and that the triune powers of the Creator on December
22nd where miraculously engaged in assisting Cêd in

and, in English, Cowbridge. Mr. Bonwick states that "Athor, as a goddess,
is the daughter of the Sun" Old Sun, for the Old Sun of one year is, in the
East, represented as the father of all the minor gods and goddesses of the
year following, hence so many have confounded the Old Sun with the
Almighty The Amen of Egypt, "she is represented with a wheel of eight
spokes," engaged in spinning the beautiful fabrics which the earth produces
into leaves, flowers, fruit, &c.' Athor, or Hathor (of the Egyptians), was a
spotted Cow, with gilded neck and head" (golden tints of Autumn) "she was
Hera, the Cow of Troy, and so allied to Isis" (the Second), "She is the
companion to Harmachus Tum, the infernal god." The spots indicate the
ferocity of the Dyrraith attribute in conjunction with Tynghedwyn, as
described in the text. The ferocious attribute is here described as an
infernal quality, and yet exercised by Nature in defending its offspring.
She is described as the being in which is enclosed Horus, or the next year's
young Sun, that is to say the substance of his physical frame, which implies
the same thing as Semele containing the *essence* out of which the physical
frame of Bacchus was annually created anew, but his divinity, or soul,
coming into him direct from the Almighty, allegorically described as the
"thigh"—strength—of Jupiter Amon, or In, the Hidden Father.—
                    Vide Bonwick's *Egyptian Belief.* p. 110.

defending and to re-deliver the infant Sun, Hu Gadarn, on the morning of every solar New Year's Day (*Vide* Shrine containing "Agruerus"). We again repeat those three attributes or emanations of the Almighty were poetically personified in the following order:—Alawn (vernal point), Plennydd (summer solstice), and Gwron (Hero) at the winter solstice, or shortest day. But the Druidic trinity are generally named in the following order:—Plennydd, Alawn, and Gwron (Hero). In all the other Gentile trinities the character of the last-named has been mixed with the character of evil, viz. : Pluto (Roman); Dis or Hades (Greek); Typhon (Egypt); Siva (India); Ahriman (Persia), &c.

The Druidic trinity, whose operations were illustrated thus \/, meeting in the middle of the Druidic circle, as symbolising the round or circular earth above the rational horizon—the original Mount Meru—were the emanations of the Great Creator and not of the sun itself. The sun—formerly spelt "son"—was regarded as the first begotten son of the Almighty by the Black Virgin, or Cêd, otherwise Latona, &c. (the feminine or passive principle of chaos) before the worlds were made. He (Sun or Son) became the agent of the Almighty in the work of creation, by becoming the transmitting agent from three principal stations, by means of his solar beams, of the various attributes of the Deity necessary to the work of creating, adorning, and defending the world. But on each December 20th in the afternoon he was said allegorically to die in the Heavens and to fall into the sea at sunset (four o'clock) on that afternoon every year opposite St. David's Head, Pembrokeshire.

In describing the sun as being, in winter, gradually defeated by the power of darkness, it was implied the *material* sun, as containing within it the divine emanations of God —hence the sun is called Huan (Hu Annedd, or abode of Hu)—was being defeated at that season of the year, and the sun, as the material agent of the Divinity within it, became in consequence disabled to perform his duty as transmitter of the attributes of the Divinity to the earth. Those attributes, quite apart from the material sun itself, were symbolised, as already pointed out, by the three horns of Taurus—the central one being a linga; by three oxen; by three apples, whose juice, or essence, symbolised the divine essence, which was another symbol of the divine emanations in the concrete; by dove and wings; and by a wren and wings; and, in later times, when the sun rose in spring (2505 until 125 B.C.; others say, 389 B.C.) in the sign of the Ram-Lamb, by Jupiter, Amon with Ram's horns. When, therefore, the Druids symbolised the sun as a Beaver, and Cêd (Cetus) as a shrine, and as being drawn out of the lake with the Beaver (sun) in it by the oxen of Hu Gadarn (Hesus the Mighty), what was implied was that the Divine Father himself by his powerful emanations drew him forth, and not his own energy. It is most curious to find that the Druids regarded the detached Divinity in the sun as strong or weak in accordance with the condition of the sun itself. When that Divinity is disabled in the sun, in consequence of the feeble, physical condition of the sun's material body, the Eternal Father comes to his aid, that assistance being symbolised by the three regal bulls of Britain, called Ychain Banawg. Faber has the following :—" Agruerus was highly venerated by the Phœnicians, and his shrine was drawn about from place to place by a yoke of oxen ; while among the Byblians he was esteemed in a special manner as the greatest of

gods." [1] Agruerus was evidently the old sun of the old
year, renewed to be the young sun of the new year.

Judging by the practice of the Phœnicians, who were in
constant intercourse with the Druids of Britain, they no
doubt learned of them that the Avanc or Beaver was
symbolised as being in the boat-shaped shrine.   In
Phœnicia a shrine and a white dove in it also were used to
denote the same objects, and we trace the same things in
Egypt and other Eastern countries.   In Britain another
set of symbols, signifying the same ideas, were a small
wooden "house," and a wren in it.

DEAD OSIRIS (SUN) AND HIS FLYING SOUL.

Funeral Car of Osiris, as the Old Sun, dead.   The Dove his Divinity escaping.
The Arch The Vault of the Heavens.   Isis f. and Isis ff. lamenting him.

It now becomes important to inquire, what or who was
implied by Agruerus ?—In Druidism, Adam was the sun,
named Tegid, Taliesin, &c., in spring ; and Eve (Venus—
Morwyn Mali) was the earth, his wife, and the whole earth,
according to another figure, was the garden of Eden,
bordered by the Druidic stone circle.   Then we begin the

[1] *Mys. Cabiri,* vol. i., pp. 35, 43, 45, and 215.

Hebrew patriarchal pedigree with Seth, second son of
Adam and Eve, and that of the Phœnician Patriarchs with
Protogonus :—

THE HEBREW PATRIARCHS.		PHŒNICIAN PATRIARCHS.	
1	Seth	1	Protogonus
2	Enos	2	Genus
3	Cainan	3	Phos
4	Mahalaleel	4	Cassius
5	Jared	5	Memrumus
6	Enoch	6	Agreus
7	Methuselah	7	Chrysor
8	Lamech	8	Zeerhuties.
9	Noah	9	Agruerus

In the above we see that Noah and Agruerus corres·
pond as to number in the lists of the two sets of patriarchs.
Cain's pedigree consists of seven personages. They are the
sun in the seven planetary spheres, explained elsewhere.
Abel, being the destroyer, has no descendants. The
identity of Agruerus with Noah and with the Beaver
symbol of the Druids is still more strikingly implied by the
statement of the Phœnician Sanchoniathon, quoted by
Faber in his *Cabiri*, as to oxen drawing the shrine of
Agruerus.[1]

" Agruerus," states Faber, " is identical with Cronus,
and he is said to have had three sons, namely, Cronus the
younger, Jupiter-Belus, and Apollo." Cronus the younger
is said to be the son of Uranus (Arawn, the old sun) and
Ge (Earth), the earth as Cêd's belly. Moreover, the elder
Uranus is identical with Saturn, and Saturn also is said

---

[1] " In memory of the Ark, the ancients were not only accustomed to carry
about small navicular shrines, but sometimes built temples in the form of ships."
- *Mys Cabiri*, vol. i., p. 215. " Nave" implies Navis (Ship or Arc), and Navel.

to have had three sons, Jupiter, Neptune, and Pluto. Noah also had three sons, Japheth, Shem, and Ham. Ad Hama is the Persian name of the sun. Like Pluto, the third son of Saturn, Ham, the third son of Noah, is said to be black. In Druidism the sun in the ninth sign of the Zodiac is called Gwydd-Naw (the Ninth Presence), and Ban-Naw (the Ninth Station), &c.

Now comes the most extraordinary coincidence. The sun, on November 22nd, enters the Ninth Sign of the Zodiac, viz., Sagittarius (Archer). In the tenth month, on December 22nd (from March 21st), the sun enters the sign of the Goat, which is the Jewish tenth month, Tebeth or Tebah, which signifies both Cow and Ark. December 22nd is the first day of the Druidic solar year, and the sun, 40 hours *before*, will have reached his greatest southern declination, and descended into his mother Cêd in the ocean.

CROMLEACH.

Thebes is said to have had a hundred gates, and the great Druidic temple of Avebury, Wilts, had an outward circle of one hundred great blocks of stone. The enclosed area of both places symbolised the circular earth above the rational horizon, and the "one hundred" in each case symbolised illimitable space beyond that horizon. We have a clue in the "hundred gates" as to the signification of the cow of Thebes, that she symbolised what Venus did afterwards, viz., the earth's fecundity. She was identical with the second Isis, daughter of Isis the First (Cêd), and the same as Gwen y Môr or Morwyn, daughter of Cêd, in Druidism. The Druidic symbol for the belly, or source of the earth's essence, that is, of Cêd, containing in herself all the feminine attributes as the consort of the Almighty

Celi, was the top slab of the Cromlech, held up, or sustained, by the reverberation of the Word /I\, which existed
before the material sun and earth were created, existing from eternity in the dual nature of the Almighty
Celi Himself. The name "Cromlech" is a compound
of three words—Cromen, Lle, and Ach. The ancient
Druids, as we very frequently find exemplified in the
compound words of the Welsh language, clipped words
formed into a compound word. Thus the above Cromen (Dome) is abbreviated into *Crom* in "Cromlech,"
or correctly, Cromleâch; *Lle*, mutated to *Le*. in the
compound, signifies Place; *Ach* signifies Root of Lineage,
or Pedigree. In Welsh, the human groin, including, as it
appears, the scrotum, is called Âchvan, which signifies the
Place holding Lineage. Cromleâch implies, the Dome
Place of Lineage, or Progeny's Source. In South Wales,
crombil is the name given to the first stomach of a
bird. Now, the termination *bil* signifies the Mouth of a
Vessel. Therefore it is clear *Crom*, in this compound, also
signifies Cromen, and that it implies belly. In the light of
what we have stated, that the Cromleâch, standing on a
tripod of stones, signifies the earth as the middle protuberance of Mother Cêd, the Consort of the Almighty, it
will be seen Cromleâch implied, in Druidic symbolism, that
protuberance of Cêd, the Great Mother, as the Source of
all Animated things. In the course of countless centuries
the name Llech, or Lleâch, came to be applied to any flat
stone. Some employ the figure of Atlas (Welsh, Adlais—
Echo,) sustaining the earth as a globe, but formerly supposed to be flat, on his shoulders; others an Elephant,
and others a Tortoise, sustaining it on its back.
Each figure symbolises the power of the Creator. But in
Druidism Adlais (Atlas) symbolises the reverberation

of the Commanding Voice of the Almighty, pronouncing most musically the majestic Word of three syllables, and filling all space with its force, and its e ho (Adlais—Atlas) coming back against the earth beneath and acting as a fulcrum, sustaining its stupendous weight above the awful abyss! As said elsewhere, Atlas's seven daughters (Atlantides) are the seven mythological divisions of the earth's Anima, corresponding with the seven emanations of the sun in his annual journey through the seven planetary spheres. Ced was regarded as both mother and Ark of Refuge, or grave, of the old sun at the close of the solar year, on every December 20th, and also his birthplace, as a babe, on every new year's first morning, as the old sun rejuvenated on December 22nd.

Note.—In page 12, after the word "Capri" (line 6) read "Pan," and instead of "she-goat" (line 7) read "young he-goat, Bacchus."

CHAPTER VI.

NE of the most remarkable of the solar myths of our Druidic ancestors, which popular customs have preserved for us, is associated with the apple. It is certain that the name Hâv, now used for summer, was anciently one of the Druidic titles of the sun as a fertiliser. An apple is called Haval (Aval is clearly an erroneous mode of spelling the name). Haval, apple, is compounded of Hâv (sun), and mal (like), and signifies: Like the Sun as regards its shape. In the sun's annual journey the sun, in three stages, was symbolised also by three apples in the Druidic circular "church." Those three golden apples are those which it is stated Hercules robbed from the garden of the Hesperides, stationed in Western Europe. Those three golden apples were similar to those seen now as a sign above the entrance into certain shops in England and Wales.

In Wales, Ireland and Scotland, where ancient Celts abound, are preserved three deeply interesting solar customs, in which the apple plays a part. (1) Near the winter solstice, a large tub containing water is placed in the centre of the public room of the house. An apple is then thrown into the water in the tub, and a competition takes place between the members of the household as to which of them can, while blind-folded, and the hands on the back, snatch the apple out of the water with his or her teeth. The apple symbolises the sun dropped into the sea of Annwn (Great Deep) at the winter solstice, and snatching it with the teeth, the action of Cêd, Ketos, or Cetus, Latona or Ark, in rescuing him from destruction. The reader will recollect the brazen sea of the temple. (2) On the early morning of New Year's day, children, in the said countries, carry from door to door an apple dressed with evergreens, and holly with red berries. A wooden skewer, which serves as a handle, is thrust into the side of the ornamented apple. Underneath the apple, and thrust into it thus ⚘ are three other skewers arranged like a tripod. Oats are thrust all over into the apple. Each child carrying the apple is accompanied by a small group of other children, and as soon as the little party reach the entrance of a house they sing a joyful song, concluding by wishing the household a happy new year. The apple is a sun symbol, and implies the sun's safe return from the realm of Pluto, or Darkness, called in Welsh, Avagddu, and signifying, literally, the Evil Nursing Place. The oats scattered all over in the rind of the apple symbolise fertility. The three pegs beneath symbolise the triune Word or the Druidic trinity in unity in the sun, and as attributes transmitted to the earth during each solar year. The evergreens symbolise the perenniality of the vital force in the sun.

The following are other of the solar rites relating to the sun as an apple in the cauldron of Avagddu, or Pluto (the sea of the great deep or Annwn) at the winter solstice :— "In Herefordshire, under the name Wassailing, the following rites are observed :—At the approach of the evening of the Vigil of the Twelfth Day, the farmers, with their friends and servants, meet together, and, about six o'clock, walk out to a field where wheat is growing. In the highest part of the ground twelve small fires, and one large one, are lighted up (the sun and the twelve signs of the Zodiac). The attendants, headed by the master of the family, pledge the company in old cider (juice of the apple), which circulates freely on the occasion." This reminds us of the conduct of the Corinthians in converting the Holy Communion into a festive banquet. "A circle is formed around the large fire, when a general shout and hallooing take place, which you hear answered from all the adjacent villages and fields. Sometimes fifty or sixty of these fires (groups of) may be seen at once. This being finished, the company return home, where the good housewife and maids are preparing a good supper."

A large cake is always provided, with a hole in the middle. After the supper, the company all attend the bailiff or headman of the oxen to the wain house, where the following particulars are observed :—The master, at the head of his friends, fills the cup, generally with strong ale, essence of barley, and standing opposite the finest ox (Bull meant), pledges him in a curious toast. * * That being finished, the large cake is produced, and, with much ceremony, put on the horn of the ox, through the hole above mentioned." [1]

The ox in the foregoing signifies the sun in the zodiacal sign of the bull, and the sun rising in that sign in spring, 200 years before the Deluge, according to Archbishop Usher's calculation as to the time that disaster occurred. The round loaf is the round earth, and the bull's horn is the sun's rays opening the earth in the springtime. Sometimes the same idea is symbolised by the bull's horn breaking open an Easter egg.

In the *Gentleman's Magazine* for February, 1784, p. 98, it is stated that, near Leeds, Yorkshire, it was customary for many families, on the Twelfth Eve of Christmas,

---

[1] Brand's *Popular Antiquities*, vol. i. p. 30.

to invite their relations, friends, and neighbours to their
houses, and to partake of supper, of which mince pies
('cakes of the Queen of Heaven') were an indispensable
ingredient. After supper, was brought in the wassail cup
or bowl, of which every one partook, by taking with a
spoon, out of the ale in the bowl, a roasted apple—essence
of the apple and barley mixed here—and eating it,
and then drinking the health of the company out of
the bowl, wishing them a merry Christmas and a happy new
year. The ingredients put into the bowl were ale, sugar,
nutmeg, and roasted apple, and they were usually called
Lamb's Wool. In the first narration we seem to have a
springtime rite dragged out of its place and transferred to
Christmastime, unless the bull's horn passing through the
cake, implies the sun opening the barrows, or round
graves, at the resurrection. In the last narration we have
the sun as an apple roasted in the cauldron of Avagddu or
the devil, and the worshippers eating it in the same way
as Typhon of Egypt is said to have given the body of
Osiris to be eaten by his murderous followers.

In a future page we point out that the wren's feathers
symbolised the sun's rays in a solar ceremony in the
Isle of Man on every December 26th. In the "Lamb's
Wool," we have the juices, implying the sun's rays in
the concrete, referred to as the "wool" of the sun in
the sign of the Lamb Ram of the Zodiac. The sun ceased
to rise in spring in the sign of Lamb Ram about 125 B.C.
or 389 B.C.

Ale, as the essence of barley, and cider, as the essence
of the apple, both being indigenous of Britain, are used
in Britain in the same sense as representing the sun's
rays or essence, as the essence of the grape was used in

vine-growing countries by the worshipper's of the sun's emanation, as Bacchus, and under other titles.

Does not the wassail bowl and its liquor remind the reader of the Holy Greal and its contents? And is not the whole of the island of Britain the *real* Insula Pomorum or the Island of Apples? Is not Glastonbury supposed to be Avalon? and does not *that* name signify in the Welsh language the Everlasting Apple? Moreover, the *As. Res.* states Britain was the original island of Delos, which floated, symbolically setting forth that the earth was loose on the ocean. Another symbol of Cêd's belly.

THE HOLY GREAL.

For the sake of those who are not familiar with the story of the Holy Greal, we supply an outline of the story. In the first place, what does the name " Greal " signify? We answer, unhesitatingly, Cread or Creation. Cread is mutated in Welsh to (ei) Gread, and somebody in ancient days mistook the terminating d for an l. Cread is analagous with the Sanscrit *kri* (to make). In Sir William Hamilton's letter, published as an introduction to Payne Knight's *Worship of Priapus*, will be seen that the Church of Rome has personified creation; and, in an island near Naples, the linga is called the "big toe of St. Cosmo" (Gr. *kosmos*—the world). The reader will recollect the ceremony of kissing the Pope's toe: a well-known Phallic rite transformed into toe kissing. The horn of the ox through the hole in the centre of the cake, implies that Phallus, and the church, with a view to lead the masses away from a Phallic vernal ceremony, which, owing to its real import having been lost, and the changed condition of human thought respecting such symbolisms had become highly objectionable, employed a pious fraud, and told the people the symbol was

" the big toe " of the husband of the church on earth,
and father of the church " members." The fact that the
church succeeded in pursuading the masses to so regard
the objectionable symbol, which for thousands of years had
been popular, proves how totally ignorant the masses had
become as to its original import as a symbol—that it
symbolised the masculine principle of the Creator transmitted in spring through the sun. In the May-pole we have
that symbol still in a popular form in England, and in the
May Queen we have the earth's fecundity represented, the
Queen of the May being Venus's representative.

The round half of the earth above the rational horizon
was thought to be surrounded by water, and that it
extended in all directions through illimitable space, as
described by Homer in his description of the Shield of
Achilles. The round earth, within the sea circle, was set
forth under the similitude of a round dish, and whether the
dish used as a symbol was large or small, it was called the
Cauldron of Ceridwen, or, of Holy Love. The Welsh
bards still refer to the "boiling of the Cauldron of Ceridwen." Primarily, that implied the earth's fermentation in
spring under the influence of the sun's rays. The sun-
beam, they inferred, transmitted the fermenting masculine
influence of the Creator. That transmitter, the obelisks
also symbolise, as, moreover, do the mysterious ancient
round towers of Ireland. The apple being used as a
symbol of the sun, the essence or juice of the apple came,
naturally, like the essence of the grape, to be used
emblematically as the " blood " of the Divinity, the source
of every nourishment. The essence of the grape is referred
to in the Bible as " blood "—" He washed his garments in
wine, and his clothes in the blood of grapes." The dish
or cauldron referred to, contained the symbol of the said

E

essence as the substance or element, by giving vitality to the passive essence in the material earth, caused vegetation and fruit of all kinds to come to be the sustenance of man and beast.

But the *roasted* apple in the winter solstice custom refers to the "death" of the old sun at that season, and, in Druidism, his being *roasted* in the Cauldron of Avagddu (Pluto or Dis), and the carrying about a dressed apple forty hours later, refers to the sun's renovation or rejuvenation through the combined Divine influence of Almighty Celi and his consort Cêd from the sea of Hades, the entrance into which is where the sun sets on the afternoon of December 20th, and the outlet from which is where the sun reappears on the morning of December 22nd, to begin the new year, and celebrated earliest of the new year at Dunwich, Suffolk. Dunwich signifies Din (Hill or Mound) and 'Wych (Magnificent)—Magnificent Mound. It is there still, and now used as a "look out" by the coastguard. The Seal and Arms of Dunwich are the following :—

THE CROWNED BABE.

The figure represents the sun of the new year rising from a boat on the sea as a " Crowned Babe " to govern the world during the year then commencing. The boat is the coracle of the sun and symbolises Cêd, the sun's mother. These were once serious observances.

In page 276 of the *Iolo MSS.* are the following lines to the " Crowned Babe," which are strikingly corroborative of what we have been stating, viz. : by the " Crowned Babe " is meant the same thing as the Divinity in the Young Sun issuing out of Cêd (his Divine Mother), as a White Dove in some eastern counties ; under the figure of Adonis from a boat, in Phœnicia ; under the figure of a Wren from an ark, in all parts of Wales ; and as a Babe, called Taliesin, from a coracle, at Borth, Cardigan Bay. By the figure of a human child is implied that the sun has received a new *body*—the " old man renewed." It will be recollected that, in the East, Cêd goes under the figure of Cetus, or Der Ketos (a whale), and that Iona, or Jonah, signifies Dove. The following is a stanza in a poem in the said page, to the " Crowned Babe," composed by " Gildas, the Prophet," who is identical with the Prince-Poet, Aneurin, author of " The Gododin," who flourished about the middle of the sixth century, dying A.D. 570 :—

> "The Crowned Babe will come, like Iona,
> Out of the belly of the Whale; great will be his dignity.
> He'll place every one according to his merits;
> He is the principal strong tower of the Kingdom."

In many of the said most curious stanzas, the Druidic-Christian bards of those early ages naturally confound the " Crowned Babe " with Jonah and with the Infant Jesus. Moreover, Joshua, otherwise Jesus, who, on the death of Moses, succeeded him, and is said to have ascended out of the Jordan, was the son of Nun, or Fish. "Nuns" signifies Fishes, or Children of Fish.[1] It is hardly necessary to state the Fish is Cetus or Der Ketos (Whale) the Oriental symbol of the Druidic Cêd, wife of the Almighty, and Mother of "gods" and "goddesses," or priestly representatives of the masculine and feminine attributes, as emanations, of the Almighty Celi and the Almighty Cêd, His consort.

The following are the introductory lines to "*The Roll of Tradition and Chronology*," copied by Mr. Llewellyn John, Llangewydd, from ancient writings in the library of Raglan Castle, Monmouthshire, which castle and contents were destroyed by General Fairfax, towards the close of the war between Charles I. and the Parliament :—" God delivered His Name vocally not otherwise than thus : \|/ ; and with the Word all worlds and animations sprang co-instantaneously to being and life, shouting in ecstacy of joy /|\ ; echoing back the name of God in sweetest sopranoimic cadences (iselfain perciddlais)," &c.

Taliesin, called by the Welsh, "Chief of Bards," (A.D. 600), referring to himself in the character of the incarnate Sun, states :—

<blockquote>
" Bum bont ar Dri Gair "—/|\
" I have been a bridge on Three Words "—/|\
</blockquote>

The Name of God in Druidism is set forth as in Three Syllables, illustrated thus \|/ ; and, as an Echo, thus /|\, which is the figure propping up every Cromleách. The words "in sweetest sopranoimic cadences" refer to the sound of the Echo of the Voice of God returning back against the bottom, and through, the earth, personified as

---

[1] Dr. Inman's *Ancient Faiths*, Vol. I., p. 96; also Vol. II., p. 168.

Miriam, or, in Druidism, Mali or Mary-Mother, otherwise Venus Marina. Literally, Mali signifies " Like the stroke I," the I being the Druidic symbol of the Equinoctial Line. This is the wand of Titâenia. Titi is the Welsh for mother's Teats. The story of the Statue of Memnon on the Plain of Thebes echoing back the music of the rays of the sun will occur to the learned reader.

Memnon is said to have been the son of Eos by Tithonos. Eos is the Welsh name of the nightingale which sings in the night. In that language the ancient mode of spelling the name of that bird is Eaws. Evidently it is a compound of two words, viz. : E and Aws. The E should be the article Yr (The). Aws signifies *beginning to move,* implying here the melodious voice of the Creator pealing through the primeval night was the active cause of the beginning of movement in the work of creation, and the name was applied to the nightingale because it also sings in the night time. But the Greek poets borrowed the Druidic Eaws or Eos, and used the name to denote Aurora, or the Dawn, which is called Gwawr by the Druids. *Dawn* signifies grace or gift in the Welsh language, and what is a finer gift of grace to the world than the dawn of day ! Aurora is said to have been the mother of Memnon, whose father was Tithonos. The last name seems to be the personified splendour of the face of the earth before the eyes of Aurora. Mythologists state, " Tithonos was so beautiful that Aurora (Eos) became so enamoured of him that she carried him away." Another way of saying the splendour of the face of the earth disappears with the disappearance of the the light of day. But the Greeks gave also the name Eos, or Eous, to all eastern parts of the world, and it is a name given by Ovid (Met. 2, v. 153, &c.) to one of the horses of the sun, which sufficiently proves that Eos was referred to also in a masculine sense for the sun itself, which, according to Druidism, leaped into existence as the result of the melodious utterance of the Creator pealing through the darkness of unfathomable eternity. We are told " Tithonos asked Aurora to be made immortal, and the goddess granted it ; but as he had forgotten to ask for the vigor, youth and beauty, which he then enjoyed, he soon grew old, infirm, and decrepid, and as life became insupportable to him he prayed Aurora to remove him out of the world. As he could not die the goddess changed him into cicada or grasshopper." The fading splendour of the face of the earth in autumn and winter is meant by Tithonos growing " old, infirm, and decrepid." We associate the chirping sound of the grasshopper with summer bloom, and the creature with the brightest of green pastures and sunshiny days. Like the beauty of the landscape, the grass·hopper is supposed to sleep in winter, hence the allegory. Besides Memnon, Tithonos had Acmathion by Aurora. Amaethun is the name given by the Welsh to this day to any rare, delicate produce of the earth ; from Maeth—nourishment. A husbandman is called Amaethwr by them. It was the custom of ancient religious philosophers to personify ideas and actions. Ideal beauty was personified as Venus ; strength as Hercules ; youthful manhood as Apollo and Adonis ; speed was symbolised by wings, and the sun's rays by feathers, and one ray or emanation by a single feather ; water was symbolised by a wavy line, &c. From those pictorial or illustrations of mental representations of objects and actions have sprung our alphabets, the letters of which were originally simply pictures, or in the words of Sharpe, in his *History of Egypt*, " the characters were used for the objects only ;" and he adds, " the first great change in the art was to use the figures for the *names* of the objects, and not for the *objects* themselves."

In Egypt Amen-Ra was set forth by the figure of a round ball, symbolising the sun, and with open wings, symbolising its out-coming emanations, one on each side of it, each wing representing many emanations. On each side of the disc of the sun, and as if descending on each side from it, is a crowned-hooded serpent. The heads and tails of the two serpents are held up, and thus the middle of each serpent is greatly bent down in the centre. Each serpent's bent body passes through a ring, which appears as if engaged in sustaining something below. Those two serpents symbolise the good and evil principles, or light and darkness respectively, sustained and kept apart by the sun, who is acting as a mediator. The same idea is implied by the teaching that Osiris and Typhon were brothers, but the latter the deadly foe of the former, but with Horus, the centre character of Egyptian trinity, and meaning the sun's fertilising influence in spring—*i.e.*, time of the Passover, standing between the opposing two forces of summer and winter.

Ra was the Egyptian name of the sun; and Amen, or as the name is often spelt, Amon and Ammon—Jupiter (Iu —Pater or Father)—signifies Hidden, precisely identical in meaning with the Druidic Celi or Keli, and after whom the Celts are so called. Therefore, Amen-Ra signifies the Hidden Sun, or the Creator, who, according to ancient religious philosophy, transmits His emanations to the visible universe by the physical agency of the sun, which, in Welsh, is called Hu Ail or Haul, the *second* sun. The ancients regarded the spiritual or intellectual life within us, apart from the physical life, as a Divine emanation, and, therefore, as immortal as its source, the Creator Himself. The Druidic High Priest, representing the soul-life on earth, was called Menw (oo) the Ancient, also in other

languages Manu, Menu, Minos. The *men* in the name
"Menai" straits, which should be spelt Menau (souls),
signifies the same thing as Amen (Hidden Spirit). In
Welsh brain is called *men*, as in *Men*-ydd. Menwyn (sacred
men) is the Welsh name for mental gift or talent. As the
mind is concealed in the human head or skull, so the
ancients compared the orb of the sun to the head or the
skull of Hu Ail or second Hu, or sometimes Iu, as in
"Jupiter." He was Amen-Ra's Regent in the government
of the universe. Memnon, son of Dawn (Aurora), and of the
Handsomeness of the Landscape, personified by the Greeks
as a masculine personage, is represented as the earthly
priest of the sun, and the light of the moral world, at
Thebes echoing back from earth to heaven at the rising of
the sun, the music which the Voice of the Creator had
imparted to the earth by the agency of the sun at the
beginning of creation. The same idea is found in that
most ancient of poems the Book of Job, where, in the
38th chapter, dealing with the creation of the earth, it is
asked, " Where wast thou when I laid the foundation of
the earth? . . when the morning stars sang together,
and all the sons " (creations?) " of God shouted for joy ? "

It seems the most learned Egyptologists have been
unable to distinguish between an Egyptian priest's priestly
character and his character as a man. The same inability
to distinguish between the priesthood and the individual
invested with the priestly representative character is seen in
numerous commentaries on the High Priest Melchizedec,
whom St. Paul describes as " man," and yet as being
" without father, without mother, without descent, having
neither beginning of days nor end of life." It is almost
trifling with intelligence to remind the reader St. Paul is
referring to the *priesthood* of Melchizedec, and not to the
individual man himself.

The sacred bull Apis, of the Egyptians, symbolised, in the Egyptian Church on earth, the sun in spring rising in the zodiacal sign of the Bull, from, according to M. Dupuis' calculation, 4619 B.C. to 2504 B.C. The bull Apis had a priestly character and an animal character. The priests said that it (Apis) had no earthly father, but that a ray of light came down from heaven upon the cow, his mother, and that this was followed in due time by the birth of the god."[1] Let the reader recollect the white bull, Elgan, of the Druids, and the white cow, Môn, called also Y Vuwch Lacthnen.

We now return to the Memnon statue. It should be stated here that the name "Memnon" is, according to Sharpe, a Greek corruption of the name of Mi Amen, or Amun Mi of the Egyptian language, which is the *priestly* title of the great King Ramesis II., the Sethos (the King) of Manetho's writings. It should be borne in mind that the great monarchs of Egypt were both priests and kings.

We now come to the very remarkable personage who erected the musical statue called "Memnon" by the Greeks, after a later King, Mi Amen—Rameses II. The preceding king, who erected the statue which emits music at the rising of the sun, is called Amun Othph III., and is styled the son of Amen-Ra (the Almighty), and Queen Maut-Mes., widow of Thoth-Mosis IV. Maut, Mut, Ma, Mot, each signifies both matter and mother. "Queen Maut-Mes received a message from heaven through the god Thoth (Tad, or Father, of Druidism) to the effect that she is to give birth to a child. Then the god Kneph (Nêv of Druidism) takes her by the hand, and with the goddess Athor (the sacred Cow as Nature) puts into her, through her mouth, life for the child that is to be born."[2] There cannot be

---

[1] Sharpe's *History of Egypt*, Vol. I., p. 201.   [2] *Ibid*, p. 67.

any doubt the above is an allegory, signifying the same
thing as the generation of the bull Apis by a ray of the
sun descending upon the cow, his mother, and both imply,
through material figures, the institution of the priesthood,
representing the union of soul, or spiritual life, with
matter on earth. The name Jesus is understood to refer
to his human nature, and the name Christ to the Divinity
of the august Nazarene. "For God, who commanded
the light to shine out of darkness, hath shined in our
hearts, to give the light of the knowledge of the glory of
God *in the face of Jesus Christ*." It is that which
"shines in our hearts" that enables us to behold "the
glory of God in the face of Jesus Christ." The allusion is
to the soul, which, apart from physical life, the Creator,
according to old ideas, transmitted to us by the agency of
the sun, and which the apostle describes as a "treasure in
earthen vessels," or, in other words, in bodies made out of
the substance of the earth. The Ancient Druids refer to
the "Face of the Sun," and to "The Eye of Light,"
meaning the focussed light in the Centre of the Circle on
Earth, which symbolised the soul-life on earth. This was
focussed light. We do not know whether they were favoured
with such a manifestation of the Divine Presence in the
sanctuaries of the Stone Age, or that they contrived by art
to produce a brilliant radiating Light in the Centre of their
Holy of Holies, which the Druids called Swyngyleh (Magic
Circle). It is, however, certain they regarded that Light
as their Divine Oracle.

Naturally enough, the Oriental writers of the scriptures
employed Egyptian figures in writing, and we actually find,
in Revelations iii., 14, Christ, himself, designated "Amen,"
"These things saith the Amen." And, in Isaiah lxv., 16,
we have a reference to the "God Amen," which is the

original Hebrew expression, but which, in the Authorised Version, is translated " God of Truth."

In the Druidic System the Celi was the Father of the Sun, and the Sun's inward life, symbolised by a wren, was the Father of Mankind as Souls ; and Memnon symbolised them collectively, by the figure of one High Priest. Every morning the Statue of Memnon greeted the Sun, his Father, with the sound of music, similar to the notes of a harp ; and it is stated the sound has been heard at sunrise in recent years issuing out of the said statue.[1]

" The Egyptians, in their hymns to Osiris " (sun), " invoked that god as the being who dwelt concealed in the embraces of the sun. Not that they deified the sun, considered merely as a mass of luminous or fervid matter, but as the centre or *body* from which the pervading Spirit, the original producer of order, fertility, and organisation, amidst the inert confusion of space and matter, still continued to emanate to preserve the mighty structure which it had formed."[2] The sun has a title of Huan in Welsh (Hu and Anedd, or Abode of Hu).

In the Egyptian hieroglyphics, Amen-Ra, or Hidden Body and Soul of the Sun, are symbolised, as we say elsewhere, by a round orb, and the Divine emanations shooting out of it under the figure of two wings of feathers. But when Amen, without the Ra, is illustrated hieroglyphically, only a single feather is employed. It would appear as if the full wings symbolise the entire operations of the sun in the kingdom of physical nature, and the single feather for " Amen " symbolises, exclusively, the soul coming from the sun to the human " earthen vessel."

[1] Chambers' *Encyclopedia.*
[2] See *Plutarch Qu. Rom.*, p. 138, and *Fragment Orphic.* Quoted by Payne Knight, *Sym. Language*, s. 55.

The great Sphynx, near Gizeh, the second Pyramid, having a man's head and face, and the body of a lion, is doubtless a symbol having direct reference to the gigantic nature of the structure of the Pyramids, representing the power of human intelligence: the human head symbolising the intelligence, and the body of the lion symbolising the might or force of that intelligence, as evidenced in the neighbouring tremendous erections reared by human hands directed by the human Mind enclosed in Matter, or Maut-Mes.

That Memnon is identical with Adonis, Tammuz, Arawn, and Arthur of the Druids, seems certain from the fact that it is said that the river Paphlagonios flowed from his blood, like the river Adonis, in Phœnicia, is said to flow from the blood of Adonis.   That he is, like Adonis, identical with Tammuz, or the sun at the end of the solar year, is proved by the fact that he is said to be a vassal of the Assyrian monarch, Teu Tamus, which appears to be Duw Tammuz (Old Sun), the "Teu" being the Druidic Duw (God).   The old sun, it will be borne in mind, was said, in the East, to be the father of the young sun of the new year.   Strange to find that thus Memnon of Egypt is identical with the Messiah of Israel, who is supposed to be alluded to by the Prophet Haggai ii., 7, in the words "the Desire of all nations shall come."   Or did the Jews commit the mistake of supposing the allusions of the poets to the new sun of each succeeding year, as a "Crowned Babe," was to be a living human Divine personage to come to govern the whole earth ?

During the prolonged struggle for supremacy between corrupt Druidism and Christianity on the continent of Europe, and in the East, Christianity adopted from

Paganism, otherwise corrupt Druidism, those rites and customs which were unobjectionable on the ground of morals; and now, some people, because Christianity is found to be travelling on the old railway of Druidism, object to it altogether. It is a foolish objection, inasmuch as Christianity is a teacher of morals, piety, and faith in the Fatherhood of the Almighty. But the early ecclesiastics, in their intense zeal for the then newer creed, went too far in their policy of adaptation; they positively lied with a view to popularise Christianity. The blame for that cannot be placed at the door of Christianity itself. The story of the Holy Greal is a striking example of the pious frauds of the early ecclesiastics. The following in brief is the invented story of the Holy Greal as a substitute for the Cauldron of Ceridwen with its cider symbol of the Divine Essence—the suns rays in the concrete—and the "Lambs Wool" symbols in the dish already described, both symbolising people feasting on the essence which the sun had left behind in the ripened ingredients of the earth, the contents of the Cauldron of Ceridwen or the earth in the springtime.

"Joseph of Arimathea," state the adapting ecclesiastics, "had a dish made. With it he caught the blood running from the Saviour's body as it hung on the cross. He afterwards begged the body of Pilate. For the devotion showed to the Greal, he was denounced to the Jews, thrown into prison, delivered to the Lord of the land, and exiled, together with the sister of Nicodemus, who had an image of the Lord. Joseph and his companions came to the Promised Land—the White Island—a part of England." We observe in the Legend of Gautier de Douleus that the name also of Logres is given. Lloegr is still the name by which alone England is known to the Welsh unacquainted with the English language, and in Welsh literature generally England is always called Lloegr. "There," the story goes on to state, "they warred against them of the land. When Joseph was short of food, he prayed to the Creator to send him the Greal, wherein he had gathered the holy blood; after which, to them who sat at table the Greal brought bread, wine, and meat in plenty. At his death, Joseph begged that the Greal might remain with his seed; and thus it was that no one, however high a condition, might see it save he was of Joseph's blood."

In the same legend the locality in the White Island wherein the Holy Greal is located is the Island of Apples, said by the ecclesiastics to be Glastonbury! Fabricators are generally eventually caught in the meshes of their own deceit. The name of the mysterious island in Welsh is Ynys 'Avalon, and it was translated into Latin *Insula Pomorum* (the Island of Apples). Now, the translator of the name 'Avalon from the Welsh into Latin fell into the error of supposing the termination "on" in 'Avalon was a plural sign, and therefore translated the name the Island of Apples. In Welsh, impersonated nouns have the "on" as a plural sign, but in the plural names of inanimate natural objects, "on" is never used as a sign plural. We say dyni*on* (men) Derwydd*on* (Druids) in reference to persons; but "on" in Cal*on* (heart), Ffyn*on* (spring of water), &c., is a sign of perenniality and nothing else. In Welsh, the plural for apples is 'Aval*au* and sometimes 'Avalenau. A Welshman would never recognise in the word 'Aval*on* a plural sense. 'Avalon clearly implies the Everlasting Apple, and Ynys 'Avalon the Island of the Everlasting, or ever-durable, Apple, and refers to the apple as a symbol of the perenniality of the sun, and to the *whole* of Britain as its sacred island.

It should be carefully observed also that Yr Ynys Wen, though literally to mean The White Island, signifies Holy Island—" white" being in Welsh used as an adjective, the same as " holy" in English. Arthur signifies the sun as a husbandman ; Garddir or (ei) Arddir ; the " ir " termination being the same as the Latin *Vir*, but with the *v* left out. Arthur and St. George are each names of the sun as a husbandman.

As we have pointed out, the annual " death " of the sun at the winter solstice was symbolised in many ways. (1) By being represented as regards his physical nature falling into a cist in a tumulus. (2) Into a cromleâch, both cist and cromleâch symbolising the earth, the former as a navel and matrix, and the latter the entire fabric of the earth as a belly, when the earth was supposed to be either beehive-shaped, like a tumulus, or like the top slab of a cromleâch or Dolmaen. The reason why a tumulus was used to symbolise Cêd, the Mother of the sun and nature, was the notion that all the attributes of the said great Mother—often called Anian or Anima by the Welsh—operated from below the earth as forces in the work of generation in the earth's loam. Those attributes, we repeat, were poetically personified as three white cows ; three holy maiden goddesses ; by three wives of Arthur ; by three sisters of Arthur ; by three noble ladies of Arthur's Court, or Circle, &c. Symbolically, the tumulus was another figure denoting the whole earth as a protuberance over the hollow containing the matrix of Cêd herself. We repeat, that hollow is the original " Cave " from which so many " gods " (High Priests, representing the sun) of the old world were officially born, and which " Cave " has puzzled so many learned archæologists as to its signification. Primarily the " Cave,"

as the symbol of the Womb of Cêd, is the birthplace and
grave of the sun, and *vice versa*. The Druids buried their
dead in a similar tumuli, and in the new birth of the sun, on
the morning of the new year, they saw, or thought they
saw, the glimmer of hope that the dead also will be raised
into a renewed life like the orb of day is annually
" renewed."   (3)[1] By the Cauldron of Ceridwen (Pair
Ceridwen) symbol of the earth as a circular dish in which
the essence of the sun's virtue acted as yeast, and dealt out
fermentation to the passive or feminine principle already in
the seeds in the earth's loam, which results in a resurrection
of the earth's offspring in spring in endless varieties of new
creations of indescribable beauty. The bodily remains of
the dead as "seeds" of the bodies in the centre of the
tumulus, or mound, were the only " seeds" of the mound,
considered as the garden of the sun, which did not shoot
forth into *new life* in the springtime. They and the sun
are annually " renewed." The Druids, no doubt, often asked
" When is also the spring time of dead *humanity*?"

Job was not the only patriarch of the ancient world who
murmured in the contemplation of the phenomena of nature
—"There is hope of a tree, if it be cut down, that it will
sprout again, and that the tender branch thereof will not
cease. Though the roots thereof wax old in the earth, and
the stock thereof die in the ground, yet through the scent
of water it will bud, and bring forth boughs like a plant.
But man dieth, and wasteth away; yea, man giveth up the

---

[1] By Cêd, symbolised in the East as a Whale (Cetus), as already described,
symbolising the passive principle in matter, Anima (Anian), as Latona, the
mother of Apollo (Sun); Black Virgin, serpent, as symbol of Athene or
Divine Wisdom, often described also as Minerva, all symbolising the feminine
principle in matter welling forth from Cêd.

ghost, and—WHERE IS HE?"[1] Every raised green tumulus in Britain, and wherever seen, and containing remains of the dead, is, to this day, an expression of humanity, in the face of high heaven, of the humble hope of mankind, in the olden days, of a resurrection of the dead.

> " * *   the Tomen, on its lonely hill,
> Bears silent record of the mighty still!"

[1] Job xiv. 7, &c.

CHAPTER VII.

F all the curious solar myths of the Druids, the most extraordinary is that relating to the annual death of the sun under the title of Arawn (To Wait), and, sometimes, under the title of Saidwrn (Linga of the Urn), corrupted into Saturnus; and also named Arthur, Taliesin, &c. The "death" took place on December 20th, the end of the solar year, and he was supposed to rest in his ark—grave, otherwise the matrix of Cêd (Cetus of the Latins, and Der Ketos of the Greeks)—on December 21st, and to be re-born a babe, and named Hu Gadarn (Hesus the Mighty), and known also as Taliesin, &c., renewed on the morning of December 22nd, after an absence of forty hours, from 4 o'clock on the afternoon of the 20th to 8 o'clock on the morning of December 22nd. The 21st was not reckoned with the days of the year, for it was the period of the sun's absence, and the suspension of his labours in the government of the universe, and when it was supposed Time itself *waited* for the reappearance of the brilliant guide in the heavens. Nevertheless, the forty hours are referred to in the phrase a "year and a day," the "day" being the said forty hours. It appears probable the solar allegory originated at a period so remote as that when the sun did not come into view in the latitude of Britain between sunset on December 20th and sunrise on the 22nd. Or, is the legend a type given to the Druids, thousands of years before the actual event, of the interment of Jesus at sunset on Friday, and his resurrection at sunrise on Sunday morning, at the end and the beginning of the sacred year of the Jews? There are most curious agreements between the incidents of the solar allegory and the death, interment and resurrection of the Lord Jesus. Alawn, or Hermes, otherwise Tegid, &c., the Druidic name of the sun on March 21st, was a mediator between the powers of summer and winter; between the creator and the destroyer; he was Horus, between Osiris and Typhon; Mithras, between Ormuzd and Ahriman; Jupiter, between Neptune and Pluto; Poseidon, between Zeus and Dis; Vishnoo, between Brahma and Siva. The Lord Jesus, on the cross, was between good and evil—the penitent and the impenitent thieves—like Seth was between Cain and Abel. In the Egyptian solar allegory it was Typhon who killed Osiris, which is tantamount to Abel killing Cain.

Jesus was interred in a stone grave (kist?) in a garden. The Druidic tumulus or circular heap, as the symbol of the round earth above the rational horizon, and regarded as the Garden of the Lord, had a stone kist in it, called by the Druids, as a coffin is still named in Welsh, Ark, wherein the dead body is deposited in the midst of the symbolical garden. In Druidism the soul which had tenanted the body had, if tarnished by evil deeds, returned to some part of the Circles of Abred, the Druidic name of their circles of transmigration, which circles begin in the sea of Annwn, the Great Deep or Hades, and ascend to the "line of free will" compared to the equinoctial line dividing the southern and northern hemispheres from each other. The Druids taught that at the "death" of the sun at sunset, on December 20th, his divinity was received for safety and rejuvenation back by Cêd into her matrix in the sea of the elements or Mor Annwn, symbolised apparently in the Hebrew temple by the Brazen Sea. It is clear a tumulus, with a stone kist in the middle of it, was, in Druidism, used as a symbol of Cêd's Womb as the Cave of Delphi was.

Delphi signifies Dolphin, which is the symbol Der Ketos
(whale), the Druidic Céd, represented by another kind of
fish.   The hairy appendages of the human Vulva are still,
in Welsh, called Céd-dor, or The Door of Cetus, or Der
Ketos.   The principal garden-grave of the sun in this
country is Silbury Hill (Sol Barrow), to the south from,
and close to, the vast ruins of the stupendous Druidic
temple of Avebury, Wilts.   The dimensions of the garden-
grave are as follow, taken from the *Imperial Gazetteer:*
"It is a mile-and-a-half from the Druidic temple.   The
meridian line of the temple cleaves it in two.   It measures
1680 feet at the base, and 315 feet at the top; is 180 feet
high, and if formed in our day would cost £20,000."
The Druidic name of the mound is *Cluda'r Cycrangon*
(She carries the Mediator), the reference being to Céd, or
Cetus, "carrying" the old sun, as Arawn, that is, Saturn,
otherwise Tammuz, Arthur, Adonis, Taliesin, Osiris, &c.,
in her hollow, the mound being symbolical of her matrix.

ANNUAL DEATH OF THE OLD SUN, AND ANNUAL BIRTH OF THE NEW SUN.

We will now proceed to give what we have culled from
the records of antiquity relating to the "death" of the old
sun at the winter solstice on December 20th, and his new
"birth" as a babe, forty hours afterwards, on the morning
of December 22nd.   The dove was the Persian symbol of
Mithras, the second person of the Persian trinity, and also
of Adonis of the Phœnicians, &c.   The fact is, the white dove
was the symbol of the whole solar trinity; the body of the
dove symbolised the sun as a material fertiliser of the seeds
of the earth in spring above the eastern end of the equinoctial line, and the two points of the wings indicated the sun

in the north in the tropic of Cancer, and in the south in the tropic of Capricorn respectively. At Hierapolis the dove, which was of gold, was exhibited between the figures of Linga and Yoni [1] (the concomitants of the Fatherhood of the Creator and of the Motherhood of Cêd, his Consort, and personified as Jupiter and Venus.

It should be borne in mind, in reading what follows, that the Druids represented the sun as a material substance, containing the Divine Spirit. It is often referred to as a skull or round head, and the places of a skull, or Golgothas, were old sites of the temples of the sun, as a round head. As the Mind is located in the human head, so they represented the Divine expression (Menu, Minos, 'Menydd, or Menw—Brain), as the will of the Creator, in the sun, as a head, and they represented it also by the symbol \//, and, in the case just mentioned, by a golden dove, gold being, in all antiquity, an emblem of the colour of the sun.

One of the most remarkable characters in all the antiquities of the East is Tammuz. Cyril, of Alexandria, tells us that Adonis and Tammuz were one and the same character. Adonis was the sun in spring, and Tammuz is the sun at the winter solstice. St. Jerome tells us a very important fact that "the winter solstice was the time when Tammuz was believed to have died, though the wailing for him took place in June" (when the sun is in the Tropic of Cancer), that is, by the Hebrews, as shown in Ezekiel, describing the weeping women with their faces directed towards the north (*Ezekiel* viii., 14), but in the middle of March, or a little later, by the Phœnicians, their neighbours. The following is stated by the Rev. Thomas Godwin, B.D., in reference to the

---

[1] Knight's *Symbolic Language*, Section 220.

death and regeneration of Adonis (sun), taken from the Orphic Argonaustica, and refers to the performance of the rites in Phœnicia, Syria, &c. :—" An oath of secrecy was administered to all who were to be initiated. Then commenced the ceremonies by a description of chaos or great abyss (Annwn, or great deep sea of the Druids), and the confusion attendant upon it. Then is described by the poet, a person as a man of justice (Arawn—old sun) about to be born (as young Adonis and Hu Gadarn, or Hesus the Mighty, in Druidism), and mentions the orgies, or funeral lamentations on account of the just person (Tammuz, Arawn, Adonis, Arthur, Saturn, Noah, and known by other names) and those of the Arkite Athene (Ark, and the Dove, as Divine Wisdom within it, floating on the Sea of Chaos). The celebration took place at night (the old sun being at the time in the Ark on the Sea of Chaos). " In those mysteries, after the attendants had, for a long while, bewailed the death of the just person, he was understood to be restored to life ; to have experienced a resurrection, signified by the re-admission of light into the temple " (the emblematical firmament). " On this the priest addressed the company, saying : ' Comfort yourselves, all ye who have been partakers" (sympathisers, and therefore, fellow-sufferers) " of the mysteries of the Deity thus preserved, for we shall now enjoy some respite from our labours'" (lamentations). The priest, now himself assuming the character of the newly-born Adonis, or Hesus the Mighty, says, " I have escaped a sad calamity, and my lot is greatly mended." The hitherto wailing congregation now answer by the invocation, " Hail to the Dove ! Giver of Light ! " [1]

The Rev. Thomas Godwin, B.D., states also[2]:—" Concerning Adonis, whom sometimes ancient authors call

---

[1] Calmet's Dic. Fragments, vol. iii., p. 577.   [2] Moses and Aaron, p. 152.

Osiris (sun again), there are two remarkable things—the death or loss of Adonis, and the finding him again. As there was great lamentation at his loss, especially among the women, there was great joy at his finding. By the death of Adonis, we are to understand the departure of the sun; by his finding again we are to understand his return. Now the sun seems to depart twice a year; (1) when he is in the Tropic of Cancer (longest day of summer), and (2) when he is in the Tropic of Capricornus (shortest day)," or north and south, touched by the two open wings of the symbolical white dove, the body of the dove indicating the sun in Aries (Ram-lamb).

The Druids had two animal figures to symbolise Côd, the mother of the sun, namely, a huge serpent, at Avebury, or Ab-Ri (Son of God), Wilts. It was over two miles in sinuous length, with the awful face directed towards that part of the heavens where the young sun, named Hesus the Mighty, reappears on the morning of December 22nd (New Year's Day). She, as Divine Wisdom, having slipped up through the earth from Gwenydva (Paradise), a district of Hades, is stationed there to encourage his advance, like a mother encouraging her child to "walk," and also to threaten the Power of Darkness, which pursued him into herself as Côd (Aid) into the sea of Hades forty hours before. The serpent here also symbolises the Dyrraith attribute associated elsewhere with Tynghedwen (Ceres). It should be borne in mind these symbols were the orthographies of the ancients, which conveyed to their minds notions or ideas beyond the symbols themselves, as letters of the alphabet in combination do to us to-day.

The Avanc (Beaver) has the fore-feet of a land animal, and the hind ones are like those of a water bird, being web-footed. The sun at the winter solstice was always seen sinking into the Atlantic Ocean—hence the Beaver, with its remarkable feet adaptation for both earth and water, came to be employed by the Druids as a symbol for the sun.

The Druids, instead of a dove, employed a wren to symbolise the sun's divinity escaping into an Arkite shrine, to save himself from his murderous pursuer, and also to be regenerated and restored, forty hours later, to the government of the universe.

As before mentioned, Taliesin is one of the titles of the sun, and in the solar legend, he is said to have been found in a skin coracle—we shall come to that presently. This is the same idea, but conveyed in another form, as the white dove Iona (Jonah) swallowed by a whale (Der Ketos), and the wren being received into a "house," the same as the Arkite shrine. It should be borne distinctly in mind that Ceridwen and Cêd are the same. We remind the reader that another symbol of Cêd is a naked ship or ark, or coracle, called *y Llong Voel* (Naked Ship) in Druidism. In the East the figures of a whale and dolphin, both symbols unquestionab y derived from a mistaken notion respecting the Druidic Cêd (Aid), were used to symbolise the consort of the Creator and mother of the sun, floating below and around the earth—and often the earth is represented as the middle of Cêd's body—floating in the sea of the elements, the Annwn of the Druids, and on the afternoon of each December 20th eagerly receiving the sun back into herself. In figure 12, plate 50, of Calmet's *Biblical Dictionary*, we find a medal of Ancient Corinth with the figure of an old man who had entered a whale. He is shown in a state of decrepitude. But on the same medal the old man is shown to have come out of the same fish in a state of infancy. Taylor on Calmet's goes on to state, "the tutelary deity" (Cêd) "nurses and suckles the babe, so that the child grows up to maturity." "The combination," Taylor goes on to state, "of *two* periods of time into *one* representation has rendered this medal hitherto inexplicable to the most learned antiquarians."

In plate 14 of Calmet's, we have the medal of Bezer, or Bozrah—the Bozrah to the south east of the Dead Sea. On one side of the medal is the head of Tre Janus Decius. On the reverse is a female figure, her head is crowned with turrets (symbol of power); in her right hand is a staff terminating in a cross; in her left hand is a cornucopia, or The Horn of Plenty. By her side, and grasping her hand, is the infant Bacchus (or old Silenus "renewed") dancing with a skin wine-bottle on his shoulder. The cornucopia, which is full of seeds, is the round half of the earth above the rational horizon, as the belly of Cêd. The dancing little boy is the young sun of the new year, called Adonis, Hu Gadarn, Bacchus, &c. The wine bottle implies that he has brought with him the element necessary to ferment the seeds in the earth's ovary, personified as Venus, symbolised by the cornucopia on the arm of his mother. The cross appears to symbolise the triumph over the Power of Hades, which, forty hours before, had sought to annihilate the old sun, and that his mother, whose Vulva is now absent from the top of the cross Tau, had carried it (the cross) away in triumph. The straight, upright beam of the cross is the solstitial colure, with the path of the sun crossing it along the tropic of capricornus on December 20th. On other medals Cêd is shown standing with her left foot on a round heap (tumulus as a grave), and, on another, she stands in a temple, and her foot is placed on an ark; both ark and tumulus representing the same attribute in Druidism. In reference to the above, Calmet's states, "Venus was born from a ship." That would imply that Venus is one of the three emanations of Cêd—pervading the substance of the earth—which is symbolised as an ark-ship navigating the Sea of the Elements, otherwise as a heap or tumulus, otherwise belly of Cêd, as the grave of the sun each December 20th. Britain and the Island of Delos, each symbolising the round earth, were said to float. The earth, as a conical heap, the belly of Cêd, was set forth as resting on the surface of the ocean.

"Hercules (sun) went into a sea fish, where he continued part of three days and three nights" (really from December 20th, at 4 o'clock p.m., to December 22nd, at 8 o'clock a.m.) "When Hercules came out again, he had lost his hair" (rays) "and appeared as a beardless babe." "At Corinth the young sun was named Palemon, that is, 'The Old Man,'" states Calmet's, and the great Biblical critic, Taylor, adds, naturally enough, "strange indeed that a child should be called old!" The reason for it is evident enough by the light of the Druidic mythological system. It is said of Hercules (the sun), that he traversed a vast sea in a cup or skiff (Cêd, a boat), which Nerus, otherwise Bacchus or Oceanus (Neptune or Plennydd) lent him for his preservation. Nerus (Humidity) is the Nêr (Power of the Most High God in Druidism). The following is to be understood thus: Hyperion is the son of the Most High Coelus (Celi) and Terra (Earth, as Cêd). That implies the sun of this year is Hyperion, the father of the young sun of the succeeding year.

Now, in reference to the Ark, called Cup, in which Hercules is preserved at sea, the following verses of Stesichorus, preserved in the Athenæus, are quoted by Bryant: [1]

> " 'Twas in a golden Cup
> That Helius (sun) passed,
> —Helius, Hyperion's son,—
> O'er floods and oceans wafted far away :
> To Erebus he went, and the sad realms of night.
> *His aged parent* there he found,
> And the kind comfort of his better days,
> And all his blooming offspring.
> Then to the sacred grove he sped—
> The sacred grove of laurel."

Erebus is Hades, the Annwn of the Druids. The "parent" is Cêd, or Ceridwen, of the Druids, the Consort of the Almighty; Mother of the sun and earth, or of Venus, as a conceiver. The Cauldron of Ceridwen is Venus. As stated repeatedly, the sun's annual stay in Cêd was during forty hours only. In the Ancient Laws of Wales, under the subject of "Havod un Nôs" (Summer's Night Abode), it is enacted, that if a man erects a cot on a Common in one night, and a family sleep in it forty hours (some say forty nights, but it is a mistake) the man is given a free title to it, together with a certain quantity of land round it, which is to be marked out with a plough. No doubt the privilege implied, originally, a right to bury and to erect a tumulus and to construct the usual water moat or trench around it. The number "forty" appears to refer to the time the sun was said to be in his Ark—in his mother Cêd—as already described.

---

[1] *Analysis.* Vol. II., p. 405.

CHAPTER VIII.

A S stated in a former page, among the British Druids the wren was used in the same sense as the white dove was used in the East, viz. :— as symbol of the Divinity in the sun. In the Welsh language the wren to this day is called "Druid," as "Derw," "Drew," and "Dryw." The reason of the Druids for selecting this wee bird for so sacred a purpose, was, no doubt, the fact that its nest is round, as they symbolised the belly of Cêd to be, and with a hole in its centre (umbilicus), like one of their own beddrods or tumuli. We seem to detect in the selection, a trace of the hope of the resurrection of the dead; for the Almighty, by the instrumentality of warmth, converts the chaotic eggs in the round beddrod (round grave) like nest into singing birds, and the same Almighty power can also restore dead humanity to corporeal existence from the round barrows. The weakness of the wren symbolised the apparent feebleness of the sun in its operations upon the earth at the winter solstice. The wren, therefore, was sacred to the sun at the winter solstice.

The following is quoted from the *Cambrian Journal* [1]:— " A mode of levying contributions at Christmas was by means of the Cutty Wren "—" Cutty " seems to be derived from Cêd, Ketos, or Cetus—" Having procured a wren, and placed it in a small ornamented box or paper house, with a square of glass at either end, two or four men would carry it about, elevated on four poles fixed to the corners,

---

[1] 1857. p. 183.

singing the while a long ditty. The words, though rough and unpolished, serve to describe three divisions of humanity. (1) The fault-finding inquisitives; (2) The know-nothings; and (3) The know-alls. The four men would enter the doorway, groaning under the weight of their burden, and looking as if they had just relieved Atlas of his load."

We have heard it said, the men would declare the occupier of the small box on the poles was now very poor. That he had once been wealthy, and would be so again, and the contribution asked would be applied to succour him in his need. In most European languages, according to Brand's *Popular Antiquities*, a wren is known by a name signifying king. Brand quotes the following popular doggerel :—

> " Tom Tit and Jenny Wren,
>   Are God Almighty's cock and hen."

In the Welsh language there is a popular rhyme to the following effect :—

> " He who robs a robin's nest shall surely taste the rope ;
>   He who robs a wren's nest to see God's face he cannot hope."

Brand quotes the following :—

> " I found a robin's nest within our shed,
>   And in the barn a wren has young ones bred ;
>   I never take away their nests, nor try
>   To catch the old ones, lest a friend should die ;
>   Dick took a wren's nest from his cottage side,
>   And ere a twelvemonth passed his mother died."

In French a wren is called, among other names, Boeuf de Dieu, or Divine Meat. This reminds us of the allegory in which it is stated the body of Osiris (sun), one of the gods of Egypt, was cut up by Typhon (the devil) into fragments, which Typhon divided among his friends; of the "blood" of Bacchus (sun) — wine — being divided among his votaries; and most astonishing of all, of the blessed Eucharist, consisting, according to one school of Christians, of the real flesh and blood of the Lord Jesus Christ.

The sun's rays, continued in a concrete form, and eaten in the produce yielded by the earth and retained in them through the winter, after the fertilising force or essence of the sun from whence it had come in spring and summer had ceased to come, is what is meant by "partaking of the fragments of the gods." As already said, bread is personified by the goddess Tynghedwen (Ceres); and the "blood" of the sun by Bacchus, or the sun's nocturnal heat influence.

HUNTING THE CUTTY WREN.

In the Isle of Man, it is customary to hunt the Cutty Wren at the winter solstice. "A wren is affixed to a long pole, with its wings extended." In that way a cross is formed; "and it is" in that shape "carried before the hunters, who march to every house chanting. After making the usual circuit, and collecting what they can obtain, they lay the wren on a bier, and then carry it in procession to the churchyard, where, with a whimsical solemnity, they make a grave, bury the wren, and sing dirges which they call "her Knell." After the funeral the mourners form a circle outside the churchyard, and dance to the music provided for the occasion." All this, we are told, takes place on Saint Stephen's Day (Dec. 26th, the morrow after the winter solstice of the Julian Calendar— by the 26th the 21st would be implied now, being the

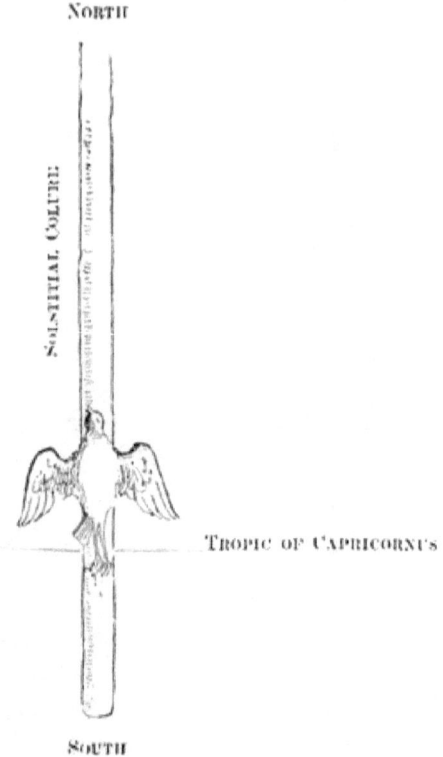

morrow after the present period of the winter solstice; in Druidism, the solar one is on the 20th of that month), and the allegorical laying of the wren in the grave would be from sunset, 4 o'clock on the 20th, until sunrise, 8 o'clock on the 22nd—forty hours. The statement goes on describing another mode of carrying the crucified wren—"The wren" in the procession "is suspended by the legs in the

centre of two hoops, crossing each other at right angles.
The hoops are decorated with evergreens and ribands, and
the company sing 'The Hunt of the Wren.'"   The two
hoops crossing each other at right angles, illustrate the
apparent convexity of the heavens above the rational
horizon, and the wren suspended in it symbolises the sun
crucified in the heavens at noon on the shortest day.
"At the close of the song, if they be fortunate enough to
obtain a small coin, they give in return a feather of the
wren." This feather symbolises a ray from the sun. "And
before the close of the day the little body is almost
featherless."[1]

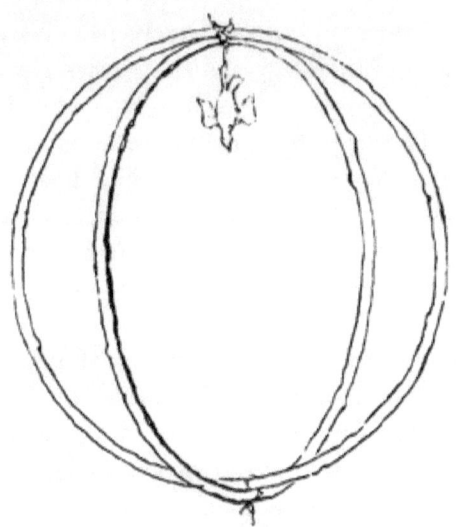

    This symbol refers really to the death of the old sun
while on the middle of the path of the equinox colure
(March 21).   It is a Phœnician one, and due to the
Eastern error intruding into Britannia.

---

[1] Train's *Isle of Man*, quoted by Brand.

Brand states—"The Irish also have a wren hunt, a whole parish running from hedge to hedge wren-hunting; and they teach their children to *thrust them with thorns.*" The reader will remember the crown of thorns.

The sun, as a head, was the seat of the Divinity, hence Taliesin, speaking of himself as the sun, states—

> "Fy Nuw, fy nerthiad,
> A ddodes, trwy fy Iad,
> Enaid ym pwllad."

> My God, my strengthener,
> Placed, through my temples,
> A soul in my head.

The middle of the crown of the human head is called " Iâd " in the language of the Druids. It signifies Hu (*e* sound to *u*,) and Hâd (seed)—soul described as spiritual seed from God (Hu). It was supposed the soul entered the head through the middle of its apex. The soul comes, like everything else, as the Druids supposed, from Cêd, by the instrumentality of Celi. Hence the name given to the part of the head through which the soul enters.

Col. Vallency, in the 13th number of his *Collectanea de Rebus Hibernicis*, page 97, speaks of the wren, and says that the Druids regarded the wren as the king of all birds. The superstitious respect, he adds, shown to this little bird gave offence to our first Christian Missionaries, and, by their commands, he is still hunted and killed by the peasants on Christmas day.[1] Train, in his *History of the Isle of Man*, states, that the Manx herring fishers dare not go to sea without a dead wren with them, for fear of disasters and storms at sea. Their tradition is of a sea spirit that hunted the herring tack, attended always

---

[1] Aubrey's *Miscellanies*, 2nd Ed., p. 45.

G

by storms, and that at last it assumed the figure of a wren
and flew away. So they think when they have a dead wren
with them all is snug.—Quoted from the *Scottish Gallovi-
dian Encyclopædia*, p. 157. But what the originators of
of the custom really believed was, that storms and disasters
were caused by the evil spirit, Avagddu (Pluto), the enemy
of the sun, and that nothing was better calculated to mollify
him than the tribute of a dead wren—the Druidic symbol,
when living, of Divinity in the sun. But the Manx fishermen simply do as their forefathers did, and know nothing
as to the original meaning of the custom—that the dead
wren was a sacrifice to the devil ! The goat "for Azazel"
on the Jewish Day of Atonement, implied precisely the same
kind of sacrifice.

Train mentions other customs observed by the inhabitants
of the Isle of Man. The Druidic Divine Triad are associated with the following : "Before marrying, the party
walk three times round the church. Every funeral goes
thrice round the cross in the churchyard."

Since writing the foregoing we have visited the ancient
city of St. David, Pembrokeshire, a place under the line of
the setting sun on the shortest day. The whole district is
teeming with Druidic traditions and remains. Quite acci-
dentally we discovered that, within living memory, it was
customary there, about the time of the winter solstice
(St. Stephen's Day), to carry about a wren in a small
' house,' such as that given in the foregoing illustration.
On reaching each habitation to be visited, the processionists,
four of whom carried the bier on which the ' house ' stood,
and which was decorated with tricoloured ribbons, sang
verses most plaintively. It appeared the custom ceased to
be observed about forty years ago, and it was by searching

out aged inhabitants we at last discovered a few of the verses that were sung by the processionists on such occasions. An aged Welsh woman, working in a garden in April, 1892, recited for us the following verses :—

I.

Dryw Bach ydyw'r Gwr,
Am dano mae stwr;
Mae cwest arno fe,
Nos heno'n mhob lle.

II.

Fe ddaliwyd y Gwalch :
'Rhoedd 'neithiwr yn falch,
Mewn 'Stafell Wen Dég,
Gyda'r Unbrawd-ar-Ddég.

III.

Fe dorwyd y Twr;
Fe ddaliwyd y Gwr :
Fe 'i ro'w'd e' mewn llèn,
Ar elor fraith wen.

IV.

Rhibanau pob lliw,
O amgylch y Dryw :
Rhibanau tri thro,
Ar ei ben yn lle tó.

V.

Mae'r Drywod yn scant,
Wedi hedfan i bant :
Hwy ddenant yn ôl,
Trwy lwybrau'r Hen Ddôl.

Without attempting to reduce the interesting old verses into English rhyme, we freely translate them, care being taken to convey in the translation the Welsh idiomatic expressions :—

I.

The Little Wren is the Hero,
His renown is everywhere ;
Tonight, in all places,
An inquest upon him is held.

II.

The Sly-wretch was last night very proud,
In a holy, fine, upper chamber,
In the society of the brethren eleven.
He, however, was found out and captured.

III.

The stone-grave was burst open ;[1]
The sly-wretch was found out and captured—
In a great winding sheet He was placed
And caried on a bier —colours white and black.

IV.

All coloured ribbons
We place round the Wren ;
Thrice-twisted ribbons
Above him for roof.

V.

The wrens are now scarce—
They've winged away ;
But again they'll come back,
Over the tracks of Old Mead.[2]

---

[1] A Kist grave is referred to by Taliesin in the words :—
"Bôl Tor Meinin" (The Belly of a Tower of Stones).
Myr. Ar., p. 35, Ed. 1870.

[2] "Hen Ddôl" (translated Old Mead) is the name of a locality in the lowlands below the Cathedral of St. David.

In the first verse we find the word " Cwest," which is the Latin *Inquisitus* altered, and adopted into the Welsh language. This indicates that the verse came into existence subsequently to the period of the Roman Imperial domination in Wales. The expressions "Holy, fine, upper chamber," " brethren eleven," &c., prove they were composed by one under the influence of Christian ideas and history. We seem to detect in the word " Cwest," the hand of a Roman Catholic Scribe of a later period than that of the first visit of St. Augustine to Wales near the close of the Sixth Century of the Christian Era. It will be observed that the verses are most curious for the dual characters given apparently to the Wren. In one place he is " Gwr " (Hero) ; then he is, apparently, " Gwalch," a Welsh idiomatic word signifying Sly Wretch. Then there is an allusion to the " Sly Wretch " as being " proud," and " in a holy, fine, upper chamber," with the eleven disciples, which clearly identifies the " sly wretch " with Judas Iscariot. Then the display of coloured ribbons streaming from the summit of the small "house " in which the wren is located, seems to identify the wren inside with the victorious Divinity of the Lord Jesus—Judas being added to the " eleven," Christ making the thirteenth. It is quite possible the rite and the verses, like our " Mary Lwyd " (Holy Mary) rites, still performed in Glamorganshire and Monmouthshire during the Christmas festivities, are fragments of the Miracle Plays of the Middle Ages, and that some of the verses have been lost, and that the present ones are not given in their original order. But what is more probable is, that we behold in the confused order of the ideas in the verses, an attempt on the part of Ancient Roman Catholic Ecclesiastics in the Ancient British Church of Wales to mix the character of the Wren symbol, which continued to be sacred in the eyes of the Welsh masses, with the traitor Judas Iscariot.

This may be true, but the "hunting the wren" was, apparently, customary among devil worshippers before the advent of Christianity.

Now, the name Taliesin signifies, primarily, the sun, and secondly, one of the titles of the high priest of the sun, being the sun's representative in the Zodiacal circle, or church, on earth. Taliesin, speaking in his representative character, states (600 A.D.) as follows:—

> "Wyv Dwr, wyv Dryw,
> Wyv Saer, wyv Syw."
> I am a Tower, I am a Wren,
> I am a Carpenter, I am Wise.

both antithetical conditions or characters. In "Cad Goddeu (Myvyrian)" he says of himself as the sun's representative:

> "Mwyav tair ar gyvryd,
> A chwerais ym myd,
> Ac un a deryw,
> O ystyr dilyw."
> The chief of the wise ones,
> Who played in the world,
> (Am) identical with the wren,
> Of the deluge signification.

Taliesin also describes the sun as :—

> "Tarw trin, Teyrn Byd,
> Morawg a Morydd."
> I am a Bull cultivator,
> The King of the World,
> One who loves the sea,
> And is a Sailor.

In "Ymarwar Lludd Mawr," Taliesin describes the priest of the sun as :—

> "Dwvn ddarogan (ydd ?) Dewin Drywon."
> Deep diviner of the Living Wren.

The "on" in Drywon is not used as a plural sign, but is a sign of perenniality, as in calon (heart), and the sun's Divinity being referred to as ever living.

> " Derwyddon doethur,
> Darogenwch i Arthur :
> Yssid y sydd gynt,
> Neu'r cighenynt?
> A Christ y crocaw (crogedig),
> A dydd brawd Rhaglaw.
> Ac am un a deryw,
> O ystyr Dilyw."

Wise Druids, sing among the oaks to Arthur (sun),
What is there more early than me they can sing of ?
And of Christ crucified—the Vice-Roy of the judgment day,
And of the Wren of the Deluge signification.

Typhon is the Arabic name for Deluge, and it is also the
name of the Destroyer, or Satan.   Dilyw, translated
Deluge, signifies literally Anarchy (Di and Llyw).   The
Latin *diluvium* appears to be derived from the above
Welsh compound word.

A symbol by which the Druids typified the earth as
a globular object was a pure white egg, called by them
Corwgl Gwydrin (Glass Coracle).   The fecundity of the
earth, meaning Venus or Virgo, an emanation of Cêd, was
symbolised by a hen, called Y Iâr Ceridwen (Hen of Holy
Love).   Instead of by a dove or a wren, they now symbolised
the sun's divinity by a cock with spread wings (rays), his
body and *beak*, as in the other birds, the virility of the
sun in spring.   Payne Knight, in his *Worship of Priapus*,
has the illustration of a statue of a cock with a Priapian
beak.   In front of the marble and below the bird are the
words in Greek characters, Zeus Soter (Jove, or Jupiter,
the Saviour).   Suidas states, " Amongst the Egyptians
Priapus is called Horas" (like the beak as a Linga,
between the two wings of the cock, Horus is the *middle*
person of the Egyptian Trinity).   " Horus," Suidas proceeds to state, " is represented in the human form, holding
in his right hand a sceptre, because he " the fertilising force
" bears sway over everything on land and sea.   .   .   He

also bears wings." One wing is Osiris, and the other
Typhon, in corrupt Druidism; in pure Druidism, however,
the last-mentioned wing is Gwron (Hero). Suidas also
mentions, "Horus bears a disc or circle to show he is
identified with the sun."[1] In all creeds the second person
of the trinity is what Justin Martyr designates the "Seminal
Logos" by the instrumentality of which all things were and
are made. The sun rising east in spring between the
tropics of Capri and Cancer. The Glass Coracle symbolised
Côd, and the Isle of Britain, secondarily, as representing
the Vulva of Côd as afloat. We have, in Welsh, a prosody
which clearly has come down from Druidic times. It is
called "Mic Dinbych." Mic now signifies a shout. No
doubt it originally signified a chorus. Din-bych signifies
high hill (of worship). The following are translations
from archaic Welsh of portions of two stanzas:—

> Amiable the circle cover (or belly), which is on the
>   surface of the ocean,
> Her chief will be merry at her splendid calends.
> When the sea will work an expanding energy.
> Amiable is the circle which is on the broad lake,
> A fortress without bounds, the sea encircles it :
> The Salutation House of Britain.

The last expression seems to refer to Avebury Circle, Wilts,
as representing Britannia's Isle, which represented the whole
round earth above the rational horizon. "Fortress without
bounds" signifies the sea and the illimitable space beyond
the ring of the horizon, which the deep trench around,
and full of water, and the circle of one hundred stones
running round the rim of the green flat arena enclosed
by the trench of the temple of Bryn Gwyddon (Avebury) symbolised.

---

[1] Dr. Inman's *Ancient Faiths*, vol. ii., p. 258.

CHAPTER IX.

T appears that in remote times a Druidic temple stood on Mount Libanus, Palestine. It is said Adonis (sun) used to be much on Mount Libanus, where Venus (the personified conceiving power of the Earth in Spring), frequently descended to meet him, but Mars (Pluto), or the devil, envying Adonis, assumed the shape of a wild boar, and attacked Adonis when hunting, and struck him in the groin. The story, of course, is an old-world parable, and refers to the sun at the winter solstice losing his virile power, and the Phœnicians dragged the rites to Easter time, the end of their sacred year. It is well to remind the reader that several Eastern nations ended and began their year at the vernal equinox instead of at the winter solstice, and dragged ceremonies relating to the latter to the former. We have already hinted that the Hebrews, by extolling Abel and employing blood in their religion, mixed the Typhonic character of the third person of the Egyptian trinity with the real or uncorrupted worship of Jehovah—the Creator's Name. Here, again, it appears as if their not being permitted by their law to eat of the flesh of swine was not really due to its being unclean, at least at the beginning, but to the fact that Typhon here, in the character of a Wild Boar, was said to have assumed the form of the third person of the Egyptian trinity, who is actually addressed as "Jehovah" by Abraham when the third person of his three visitors was on his way to *destroy* the Cities of the Plain. The two others, who had visited the patriarch under the oaks of Mamre (Memra-Word), had

gone on their merciful errand, warning Lot of his danger.
Other nations who did not worship Mars, that is, the devil,
Typhon, or Pluto, ate the flesh of swine ; and they were
particular favourites with the Druids because they fattened
on the Sacred Acorns of the Sacred Oaks. Strange to say,
the bee was also " unclean " under the law of Moses. It
was sacred in Druidism, and the clergy were called after
it Clêr (Bees), hence Cleros and Clergy.

We have, in the above, the reason for the custom of
serving up with joy the boar's head at Christmas. The
custom implies victory over the asailant of Adonis on Mount
Libanus. The custom was formerly very popular in Britain,
and is, we believe, still observed in the palace of the monarch,
and in some other great houses, and at the Oxford
University. The songs which were sung on the festive
occasion are still preserved, such as :—

> " The bore's heade, I understande,
> Is the chief servyce in this lande :
> Loke wherever it be fande,
>   Servite Cum Cantico.
>
> The bore's heade in hands bringe I,
> With garlandes gay and rosemary :
> I pray you all synge merely,
> Qui estis in Convivio."

Aubrey states (1678), it was customary to bring in the
boar's head *with a lemon in its mouth*.[1] The golden apple
(lemon) in the mouth of the boar, signified, in Druidism, the
sun (Adonis) in the similitude of an apple. The rite implies
slaying the Destroyer with Adonis in his mouth, but the
Divinity which was in it flown away. The following further
particulars are given by the poets, respecting the attack
upon Adonis, otherwise Jupiter, Arthur, &c., on Mount

---

[1] Brand's *Popular Antiquities*, Vol. 1., p. 484.

Libanus—" Venus, when she heard the groans of Adonis, hastening to his assistance, pricked her foot with a thorn, and the blood which issued from the wound, falling on a rose, turned it from a lily to carnation colour, and the blood of Adonis was converted into a flower called Anemone. Venus laid Adonis down on a bed of lettuce in a garden. She then proceeded, herself, to Hades, and there saw Proserpine, the Queen of Pluto (Pluto is the Druidic Avagddu, and is identical with Mars), king of the infernal regions, and she succeeded in obtaining conditions as to Adonis's future. Proserpine agreed that Adonis should live with Venus during six months of the year, and with herself the other six months. Venus signifies, in the above fable, the earth during the six months of summer, and Proserpine during the six months of winter.[1]

During the religious processions of Adonia, the Egyptian, Phœnician, &c., women carried shells, called " Gardens"— Adonidis Horti—in which grew several sorts of herbs, especially lettuces, in memory of Adonis having been laid by Venus upon a bed of lettuce. Each bouquet signified the whole summer earth as the beautiful garden of the sun. The custom still observed of a bride, at her wedding, carrying a bouquet in her hand, had its origin in this custom, and originally signified she would be her husband's fruitful garden. The Ancients believed lettuce caused impotency, and the signification of the fable about Venus placing Adonis upon a bed of lettuce, while she went from home to visit Proserpine, is obvious. It is important to bear in mind that Adonis was described as being *annually* wounded by the wild boar, and appearing as one dead or " dead alive."

The river now called Ibraim Bassa, issuing from Mount Libanus, was called " Adonis " in ancient times—a name

---

[1] Bell's *Pantheon*. " Adonis " and " Adonia."

still given to it in the maps—on whose banks were anciently performed the rites and lamentations for Adonis, who was said to have been wounded by a wild boar on the mountain out of which the river rises. Lucan relates concerning this river, that this stream, especially about the feast Adonia, is of a bloody colour, which the Phœnicians regarded, states Lucan, as proceeding from a kind of sympathy in the river for the "death" of Adonis (as Tammuz). Marmorell relates[1] that on Wednesday, March 17th, he saw the water of the river "stained to a surprising redness."[2] If the Adonia was celebrated about March 17th, it was held about the period of the Jewish passover, the end and the beginning of the sacred year of Israel, corresponding, it will be recollected, with our March (Old Style). The death and resurrection of Adonis at that season of the year imply precisely the same thing as the death and resurrection of Tammuz; but the solar rites observed really belonged to the winter solstice, to December 20th and 22nd respectively.

ALTERING THE YEAR.

Now, who dislocated the Solar Year? Was it done by the Hycsos, the Shepherd Kings, who were Phœnicians, and who settled in Palestine, according to Manetho, and built Jerusalem? Manetho was an Egyptian by birth. Now, let us seek for the motive in shunting the Egyptian rites, relating to the Murder of Osiris by Typhon at the winter solstice, to the vernal equinox, or the Passover. In the year 2504 B.C., the sun at the vernal equinox commenced to rise in the sign and constellation Aries or Young Ram. Until then, the sun at that season rose in the sign of the Bull, and the Bull Apis was the Egyptian

---

[1] *Journal* pp. 34, 45.

[2] Calmet's *Fragments*, vol. iii. p. 576.

symbol of the sun, as mediating on behalf of the world
between light and darkness—life and death.   But when,
by the law of the precession of the equinoxes, the vernal sun
moved, so to speak, to Aries instead of Taurus, the
Egyptians adopted the Young Ram instead of the Bull, as
the sign of the mediatorial sun in spring, and that Young
Ram was called Iupater (Iu Father) Amon (Hidden), and
came to be shown as a dignified man with Ram's horns.

We do not discover in the Adonia of Phœnicia any connection with ram slaughter as a religious rite.   But the Jews
themselves admit that they first slew the Passover Young
Ram in Egypt itself, and continued the practice in memory
of what they did in Egypt.   At this very time the principal
religious symbols of Egypt were the Ram, the sacred bull
Apis, and the sacred cow Tebah or Athor.   The last two
(Bull and Cow) were gradually giving way before the young
Ram (Jupiter) symbol, which the religious astronomers had
directed should be substituted for the bull Apis, because
in spring the sun no longer rose in the Sign of the Bull.
In Exodus viii., 25 and 26, we find the following :—"And
Pharaoh called for Moses and for Aaron and said, Go
ye, sacrifice to your God *in the land*.   And Moses said,
It is not meet so to do ; for we shall sacrifice the *abominations* of the Egyptians to the Lord our God : lo, shall we
sacrifice the *abomination* of the Egyptians before their
eyes," (in the land) "and will they not stone us ?"   Observe
" abomination " is in the singular number, therefore, it was
the *one* particular creature which the Egyptians held in
pious reverence, the Jews were about to sacrifice to " their
God."   Did they not, ultimately, sacrifice the Young Ram,
symbol of Jupiter Amon " in the land ?"   Most remarkable
they should offer to " their God " what *they* regarded as an
" abomination," but what was most holy in the eyes of the

Egyptians, who would have avenged the sacrilege by stoning the guilty. Was it as an "abomination" Abraham sacrificed a ram on the mountain? which was an event which cannot have occurred prior to 2504 B.C.—probably much later—when the Young Ram was adopted, for the reason given above, as a symbol of the vernal sun. Was it offered to Typhon? It is interesting to note that it is said when the Jews, on the march from Egypt, fell into idolatry, it was the older symbol of Egypt, the bull (Apis)—Golden Calf—not the ram (Jupiter Amon) they set up as the symbol of worship. No doubt they supposed they had degraded Jupiter Amon too much by killing him as a Passover lamb to venture to approach *him* again, and they fell back instead upon the older Egyptian symbol, which was being supplanted by the Ram, or Aries. We here refer the reader to what we say elsewhere about the goat sent to Azazel. Now comes the question, did the Hebrews transfer from the winter solstice (December), to the vernal equinox (March), the Egyptian rites relating to the murder of Osiris by Typhon (the old sun by the devil) to enable them to apply the said rites, which were popular, to the slaughter of the Young Lamb, In Pater Amon, the great Mediatorial God of the Egyptians? The nature of the great Christian sacrifice, and the question to whom made, rest on the answer!

St. John, in Rev., ch. xiii., states the Ram-Lamb was "slain from the beginning of the world." No doubt the Jewish "world" is meant.

Byblus, otherwise Gebal, Phœnicia, is a port of the Mediterranean, nearly opposite Mount Libanus, from which the river Adonis issues out. The Adonia was observed in March, when the sun rises due east, and, therefore, sets due west. But Alexandria, Egypt, is about

250 miles to the south-west, the direction the sun sets
at the winter solstice, so that the Phœnicians, while
observing the "wounding" of the sun at the vernal equinox
when rising due *east*, imply that he dies *south-west* at
the winter solstice, as will be seen by what follows. Thus
they clung to the older south-west ritual point of the
heavens as being the place of his death. St. Cyril saw
the solar rites of the Adonia performed in memory of the
death and the return of Adonis from Alexandria.

In the first place, it will be borne in mind, it is related
that Adonis was *annually* mortally wounded by the devil
(Mars or Pluto) disguised as a wild boar on Mount Libanus,
and the "red" river, Adonis—red at the vernal equinox—
was really supposed to be so coloured by the blood of, or in
sympathy for, Adonis. The appearance of the redness in
the river (like the "Red" Sea) at this season—and, as
already stated, a traveller has seen it recently—was the
signal for celebrating the Adonia, or lament for Adonis.
"It was not lawful," states Taylor, "to omit the observance of them." Taylor goes on to state, "great
lamentations were made at this time through town and
country; they cried dreadfully, whipped themselves"
(to be fellow-sufferers with Adonis), "and imitated all
the ceremonies of a most afflicting mourning for a dead
person. After this mourning ended, succeeded the interment and funeral solemnities." "At the funeral," states
Bell's *Pantheon*, "flutes, emitting melancholy sounds,
were played in imitation of the cries of Adonis" Tammuz,
Osiris, Arawn, Arthur, &c., "when being wounded by
Mars" Pluto. "The women appeared with *shaven heads*"
in imitation of the sun's rayless condition. "The common
people were persuaded to believe that the Alexandrians"
who dwelt in the direction of the setting sun, the direction it

set on December 20th, had sent an Ark" not *box* " made of bulrushes, or of the Egyptian papyrus, containing a letter, informing the Phœnicians that Adonis had been found alive," and some say the figure of a babe, like our Taliesin in the coracle, in it. Then, after the arrival of the Ark of bulrushes, the festivities of joy commenced throughout the country. The lamentations are the same solar rites as the Saturnalia, and the merry-making the same as the Bacchanalia of the Romans and of other nations, and refer to the "death" of the "old" sun and the birth of the "new" sun, referred to also under the title of Myses or Moses. What is of extreme importance is that both in Palestine and in Egypt the death of the old sun on a mountain, and his "renewed" birth, forty hours later, were celebrated there at the time of the Passover, untold ages before the death of Jesus at that season of the year, and continued to be observed until the time of St. Cyril and of Julian the Apostate. The figures of the "old" and "renewed" sun, are actually borrowed by St. Paul in the following verses, to denote the death and resurrection of the Saviour:—" Knowing this, that our *old man* is crucified (as Saturn, Tammuz, Adonis, Osiris, Wren, &c.,) with him."—Rom. vi., 6. "That ye put off, concerning the former conversation, the *old man*, which is corrupt according to the deceitful lusts."—Eph. iv., 22. Saturn and Silenus, both titles of the old sun on December 20th, had, in the East, been associated most erroneously with the character of Typhon, the Avagddu of the Druids, hence the bad character given by the Apostle to the "old man." "For ye know the grace of our Lord Jesus Christ that, though He was rich, yet for your sakes He became poor" (like the Wren) "that ye through His poverty might be rich."—2 Cor. viii., 9. After the resurrection, according to St. Paul's words, "God hath highly exalted Him,

and given Him a NAME" (M/) "which is above every
name."—Phil. ii., 9. The frontal of the crown of the
"crowned Babe" of Druidism (vide the three points of the
crown of the human figure in the Arms of Dunwich), and
perpetuated as the three feathers in the diadem of Wales.

Now, the Welsh name of Severn is Havryn, and Dr.
Owen Pughe states it signifies a gelded goat. The Welsh
for goat is Gavr. There is nothing in the etymology of
Havryn to lead one to suppose the name itself had any
reference in it to such a condition. We infer, therefore,
the name Havryn came to be applied, and continues to be
applied, to a gelded goat arbitrarily, and in consequence
of something with which such a goat was associated. Hàv
is the Welsh name of summer, and ren (yr en), the
termination of Havryn, would imply "the birth."
Therefore Havryn signifies, primarily, the birth of
summer. Hàv—called Hàvgàn (Bright Hàv)—is the
Druidic Bacchus, who is also called Gwy Iên, meaning
Warm Dew, and he is the personified vital force in the warm
humidity of the atmosphere. Hàv, therefore, signifies
the sun, for all warmth comes from the sun, and warmth
was regarded as being one of the Creator's emanations
passing through the sun. The name Havryn was, as it
appears, given to the Severn because it indicates the
direction, to those in South Wales, where the young sun
reappears as Hu Gadarn (Hesus the Mighty) named also
Taliesin on the morning of the Solar New Year's Day
(December 22nd), in the South-East. For a similar reason
Gloucester is called, in Welsh, Caer Loyw, or Shining
Enclosure, for, primarily, Caer means Enclosure. We do
not believe Caer Loyw has derived its Welsh name from
Claudius. In A.D. 52, Caractacus, and the whole of the
British forces under his immediate command, were stationed

in its neighbourhood, and Nero ascended the throne of Rome about eighteen months, or less, later. The Roman commander, Ostorius, dared not attack the Welsh British general in front, but outflanked him by crossing the Severn from England below the Wye to Caldicott Pill. It is highly improbable, therefore, Gloucester received its name after the name of Claudius Caesar. The "Glou" in the name is the Welsh Gloyw, corrupted. The termination is from the Latin *Castrai*, a Camp. In the Itinerary of Antoninus it is spelt *Glevum*. Richard of Cirencester's work is proved to be a forgery, therefore we take no notice of his "Glowi." It was the common practice of the Romans to associate Welsh British names with the names of their Stations, as Caerwent became *Venta Silurum*, *Isca* for Gwysc (Usk), &c. Caer Loyw, therefore, is, we think, conclusively a Pre-Roman name of the City on the Severn. At Tewkesbury ("Tew" is the Welsh Duw, God) there is an immense mount on top of which the Beltân in honour of Teutates (Duw Dad—God the Father) was wont to be kindled. As stated already, the Holy Name of the Creator Celi, apart from Himself, shown, illustratively, thus \I/, pointed to the sun in the tropic of Cancer, the Vernal Equinox, and the tropic of Capricornus or Goat, and personified as Plennydd, Alawn and Gwron (Hero). The Hero is Arawn (Aaron?) known also as Saturn, Arthur, Tammuz, Adonis, St. George, &c. It is well known that old Saturn on December 20th was said to be gelded, meaning the sun had been at that season deprived of his virile power by Avagddu (Mars or Pluto, &c., *vide* injury to the "groin" of Adonis—Saturn under another name), and those nations who obeyed the rite of Circumcision did so as a token of their sympathy with Saturn, otherwise Adonis, in the aforementioned condition. They worshipped Saturn, and Saturday was their "Day of Rest," in mournful celebration of his

H

annual " rest " in his ark, the body of Côd, in the sea of
Annwn, on each December 21st, each year, during forty
hours.   The sun enters the sign of Capricornus (Goat) on
December 22nd, but it is quite evident that, like some other
nations, the Druids hooked or joined the preceding Zodiacal
sign of the Archer to that of Capricornus or Goat, and
that, therefore, the sun on December 20th, a few hours
before he left the Archer, was represented, like old Saturn,
though a Hero still, by the figure of a Gelded Goat.
Payne Knight (*Symbolical Language*, S. 112), states,
the Archer of the Zodiac has the tail and the ears, as well
as the feet, of a horse, joined to a human body, together
with a goat's beard, and, at other times, the Archer is a
mixture of goat and man.   In Bell's *Pantheon* it is stated
that, in Egypt, Bacchus (Myses or Moses), another figure
of the infant sun, is represented as a rosy youth in a chariot
drawn by tigers and leopards, and with goats surrounding
him.   The tigers and leopards symbolise his heroic qualities.
Young Æsculapius (another figure of the young sun), is
said to have come from the egg of a crow (Coronis), which
signifies that he came at his birth from Chaos and Night, or
Annwn (Hades).   In Welsh, the West of England is still
called Gwlad-yr-Havryn (Country of the Gelded Goat),
because it borders on the Severn, which seems to have been
sacred to both the old sun of the dying year and the infant
sun of the new year.   It was translated Summer-set, by
the Saxons, implying, as it appears, the setting of the sun
from Wessex at the winter solstice, when rites relating to
the annual event were observed.   The sun follows the
course of the Severn (Havryn) in his descent at the winter
solstice, and hence the Severn is called Havryn, or the
Gelded Goat.   As St. George, he is, later in the day
(December 20th), in the south-west of the Severn Sea, and
beyond its junction with the Cardigan Bay, fighting heroic-

ally the dragon of Annwn or Hades. The Rev. Baring
Gould, M.A., with that intuitive power which so greatly
distinguishes him, points out (*Myths, &c*, p. 284), that
St. George and Tammuz are identical personages.

The connection of the Severn with the Druidic Solar
Drama, is implied in the chronicles of Walter de Mapes
and Geoffrey of Monmouth. Arthur is introduced as
saying, "There is a Llyn (Lake) near the Severn (Havryn)
called Llyn Llionwy, which swallows all the water that
flows into it at the tide of flood, without any visible
increase; but at the tide of ebb it swells up like a mountain, and pours its waters over the banks, so that, whoever
stands near it at this time, must run the risk of being
overwhelmed." Some think this allusion is to the Severn
"Bore" influx caused by more water rushing into the
Severn from the Atlantic than the various waterways
flanking the Severn can admit into them at the instance
when the violent influx takes place. But the allusion is to
a "Lake near the Severn," and not to the Severn itself.
We believe the allusion is to the sea on the east coast of
England, opposite Dunwich—Din Wych (Grand Hill)—
Suffolk, 98 miles N.E. of London. It is the opposite of
Gwyllionwy, which is the sea of the setting sun, while
Lli-Onwy refers to the rising sun.—*Vide* Dunwich and the
story of the Crowned Babe, pp. 66-7. The violence of the
sea at Dunwich is such that it has "demolished its churches
and convents, ruined its haven, and swallowed up its
streets."

Now, as to the meaning of the names of these Llyns or
Lakes in Druidic mythology, namely Llyn Gwyllionwy,
and Llyn Llionwy—Gwyllionwy is compounded of the
following words :—Gwyll (Darkness), Ión (the Creator),

and Wy mutated from Gwy (Water); therefore, the name
signifies the Dark Waters of the Creator, and it refers to
the sea beyond the mouth of the Severn, in the direction
of the South West, where the sun sinks or sets into it on
the darkest and shortest day of the year (December 20th),
compared to a beaver in the evening entering into his
"house" in the water. Llionwy is compounded as follows:—Lli (Flood), On (Perennial), and Wy mutated
from Gwy (Water)—the Perpetual Water Flow or Flood.
We think there can be no doubt the following refers to
arkite rites performed by the Britons of Wales and England
on the upper waters of the Severn, somewhere about
Gloucester or Worcester, and on the coast of Suffolk,
notably at Dunwich, in the direction of where the sun rises
on the first day of the new year, as the perennial source of
life. In the Ark, during the ceremony of the winter solstice,
would be the emblems of the masculine and feminine principles (Linga and Yoni) preserved from decay during winter.
In the Triads we read of the master works of the island of
Britain, viz:—building the ship which carried in it a
male and female of every species, when the lake of Llionwy
burst forth; and the second great achievement was drawing
the Beaver (Avanc) to land by the Oxen of the Many
High Hills. Clearly the references are to solar rites on
the Severn and the eastern coast of England, as described
in other pages. The Atlantic, beyond the junction of
Cardigan Bay and the Severn, is the river Styx of
Druidi-m.

Now, the Severn, between Gloucester and Worcester, bears
precisely the same relation to the sun rising, and the outlet
of the Severn the same relation to his setting, at the end of
the solar year, as Bozrah of Edom and the Red Sea do to
the rising and setting of the sun at that period of the year.

Both dual localities describe south-east and south-west in their relation to the apparent path of the sun at that season. Let not the reader confound the Bozrah to the east of the Jordan with the other Bozrah. In another page we stated the Druidic name of Silbury Hill is Clnda'r Cyvrangon, and it signifies, "She carries (or bears) the Mediator." The ancient Druidic name of Worcester is Caer-Wrangon (Enclosure of Wrangon). The last word is a compound of two words: *Wr* mutated from *Gwr* (man and manly); it is an intensitive, and is used like the Latin *Vir*, and signifies a being endowed with power. It was used by the old poets as one of the titles of God—

> " Penav *Gwr* a'r pena' 'gyd,
> Goruwch byd, yw'r *Gwr* uwch ben."

The chiefest *Gwr* of all the chiefs, above the world, is the *Gwr* above.

The second word of the compound is spelt "*angon*." There is no such word in the Welsh language, and, evidently, it is a mutilated word. It should be "*Rhyngon*," which signifies Between-us, in another word, Mediator. This agrees with what Plutarch states, that the Persians regarded Mithras (the sun), the Alawn of Druidism (the same as Iupater), and meaning the sun in spring, as a mediator between Ormuzd (sun in summer) and Ahriman, the power of Death dominant in winter (Volney's, p. 112, and note 66). 'Wr-Ryngon seems to imply, the Power—or Manly Power—between us and the Devil or the destroyer, and was applied to the young sun on his reappearance, returning, crowned, from Hades, or Annwn, on December 22nd, over Dunwich and Worcester. The great mound, called "Barrow," near Worcester, and another near Tewkesbury, were the exact spots on the border of Wales; the great mound at Dunwich, Suffolk, another; and the great mound near the Temple of Avebury, Wilts, a fourth. Probably the said

Caers, or enclosures, were, originally, Druidic circular "churches," where the young sun was welcomed, on each December 22nd, with the joyful hosannas of the assembled Druidic worshippers.

Isaiah (ch. lxiii.) borrows the figure of the young sun of the new year's morning, rising over Bozrah:—"Who is this *rushing* up (so in Hebrew) from Edom, with dyed garments from Bozrah? This that is glorious in his apparel, travelling in the greatness of his strength? I that speak in righteousness, mighty to save. Wherefore art thou red in thine apparel, and thy garments like him that treadeth in the wine-vat?" Forty hours before, he had fallen into the sea—Red Sea—which, in allusion to his bleeding condition, bleeding from the wounds inflicted upon him by the Prince of the Air, Mars, otherwise Pluto, Avagddu, &c., that sea was named the Red Sea. It was called "Red" for the same reason that the river Adonis, issuing from Mount Libanus, and entering the Mediterranean at Byblus, was called "red," viz., that the sun-god, as was supposed, had bled into it. In the Red Sea, Cêd (Cetus) —often symbolised as an Ark, and often as a great fish, whale, and sometimes as a dolphin (Delphus—womb)—had received his *divinity* in the shape of a white dove into her own body. After bearing him for forty hours, Cêd delivers him in the south-east, and he rushes up—up from Edom-Bozrah and from the sea opposite Dunwich, in England—having been rejuvenated, and to increase in power for another encounter with the power of darkness and decay. It appears the Hebrews regarded the "new" sun as still old Saturn, and they would not acknowledge the truth of the poetical myth, that the young sun was a "new" one, in the sense we say now a "new" moon. In the 13th verse of the above-mentioned chapter, Isaiah seems to have had the Zodiacal

Archer and Horse—the Zodiacal sign from November 23rd to December 22nd—before his mind. Isaiah asks where is he "that led them through the deep, (and) as a *horse* in the wilderness, that they should not stumble." But we shall, in another place, deal with Moses and Miriam, the passage of the Red Sea, and the "fish" that left the Red Sea, to teach the Babylonians, only let the reader revert to these pages when we come to treat of them. Calmet, in his *Dictionary of the Bible*, under the word "Bezer," or Bozrah, has the following, after stating a ship was one of the emblems of Bozrah, he goes on to remark :—" It deserves particular notice that this figure (ship), though appertaining to a city not only inland, but also in some degree situated on the edge of, if not in, a desert, yet should have a ship" (Ark of the sun) "as the type on its coins."

CHAPTER X.

THE Cain and Seth pedigrees in Genesis are not human ones at all, but solar ones, drawn up after the fashion of human pedigrees. That of Seth is the Nine Signs of the Zodiac, beginning with Aries (Ram), and concluding, for the purpose of the diluvian solar allegory, with the Archer and Horse, the Ninth Sign, and continued into Capricornus (Goat), which is the Hebrew month Tebeth, signifying both Ark and Cow. Tebah, or Tebeth, signifies in Hebrew both Cow and Ark, and both signify Côd, and Isis I., of Egypt.

The pedigree of Cain, beginning with Adam (Sun—Ad Hama, of Persia), consists of seven characters, and relates to the sun passing through the seven planetary spheres. This pedigree was symbolised in the temple of Jerusalem by the seven lamps of the Golden Candlestick, while the twelve signs of the Zodiac were symbolised by the twelve loaves of shewbread. In the Holy Place the seven lamps stood on the south side—the gloomy region of the heavens —and the twelve loaves on the north side—the bright side of the heavens—of the western side of the equinoctial line, being the line passing over the Golden Altar of Incense, and running east and west, the "line" indicating the middle equatorial passage, running from west to east through the middle of both the Holy Place and the Holy of Holies. The seven days of the week, beginning with the sun (June 21), and ending with the sun as old Saturn (Dec. 20), with Mercury, the Minister of God, in the middle on the equinoctial line (March 21). Thus we describe the pedigrees of Cain and Seth :—

1 Adam	Adam	Adam
2 Cain	1 Seth	Abel
3 Enoch	2 Enos	Symbol of the Destroyer.
4 Irad	3 Cainan	The Orientals deified the
5 Mehujael	4 Mahalcel	Devil, and Abel agrees
6 Lamech	5 Iaread	with the Egyptian Ty-
7 Tubal Cain	6 Enoch	phon, and with Pluto,
	7 Methusalah	Siva, &c. He had no
	8 Lamech	pedigree.
	9 Noah (Nine)	

The right hand stroke of the sacred sign, \/, points to the seventh planet, Saturn, and also to the *Ninth* sign of the Zodiac. Therefore, Tubal Cain, the seventh in the pedigree of Cain, corresponds with the Ninth in the pedigree of Seth, namely, Noah, or the Ninth position of the sun in his annual progress through the Zodiac, and also with Agruerus in the Zodiacal patriarchal pedigree of the Phœnicians.

The three sons of Noah, viz:—Japheth, Shem, and Ham, three added to the Ninth or Noah, complete the twelve signs of the Zodiac. Counting from Aries, Japheth is the tenth sign (the Goat); Shem the eleventh (the Waterer); and Ham the twelfth (the Fishes). The three sons of Noah are said to have been the second progenitors of mankind. Japheth of the Northern population; Shem of the Eastern population; and Ham of the Black population of the South. Their wives are identical with the three sisters of King Arthur. Instead of "Wales," in the Arthurian narrative, is to be understood the heavens and the earth above the rational horizon. Arthur's sisters are described as follows:—Queen of North Wales, Queen of

East Wales, and the Queen of Desert Places.   In reference
to the sun in three of the seven planetary spheres, the
sons of Noah, respectively occupy the following positions:—
Japheth is the sun on the longest day (June 21st) in the
northern sky; Shem is Mercury in the eastern sky
(March 21st); and Ham is Saturn in the southern sky
(December 20th).   Saturn, the old sun, at the end of his
annual return downwards to the south, finishes his annual
work in the sixth planetary point of the ecliptic, enters into
his "rest" on the seventh day—the day of Saturn;
meaning the Archer-Goat period, or December 21st,
hence the Jewish Sabbath is on the day of Saturn, or
Saturday—the seventh day, and hence the Saturnalia of
the Gentile world at the close of the solar year; in
Druidism on December 20th at Sunset.   It was not the
Almighty "resting"—the idea is absurd—the Druids
meant, but it was a poetical figure in reference to the
personified abstraction of the Deity, symbolised by a
Wren, and also by a Beaver (Avanc), which escaped into
Cêd, the divine mother, at the moment the corporeal body
of the old sun was being annihilated in the heaven by
Avagddu, otherwise Typhon, Pluto, Dio, Ahriman, Siva, &c.,
and entered into his "rest" at sunset, on each December
20th, in Cêd (Cetus or Der Ketos), his great Mother, in
the South Western Ocean.   As repeatedly stated, various
figures were employed to denote Cêd, namely:—Ark
(instead of Tebah or Cow; for it would have been too
absurd to represent the Cow as taking him to the sea of
Annwn or Hades, beyond the earth's circle); Cetus and
Der Ketos (Whale).   In reference to the sun's journey
through the said seven points or planetary spheres, he is
named in Druidism, Scithun Saidi (the Seven Causitor);
Saithwedd (the Seven Featured);   Septimianus by the
Romans; and in reference to his being in the ninth sign of

the Zodiac he is named Ninius, Deo Nisios, Naus, Deva Naus, Gwydd Naw (Ninth Presence), Nuh, Noah, &c.

Let us now, in the name of Eternal Truth, "the eldest Son of God," proceed to examine the Scriptural narrative of the Deluge. As stated already, Tebeth and Tebah—the former name obviously derived from the latter—signify both Cow and Ark, but the name seems to have been used for ark or tub—Twba (Tooba) in Welsh—before it came to be applied to designate the sacred cow and ark. Now Tebeth is the Jewish name of the tenth month of the sacred year, and that month corresponds with December (Old Style).

Let us now turn to the narrative of Noah's Deluge. The Ark rested on the seventh month, on the seventeenth day of the month. The earth, as the sacred Tebah (cow or Ark), "resting," signifies her fermentation had ceased for the year. That is in the month Tishri, coresponding with our September (Old Style), Medi of the Druids—the autumnal equinox—when the earth's produce has ripened in Britain, and when two of each species—male and female —have dropped into the earth (cow), considered as a sacred ark of safety.

" And the waters decreased continually, until the tenth month: in the tenth month" (Tebeth—December), "on the first day of the month, were the tops of the mountains seen. And it came to pass at the *end* of forty days" (forty hours) "that Noah opened the window of the ark" (Tebah) which he had made: And he sent forth a raven which went forth to and fro: until the waters were dried up from off the earth. Also he sent forth a dove from him, to see if the waters were abated from off the face of the ground; But the dove found no rest for the sole of her foot, and she returned unto him in the ark, for the waters were on the face of the whole earth : then he put forth his hand and took her and pulled her in unto him in the ark. And he stayed yet other seven days; and again he sent forth the dove out of the ark ; And the dove came to him in the evening ; and, lo, in her mouth was an olive leaf pluckt off: so Noah knew that the waters were abated from off the earth. And he stayed yet other seven days; and sent forth the dove; which returned not again unto him any more. And it came to pass in the six hundredth and *first* year" (day), "in the first month" (Nisan, corresponding with our March, Old Style, the time of spring), "the first day of the month, the waters were dried up from off the earth : and Noah removed the covering of the ark, and looked, and, behold, the face of the ground was dry."

In Calmet's Biblical Dictionary, it is stated the name of Noah's wife was Neuratio, according to the Syro-Chaldean, and in Syriac the name signifies Fire (Heat), hence Pyrrah, or Fire, is said by the Greeks to have been the wife of Deucalion (Duw-Celi-on of Druidism), which name signifies the Creator : the Most High. Etymologically, it signifies the Everlasting God Who is Hiding. But when it is stated that Heat was the wife of Deucalion, and also of Noah, the old sun, as Deucalion, is confounded with the Almighty himself, and, by identifying Deucalion with Noah, it is implied that the Almighty is the old sun, instead of the Father of the sun—whether old, as Saturn, or young, as Adonis, or Hesus, the Mighty, otherwise Taliesin and Hu Gadarn. No doubt the confusion was caused by the practice of ancient mythological religionists of representing the old sun as the father of the new sun. Heat was regarded as but one of the varied emanations of the Creator and his consort Cêd.

In Druidism, the name of the earth, as the consort of
the old sun, in winter—November and December—is
Dyrraith (Barren), and is identical with Beroe, the old
nurse of Semele; the lubricity, or grease, of the following
spring. By Dyrraith the Druids implied the dry outward
crust of the earth in the said months. But the internal
heat of the earth is an emanation of Cêd, and matches the
divinity within the body of the sun identical with the Eternal
Father himself, from whom that divinity is an abstraction.
Both the father, Celi, and the mother, Cêd, never grow old.
Noah, as an old man—the old sun—has for his wife
Dyrraith, identical with the Greek Beroe, and when the
earth is used as a personification of Cêd, the outward
framework of the Ark—like the dry crust of the earth—
would be the wife of Noah, or the old sun. But the male
divinity within the Ark, which divinity is symbolised by the
body and wings of the white dove, was to be the husband of
Neuratio, or Pyrrah (Heat), whose name, as a virgin wife,
is Venus (the conceiving power of the earth on March 21st),
being the daughter of Cêd. But to return to the Scriptural
narrative. The " six hundred and *one* years " of Noah are
the six months of winter, between September 23rd and
March 21st. The " one year " in addition to the six
hundred years is the *one* day of forty hours from 4
o'clock, December 20th, to 8 o'clock on the morning of
December 22nd—shunted to the vernal equinox by either
the Phœnicians or the Hebrews. The Druids taught that,
during the said forty hours, the old sun was in his " grave,"
otherwise in the womb of Cêd, his mother, whom the Ark
symbolised. In the Biblical narrative, we discover *two* solar
allegories intermixed. The first day of the first month of
the Diluvian allegory, refers to the first day of the first
month, Nisan, regulated by the new moon (March, Old
Style), of the sacred year, when the " covering of the Ark "

was "removed." That refers to the protective coatings given to the seedlings and bulbs to defend them from the destructive elements of winter. Then all leaving the Ark on the 27th of the "second month" refers, as it appears, to the second month, called Ve Adar, the intercalary month, or a second February, proclaimed every three years. It is named "The Second." The seedlings, two of every species, leave the earth, considered as an Ark—and a coffin is so named (Arch) to this day in the Welsh language—leave it in pairs.

But what is meant by Noah's raven and white dove? In the ancient world, Darkness was regarded as being as much a creation of God as Light was. The raven symbolised the cause of night; the white dove symbolised the cause of light from the sun. The dove symbolised Adonis, or, in Druidism, Hu Gadarn (Hesus the Mighty), returning "renewed" as a young new sun, after an absence of forty hours, parts of two days and one whole one, in the Ark in the body of his mother, Cêd, during the before-mentioned forty hours. The raven was a symbol of Night, and the dove of Day, and both came from the mother Ark, otherwise Cêd. The said forty hours correspond with the forty hours each of the following "gods" is said to have been absent, viz., Arawn, Osiris, Adonis, Bacchus, &c. Iona (Jonah), which means Dove, was forty "days" at Nineveh; Jesus, forty "days" in the wilderness, after ascending from the waters of Jordan; Iona, or Jonah, three days and nights in the hollow of Ketos (whale), Cetus, or Cêd; Jesus, in his stone grave in a garden from sunset on Friday until sunrise on Sunday, which, at the winter solstice, would be during forty hours; Jesus was forty "days" on earth after his resurrection from the dead, then he ascended into the heavens, as Druidism teaches the young sun does every year, after an absence of forty hours, on the morning of December 22nd.

The conclusion is that the story of the deluge in Genesis is not a literal event, but a solar allegory; that Noah is the sun, as Saturn, in his old age, identical, too, with Silenus, the foster-father of the succeeding year's young Bacchus. Silenus is symbolised as always fuddled, and the handle of his jug is shown almost worn out with frequent use. His eyes were red by reason of wine. Everybody recollects the story of Noah's intoxication. Apollo and Bacchus are said to have been two brother gods. Apollo was the heat of the sun; Bacchus was the heat in the atmosphere at night, descending in dew, giving nourishment to vegetation, and therefore, Bacchus was the cause of the fruitfulness of the earth as Venus. Silenus is a figment of the mythologists, to supply Bacchus with a paternity. The Dove coming out of Noah's Ark is the Divinity in the young sun of the new year, and is identical with the white dove Adonis of other nations, and the wren of the Druids. Jonah, we repeat, is Iona, a dove; and Iona in the whale's belly is the sun's Divinity in Cetus or Der Ketos (whale). The Lord Jesus, according to the Greek Testament, Matthew's Gospel, ch. xii., 40, states distinctly that Jonah was in the hollow cavity of Ketos or Cêd. Jonah states he went to Sheol or Hades, in the sea of which Ketos (Cêd), consort of the Creator, was said to roam. "Nineveh" seems to be a name associated with Nine or Noah.

We take the following from vol. iii., p. 735 of the "Fragments" added to Calmet's *Dictionary of the Bible*:

NOAH	JONAH	JESUS
In the Water	In the Water	In the Earth
Is Preserved	Is Preserved	Is Preserved
By Divine Power	By Divine Power	By Divine Power
In his Ark	In the Whale	In his Tomb
In which he was	In which he was	In which he was
1 Part of a year	1 Part of a first day	1 Part of a first day
2 The whole of a second year	2 The whole of a second day	2 The whole of a second day
3 The beginning of a third year.	3 The beginning of a third day	3 The beginning of a third day

The "Fragments" omit other striking agreements, namely, Noah's forty days, Jonah's forty days at Nineveh, and Jesus, from sunset on Friday until sunrise on Sunday, exactly forty hours, in his stone grave in the garden!

As the Word of God in the old sun, descending for protection at sunset on December 20th into Côd, the consort of the Creator, in the sea of the elements, and leaving her with renewed powers at sunrise on December 22nd, that Word was symbolised by a white dove, or Iona, while the Almighty Himself bore, in Druidism, the name Iôn (Leader-Lord). Other nations symbolised the young sun as a babe born of Côd, called by the Druids also Black Virgin, on December 22nd, or, according to the Julian Calendar, on Dec. 25th, Christmas Day. We maintain Noah's dove departing from the Ark signifies the birth of the Word of God from the Black Virgin, Côd (Cetus or Der Ketos), Delphus (Womb, of the Greeks), symbolised by the Ark, or Tebah, of Noah! Some say the Dagon of the Phœnicians meant Dag-aon, or Dag-Nau: in

English, the Fish of Noah (old sun), or Nine or Ninth. Dagon was the figure of a Dolphin fish, with a rosy youth emerging out of its mouth; the youth was the young sun, Hesus the Mighty.   "Great ships," states Hesychius, "were often called *Katene*, from Ketos (whale)." Berosus, a priest of Babylon, states that Oannes, who was half man and half fish, rose in the Red Sea—sometimes the Indian Ocean is meant by "Red Sea" in the writings of ancient authors—"and came to Babylon, where he taught several arts, letters, and astronomy. He then returned to the sea." The meaning of the foregoing appears to be that a priest of the young sun came to Babylon in a Katene (a great ship) and instructed the Babylonians.   That he afterwards returned to the Katene, or the great ship, and the name, being the same as Ketos (a whale), induced writers to suppose that Oannes came out of a fish and nightly returned into it!

Now comes a curious thing.   The name John is, in the original Greek, Oannes, and in Welsh, with a view to keep near the original form of the name, it is rendered Ioan. In the history of John the Baptist, care is taken to describe his outward appearance.   "And John,"—Oannes (Man-Fish)—states Mark, "was clothed with camel's hair, and with a girdle of a skin about his loins."   Was this intended to represent him as appearing like the Oannes (Fish-Man) of the solar allegory, or, to be more explicit, of Der Ketos or Cetus (whale) out of which the young sun, Hesus the Mighty, was represented annually as emerging on the morning of each December 22nd ?   John's hairy and skin raiment implied the same thing as the hairy and skin symbols in the eastern front of the tent of the Ark of the Covenant, viz., the Vulva of Cêd.

I

Among ancient nations, the meridian line—the path of the sun's mid-day elevation during his annual journey from the morrow of the shortest day (December 22nd) to the longest day (June 21st)—was the River of Life, and, while daily ascending it, the power of the sun's divinity drew lives out of Hades in the south. The equinoctial line was the River of God and the Lamb, or Aries, where the Creator poured, through the sun in Aries, the chemical properties necessary to fertilise the seeds of the earth. The solstitial colure line—north and south—was the Creator's spiritual channel.

The river Jordan was employed by the Jews to denote both "rivers." The Jordan ran north and south. At its southern end is the Dead Sea, which was Israel's symbolical Sheol, Hades, or Hell, pre-figured by Sodom and Gomorrah, the alleged Cities of the Plain, but they never existed literally, as geology has proved clearly. In Druidism, the Sea of Annwn, or of Hades, where *new* souls are waiting to be called up to inhabit human bodies on earth—the wicked dead, who formerly lived human lives, are in the circles of transmigration, passing through processes of purification, and the bottom of those circles is in Annwn—is located in the southern regions of the setting sun. The baptism of John (Man-Fish) was really an act of symbolical regeneration, precisely—and the idea was borrowed from it—the regeneration of old Saturn rejuvenated, as Hesus the Mighty, from the Der Ketos (Dolphin or Whale,) and the Sea of Annwn. The Lord Jesus, referring to his own baptism by John, states:—"Verily, I say unto you, that ye who have *followed* me in the regeneration, when the Son of Man shall sit on the throne of His glory ye also shall sit on twelve thrones, judging the twelve tribes of Israel."

"Then cometh Jesus from Galilee to Jordan unto John, to be baptised by him.   *   *   And Jesus, when he was baptised, went straightway out of the water"—John apparently staying behind in the water as the fish Der Ketos, out of which Jesus had, symbolically, emerged—"and lo, the heavens were opened unto Him, and He saw the Spirit of God descending like a dove, and lighting upon Him; and lo, a voice from heaven, saying: This is my beloved Son, in whom I am well pleased." In the Cambridge MS., last words added are, "*to-day I have begotten Thee.*"

That Dove was identical with the Dove of the Phœnicians, Syrians, &c., which, among the Gentile nations, symbolised the Divine Spirit of the Creator returning into the sun, renewed or regenerated from his mother, Cêd in Druidism, and Cetus and Der Ketos, which the Romans and Greeks and others erroneously represented as being a whale or dolphin, and others as being Oannes, or Man-Fish, which the Philistines symbolised by Dagon, or Dagaun, and Dag-Nau, a rosy youth emerging from the mouth of a great fish; and the fish and the youth so emerging from it were called collectively Dagon, which signifies the same thing as Oannes. It is hardly necessary to repeat, the rosy youth is the new sun personified, and that he was Old Saturn or the old sun of the preceding year regenerated, or rejuvenated, by Cêd in the water, by the joint influence of Iôn, acting now spiritually as her husband. We think it necessary to repeat again that the young sun was called Hu Gadarn (Hesus the Mighty) by the Druids, and also Arthur, Taliesin, &c.; and in the East, Adonis; and in Greece and Rome, Saturn, Bacchus, Apollo, Esculapius; in Egypt, Horus, Osiris, &c. That Dove symbolised the Holy Spirit, which had escaped out of the old sun, Arawn or Saturn, when, on the afternoon of December 20th—forty

hours before—the old sun was physically annihilated in
the air by the Power of Darkness.   The body and two
wings of the Dove were symbols of \V/, which, illustratively,
symbolised the Word of God, which the Greeks called
Logos, and the Latins Verbum, and the Druids *Gair Duw.*
But what was the " voice " which is said accompanied the
descent of the Dove on the head of Jesus ?   Was it not
the Bath–Kol of the Talmudists?   " The generality,"
states Calmet, " of Hebrew traditions are founded upon
what is called Bath-Kol, which they *pretend* was the
Voice of God, as being the mode the Almighty communicated with them after prophecy had ceased.   The
Bath-Kol," he continues, " as Dr. Prideaux shows, was a
fantastical way of divination *invented* by the Jews, like
the Sortes Virgilianæ among the heathen."   " Bath-Kol "
signifies " Daughter of the Voice."   It will be remembered
that in Druidism there is a saying "The Voice of God is
heard in the Voice of Anian," which is the Anima Mundi
personified as a daughter of the Creator and of Cêd, his
Consort.

As already mentioned, the Ark, the Wren, the Shrine and
the Beaver, symbolised, in Druidism, the same allegorical
fancies of the Druids and other religionists, as did John
(Oannes) in the Jordan, and the Dove descending into the
head of the Sun of Righteousness, immediately after his
regeneration in the waters of the Jordan, out of John,
otherwise Oannes, the Man-Fish ; the " Man " being the
new sun coming out of Cêd, Cetus, or Der Ketos (whale).
Instead of "Man" is to be understood here the " Dove."

Was the Bath-Kol tradition *used* by the Christianised
Hebrews of the school of Alexandria to give apparent Divine
sanction to the claims of Jesus to the Messiahship?   But

both Calmet and Dr. Prideaux declare the Bath-Kol as
sanctioning the traditions of the Talmud was an invention,
and "a fantastical way of divination" common to both Jews
and Gentiles. In the Gospel narrative the Holy Spirit
descends into the *head* of Jesus whilst He is in the
act of emerging from Oannes (John) and the waters
of the Jordan. Were the Bath-Kol of the Hebrews and
the Sortes Virgilianæ of the Heathen derived from the
Druidic teaching that the Voice of God is heard in the
Voice of Nature's living principle? Then succeed Jesus's
absence in the wilderness forty *days*. In the old parable
of the Druids, the sun is absent forty hours *before* he
ascends from his mother Côd, stationed in the water or the
Sea of Annwn.

From a Druidic point of view, Jesus, ascending from hairy
John (the "Man"-Fish, or whale, or, sometimes, a dolphin
[Delphus--Womb] and a rosy youth leaving its mouth,)
in the river Jordan, and the dove appearing at the same
moment are identical with the dove leaving the Ark of
Noah; the dove welcomed by the Syrians with the invocation, "Hail to the Dove! The restorer of light!"; with
Taliesin ascending from his skin coracle; with Aaron, the
high priest, emerging from the eastern front of the Holy of
Holies of the Sanctuary; and with the new sun of the
new year ascending from the South-Eastern Sea on the
morning of December 22nd, as Hu Gadarn, or Hesus the
Mighty!

It will be remembered that the moment the Divine
Sufferer, on Golgotha, died, the western veil of the temple
hiding the eastern sanctum sanctorum, rent from the top
to the bottom, implying that the Divinity (Dove) of Christ
had escaped into his mother Côd, which the outer dolphin

skin enclosing the Ark of the Covenant in that place
symbolised. The sun sets in the west at the vernal
equinox, the time the crucifixion took place, and he
reappears in the east. Jesus told the penitent thief He
would be in Hades that day.

It is curious to find that Jesus had three disciples who
constituted, as it were, his inner cabinet, viz., Peter, James,
and John. It seems the said three were intended to represent the personifications of the sign \I/ already explained.
The right-hand stroke indicates the sun in the tropic of
Capri, where, in the solar myth, the sun is received into
the great fish emblem of Cêd, and comes out again, after
an interval of forty hours, renewed. This John also is
Oannes, or Man-Fish, and it is alleged Oannes, the Apostle
of Love, was engaged in the fish trade at Jerusalem.
The hoods of the clergy and the mitres of the bishops, to
this day, are fish emblems. The sun now, during Lent,
is in the sign of the Fishes, and it is the reason why fish
is eaten as a religious rite during Lent. John, in the
arrangement, agrees with the sun's astronomical position in
reference to his relation with Der Ketos (whale or dolphin).
James, in this arrangement, would correspond with the sun
in the vernal equinox, and Peter with the sun in the
summer solstice, that is, with the tropic of Cancer. In the
Druidic church on earth, three chief priests represented the
three divine attributes indicated by \I/, and they were named,
always, Plennydd, Alawn and Gwron. According to the above
arrangement, Peter would indicate the sun at the top end
of his annual path (June 21st), the sun's meridian line on
the longest day, and he would, therefore, according to the
old Druidic system, be both Plennydd, and A-wen (the
Spirit of the Muse) the instrument in the regeneration
of souls. James would be the chief of the physical or

temporal church, and in Acts xv. we find it was he, and not Peter, who presided over the Council of the Apostles. In Druidism, the Spirit of God is called Awen. literally White A, but implying Holy A. The A figure, without the cross-bar, is that letter in the old Druidic alphabet which is named Coelbren-y-Beirdd (the Bardic Letters of Credibility). The Roman Alphabet was called Coelbren-y-Myneich, or, of the Monks. The Awen is named Awen Hevin, or, the Spirit of God at the Summer Solstice. The symbol is understood as descending from the sun then, thus V. The following is a startling confirmation of what we have frequently hinted, viz., that the Christian religion is scientifically arranged on the most ancient framework of British Druidism. "And when the day of Pentecost" (Whitsuntide, or summer solstice, June 21st,) "was fully come, they were all with one accord in one place. And suddenly there came a sound from heaven, as a rushing mighty wind and it filled all the house where they were sitting. And there appeared unto them cloven tongues (V) like as of fire and *it* sat upon each of them. And they were filled with the Holy Ghost" (Spirit, not "Ghost," is the word which should have been used,) "and began to speak with other tongues, as the Spirit gave them utterance. * * Peter, standing up with the eleven, lifted up his voice, and said, Ye men of Judea, and all ye that dwell in Jerusalem, &c." About 3,000 were "pricked in their hearts" by the Holy Spirit through the instrumentality of Peter's "voice." Whitsuntide is called in Welsh *Sul Gwyn* or Holy Sun. It was believed by the Druids that when the sun had attained his highest northern ascension all the power of the Almighty was focussed in him, and that it was by the exercise of that power the produce of the earth was then being garnished, and the souls of the good perfected through the agency of the sun; it is the very time—at twenty minutes to four o'clock in the morning

(June 21st,)—the first beam of light from the sun strikes the altar in the temple of Stonehenge.   It will be observed in the above that the plural "cloven tongues" is employed to describe the appearance of the outer manifestation which "sat upon each of them," nevertheless, the singular "it" is used to refer to the "cloven tongues" collectively.   Thus it is left to be understood the "cloven tongues" radiated from one common centre.   It appears the Jewish symbol of the Awen, or the Holy Spirit, was, and is still, the letter *Shin* (ש), which each Jew still wears on his phylactery on his forehead during prayer.

In Druidism there is also the A-ddu (Black A), generally rendered Avagddu, which signifies A—Nursing Darkness, or Evil, and is the direct negative of Awen.   The Awen (White A) and the A-ddu (Black A) are precisely identical with the Dove (no doubt white), and the Raven (black), of the Noahic allegory.   Probably, the Druidic original ideas having been lost, the Greeks declared that Jupiter had let loose two "doves" from the extremities of the earth—north and south, the zenith and the nadir of the celestial meridian —and that they met at the shrine of the Oracle at Delphi, meaning the middle of the surface of the round earth, above the rational horizon, otherwise, on the summit of Mount Meru (Marw—Dead), otherwise, Mount Moriah, symbolised in India and Egypt by the apex of the Lotos flower.

CHAPTER XI.

THE following was penned by an eminent bard, about A.D. 600, who as priest of the sun, bore one of the titles of that luminary, namely, Taliesin. All his poems in the "Myvyrian" indicate, in a most interesting manner, the influence which Biblical literature had already exercised on the British Druids of his time. The bard, who evidently was a Christianised Druid, writes as if he himself were the sun, or Taliesin, whom he represented by his office of Archdruid.

The primary Bard universal
Am I to Elphin,[1]
And my original country
Is the region of the Cherubim.
Ioannes the Divine
Called me Merddyn[2]
At length every king
Will call me Taliesin.

I was fully nine months
In the womb of Ceridwen :
I was Gwyion heretofore,
Taliesen am I now.
I was with my Nêr[3]
In the superior state,
When Lucifer did fall
To the infernal deep.

I have borne a banner
Before Alexander ;
I know the names of the stars
From the North to Awster.
I have been in the Circle of
Odin[4]—
Tetragrammaton :
I conducted Heon[5]
To the depth of Ebron Vale.

I was in Canaan
When Absalom was slain ;
I was in the Court Dan
Before Odin was born ;
I was the attendant
On Elijah and Enoch ;
I was on the place of the Cross[6]
Of the Son of the Merciful God!

---

[1] Awen, and the same as Alpha. [2] Merddyn (Merlin) signifies, literally, Water Man; Born from the Water. [3] God (literally, Ner, which means Strength). [4] Gwidian, Gwyddon, or Odin is said to be the Tetragrammaton, or the unutterable Name, or Word, of God. [5] We are inclined to believe it should be Deon, a title of the Sun in the "Vale" of the southern heavens, on the shortest day; from "De" (South) and "On" (ever living). [6] "Vran" in the original obviously should be "Van" (place).

I have been chief Keeper of
The work of Nimrod's Tower;
I have been in the three Circles *
And the Enclosure of Eirian-
    Rôd.
I was in the Ark
With Noah and Alpha;
I beheld the destruction
Of Sodom and Gomorra.

I was in Africa
Before Rome was built;
I am come here
To the remnant of Troia.[8]
I was with my Rhên[9]
In the manger of the She Ass.
I strengthened Moses
Through the water of Jordan.[10] *

I have been in the Firmament
With Mary Magdalen:[11]
I have been gifted with genius
From the Cauldron of Ceridwen;
I have been Bard of the Harp
To the Thane of Denmark.

I have endured hunger
For the Son of the Virgin. †

I have been on the White
    Hillock,[12]
In the Court of Cynvelyn,
In fetters a year and a day.
I have been for profit
In the Kingdom of the Trin-
    ity ;[13]
It is not known what is my
    body
Whether flesh or fish.[14]

I have been Instructor
To the whole Universe ;
I shall remain till the day of
    doom
On the face of the earth.
I have been in an agitated seat
Above the Circle of the Zodiac,
And that continues revolving
Between three elements.
It is not a wonder to the world
I cannot be cooped up !

---

[7] By Alpha—the beginning—is meant the White Dove as the Spirit of God beginning the New Year (Noah—the Old Sun).   [8] The Britons.
[9] Rhen (God).   [10] The Bard, in this instance, wrong in Biblical History.
[11] In Welsh, Lady Day is called Gwyl Vair y Cyhydedd, which signifies the Festival of Mary of the Equinoctial line, the earth being then in the Constellation Virgo or Virgin.   The old Bard avoids heresy by saying the Sun was in the heavens with *another* Mary—Mary Magdalene.
[12] Holy Mound, or, literally, Whitehall.   The Sun is called Cynyn (The First), Cynvelyn is Cyn Belin, or the First Belus.   [13] Llogawd, in the original, is from Llôg (Benefit) and Awd (opportune). The Ancients believed the Sun brought souls, and a supply of fermenting essence, within him, on his return from Annwn or Hades on the morning of the New Year, hence the babe Bacchus shown with a skin wine-bottle on his shoulder.   The expression " in fetters a year and a day" is incomprehensible, unless it implies the " shutting " of the Gorsedd authority for "a year and a day," still observed by the Bards. It implies the same thing as the Septennial Act of Parliament when the authority of the Country vested in the House of Commons is dissolved, and a fresh appeal is made to the Country. Taliesen refers, here, to himself as the Prime Minister of Britain circumscribed by the law during a "year and a day."   [14] In the East the Sun's Mother was represented to be Der Ketos (a great fish), hence the Bard's allusion to the nature of the substance of the Sun's body.   † He speaks here as the priest on earth.   * See p. 426.

It will be understood that Taliesin is one of the numerous Druidic titles of the sun. It is composed of two words, viz., Tal (lofty) and Iesin, which is identical with Esus, or Hesus, of the Gauls.

The following is to be found in the " Myvyrian," but is translated into English in *Rites and Mythology of the British Druids*, p. 238 : —

"In those times Gwydd-No's weir stood out in the beach between Dovey and Aberystwyth, near his own castle." Borth facing Cardigan Bay is meant.

" In that weir it was usual to take fish to the value of a hundred pounds every year upon the eve of the 1st of May.

Gwydd-No (old sun) had an only son named Elphin, who had been a most unfortunate and necessitous young man (poor as the wren). This was a great affliction to his father, who began to think that he had been born in an evil hour. His counsellors, however, persuaded the father to let the son have the drawing of the weir on that year, by way of experiment, in order to prove whether any good fortune would ever attend him, and that he might have something to begin the world.

The next day being May Eve, Elphin examined the weir and found nothing ; but as he was going away he perceived a coracle, covered with a skin, resting on the pole of the weir."

" The coracle, covered with skin, was opened, and the opener, perceiving the forehead of an infant, said to Elphin ' Behold, Taliesin ! ' " or Lofty Esus.

It is customary to translate Taliesin " Radiant Front." But Tal is not front, but high or lofty, and Iesin is like Iu,

or Hu, one of the titles of the sun, as Hu-an (Annedd
Hu—Abode of Hu).

A shocking error too has been made in translating
Ceridwen Wrâch, Ceridwen the "Hag." Wrâch is compounded of Gwr (manly or brave) and ach (characteristic),
and simply means the masculine energy of the Goddess.
Why she is described as a fury will be seen farther on.

The skin coracle in the weir of Gwydd-No, containing the
lovely babe Taliesin, is identical as regards import with the
ark of bulrushes which the Alexandrians were wont to send
across the Mediterranean, to the inhabitants of the port of
Byblus, in Phœnicia, containing the feigned lost Adonis or
Tammuz.   Let the reader not forget the ark of bulrushes
in which Moses (Mysus or Bacchus) was found on the Nile.
The sun at the vernal equinox, March 21st, rises due east
over Yarmouth, and sets in the west over Borth, between
Dovey and Aberystwyth.   " Y " in " Yarmouth " is, doubtless, a corruption of Hu (pronounced Hee).   Directly
opposite Borth, Cardigan Bay, is Arklow, on the coast of
Ireland.   Arklow is manifestly a corruption of the Welsh
Archle, or, Place of the Ark.   Arklow has been spelt
Arklogh and Alercomshed.   The last compound is made
up of the following words, Al (sun), erc (ark), om (omen),
shed (to protect or ward off).

No doubt the whole locality of Arkle became identified
with the Ark of Taliesin or of the sun, and in the course of
long ages the place came to be regarded, like Delphi and
Jerusalem, with awe and pious reverence, owing to the
presence of the ark, though, in this instance, consisting only
of a sacred coracle covered with skin.

Apparently the Sacred Arkite Coracle, or Ark of the
Sun, was annually launched into St. George's Channel

(St. George is identical with Arthur, and is one of the
titles of the sun in the sign Archer, from November 23rd
to December 22nd), on the Irish coast at Arkle, and the
wind being favourable was directed to the Welsh coast at
Borth, Aberdovey, Cardigan Bay, a distance of about eighty
miles in a straight line from Archle or Arklow.

The Rev. Thomas Godwin, B.D., in his *Moses and Aaron*,
p. 152, referring to the losing and the finding of Adonis or
Tamuz, and the solemnities observed on those occasions by
the worshippers, states, " Those solemnities were chiefly
observed between the people of Byblus and the people of
Alexandria. The manner was thus: When the Byblians
solemnized the death or loss of Adonis, the Alexandrians
wrote a letter. This letter was enclosed in an ark of bulrushes, therein they signified that Adonis, whom they
lamented, was found again. The said ark being, after the
performance of certain rites and ceremonies, committed to
the sea, forthwith it was carried by the stream to Byblus," a
distance of about 250 miles; " and upon the receipt whereof
the lamentation of the women was turned into joy." Others
state the image of Adonis was conveyed in the Ark. The
reader will recollect that Osiris was killed by Typhon
(Avagddu) his brother, who enclosed him in a box, and
threw the box and its contents into the Nile. It was carried
to sea. The goddess Isis found the box, and Osiris in it,
on the coast of Phœnicia, where Byblus is situated.
Typhon stole the box, whilst it was being carried by Isis
to Memphis in Egypt, and gave the body of Osiris to be
eaten by his hellish companions! Osiris is the sun at
the summer solstice. Here Adonis seems to be the sun at
the vernal equinox. Both are, in reference to the tragedy,
identical here with Tammuz, the sun at the winter solstice.

Now, on the inland or east side of Borth, Cardigan Bay,
is a vast morass called Cors Voch-No. At its eastern end
is shown, to this day, a spot called the Grave of Taliesin,
and a village close by is named Taliesin. The said Morass
of Voch-No was, in ancient times, covered by high tides,
and, indeed, until the present railway bank was constructed, the high tides entered it.

It will have been observed that the name Gwydd-No and
Voch-No have the same termination. That " No " means
Naw, Nau, Noah, or Nine, and Gwydd-Naw signifies Ninth
Presence, or the sun in the ninth sign of the Zodiac or the
Archer, otherwise St. George, and is identical with Saidwrn
or Saturn, and with Saithun Saidi (Seven Causes in One),
and called also Saithun Veddw (drunk), and is identical also
with Silenus, the foster-father of Bacchus, or the sun as the
fermentor of the earth's juices. Saithun is the foster-father
of Gwylôn Bach, the Druidic Bacchus as a child.

The Druidic priests were called Swine, an honourable
appellation, as also were the priests of the Cabiri, or the
Seven Gods of Phœnicia, meaning the sun in his annual
stations through the seven planetary spheres in his annual
journey, the mid-day ascent northwards up the ecliptic, as
understood by the ancients.

The name Voch-No implies a place sacred to the Swine,
or priests, of the sun, when in the Ninth sign of the Zodiac.
That inlet or cove of Cardigan Bay was, evidently, in
ancient Druidic times, on March 21st, sacred to the Arkite
mysteries of Taliesin or the sun, exactly as Byblus, in
Phœnicia, was to the death and restoration, as a babe, of
Adonis ; and Arkle, in the west, on the Irish coast, corresponded in significance with Alexandria, which is south-
west from Byblus, Phœnicia, where (Alexandria) Adonis

was feigned to be found again and despatched back, as a newly-born babe, in an ark of bulrushes to Byblus, the same as we find Taliesin sent as a babe from Arkle, on the coast of Ireland, and arriving in a coracle, covered with a skin, at the weir of Gwydd-No —Garau Hir (Long Shanks, and Dadi Long Legs of folk-lore, and the three "legs" of the Seal and Arms of the Isle of Man authorities)—between the Dovey and Aberystwyth.

It will be remembered that on Mount Libanus, to the north-east of Byblus, it was feigned that Adonis was put to death by Typhon (Mars, Pluto), disguised as a wild boar. On the east side of the Morass of Voeh-No is shown, to this day, the grave of Taliesin! His grave, and his birth, from the coracle, it will be noticed, are near each other.

The skin coracle, like the ark of bulrushes, is one of the representations of Cèd (Cetus or Der Ketos), one of whose emblems in Druidism is the Llong Voel or the Mastless Ship or Ark. The sun of the old year, as Gwydd-Naw or No, is feigned to be old at his death (December 20th), and called both Saidwrn and Silenus or Seithun Veddw (drunk). It would appear the Druids did not always observe the nice distinctions of their mythological nomenclature, and applied the name Taliesin to the sun in his old age, and also at his new birth, in the same way as we find the Phœnicians applying the name Adonis both to the old sun, and also to the young sun of the new year.

But there is a remarkable divergence here from the correct ancient usage of the Druids of Britain in observing, by a section of those of Wales, the death of the old sun and his new birth, at the vernal equinox, instead of at the winter solstice, or December 20th and 22nd respectively. We know the Phœnicians were, during many centuries,

closely associated with the import and export trades of
Britain, and they appear to have so influenced some of the
Druids as to induce them to adopt the period of their
Adonia, instead of their own most ancient British correct one—the period of the winter solstice—as those of
the death and new birth of the sun under his title of
Taliesin. The name of the Morass of Voch-No, or Naw
(Nine), proves, however, all the Druids continued to regard
the solar rites performed, as relating to the Ninth Presence
of the sun from the time of the vernal equinox, or the
sign Aries, to the Ninth sign, Archer (November 23rd till
December 22nd), although, for the reason given above,
they came to observe them the same time of the year as
the Phœnicians did. But the fact of the innovation proves
the Phœnicians came to exercise great influence in Britain.

We must not forget to mention that Gwydd-No is sur-
named Garau Hir, or Long Shanks, a way of describing the
apparent long strides the personified sun is travelling across
the heavens from his rising to his setting. As illustrating
the fog of ignorance in which writers on this subject have
been groping, may be mentioned " Garau Hir" has been
rendered Garan Hir, and translated Long or High Crane!

Since writing the foregoing, we have come across what is
to us a startling confirmation of what we stated as to the
connection of " Arklow," on the coast of Ireland, with the
Taliesin solar legend. The following is a summary of
what the Rev. Robert Williams states in his " Eminent
Welshmen," *vide* " Taliesin." His authorities are Iolo
MSS., pp. 459, 467 ; Jones's *Bardic Museum*, 19 ;
Guest's *Mabinogion*, vol. iii. ; *Myv. Arch.* ii., 19. We
omit those parts about Taliesin fishing, &c., which are
evidently simply excrescences which have grown on the

pith of the allegory in the course of many centuries. We may state that Urien, his alleged patron, appears to be " Yr Huan " (Sun), here signifying the old sun of the preceding year, who, like Arthur, has been converted by benighted scribes into a great warrior. Like the sun at the longest day, Urien is said to have returned to the North, "where he recovered his father's dominions." As we have shown, a cause of endless confusion has been the practice of the Druids and others of giving the same poetical name to the old sun and the new, father and son, in the solar allegory. To proceed with Taliesin. " An Irish pirate ship seized him and bore him away towards Ireland, but while his captors were at the height of their drunken mirth, Taliesin pushed his coracle into the sea, and got into it himself with a shield in his hand, which he found in the ship (coracle), and with which he rowed the coracle until he approached the land. But, losing his shield (sail), he was tossed about at the mercy of the waves, until at length the coracle stuck to the point of a pole in the weir of Gwydd-No (Naw or Nine), at Aberdyvi, Wales." It will be recollected that elsewhere it was stated it was as a babe he was found in the coracle in the weir. The "shield" referred to is the skin which covered the coracle, and doubtless part of it was arranged so as to serve as a small sail. The myrmidons of Annwn (Hades— Ireland), which in the allegory sought to destroy the old sun Taliesin, when he was seen sinking in the west into the sea, are converted into drunken Irishmen by later scribes who had not the key to unriddle the solar allegory.

Undoubtedly the strange legend about the Land Beneath the Sea, called in Welsh " Cantre'r Gwaelod " (the Hundred of the Lower Region), Cardigan Bay, at this spot, is an echo of the ancient Druidic allegory of the lower region of Annwn (Hades), into which the old sun was supposed to descend

J

at his setting, originally on the shortest day, and afterwards, as we have seen and explained, at the vernal equinox, from the east to Ireland in the west of the said locality of Aberdyvi, or Aberdovey, as the English now spell the name of the locality. "Drunken Seithynun" (Silenus) is said to have caused the disaster of the Hundred of the Lower Region, the entrance into which is said to have been here in ancient times.

It will be seen we state elsewhere, particularly where we deal with "the place of a skull," that the sun was often referred to throughout the Gentile world as a "Head." In Professor Rhys's *Hibbert Lectures*, Ed. 1888, p. 96, the learned Cymro quotes from ancient lore the story of the miraculous head of Brân, who had gone to Ireland with his head on right enough, being brought back without the body to Harlech, where the society of the head was pleasant. "Brân" is evidently Ab yr Huan (Son of the Sun) abbreviated.

By Ab yr Huan (Brân) is meant the sun as the son of Hu Cylch y Ceugant, that is to say, the Almighty, as the Sun of the Highest Heaven or Gwynvyd. And it actually seems, from p. 97, "Uthr Ben"—called "Uthr Ben Dragon"—signifying Dignified "Head," is the humanised father of King Arthur (the sun), in the same sense as the old sun is the father of the young sun of the new year. In p. 90, Professor Rhys makes the important statement that sometimes in the Celtic mythology visits to Ireland are regarded as visits to Hades (Annwn); of course, in a mythological sense, because Ireland is in the direction of the setting sun from Wales. In the sun worship it was customary for women to cut off their hair (rays) and cast it into rivers, symbolizing the south western sea, where the sun was represented to have lost his rays.

CHAPTER XII.

THE Isle of Man was, clearly, like the Isle of Delos of the Greeks, sacred to Apollo (Ap Haul—Son of the Sun of the Circle of Infinitude or the Almighty), but much before the time that Delos was consecrated. In Welsh, the Isle of Man is now called Ynys Manwy. It ought to be spelt Ynys Mônwy. Môn is the olden name of a Cow in Welsh, and Mônwy signifies the Cow of the Water, the termination "wy" being the mutated form of Gwy (Water). As might be expected, the Isle of Man is still teeming with old Druidic customs, but, in many instances, they have become mixed. Train, in his *Isle of Man*, page 124, quoting Waldron's (Ed. 1744), &c., states, "The inhabitants of the Island of Lewis come to the church of St. Mulvay, carrying ale. One of their number is picked out to wade into the sea up to his middle, and carrying a cup of ale in his hand. Standing still in that posture, he cries with a loud voice, saying, 'Shony, I give you this cup of ale, hoping you will send us plenty of sea ware for enriching our ground for the ensuing year.' He then throws the cup of ale into the sea. This was performed at night time. At the return of the man to land, all the people went to church (Christmas Eve) where there is a candle burning on the altar. Then standing silent for a little time, one of the people gives a signal at which the candle is put out (extinguished), and immediately all go to the fields where they fall to drinking their ale, and spend the remainder of the night in dancing and singing."—Martin, quoted by Ellis. Note in Train's book, page 124, &c.

J 2

To this day, Shony, in Welsh, is slang for John. John, again, is the English form of Oannes, which is identical with the Philistine Dagon, or Dag-aun, and signifies, half fish and half man. Really a great fish projecting a child out of its mouth.

It will be observed that the fish, being a symbol of Ced, is feminine, and that the Divine child is masculine. And that the mythologists, having lost the original meaning of the symbol, made *one* symbol of the mother and child, and called it Oannes, or John, that is, Man-Fish. How came the mixed figure to be known in the Isle of Man by the name "Shony," the slang for John? Like the Baal Fire, called, corruptly, Beltane and Beltein—the termination should be tán—we discover in "Shony" an Eastern error, introduced no doubt by the Phœnicians. The cup of ale libation is offered to Oannes, the foreign god of the sea. But in pure Druidism, the cup of ale, and the drinking in the darkness after-wards, is a sacrament offered to Ced, the giver of the sun of the new year and the seeds (Satus) of the earth. "On Christmas Eve, the people of the Isle of Man flock to the churches bearing the largest Candles they can procure, and producing a brilliant illumination. The churches are all decked with holly, and the service in commemoration of the birth of the Saviour is called "Oiel Verry." Oiel is evidently O, Haul! (O, Sun!); Verry is, apparently, the Latin *Verus* (True), and the phrase signifies O, True Sun! The Christian fathers probably added the Verus with a view to convert the old solar rite to commemorate the birth of the Sun of Righteousness. On the night before January 6th (Epiphany), singers go round the town, carrying, in the midst of the choir, a lighted torch (Star of Bethlehem symbol?). On that night one of the fiddlers lays his head in the lap of one of the maidens, and the Mainstyr Fiddler asks who such a man or such a maid will marry. His answers are regarded as oracular. The ceremony is called 'Cutting the Fiddler's Head.'" They were devil worshippers when cutting off the " Head," for it signified the Power of Darkness cutting off Saturn's, or the Old Sun's " Head."

As already intimated, Taliesin is one of the many Druidic titles of the sun, and was used in Britain precisely in the same way as Adonis was used in Syria. In the history of Taliesin and the coracle in which he was found we are told that he was placed there by his mother, Ceridwen, which is another title for Cêd, God's Consort. As a crescent the coracle or ark is also called Latona, and the moon six days old, then shaped like a boat, ark, or coracle. We now proceed to learn how Ceridwen, or God's Consort, named here Holy Love in the sense a wife is designated " My Love," came to have Taliesin, and the story relates to the Druidic Cosmogony, or Theory of the Creation of the World.

" In former times," we are told, " there was a man of noble descent in Penllyn (Top of the Lake). His name was Tegid Voel (Tegid—All Lovely, and Moel—Bald), the rayless sun in winter. Tegid Voel's paternal home was in the middle of the lake—Bala Lake, called Tegid's Lake in Welsh. " His espoused wife was Ceridwen." This is precisely the same mistake as we often find in Egyptian history, where Isis is said to be the wife of Osiris, instead of saying correctly she was his *mother*. There was a second Isis (Venus), her daughter, and doubtless there was likewise a second Ceridwen, but signifying Venus. The earth in spring (Venus) as exercising the fecundating emanation of Ceridwen, or Cêd, is the wife of Tegid Voel in

his prime, that is to say, on March 21st.   Tegid is one of
the general names of the sun, and is the husband of Flora,
the earth's emanation at the summer solstice, and is identical
with Osiris.   By stating that Ceridwen the First is the
wife of Tegid Voel we confound the sun with the Creator,
the sun's real father.

"By his wife, Ceridwen, he" the Creator, to whom is
mistakenly given the name Tegid Voel, a title of the old
sun—we correct the mistake—"had a son named Môrvrân
(Sea Crow, personified Night)."   Night is the son of the
Almighty Celi, and Môrvrân is identical with Noah's raven !
" There was also born to them a damsel named Creirwy."

Creirwy signifies created egg, and implies plastic chaos,
and personified as Calen (orderless lump).   In Druidic
personifications, Creirwy or Calen, signifies also, as well
as a conglomerate mass, like the contents of an egg,
Beginning.   She is the sister of Hu Gadarn, Hesus the
Mighty, or Taliesin, who is born afterwards, as will be
shown presently.   Those two offsprings, Môrvrân (Night)
and Creirwy (created egg) had a brother named Avagddu
(the first of the trinity of evil causes).   " Avagddu was the
most hideous of beings.   Ceridwen, the mother of the black
deformed son, concluded in her mind that he would have
but little chance of being admitted into respectable
company, unless he were endowed with some honourable
accomplishment or science ; for this was the first period of
Arthur and the Round Table."   Of course, it was the
beginning of Creation.

In the above allegorical narrative, the paternal home
(trefdad) of Tegid Voel (old sun) is in Cêd, otherwise
Ceridwen, on the Sea of Annwn (Great Deep), symbolised

by the coracle on Tegid (or Bala) Lake. Tegid and Taliesin are one and the same character—the sun, under different names, and no doubt a coracle carried a symbolical babe, Taliesin or Tegid, on Bala Lake, as St. George's Channel did between the Irish coast on the west and that of Wales on the east.

In correct Druidism, the coracle would reach port at Dunwich, on the south-eastern coast of Britain (Suffolk), with the dawn each December 22nd, to begin the solar New Year.

The sacred Dee flows from Bala Lake, and to this day its waters are called Dwvr Duw, or Divine Water. We have it on record that a Welsh army, on its march to avenge the murder of the Welsh students at Bangor-Iscoed, Flintshire, about A.D. 600, was directed by Abbot Dunawd (Dinoot Abbas) to drink water from the sacred river Dee, in memory of the blood of the Lord Jesus, and to kiss its banks, in memory of his sacred body![1] At that epoch Wales, no doubt, was redolent with Druidic traditions. The probability is, that wherever the solar rites relating to the ancient worship had been performed, often on inland lakes and rivers, those places were still regarded by the masses as sacred. In such localities we have hazy traditions about sunken towns, fairy damsels, oxen, bulls, beavers, &c. They were the *dramatis personæ* of the ancient solar drama of our Druidic ancestors.

To proceed with the Taliesin narrative. "Then Ceridwen (Keridwen) determined, agreeably to the Books of Pheryllt (Chemist), to prepare for her son" Avagddu, or Mérvrân —Darkness, unless Avagddu is intended to symbolise the evil emanation of Night "a cauldron of Awen and Gwybodau."

See 1 *Corinthians* x., 1-4.

It will be observed one is called A-ddu or Black A, and
the other A-wen, or white A, that is, holy A.   In the
middle of the compound "Avagddu" is vag, mutated from
magu, with u (e) left out for the sake of euphony. Magu
signifies to nurse, as explained in a former page. Both A's
were Druidic symbols ; the black Λ (raven) from the door
of Annwn or Hades, down in the south where the sun sets
on the shortest day ; the white Λ (white dove) from the
door of Gwynva, in the northern heavens on the longest day.
We observe here the Druids regarded Avagddu, called also
Sea Crow, as the brother of the Sun, precisely as the Pagan
Romans said Pluto and Jupiter were brothers, and the
Egyptians, that Osiris and Typhon were likewise brothers.
We find here a trace of a Druidic meddling with the problem
as to the origin of evil, which has in all ages baffled the
master minds of all nations.

The Hebrews supposed they settled the question by
stating that a rebellion broke out in heaven, and that the
Evil One and all his angels were hurled out of heaven.
But then, we are met with the puzzling questions, "How
did the evil spirit, which caused the trouble, get there?"
and, "If it got there once, is it impossible for it to break
out there again among the ancient friends of those who
were hurled out?" According to this, the place is not a
safe one.   What is most astonishing in the story of
Ceridwen and the cauldron is, that she, the Consort of the
Creator, intended, according to the Druidic philosophy, the
inspiration prepared in the cauldron, in the first place for
her monster and deformed son Avagddu, and not for
Taliesin, her lovely boy, who, in spring, would receive the
title of Tegid or All Lovely. He, however, was yet
uncreated. Avagddu (Night) was Ceridwen's *first* born,
and, therefore, she was rather partial to him, ugly and black

though he was. The Sun was uncreated, but Time was in existence, and "the year and a day," during which the cauldron was to boil, to prepare the inspiriting liquid for Avagddu's benefit, was Time. The narrative goes on to state : " The cauldron began to boil, and it was requisite that the boiling should be continued for a year and a day " —from December 22nd until the following December 20th, and 40 hours over : a period, except the darkness of forty hours on earth, each year aftewards monopolised by Taliesin, to the eternal chagrin of his brother, Avagddu, or the devil.

" Ceridwen placed Gwyion the Little to superintend the preparation of the cauldron," the essence of the contents of which was intended by Ceridwen to convert her ugly black son into the resemblance of a genius, and of what is good and noble, however unpresentable he might be outwardly. " She appointed a blind man " light not being yet created, eyes, therefore, were not yet necessary " named Morda, with a strict injunction that he should not suffer the boiling to be interrupted before the completion of a year and a day," when, it appears. she intended to administer the inspiriting essence to her black monster son. We are strongly of opinion this name ought to be spelt *Môr-du* (e)—Black Sea or Black One of the Sea—and that Night is meant by the character; and, therefore, that by Avagddu is meant Evil personified. In Bell's *Pantheon* the portrait of Pluto represents that god as blind, and all his worship was conducted at night. All animals sacrificed to him were black, and black bulls were the favourite sacrifice. The bulls of the Taurine Sun were white. It is said that Plutus, the god of riches, has been confounded with Pluto, and that it was Plutus that was blind. But we believe Plutus is simply an emanation of Pluto, and that both were represented as being blind. The three-headed dog of the Infernal Regions, named Cerebus, is blind also, and is represented by the side of Pluto (Typhon) or Avagddu.

" In the meantime, Ceridwen, with due attention to the books of astronomy" time counting "and to the hours of the planets, employed herself" daily " in botanizing and in collecting plants of every species of rare virtue." It is clear it was believed the sun was a distinct special creation for this world alone, and that the seed germs were created before Time, and that the Consort of God is weeding and making selections for the coming world. Elsewhere it is stated the " plants " were Pumwydd (Five Trees), and that the mixture in the cauldron out of which the inspiriting liquid was to come came from the *Pumwydd*. The five trees seem to symbolise the five senses of Côd, the great mother, namely—hearing, sight, smell, taste, and touch, and here referred to as essence. " On a certain day, about the completion of the year" Dec. 20th, " whilst she" Ceridwen " was botanizing and muttering to herself, Three Drops of the efficacious liquid happened to fly out of the cauldron, and alight upon the finger of Gwyion the Little. The heat of the essence occasioned his putting his finger in his mouth. As soon as those precious Three Drops (∴) had touched his lips every event of the futurity was opened to his view ; and he clearly perceived that his greatest concern was to beware of the stratagem of Ceridwen, whose knowledge was very great. With great terror he fled towards his native country. As for the cauldron it divided into two halves."

We stop here. What follows is a reference to the horses of the sun, which is clearly an eastern parable, added, no doubt, through Phœnician influence ; for Bryant has shown, we believe satisfactorily, that the introduction of horses into the solar allegory, is due to a mistake, though as old as the time of Homer, through misunderstanding terms in translation from one language into another.—Vide *Analysis*, vol. ii., p. 407.

CHAPTER XIII.

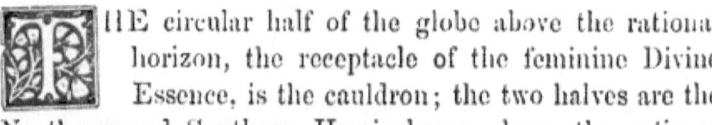

THE circular half of the globe above the rational horizon, the receptacle of the feminine Divine Essence, is the cauldron; the two halves are the Northern and Southern Hemispheres above the rational horizon, with the equinoctial line dividing the earth *into two halves.* The northern half when the sun is between the east and the northern point of the heavens, is under the dominion of Taliesin (sun). The southern half when the sun is between the east point and the shortest day, is claimed by Avagddu. It is a contest between summer and winter, and is the same as Adonis six months with Venus and six months with Proserpine.

In reference to the cauldron, whose contents were prepared for one brother, and given to the other, we are reminded of the story of Esau and Jacob. Rebekah, like Ceridwen, prepared the broth. Ceridwen prepared her broth honestly for Avagddu; Rebekah dishonestly prepared her broth, ostensibly on behalf of Esau, but really on behalf of Jacob. The lesson is on a par with robbing the Egyptians. Esau, too, was a man of unnatural and repulsive appearance. He was so very hairy, according to the narrative, as to resemble a monkey, for we are told that Rebekah placed the skins of kids of goats upon Jacob's hands, and upon the smooth of his neck, so as to make him resemble, to the touch of their father Isaac, his son Esau. Esau is " red," the Red Dragon (War) is the emblem of Avagddu, and the Golden Dragon (Peace) is the symbol of Taliesin. The ancient Druidic allegories accompanied their circular temples everywhere, and Palestine has still many of them, as reported by the Palestine Exploration Society.

Why was Ceridwen angry with Gwyion the Little? Because he had taken the Three Drops, which she had prepared so laboriously, by chemical studies and solar observations, for her son Avagddu.

What do the Three Drops, which inspired Gwyion the Little in a startling manner, signify? We reply, the Triune Word, or Logos, of the Creator. They imply the same thing as the White Dove Adonis; the Wren symbol of Taliesin; the Dove which descended on the Lord Jesus when he was ascending from the Jordan after being baptized by John; the two wings and body in each making triplets ⅃; the three pillar supports under every Cromleâch, as Adlais (Atlas or Echo) of the Voice of the Creator, returning and propping the earth as a fulcrum; the three Golden Apples stolen by Hercules from the Garden of Hesperides; the three Bulls of the Taurine period of the Druidic religion; and, finally, Plennydd, Alawn, and Gwron, of the later epoch of the humanised personification period; and last of all, the three props or legs supporting the ancient Druidic Chair of the Bards of Wales!

But what is meant by Gwyion? The name is a compound of two words, Gwy (water), and Iôn or Leader-Lord, the Druidic title of the Creator in the work of leading the elements into order at the beginning of Creation.

It will have been seen, in Chapter II., that Enid (Venus) called also Gwen-y-Môr—Wen of the name Venus—(Holy one of the Sea), is the daughter of Niwl, or Humidity, her mother being Cêd or Ceridwen—source of the vapour supposed by the ancients to be ascending through the earth). The Divine virile power, operating through the agency of dew, is warmth or heat from the Creator himself, who is called Hu Cylch y Ceugant, or, Hu of the Circle of Infinitude, while the sun is Hu Cylch y Sidydd, or of the Circle of the Zodiac, operating triunally during the year. Gwyion signifies warmth coming by the agency of dew, that warmth coming from the Creator himself. In German dew is called *Tau* (Tad, the Welsh for Father). Dew is much like the Welsh Daw (God). He having imparted into it the virtue of His Word, the active principle independently of His Consort Ceridwen, otherwise Cêd, or the passive principle in the mother of Nature, that is, the mother of Venus, (the Druidic Gwen). The same ancient idea is found in the allegory wherein it is stated the thigh of Jupiter (Iu-Father) was the second mother of Bacchus (Sun). The "thigh" signifies the Creator's Almightiness.

But, as the sequel will show, Ceridwen (Cêd) became afterwards the mother of Gwyion, but under the new name Taliesin.

We now resume the Druidic allegory: "Ceridwen entering just at that moment, and perceiving" as she supposed "that her whole year's labour was entirely lost, seized an oar, and struck blind Mêrdu upon his head, so that one of his eyes dropped upon his cheek.

'Thou hast disfigured me wrongfully,' exclaimed Mêrdu, 'seeing I am innocent; thy loss has not been occasioned by me.'

'True!' replied Ceridwen, 'It was Gwyion the Little who robbed me.'

Having pronounced these words, she began to run after him.

Gwyion, perceiving her at a distance, transformed himself into a hare, and doubled his speed. But Ceridwen, instantly becoming a female greyhound, turned him, and chased him towards a river. Leaping into the stream he assumed the form of a fish. But Ceridwen became now a female otter, and traced him through the stream, so that he was obliged to take the form of a bird and mount into the air "—the Divine soul of the sun passing through the animal kingdom before entering the physical body of the sun as a physical creation, the son of Semele. "The element afforded him no refuge, for Ceridwen in the form of a sparrow-hawk, was gaining upon him, and she was just in the act of pouncing upon him. Shuddering with the dread of death, he perceived a heap of wheat upon the floor, and dropped into it, and assumed the form of a single grain. Ceridwen took the form of a black, high-crested hen (Black Virgin), descended into the wheat, scratched him out, distinguished, and swallowed him." And, as the story relates, she was pregnant of him nine months, and when delivered of him, she found him so lovely a babe (Taliesin) that she had not resolution to put him to death. She placed him, however, in a coracle covered with a skin, and by the instigation of her husband (the Almighty, and father of Taliesin, but not in the ordinary way of Nature), cast him into the sea. Localities named Rhagod (to Ambuscade) and Treboeth Farm (Hot Quarters), near Trefeirig, on the Gwyion Dro Road (Road of Gwyion's Turning), between Bwlch Gwyion (Gwyion's Gap), on the route between Pontypridd and Tonyrefail to the west from the first named of the last two named localities, seem to be associated with the allegory. Most singular that in the allegory the Rocking Stone at Pontypridd, and the neighbourhood and Borth, Cardigan Bay, should be associated together.

The incidents of the above singular solar drama are imprinted on local place names in the neighbourhood of Pontypridd, Glamorganshire. In the neighbourhood are several Druidic remains, namely, a great Gwyddva, still

entire, to the south of the town, in the fork between the
two highways, one leading to Llanalltud Church, and the
one leading towards Llantrisant. Another great Gwyddva
(Place of Presence) called Maesycrug, is on the top of the
hill to the north-west of the former, not far from Ty'r
Arlywydd Farm, and a short distance to the south-west of
Crawshay's iron tower; but notably the Logan, or Rocking
Stone, on Pontypridd Common, to the east of the town.
The Druids, we repeat, referred to the round earth above the
rational horizon as the Garden of the Sun. The Isle of
Britain symbolised that garden, as did the Island of Delos
in Greece. Each Druidical circle symbolised that Garden
of the Sun. It appears that the original name of Ponty-
pridd Common was Prydwen-Ardd, or Britannia's Garden.
The name is now limited to a farm on the border of the
Common, and popularly called Brydwen-Ar'.

No doubt, on that Common, and in the neighbourhood,
were performed great ceremonial Druidic rites in remote
times, with the Rocking Stone as the symbolical Ark of the
Mysteries in the midst, and rocking west towards east;
bowing to the east, as the "church" does still at the
mention of the Name of Jesus, her husband, she being his
sister-spouse. In reference to the allegory of Ceridwen and
Gwyion, there are near Pontypridd such names as Craig
Gwyion, called erroneously Craig Wen; Pwll Gwyion
(Gwyion's Lake), erroneously called Pwll Gwaun; Gelli
Wyion (Gwyion's Grove); Tyle Gwyion-Dro (the Ascent of
Gwyion's Turning); Gelli Draws (Grove where she turned):
Bwlch (Gap of) Gwyion, erroneously called Bwlch-Gwyn.
The highway from Bwlch Gwyion to St. John the Baptist
Church, near Tonyrefail, a distance of about two miles, is
called Heol Gwyion-Dro (the Road of Gwyion's Turning).
Two farms in the same neighbourhood are named respect-
ively Rhiw Gwyion-Dro, or the Path of Gwyion's Turning.

We omit the date given to the event because we know it to be erroneous. The babe in the coracle received the name Taliesin. As already mentioned, the correct date of placing him in the coracle and on the sea is at four o'clock p.m. on Dec. 20th. The vernal equinox period for the ceremony, in commemoration of the event, is clearly an error brought to Britain from the East, doubtless by the Phœnicians. But the St. George's Channel Druids of Borth would perform the rite on March 20th, being the Phœnician time for the rite. The Taliesin narrative implies the sun's material body, in which is enclosed the Divine Logos or Word, which body was derived from the substance of Ceridwen during the nine months of gestation. The severance, as it were, of the Word or Logos from the Creator took place when, in three drops of Divine essence, it alighted on the finger of Gwyion, on Dec. 22nd. What is meant by the "finger of Gwyion" we cannot understand, unless it is being implied that the sun, in accordance with the system of transmigration, was a creature, as Jesus was before his baptism, before he became a Divine Son by the descent of the Dove. His incarnation in that body took place when the Word, enveloped in the grain, was swallowed by Ceridwen. That would be on March 21st, or, according to the Julian Calendar, on March 25th, or Lady Day. His quickening, as the soul of the sun, in the material body of his mother, Ceridwen, took place on each Sept. 22nd, six months since his incarnation, and which is nine months from Dec. 22nd-25th, when he came from the Eternal. Here we have a reference to the birth of the soul, Dec. 22nd, and the introduction of natural life, serving to develop the body in the womb, on March 21st-25th. His birth took place on each Dec. 22nd, or, according to the Julian Calendar, on each Dec. 25th—Christmas Day. The above are the "six months" referred to by St. Luke, when describing the visit of the Virgin to Elizabeth, the mother of John the Baptist. But in the narrative it is John who is said to have leaped in his mother's womb, not Jesus in the Virgin's womb (St. Luke, chap. xxvi., 2). John the Baptist was said to be Old Elijah returned. Eli-Jah signifies: Eli (Sun), and Jah—Shabbetha—"Jah is Saturn" (Old Sun). Observe, Elizabeth signifies: Beth (House or Grave—Welsh Bedd), and Eli—"Za."[1] It seems to be implied it was the Divine Logos which caused the leap in the womb of Eli-za-beth—Céd or Delphus (womb)—to be transferred from John (Old Sun—Elijah) to Hesous (the Young Sun) at his baptism. Everybody now knows that the birthday of the Lord Jesus, viz., Christmas Day, is simply a fiction, and that that date was fixed upon with a view to supplant the sun by placing the birth of Jesus, instead of the birth of the sun, where, during countless ages, the world had celebrated the date of the birth of the sun of the New Year from Céd (Der Ketos) with unbounded tokens of joy.

In reference to the quickening of the soul of the sun at the autumnal equinox, we would remind the reader it is the period of the Jewish Day of Atonement. We beg to refer the reader to what we state elsewhere of the birth of the priesthood of Aaron, and what the ceremonies on that occasion each year signified. It was implied that the Word or Logos was repeated annually.

The following is stated to have been said by the babe, Taliesin, when he was found in the coracle in the weir of the Morass of Gwydd-No. Observe the similarity between his experiences and those which befell Gwy Iôn Bach. Thus he sang to Elphin (Alpha):

Dr. Inman's *Ancient Faiths*—Vol. II., p. 504.

K

" I was first formed in aspect like a fair man :
I was appointed[1] to the Court of Ceridwen.[2]
Though small in appearance,[3] and in darkness,[4]
Yet I was in a Festival :
I was important on the floor of the Circle Grove[5] into
    which I was led.
Precious was my enclosed[6] sweet Awen[9] of Paradise :[7]
And (I) by law, without language and free will.[8]
(The) Ancient Scientist[9] of the black water,[10] when
    she became enraged,
Furious[11] was her purpose when she started—

        I fled with vigour :
        I fled as a frog ;
        I fled in the guise of a crow—
          Hardly resting.
        I fled vehemently ;
        I fled zigzag ;†
        I fled as a roe
          That in the bush hideth :
        I fled as a wolf's cub—
        I fled as a wolf
          In the Wilderness.
        I fled as a thrush—
          The interpreter of Omens.
        I fled as a fox,
          Bounding and leaping :
        I fled as a Marten,
          But to no purpose :
        I fled as a squirrel
          That vainly hides :
        I fled as an antlered stag,
          Freely he paddled me.
        I fled as iron in glowing fire :
        I fled as a spear—
          Woe him who desire it :
        I fled as a bull,
          Fiercely he fought :
        I fled as a boar
          That in the furrow ploughed ;
        I fled into a grain of wheat—

---

[1] Penydwys-Penodi : Appointed — to look after the Cauldron.   [2] Place of
Cauldron.   [3] Gwy fôn the Little.   [4] Sun not yet created.   [5] Llawr Llan:
Circular Grove.   [6] Parwyden: Enclosure.   [7] Parwys—Paradwys: Paradise.
[8] Rylliwys: The word rhydd (free) and the context make this word appear
Yr Ewyllys (will).   [9] Nash makes "Hen Widdon" to be "Old Hag"
Widdon is from Gwyddon, the Welsh, to this day, for Scientist.   [10] Ddulon
is Ddulyn: Black Lake or Water.   [11] Anghuriawl is Anghurawl: Irresistible.
* The Three Drops in the Cauldron was the medium of Awen (Inspiration).
† Literally, Like a Chain.

On the brow Llan Garthen (she) ensnared me :
Seeing her was like beholding the hold of a ship
Filled on the waters.
Into a dark belly she transmitted me :
Into a boundless ocean she conveyed me :
It was a place of concealment when her scales‡
    suffocated me ;[12]
God, Lord of Liberty, delivered me !

It is deeply interesting to find that the original Welsh of the foregoing is in the Gwentian dialect.

Then Alpha, or Elphin, conveyed Taliesin to the house of Gwydd-No, his father. It appears that Gwy Iôn Bach, now having become Taliesin, is the Druidic Bacchus, and that Gwydd-No is Arawn (Silenus) and that Saidwrn is Saturn. The former is the *Old* Nocturnal Sun while the last-named is the *Old* Diurnal Sun, and he is the father of Hu Gadarn or Hesus the Mighty. Gwydd-No asked Alpha if he had a good haul at the weir. He replied that he had got what was better than a fish. What was that? asked Gwydd-No. " A Bard," answered Alpha. Then said Gwydd-No " Alas ! what will he profit thee ?" Taliesin himself replied, and said " He will profit him more than the weir ever profited thee." Asked Gwydd-No : " Art thou able to speak, and so little ?" Taliesin replied, " I am better able to speak than thou art to question me." " Let me hear what thou canst say," quoth Gwydd-No. Then Taliesin sang : —

---

[12] Fygwys is Fogws: Suffocated.

‡ "Cain" in the original should be Cen (scales); The error doubtless crept in in transcribing. In the *Iolo MSS.*, p. 276, Ceridwen, in v. 19, is alluded to as a Whale or Dolphin by the name Morvarch, and Taliesin or Ionas (Iona—Dove) delivered out of her belly. This is an additional proof that the solar drama, performed at Borth, Cardigan Bay, was derived from Phœnicia.

"On the water is precipitant[1] the blessed song;[2]
  'Tis best to trust to God to make (one) rational,[3] (and)
  To God the Righteous chant[4] prayers seriously;
  Owing to obstacles there is no benefit where He is not.[5]

Thrice was I born.[6]   I know, through study,
  (That) Wretched is the man who comes not to seek
  All the sciences of the world, which troop into my brain,[7]
  For I know what has been, and what in future will
    happen.

I will address my God, who is my succourer;[8]
  Through my penance[9] His gifts will come to me.
  My Emblem of Covenant is the Son of Mary,[10]
  And my heart is fixed on him,
  For the world is held every hour by him.

God Taught me and for Him I will seek—
  True Creator of Heaven is ever my succourer.
  It is proper for the saints always to pray,
  For God-David will guide them to Himself.

---

[1] Cyv and Llwr: Those who tend forward together.   [2] Cân Vendigaw: Blessed Song.   [3] Synwyraw: to be rational.   [4] Can: Song or Chant; the first word of the fourth line is evidently part of third line.   [5] Ny ellir lludd cael budd iwrthaw: Ny (continuity) (Ni) ellir (cannot) lludd (obstacle) cael budd (to have benefit) iwrthaw (oddirthaw—apart from him). The fourth line conveys the sense.   [6] Teirgwaith im ganed: Thrice was I born. (1) As an animal; (2) As a human being; (3) Now, as a being endowed with the Divine afflatus—Awen from God (Inspiration imparted by the Three Drops (∴)—\|/). The Archdruid symbolised all Three (Births) viz., the Divine Spirit, by his office.   [7] Brue): literally, Womb, but in the sense of conceiving ideas, the Brain is alluded to. The Archdruid was called Menw Hen or the Ancient Mind (Minos or Menu), meaning Mind as an abstraction derived from God's Spiritual Nature. The sun was regarded as the abode of intelligence. The pre-existence also of Man before he received his soul is implied by the following, in the "Awdyl Vraith" Song of Varieties, imputed to Taliesin:

    "Five hundred years, without much protection,
    Was he (Adda)* lying down
    Before he obtained a Soul."

[8] Nawdd: Succourer.   [9] Cyvarchwel: Penance.   [10] Crair: Emblem of Covenant.

* Adda is translated Adam.

Now the foregoing verses are, judging by the archaic character of the language employed, extremely old; but the scriptural allusions in them indicate that they, and also many others, which bear the name of Taliesin, were penned during the Christian era. But the mixture of Druidic ideas found in them, in very old Welsh, relating to the solar allegory, proves they came into existence very early in the history of the Christian religion in Wales. We quote them here simply to illustrate the story of Taliesin. They were undoubtedly used in the solar drama performed between the Welsh and the Irish in the neighbourhoods of Borth, Wales, and Arklow, Ireland, of which sending the coracle with the babe Taliesin in it was but one of the incidents of the magnificent religious performance.

CHAPTER XIV.

KING Arthur (the Sun), the renowned Welsh British personage, occupies in the traditions of the Cymry and their kindred, the Bretons of France, much the same position as the traditions of the hoped for Messiah did, and does still, among the Jews. The Messia⁾, the Jews believed, and believe still, will appear miraculously and establish them as the ruling nation of the whole earth, with his headquarters at Jerusalem. In another portion of this work, we have shown that Arawn is one of the Druidic titles of the sun at the end of the solar year, and that it is identical with the Greek Ouranos of the New Testament. Ouranos has been erroneously translated "heaven" in the New Testament. Alford in his comments on the Greek text of the Gospel of St. Matthew, chap. iii., v. 2, &c., admits it to signify the Advent of the Messiah. Therefore, the words of John the Baptist in the said verse, translated "Repent ye: for the kingdom of *heaven* is at hand," ought to have been translated, Repent ye: for the kingdom of the Messiah is at hand; that is, if Ouranos or Arawn (Old Sun "renewed") signifies the Messiah. If it does, then the Arawn of the Druids, and the Aaron of the Hebrews, signify both the sun and the Messiah; for there is no question the Aaron of Israel is derived from the Druidic Arawn, and also that Arôn, the Hebrew name of the Ark of the Covenant, as being the Ark of the sun—the Ark deriving its name from it—under his title of Arawn. As we have shown in preceding pages, the old sun was supposed to disappear at the end of the solar year, and the new sun appearing in his place, forty hours later, to take up the government of the world. And that, in many instances, the same title was given to the new sun as that by which the old had been known, because some nations, and the Hebrews among them, held that the new sun was simply the old sun "renewed," as has been clearly shown in what we have stated about Saturn, Hercules, Adonis, &c. Now we arrive at one of two conclusions, namely, either the legend, which prevailed among all ancient nations, to the effect that the old sun restored or "renewed," as a new sun on Christmas day—but on each December 22nd in Druidism—was typical or emblematical of the Coming of the Son of God, the Messiah of the World, or—and it is a tremendous "or"!—that the whole structure of the Christian religion is based on a solar poetical fable, which was invented by the Druids in the early ages of the world, for the purpose of setting forth poetically the Cosmogony of the universe, as they understood it. Each reader must, before God and the eternal verities, solemnly determine the question for himself. Let no man dwell over the question simply in a party spirit, but in the spirit of free inquiry, and of eternal truth—"The Truth against the World!"— Truth will abide forever. Throughout these allegories, a spirit of piety, and ardent yearning for drawing nigh to God's mysterious individuality, are clearly manifest.

It appears that Tertullian—A.D. 193–220—had been pondering over the Eastern aspect of the above solar allegory, both among the Gentiles and the Hebrews, and he wrote about the incarnation of Jesus as follows :— *De Carne Christi*, c. VI.—"But you do not receive this, as you do not receive that Christ who, at that early period, was studying how to address and free and judge mankind, in the guise of the flesh, not yet born, because not yet

about to die, unless his nativity had been previously
announced." And: *Praxeas*, c. XVI.—"Thus, even God
was always studying to live with men on earth, no other
than the Word (*sermo-λογος*) who was to be the flesh. He
was, moreover, learning to *prepare* the faith for us, that we
might, by learning *that something of the kind had been
done before*, more easily believe that the Son of God
descended into the world."

King Arthur's name is interwoven with all the ancient
romances of Europe. "Arthur, when first he appears in
history, three hundred years later than the day he is said
to have lived, is found invested with all the glories of
legend, and straightway becomes the national hero" of
the Welsh and the Bretons "to whom" (Arthur) "is
attributed a series of victories of surpassing splendour,
and the empire of half of Europe. * * His name is
extolled in endless lays, as that of the ideal of Christian
chivalry, surrounded with a brilliant circle of warriors,
patterns of all kingly graces, and who, excelling even him
in prowess, are incorporated into a mystic fraternity, and
aided by the most potent wisdom and skill in the achievement of their feats of renown ; yet again, as if to none but
to him all that could stir the hearts of men in the ages of
faith and honour," could be entrusted " mysterious
symbols of the Christian Creed (the Greal, &c.,) as they
were held by those who had learnt in Eastern lands,
while they fought for the Holy Sepulchre, * * the sacred
vessel from which the Lord partook of the last supper, the
lance which pierced His side as He hung upon the Cross,
are mingled in the story."—*Woodward*, p. 104.

All the legends of Arthur, mixed up with the marvellous
story relating to the establishing of the Christian religion
in Palestine, prove one of two things, viz., either that the

Round Table of King Arthur, with the inner circle of twelve knights around it, and the Sans-Greal dish on the middle of the table, is an imitation of the earliest formation of the Christian Church, or that that institution of the Christian Round Table of the Monks is planned after the model of the Druidical Arthur's Round Table and its associates, which are simply a solar allegory.

In the history of Arthur he is presented to view with twelve knights. One of them—his nephew Modred—turns out to be his murderer.

The Lord Jesus is at the Table of the Last Supper with his twelve disciples. One of them—Judas—turns out to be the cause of *his* murder.

At "Avebury," Wilts, is the ruin of a vast circular Druidic temple. The outward circle contained a circle of one hundred stones, the same number, we beg to remind the reader, as the number of "gates" round the city of Thebes, in Egypt. Two inner circles in the middle of the vast enclosure, bordered all round by the circle of one hundred stones, contained a circle of twelve stones each, or twenty-four in all. In addition to those stones would be four others, namely, the cromleâch and its three gigantic stone pillar supports. In the formation there would be thus one hundred priests at the one hundred stones forming the vast outer circle ; twenty-four stationed at the two inner circles of twelve each ; and four at the four cromleâch stones, or twenty-eight. There was, in addition to the above, a vast cylindrical pillar stone in the middle of one of the two circles of twelve stones each.

Now, in Sir Thomas Malory's *Morte d'Arthur*, Book III., ch. i., King Leo. de Grance presents to King Arthur

the Round Table of Uthr Pendragon (Dignified " Head "),
Arthur's father, also one hundred knights. Symbolising
the outer rim of the earth above the rational horizon.

"Now, Merlin," said King Arthur, "go thou and espy
me in all the land fifty knights which be of most prowess
and worship. Within a short time Merlin had found such
knights that should fulfil twenty-eight knights, but no
more he could find." Arthur himself represented the
cylindrical pillar. Thus they number twenty-four, in two
circles, of twelve each, and four over. It is well known
each of such pillars, like the round towers of Ireland, was
sacred to the sun, who was said to be the Son of the
Almighty, otherwise, a personification of His virile power.
The four additional ones are the Druidic trinity—Plennydd,
Alawn, and Gwron, and the Archdruid, in whom, symbolically, they as Divine attributes dwelt, and in whom,
therefore, dwelt all the fulness of the Godhead bodily.

As we have shown in preceding pages, the round
earth above the rational horizon was, in Druidic times,
symbolised by the Isle of Britain, and imitated by the
Greeks by the Island of Delos ; the chief Druidic circle
of Britain—Avebury—symbolised the Isle of Britain, itself
symbolising the circular earth above the said horizon. The
circular earth would be also symbolised by a round dish—the
Holy Greal,—and its contents—personified as Venus—the
chemical fermentation of the earth under the sun's warm
influence in spring. As we have seen, the sun's round disk
was symbolised, among other ways, by an apple, and its
three annual stages by three apples ; and the circular temple,
or Britannia, was named the Garden of the Hesperides in
the west of the world, from which Hercules is said to have
stolen the three apples. The sacramental essence produced

by the sun and earth co-operating, was, owing to the apple symbol employed, symbolised by cider in Britain, but by the juice of the grape in grape-growing countries. The said dish, which was, in a sense, like the molten " sea " of the Hebrew temple, was called Pair Ceridwen by the Druids, which, translated, means, the Cauldron of Holy Love, meaning the Creator's Consort ; the Anima Mundi, the Druidic Anian, considered as a Divine essence concreted. The said dish of the Druids was, we doubt not, imitated by the inventors of the San Greal legend. And we believe the vast circle of Avebury, symbolising the round earth and the garden of the sun, is the original San Greal ; and, as we have stated elsewhere, we believe Greal is the Druidic word Cread (Creation), which would be mutated Ei Gread by employing the word His (Ei), and corrupted to " Greal."

Referring to the miraculous nourishing quality of the Holy Greal, Nutt, in his *Studies on the Legend of the Holy Greal*, p. 75, quotes the following : " In D. Queste,' we reve t to the physical gifts of the Greal, " as soon as it" the Greal dish " entered the door of the hall, the whole court was filled with perfume * * and it proceeded to every place in the hall. And as it came before the tables, it filled them with every kind of meat that a man could wish to have." The earth, of which the Cauldron of Ceridwen was the symbol, does that literally.

It appears puzzling why there are two sets of circles of 12 stones each within the area of the great circle of 100 stones at Avebury, for it is certain each circle represents the Zodiac. They represent two sects or denominations, in Druidism, namely, the party of the Linga, and the party of the Logos or Divine Word. The party of the Logos—the party who, afterwards, isolated themselves at Stonehenge—

held that the virile power of God through the sun, expressing itself at the vernal equinox, was but *one* of the attributes of W or /I\, the Word or Logos of the Creator, and that the three attributes must be expressed collectively. The party of the Said or Linga, or "The Seminal Word," as Justin Martyr styles it (p. 68)—no doubt the earlier party, the party of the acorn and cup—demurred, and it appears that, during the progress of unknown ages, both sects agreed to differ, and continued to meet regularly in the same sanctuary. But, at some unknown period, the party of the Word, or Logos, erected Côr Gawr, or Stonehenge, with simply a cromleâch—three props and a horizontal slab—as symbols of the Word /I\ and the symbol of the earth held up by its reverberation (Adlais—Atlas). Outside the Stonehenge sanctuary is a huge *flat* rough pillar as a sun dial, indicating exactly the point of the horizon, and level with it, where the sun rushes into view on the morning of the *longest day*, when it is in the north-east, in the tropic of Cancer, and in his full effulgence. The said sun-dial is so arranged that, to those standing in front of the ruined cromleâch, the sun seems on top of the sun pointer, and flooding the sanctuary with his radiant beams. In Druidism this pointer is called "Maen Porth y Nêv" (The Stone Pillar of the Porch of Heaven).

To revert to the twenty-eight knights whom Merlin brought to the Round Table, it is astounding to find the number corresponds with the number St. John, as described in Revelation, saw at the Round Throne of God, which was encircled by a rainbow, like the moat full of crystal water reflecting the sunbeams around the circular temple of Avebury. "And," states Sir Isaac Newton on the Apocalypse of St. John (p. 275), "he that sat on it (the throne) was to look upon like jasper and sardine

stone; that is, of an olive colour, the people of Judea
being of that colour.   And the sun being then" at
the time of the Passover "in the East, a rainbow
was about the throne, the emblem of glory.   And
round about the throne were four and twenty seats,
answering to the chambers of the four and twenty princes
of the priests—twelve on the south side, and twelve on the
north side of the priests' court.   And upon the seats were
four and twenty elders sitting, clothed in white raiment,
with crowns upon their heads representing" continues Sir
Isaac "the princes of the four and twenty courses of the
priests, clothed in linen.   *   *   And in the midst of the
throne, and round about the throne, were four beasts full of
eyes, before and behind."   Sir Isaac Newton did not observe
that, at one period, Zodiacal animals were literally the
emblems of the Divine attributes in the circular throne of
the Druids.   As we have shown elsewhere in this work,
bulls and cows were the symbols during the Taurine
period, when the bulls were represented by oxen where
used.   Afterwards, in the East, the bulls were invested
with wings, representing the sun's rays, and given all
manner of ideal shapes, and finally human figures with
wings.   But we are dealing now with the correspondence,
as regards numbers, between the *dramatis personæ* of St.
John's vision, the Hebrew temple, the Druidic temple of
Avebury, and the Round Table of Arthur.   The twenty-
four elders and the four beasts *make twenty-eight.*   *   *
"And lo, in the midst of the throne and of the four
beasts" each evidently pointing to one of the cardinal
points, "and in the midst of the elders" circle of elders
around the throne, "stood a Lamb   *   *   having seven
horns   *   *   and seven eyes.   *   *   And he "the
Lamb, "came and took the book out of the right hand of
Him that sat on the throne."   The sun itself, personified

in the heavens, is the last-named, and the Lamb (sun
in Aries, March 21st) his (sun) representative priest in the
circular church on earth is meant. "And when he had taken
the book, the four beasts and four and twenty elders fell
down before the Lamb" the sun's representative. "having
each one of them a harp and a vial" censer "full of odours."
We have restored the wording into proper grammatical
form. "And before the throne was a sea of glass, clear as
crystal." "The brazen sea," states Newton, "between the
porch of the temple and the altar, filled with clear water, is
implied as the antitype." The sun at that season (spring)
was the earth's fertiliser, and it rose in the sign of the Ram,
who was, therefore, the importer of life to the earth's seeds
or ova. Arthur is Arddir, or earth's cultivator, husbandman,
or St. George, which also means husbandman. In Welsh,
the language of the Druids, the double "d" has the sound
of "th" as in "then," and in the time of the adoption by the
Welsh of the Roman alphabet, when confusion as regards
Druidic tenets had resulted from the massacre of the
Druids, in obedience to the edict of Claudius to extermi-
nate them, "Arddir" became in Welsh-Latin "Arthur."
And afterwards, also in English, "Arthur," during the
gradually attained domination in British literature of half
British and half Romish monks. In Welsh a garden is
named "gardd," and a gardener is called "garddir" ("ir"
instead of "wr," mistaken for the Latin "vir")—man or
"garddwr." But by placing "ei" (his) "garddir," it
becomes "Ei Arddir, or "his Arthur," giving to the "th"
the sound of "th" as in "then." The monk Nennius confounded Arthur with "Arth" (a bear), and the world has
been since misled in consequence. "Arth" (bear) is from
"garth," which means a wild or unenclosed locality, such
as a mountain, &c. The beast became, it seems to be,
known by the name of the locality where it was usually

found to roam, and to be identified with that name among the original inhabitants of Britain.

It will be observed Sir Isaac Newton accounts for the existence of *twenty-four* elders by the existence of twelve princes' priests on the south side, and twelve on the north side of the priests' court of the temple—twenty-four priests in all. The two sets of circles of twelve stones each—at which, no doubt, in the ceremony were twelve priests in white—were also on the south and north respectively, within the temple of Avebury, Wilts.

Sir Isaac Newton remarks that the standards of Judah, Reuben, Ephraim, and Dan, were a lion, bull, man, and eagle respectively; and those correspond with the appearance of the " four beasts," one in front, another behind, and one on each side of the throne of God in the Apocalypse of St. John. " And the four beasts had each of them six wings—twenty-four wings—answering to the twenty and four stations of the people " (priests). " And they were full of eyes within, or under their wings;" implying, it appears, according to Sir Isaac's opinion, the eyes of the throngs of worshippers. But why twenty-four elders around the throne? Twelve was the number of the tribes around the sanctuary in the wilderness. What foreign influence induced the Levitical priesthood, as the leaders of the national public worship at Jerusalem, to substitute *two twelves*, instead of one twelve, as representing the twelve tribes of Israel at the temple? The twenty-four elders of St. John, and the twenty-four priests of the temple at Jerusalem, correspond with the twenty-four, in two circles of twelve each, in the Druidic temple of Bryn Gwyddon, or the Hill of Odin, otherwise, Avebury, in England ; an arrangement introduced in consequence of the Druidical theological

dissension referred to ; but their number and arrangement
do not agree with anything in the history of the Hebrews.
But the *four* " beasts" do correspond with the Shechinah,
the two winged bulls, one on each side of it, and with the
high priest of Israel (the " Man "). It is well known the
Hebrew nation in the wilderness is grouped into for separate divisions. Each division is under the banner of one of
the leading tribes, namely, Judah, Reuben, Ephraim, and
Dan. Judah, due east; Reuben, due south; Ephraim, due
west; Dan, due north. Now, Ephraim and Manasseh were
the sons of Joseph, one of the twelve sons of Jacob. Why
was there no tribe called after the name of Joseph, like the
rest of the sons of Jacob? The reply is, here, in the tribes
Ephraim and Manasseh, are *two* tribes issuing from Joseph.
What was the object in dividing the tribe of Joseph into
two ? We answer, the western position legitimately
belonged to Levi, and the position occupied by Manasseh
to the tribe of Joseph. But Levi was withdrawn from the
Zodiacal position in the circle, to serve in the sanctuary ;
and it became necessary therefore, to divide the tribe of
Joseph into *two* to fill up the gap in the Zodiacal circle
caused by the withdrawal of Levi. Ephraim, in Aaron's
place, carried the *third* standard in the march, and the
third "beast" that St. John saw had the face of a man.
No doubt he symbolised Aaron, the high priest, or the
Levitical priesthood. When the sun, at the Passover, rose
in the first point of the sign Aries or Ram (due east), the
earth was directly opposite, in the sign Virgo in the west,
and the setting sun passed through it. But at the time of
the Day of Atonement (September) the sun rose in the sign
of the Virgin, in the east, and set in the west through the
sign of the Ram. The tabernacle symbolised the imaginary
space called Sheol or Hades, *beneath the earth*, and, on
the Day of Atonement, the high priest, dressed in his shroud

alone, passed into the west of the tabernacle, and, after
traversing dark Sheol or Hades, emerged through Virgo, in
the eastern end.   He descended in the west as a " Man,"
hence the " Man " on the standard of Ephraim in the west,
in the Levi's position; but when he re-appeared through
the eastern outlet he was more than a mere man—he was
an incarnate God![1]   The intercourse between Britain and
Palestine through Phœnicia continued during countless ages,
and even at the beginning of the Christian era was still
extensive, through the instrumentality of the merchants of
Phœnicia, and the influence the Hebrew and Welsh (or
Cymric) tongues attained upon each other in those days
is still observable in the said languages.   " In the British
(Welsh) tongue there are many, some say 300, Hebrew
or Semitic roots to be found."—Rowland's *Mona*, iii.,
p. 278, quoted by Higgins' *British Druids*, p. 91.
That intercourse between Britain and Palestine being
great—it is highly probable the powerful and intellectual Druids of this country, not only frequently
visited Phœnicia, but imparted to Palestine, including
Phœnicia, the tenets of their religious philosophy.   The
fact that Palestine, including Phœnicia, is still teeming
with Druidic remains—Bethel itself still having great
Cromleâchs, structures which the world has no other than
a Welsh name to describe—proves that Druidism was once
dominant in that country.   It seems, therefore, as certain
as anything can be, the *two* sets of Levitical Priests at the
temple of Jerusalem, of twelve each, instead of one of
twelve, to represent the twelve sons of Jacob, were due to
the influence of the example of the great Druidic temple of
Avebury, in Britannia.   Tyre, one of the great ports of
Phœnicia, is only about one hundred miles to the north
from Joppa, and about the same distance, as the crow flies,

---

[1] Man was substituted for Aries, or Ram-Lamb, in *Joshua* v., 13.

L

from Jerusalem. Sidon is almost twenty miles above
Tyre. Galilee borders on Phœnicia. It is most interesting in this connection to find that the French call Wales
Galles. The country of the Galatians, in Asia Minor, is
called Gallo-Græcia by Livy. It is said the Galatians
were Gauls. Be that as it may, both Gauls and Britons
were Druids, and worshipped the Most High by the name
Celi, and there can be no doubt Gallo, Galles, Gala, are
each derived from the Welsh-British name of the Supreme
Celi or Keli—Ei Geli. It is extremely probable that, at a
remote period, and under Phœnician influence, Britons
settled in Galilee, and that hence the name, " Galilee of the
Gentiles." Gallia, Gwalia, Wallia and Wales, are various
forms of the same name, beginning with Celi, mutated to
Geli, the Druidic Supreme name of the Creator.

Nennius, in his History of the Britons (Welsh), who
wrote, according to some, about A.D. 796, according to others,
about A.D. 994, is the first to mention the King Arthur of
romance. He states Arthur fought twelve battles. In the
twelfth, he is described performing prodigies of valour,
slaying 940 Saxons by his own hand on Mount Badon,
supposed to be near Bath. Geoffrey of Monmouth, writing
a little before A.D. 1147, states Arthur was mortally wounded
by his nephew Modred in a battle on the river Cambula,
supposed to be in Cornwall. Elsewhere it is stated
Arthur's mortal wound was received in his *head*. As we
have seen, in all the solar legends the sun is described
as a skull or head. He is a black skull or head on Decr.
20th, according to Druidism. We repeat, all the places of a
skull—the Golgothas and Calvaries of the East—refer to the
sun at the winter solstice as a black skull. This skull, or
head, is the Roman Jupiter Capitolinus, or, Jupiter of the
Head or Skull. In reference to the sun as rayless at the

winter solstice, the Phœnician women cut their hair off at the end of their sacred year (March 20th), and cast it into the river, a rite really belonging to the winter solstice, like the rites relating to Tammuz, although practised at another period of the year, referring to the sun's rayless, or hairless, condition at that season. And a Jewish woman, to this day, has to cut off the hair of her head as a rite associated with the birth of a babe to herself. It is alleged that the Hebrews worshipped the old sun as Saturn, and that hence their Sabbath, their day of "rest," is Saturday (Saturn's Day). It is remarkable that Tacitus, in his History of the Jews, written in the first century of the Christian era, makes the following observations on the history of the Jews (Book v., chap. 2): "The tradition is that the Jews ran away from the island of Crete, and settled themselves on the coast of Lybia, and this at the time when Saturn was driven out of the kingdom by the power of Jupiter." Here, Tacitus, like all other Pagans, mixes solar mythology with history. He did not know that Saturn was the old sun, and Jupiter the young sun of the new year, and that that is what is meant by "Jupiter driving Saturn out of the kingdom." In another paragraph in the same chapter, Tacitus states, "It is generally supposed that they (the Jews) rest on the seventh day (Saturday) because that day gave them the first rest from their labours. Others say that they do honour thereby to Saturn." In the light of what we have been stating, the importance of this statement, made eighteen centuries ago by the great Roman historian, cannot be over-estimated. The reader should carefully bear in mind there is no reference whatever here to the *planet* Saturn, except as the sphere of the sun at that season. The foolish practice of giving the names of pagan gods to the seven planets, has caused much misleading and immense confusion. Still, the name of each of the seven planets, like the name of each of the seven days of the week, describes one of the seven attributes of God passing through the sun in the seven planetary spheres, during the sun's annual progress. It will be noticed that Mercury (Woden or Odin) is the name of the middle day of the week; three on each side of him. He is the sun on March 21. He is the minister of the Gods, and his representative in the Zodiacal circular " church" on earth is Gwyddon (Odin), one of the titles of the Archdruid when performing his high office. We beg to remind the reader that the *head* of the Saviour was attacked in a special manner, with the crown of thorns. The wounded head of Arthur gave origin, as it seems, to the order of Templar Knights, their name being derived from the Latin name *Tempora*—Head.

The Templars were charged with having an *idol*, which the Chronicles of Saint Denys (which terminate 1461,) describe as " an old skin, embalmed and polished, in which the Templar places his very vile faith and trust, and in which he confidently believes; and it has in the sockets eyes of carbuncle shining with the brightness of the sky." Abraham Bzor, in his continuation of the " Church History " of Baronius, quotes a charge brought by the Italian bishops against the Templars, to this effect : " They have a certain *head*, the face pale like that of a man, with black curled hair, and round the neck a gilded ornament, which, indeed, belonged to no saint, and this they adore, making prayers before it." No doubt a symbol of Phallus or of Yoni. And one of the questions asked by the Pope of the witnesses was " Whether they had not a skull, or some sort of image, to which they rendered Divine homage ? "

So also the Chronicle of Meaux states that " on the first day of the General Council of Templars, a *head* with a white beard," (old Saturn or Arthur) " which had belonged to a former Grand Order, was set at midnight before the altar in a chapel, covered with silken robes and precious stuffs.   Mass was sung before *daylight*, and the *head* was then adored by the Master and the other Knights."—Rev. Baring Gould. M.A.'s *Curious Myths*, p. 625.

In the foregoing reference to the Ram or Lamb, with seven horns, in Druidism the Ram would be the sun in Aries of the zodiac with the seven planets on his head (Revelation v., 6), that is the sun in the course of the year passing through the seven planetary spheres.   In Druidism, in relation to the seven planetary spheres, he is Saithynun, otherwise Seithynun, *not* " Seithyn " (Seven in One), and Saithwedd (Seven-featured or faced).

Now, Nennius's " History of the Britons," p. 408 of Bohn's six *Old English Chronicles*, gives King Arthur's twelve battles against the Saxons.   There are several indications in the words used by Nennius that, in writing his history, he was quoting from either a Welsh chronicle or chronicles, or relating traditions still extant in his time among Welsh-speaking people.   The localities of the twelve battles are said to be:—The first, Mouth of the River Gleni ; the second, third, fourth, and fifth, on a river called by the Britons Duglas, in the region Llinius ; the sixth, on the river Bassas ; the seventh, in the wood Celidon, which the Britons call Cat Coit Celidon ; the eighth, near Gurnion Castle, where Arthur bore the image of the Holy Virgin, Mother of God, upon his *shoulders*, and, through the power of Our Lord Jesus Christ and the Holy Mary (he) put the Saxons to flight, and pursued them all day with great slaughter ; the ninth, at the City of the Legion, which is called Cair Lion ; the tenth, on the banks of the River Trat Treuroit ;

the eleventh, on the mountain Breguoin, which is called
Cat Bregion; the twelfth was a most severe contest,
when Arthur penetrated to the Hill of Badon." Cât is
the Welsh Câd (Battle).

The fact that Nennius employs Welsh names of localities
favours the idea that certain actual battles were fought
between the Welsh Britons and the Saxons in localities
bearing such names. But when we find the number given
as *exactly twelve*—no more nor less—we instantly suspect
that Nennius has been adapting facts to fit in with the
legendary history of the mythical, or solar, Arthur,
or, in other words, with the journey of the sun—as then
understood—through the twelve signs of the Zodiac, and
that the twelve battles of Arthur are identical with the
Twelve Labours of Hercules, or the sun. There are two
statements in the narrative of Nennius which prove conclusively either his ignorance or his fraudulent intention to
impose upon his readers. In the reference to the *eighth*
battle, he states Arthur carried " on his shoulders " the
image of the Holy Virgin. Let the reader count the
signs of the Zodiac to the right, instead of to the left and
the correct way, and he will find that the *eighth* sign is
Virgo, or the Virgin! On turning to p. 234, we find
Geoffrey of Monmouth stating the name of Arthur's shield
was " Priwen." That is obviously a mis-spelling of
" Brydwen," the correct Welsh name, and the original
form of the name Britannia, while the sun in his relation
to the Isle of Brydwen, or Britannia, is named Prydain
(masculine). Why did Nennius omit the *name* of the
shield, which the less cautious Geoffrey of Monmouth
furnishes? But both claim the association of the shield
with Christianity; Nennius that Arthur carried on his
" shoulders " the image of the Holy Virgin, and Geoffrey

states the *shield* was called " Priwen " (Brydwen), upon which was the image of the Blessed Mary, Mother of God. That is the way it is given in the original Latin. The following remarks by the Rev. Thomas Price, in his *History of Wales*, printed in the Welsh language, is most important. Referring to Nennius's statement, that Arthur carried the image on his "*shoulders*," Mr. Price has the following weighty observations: " The expression '*super humeros suos*' (upon his shoulders) in the above Latin sentence, inclines me to think that the author" (Nennius) " translated from the Welsh, and mistook the meaning of the original. The Welsh word Ysgwyd (a shield,) and Ysgwydd (a shoulder), are so similar" (differing only in one *d*), " especially in old writings, as easily to occasion mistakes, and to cause the words to be translated ' on his *shoulder*' instead of ' on his *shield*.' " The shields of the Britons were round shaped, like the shape of each of their temples. We have seen that each circular temple symbol- ised Britain, and that Britain symbolised the round earth above the rational horizon. The shield on the arm of each Briton then was called Britannia, because it symbolised the Fatherland, the Sacred Garden of God. Therefore, it is highly probable the shield carried by the his- torical Arthur in all his battles--apart from the legendary Arthur, or the sun personified—was called Brydwen, or Britannia. Brydwen signifies " Holy Fair- Featured One." " Britain" is a corruption of the Latin Britannia, and that of the Welsh Brydwen. Nennius, how- ever, either fraudulently or ignorantly, sought to adapt the exploits of the historical Arthur and the legendary Arthur with each other, and, in localising Brydwen or Britannia, counted the signs of the zodiac the wrong way, and instead of making Brydwen, or Virgo, to be the sixth, he made her the eighth, sign. The fact that he omits the name Brydwen

altogether, and substitutes for the name that of the Holy
Virgin (Mary), proves to our mind that he was guilty of a
wilful fraud.   Geoffrey, on the other hand, blurts out the
name Prydwen, or, as he writes it, " Priwen," and implies
that Britannia and the Virgin Mary are the same individual
character.   It seems as if Geoffrey drew from the same
source as Nennius did.

Now comes a most wonderful confirmation of what we
have been stating. The Coptic Y H E, or otherwise, Y H S,
and changed by the Church to I H S, and said to signify
Iesus Hominum Salvator (Jesus the Saviour of Men), is an
old monogram signifying, enigmatically, the Sun or Bacchus.
Martianus Capella, in his hymn to the sun, addresses him
in these words :—" Latium calls thee Sol, because thou
alone art in honour, *after the Father*, the centre of light ;
and they affirm that thy Sacred Head bears a golden
brightness in twelve rays, because thou formest that number
of months and the number of hours.   They say thou
guidest four winged steeds " (the four seasons), " because
thou alone rulest the chariot of the elements.   For dispelling the darkness, thou rulest the heavens.   Hence
they esteem thee, Phœbus " (Gr. Phoibos—the Bright or
Shining One), " the discoverer of secrets of the future ; or
because thou preventest nocturnal crimes.   Egypt worships
thee as Isean Serapis, and Memphis as Osiris.   Thou art
worshipped by different rites, as Mithras, Dis, and the
cruel Typhon.   Thou art the beautiful Atis, of the fostering son of the bent plough.   Thou art Ammon of arid
Lybia, and the Adonis of Byblos (Phœnicia).   Thus,
under a variety of appellations, the whole world worships
thee.   Hail, thou true image of the Gods, *and of thy
Father's face*.   Thou whose sacred name, surname, and
Omen, Three Letters, make with the number 608—Y H E.

Grant us, O Father, to reach the ethereal intercourse of Mind, and to know the starry heaven under this Sacred Name. May the great and universally adorable Father increase these his favours "—Martianus Capella de Nuptiis, *Philologiæ*. lib. ii., p. 32.—Higgins's translation in his *Anacalypsis*, and in his *Celtic Druids*. Vide p. 128 of that work ; also Dr. Inman's *Ancient Faiths*, vol. i., p. 647. In reference to the name of God being symbolised by the Druids by Three Letters (\l/) I find the following :— " D I W are the Three Letters, and in very old books I O U because U was used instead of W in the olden times. It is the secret WORD of the Primitive Bards, which it is not lawful to speak or utter audibly to any man in the world, except to a Bard who is under the vow of an oath. The letters may be shown to any man in the world we like, without uttering the vocalization, which, under the protection of secrecy, is due to them, though he be not under an oath ; but should he utter them in speech audibly, he violates his protection, and he cannot be a Bard, nor will it be lawful to show him any more of the secret, either in this world that perishes, or in the other world that will not perish for ever and ever."—John Bradford, Bettws, Bridgend (A disciple of the chair of Glamorgan as a boy in 1730 ; Archdruid in A.D. 1760 ; died in A.D. 1780. Vide *Bardism*, p. 66-7). It is clear that "O" in the copy should be " D," and we have, therefore, adopted it.

But it is quite clear the primitive symbol of the Name or Word of God coming through the sun is as follows : \l/ but shown thus : /l\, for that is the form as Adlais (Atlas) or Echo of the Word in supporting each cromlech, or symbol of the earth, then supposed to be flat-bottomed, on the northern side of the rational horizon. The three strokes are attempts to render, illustratively, the vocal rever-

berations of the Voice of the Creator, the expression of
His Word.   Doubtless, the illustration was given as early
as the invention of the Bardic Alphabet, hence the saying
of the Druids and Hebrews that their alphabets are derived
from the beams of the sun.   The sun itself was deemed the
result of the musical vocal utterance of the Creator or the
Father.   It is said the sign /|\ is the key to the alphabet of
the Ancient Druids.

Having explained elsewhere what is to be understood by
the Wounded Head of Arthur, we proceed with the
narrative of his disappearance.   It is identical with the
disappearance of Adonis, of Phœnicia ; the Tammuz of the
eighth chapter and fourteenth verse of Ezekiel—the
Hebrews observing it at the time the sun is in the Tropic
of Cancer, and the Druids when he is in the Tropic of
Capricornus ;   and Osiris, of Egypt, murdered by his
brother Typhon ; of Aaron's official death on the Day of
Atonement (end of the Jewish Civil Year) ; in fact, with
each of the " dying " gods of the ancient world.

In the following particulars, anent the departure of King
Arthur, we find Druidic allegory and Christian ideas jumbled
together and presenting, to the uninitiated, the appearance
of a tangled mass.   But the initiated Druid can very easily
distinguish between the two elements in the story.   He can
easily detect the *pious frauds* of monkish polluters of
the clear stream of Druidism.   The perpetrators of *pious
frauds* made the world believe the Cauldron of Ceridwen
was identical with the dish used by the Lord Jesus and His
disciples at their last supper together ; they fraudulently
implied that King Arthur was a Christian Knight ; and they
actually sought to make the world believe that Britannia,
otherwise Virgo of the Zodiac, the personified Earth in
March, when the earth is in the sign Virgo in the west,

opposite the sun (sign of the Lamb,) in the east, is identical with the Virgin Mary! and they blasphemously describe her as the Mother of God ! She is the mother of the priesthood of Gwyddon (Odin or Woden), otherwise the Archdruid, as the chief Bardic priest, symbolising by his official character the union of Soul or Mind (Minos, Menu, or Menydd—Brains,) with Matter in all animated beings, for they believed the lives of all created beings—men, animals, birds, reptiles, flies, &c.,—were Souls in various conditions.

CHAPTER XV.

NOW we return to the narrative : "But," states Arthur, "I may not stand, my head works (throbs) so. Ah, Sir Launcelot, this day have I sore missed thee. Alas, that ever I was against thee, for now have I my death, whereof Sir Gawaine me warned in my dream."

Then Sir Lucan took up the king the one part, and Sir Bedivere the other part, and in lifting, the king swooned, and Sir Lucan fell in a swoon with the lift (the weight of) that part of his bowels fell out of his body, and therewith the noble knight's heart brast (burst).

And when King Arthur came to himself again, he beheld Sir Lucan how he lay foaming at the mouth, and part of his bowels lay at his feet.

"Alas," said the king, "this is unto me a full heavy sight, to see this noble duke so die for my sake, for he would have helpen me that had more need of help than I. Alas, he would not complain him, his heart was so set to help me. Now Jesu have mercy on his soul."

Then Sir Bedivere wept for the death of his brother.

"Leave this mourning and weeping," said the king, "for this will not avail me : for, wit thou well, and I might live myself, the death of Sir Lucan would grieve me evermore ; but my time hieth fast."

"Therefore," said Arthur, "take thou Excalibur, my good sword, and go with it to yonder water side, and when thou comest there, I charge thee, throw my sword into that water and come again. and tell me what thou there seest."

"My lord," said Bedivere, " your commandment shall be done."

In the foregoing it is quite evident the compiler has been using materials which he found in the Welsh language for his novel. The proper names he employs are Welsh. In the name Lucan we find the Welsh name Lleuver (Light) Latinised. It will be observed, when Arthur, the personified sun, swoons, Lucan, or Light, perishes.

Sir Gawaine is Gwyion, or the warmed humidity personified. When Arthur's power — sun's power —is diminishing, prefigured by the rebellion of Mordred, Arthur swoons; Gawaine, or Gwyion, dies; that is, the sun no longer operates on the seeds of the earth through the agency of the warmed dew which ceases to exist in the atmosphere. The name *Bedivere* is pure Welsh, but retaining the archaic form of spelling. In the modern mode of spelling its form is, Bädeivèr. It signifies the Boat (dew), His Mer or Water; to distinguish it from the coracle, which is another symbol of the ark or mastless ship (Llong Voel) as symbol of Cêd, Cetus, or Der Ketos, the consort of the Almighty. The moon, six days old, being crescent-shaped, was, it will be remembered, a symbol of the sacred bâd or boat of the sun, and it will be observed that "Bedivere" is said in the narrative to be the brother of Sir Lucan (Lleuver); *Latin*, Lucis, or of Light—Heat, brother of Light. Vèr, mutated from Mèr, is a very old Welsh name of water, and is only found now in use in the composition of compound words, such as Cymmer (meeting of waters); diveru (unwatering), and used in the sense of to drop or to drizzle. The *di*, at the beginning of the word, is a negative prefix. The word is usually spelt, erroneously, *dyferu* ; the " *dy* " being used as an intensitive, but misapplied here.

To resume the Arthurian narrative : " So Sir Bedivere departed, and by the way he beheld that noble sword, that the pommel and haft were all of precious stones, and then he said to himself, ' If I throw this rich sword into the water, thereof shall never come good, but harm and loss.' And then Sir Bedivere hid Excalibur under a tree. And as soon as he might, he came again unto the king, and said, he had been at the water, and had thrown the sword into the water. 'What sawest thou there ?' said the king. 'Sir,' he said, ' I saw nothing but waves and wind.' ' That is untruly said of thee,' said the king " (he lied by saying he had seen the wind), " 'therefore, go thou lightly" (swiftly) " again, and do my command as thou art to me lief and dear, spare not, but throw it in.' Then Sir Bedivere returned again, and took the sword in his hand : and then him thought sin and shame to throw away that noble sword, and so eft he hid the sword, and returned again, and told to the king that he had been at the water, and done his command. ' What saw thou there ?' said the king. ' Sir,' he said, ' I saw nothing but the waters wap and the waves wan.' 'Ah, traitor, untrue,' said King Arthur, ' now hast thou betrayed me twice. Who would have wend that thou that hast been to me so lief and dear, and thou art named a noble knight, and would betray me for the riches of the sword. But now, go again lightly (swiftly), for thy long tarrying putteth me in great jeopardy of my life, for I have taken cold. And, but if thou do (not) now, as I bid thee, if ever I may see thee, I shall slay thee with my own hands, for thou wouldest for my rich sword see me dead.

Then Sir Bedivere departed, and went to the sword, and lightly (swiftly) took it up, and went to the water side, and there he bound the girdle about the hilts, and then he threw the sword as far into the water as he might, and *there came an arm and an hand* above the *water*, and *met it*, and *caught it*, and so shook it THRICE—Triune Divinity (\I/)—and brandished it, and then vanished away the hand with the sword in the water."

Now, the only portions of the above narrative which appertain to the solar allegory of the Druidic Arthur, are the boat, the sword Excalibur, the lake, the arm, the shakes, and the hand. The "sword" is the decrepit *membrum virilis* of Arthur's old age ; the lake is the sea of Annwn (Hades) ; the arm and hand are those of Cêd, the consort of the Almighty and mother of the sun, rescuing the symbol of the sun's divine seminal agency from destruction in the wreck of his corporeal destruction at sunset on each December 20th. In Egypt she is Isis I. It is Isis II. (Venus) who cries after Osiris's Phallus, which Typhon had thrown into the sea. It is the same idea as Cetus or Der Ketos receiving the white dove, as Adonis (the masculine living principle in the sun), for safety unto herself in the Red Sea, and sometimes in the Indian Ocean in the solar allegory of Phœnicia, Syria or Egypt ; and the wren of the Druids received into the ark. Let us now examine the name of Arthur's "sword." It is *Excalibur*. It is amusing to witness the ingenuity which the compiler of the *Mort d'Arthur* exercised with a view to throw a thin veil over the significance of "Excalibur." We detect the meaning of the word, or name, in its middle. *Cali* or *Cala* is the Druidic name of the *membrum virilis*. The *Bur* termination is the Gaelic *Borr*, which is a verb signifying to swell. Then *Ex*, at the beginning of the name, is a Latin prefix, denoting "formerly." *Ex-Cali-Bur*, therefore, signifies, Phallus-that-Swelled-Formerly.

If the reader will refer to the Rev. J. Lempriere, D.D.'s *Classical Dictionary*, he will find the following under the name "Osiris," one of the Egyptian titles of the sun. The first portion of the account refers to the priest of Osiris, the sun's representative in the Egyptian religious system, and bearing his name in consequence of his representative character. After describing the murder of Osiris by Typhon, his brother, and that Typhon had divided the body of Osiris amongst his murderous companions, Isis II., the wife of Osiris, "recovered the mangled pieces of her husband's body, *the genitals excepted*, which the murderer (Typhon) *had thrown into the sea;* and to render him all the honour which his humanity deserved, she made as many statues of wax as there were mangled pieces of his body." * * "That part of the body of Osiris which had not been recovered (the *membrum virilis*) was treated with more particular attention by Isis, and she ordered that it should receive honours more solemn, and at the same time more mysterious, than the other members." Let the reader refer also in the same dictionary to the article headed "Phallica." After describing the ceremonies relating to the lost Phallus of Osiris, the learned rev. gentleman states :—"The public held it (Phallus) in the greatest veneration * * and the mention of it among the ancients never conveyed any impure thought or lascivious reflection." In the above, Isis, a goddess of Egypt, appears as the wife of Osiris, and she is said to have been pregnant by Osiris before she left her mother's womb. Who, then, was her mother? *This* Isis is Venus, the Morwyn or Gwen y Môr (the sacred one of the sea), of Druidism, or the fecundity of the earth in spring. *This* Isis is cow-horned Athor of Egypt. The greater Isis is "the mother of the child" Horus, who is Osiris as a young man, the sun in spring, the second person of the Egyptian

Trinity, but really the first, counting from the equinoctial line northwards, and corresponds with the Druidic Alawn and Plennydd. The greater Isis, mother of Venus (the second Isis,) is identical with Cêd or Ceridwen (Cetus, Ketos, &c.), the Consort of the Almighty Celi of Druidism, and she has taken into her care the virile attribute of the personified sun in the sea, which her daughter, the second Isis, Gwen, Enid, or Mor'wyn (Virgin), could not discover, and the sun of the New Year reappears, endowed by the great mother of the sun child with all the requisite attributes necessary, on attaining the age of puberty in spring, to propagate the seeds of the surface of the earth (Venus) that year, to ripen in her into maturity in September.

In like manner, Arthur and his " sword Excalibur " are restored, " renewed " to maturity, to the world every spring.

Again we return to the Arthurian story :—" So Sir Bedivere came again to the King, and told him what he saw. 'Alas!' said the King, ' help me hence, for I dread me I have tarried over long.' Then Sir Bedivere took the King upon his back, and so went with him to the water-side. And when they were at the water-side, even fast by the bank, hoved a little barge" (the same thing as the coracle in which Taliesin was found, only here it is the departure of the coracle for the south-west, and the old sun in it is implied), " with many fair ladies in it, and among them all was a Queen" (their mother Cêd was the coracle or barge itself). " And all they had black hoods" (night time). " And all they wept and shrieked when they saw King Arthur. 'Now put me into the barge,' said the King, and so they did softly. And there received him Three Queens, with great mourning, and so they set him down ; and in one of their laps King Arthur laid his head.

M

And then that Queen (the Virgin Venus) said, ' Ah, dear
brother,' " (she was his sister-spouse) " ' why have ye tarried
so long from me? Alas! this wound in thy head hath
caught over much cold.' " (The Annwn or Hades [Hell] of
northern ideas is cold.) " And so they rowed from the land,
and Sir Bedivere beheld all those ladies go from him."
He had lost his Phallus " sword," and consequently had
now become uninteresting to them all, except to his mother
(the coracle), Céd, Ceridwen, otherwise Isis the First.
" Then Sir Bedivere cried, ' Ah, my Lord Arthur, what
shall become of me now ye go from me, and leave me here
alone among mine enemies?' ' Comfort yourself,' said the
King, ' and do as well as thou mayest, for in me is no trust
(strength) to trust in ! For I will go into the Vale of
Avalon, to heal me of my grievous wound. And if thou
hear no more of me, pray for my soul.' But ever the
queens and the ladies wept and shrieked, that it was a pity
to hear. * * And as soon as Sir Bedivere had lost
sight of the barge he wept and wailed, and so took to the
forest." Then we are told the first Queen was Morwyn le
Fay, the second was the Queen of North Wales, and the
third was the Queen of Waste Lands. Also there was
Nimue, the Chief Lady of the Lake. The monk has
been at it concealing again. Nimue is evidently the Latin
Nimius, which name, associated with the Lady of the Lake.
signifies " Exceedingly Great Lady." She is the Céd of
Druidism, the mother of Arthur, and the greater Isis of
Egypt, mother of Osiris. It was her hand that received
the sword Excalibur under water, and she is the restorer of
Arthur as Hu Gadarn, otherwise Taliesin, Hesus the Mighty,
as a babe on each December 22nd, or, according to the
Julian Calendar, on December 25th. The Druidic names
of the three queens are Morwyn, Blodwen, and Tynghedwen-
Dyrraith, as already explained in Chapter II.

Where did Arthur go to alone in the barge, or, more correctly, in the Llong Voel (symbolised as a goddess, and also as a coracle), or naked ship or boat? The Rev. Thomas Price, in his *History of Wales*, quotes among the " sepulture stanzas " the following :—

> Bedd i March, bedd i Gwythur :
> Bedd i Gwgawn Gleddfrydd :
> Anoeth bydd bedd i Arthur.
>
> A grave for March, grave for Gwythur :
> A grave for Gwgawn Gleddfrydd (Free Sword) :
> It would be folly to provide a grave for Arthur.

We believe the word anoeth (uncertain) ought to be *annoeth* (unwise or folly). For the Welsh and Breton nations fully believed Arthur had not died, but had simply gone to fairyland, to be there renovated. Therefore, providing a grave for Arthur would be unwise or unnecessary. It was to endeavour to remove from the minds of the Welsh Britons that Arthur was alive, and would again return to lead them to battle against their foes, that Henry II., King of England, induced the monks of Glastonbury to assist him, by perpetrating another *pious fraud* by pretending to discover the grave of Arthur there for that purpose.

But what is meant by Avalon, to which it is stated Arthur said, to Bedivere, he was going in the barge? As we have already pointed out, the Druids symbolised the sun's influence in spring, summer, and winter, by three apples, and the juice of the apple was used as a symbol of the sun's divine essence, as the juice of the grape was used as a similar symbol in grape-growing countries, and it became natural, therefore, to regard the region where life is renewed after death, as the everlasting *source* of the divine essence, as an Island of Apples. Avalon, or Havalon, signifies perennial apple : or the perennial divine juice, the elixir of life. It

would be highly important, as well as interesting, to ascertain
clearly when Avalon came first to be identified with Glastonbury. The reader should recollect that the work bearing
the name of " Richard of Cirencester," a work which
poisoned the history of Britain during a century, is proved
to be a forgery, and that any reference to Avalon in it is
fictitious, except the quotations in it from other works of
undoubted authenticity. There is, we believe, no doubt,
Glastonbury came first to be associated with Aval-on—the
Insula Pomorum or Britain, as the Island of apples—at the
period when English, or rather Norman, Kings sought by
fraud to persuade the Welsh Britons to believe the body
of Arthur had been discovered at Glastonbury. The *Vita
Merlini* of Geoffrey in no way connects it with Glastonbury.
Geoffrey, its author, wrote about A.D. 1140. As already
hinted, it appears to have escaped notice that Avalon is
in the singular number, while the *Insula Pomorum* of the
monks is in the plural number. One signifies ever-durable
apple, and the other the Island of apples. The Druids, 'tis
true, had *three* sacred apples in their circular church, otherwise garden—the garden of the Hesperides from which
Hercules stole *three* apples—but the termination " on " in
Welsh primitive nouns, except personal ones, as dyni*on*
(men), Iuddew*on* (Jews), &c., is never a sign plural, but of
perenniality, as in ffyn*on* (water, spring); cal*on* (heart,
always beating) ; ffo*n* (a walking stick, because it is in
shape like the old Druidic " f," and always moving with
the walker). The three apples symbolised the sun as seen
in three stages from the earth. But as transmitter of
heaven's essence he was *one*. In the name Arthur—the
sun as Arddir, or gardener, or husbandman, it is only the
sun's *one* attribute, as a fertiliser of the seeds of the
earth, that is implied as the source of the fertilising
juice from heaven operating on the seeds of the earth in

spring, &c. The essence has it source in the Paradise (Gwenydva) of the Druids, where decay and death are unknown, and is discharged by the agency of the sun to the seeds of the earth. The sun, or Arthur, returning on the solar new year's morning, with youth renewed, is still symbolised in Wales on the morning of the new year, by the symbol of an apple, dressed with evergreens, and carried from door to door, and the carrier, and the group of children with him, singing a joyous old melody. In ancient times, the custom, no doubt, was regarded as a pious one. It implied the return of the sun from Gwenydva (Elysium) of the Druids, renewed, and charged with a fresh supply of the invigorating essence of life, derived from where the essence of the material creation began, like yeast fermenting, to renovate the face of the earth. The district of Hades beneath the earth, and beyond the " river," was the fairyland of our ancestors—the source of the passive principle of life. Neither the old sun nor the new sun had anything to do with the perfected souls already gone into Gwynva, or Heaven, in the northern sky we repeat.

In plate 25th, figure 14, of Calmet's *Biblical Dictionary*, the ideas implied by the apple or juice, are symbolised by a skin-bottle containing wine on the left shoulder of the infant Bacchus, who is accompanied by the greater Isis I., or Cêd, his mother, who carries the seed grains in the horn of plenty, which she carries on her left arm. He descended to Hades as Old Silenus, otherwise Saturn, or Old Arthur, Old Taliesin, Old Adonis, Old Tammuz, &c. ; he now returns after being restored to youth or infancy, with his mother, to renovate the face of the earth, otherwise Venus, the Morwyn of the Druids, by the agency of the essence riches he brings with him from the place where he was renovated himself.

There can be no doubt whatever the numerous localities in Wales, England, Scotland, Ireland, and the smaller islands, bearing the name of Arthur, originated in those localities when, in Druidic times, they held temples of the sun as the great agent and exponent of the Eternal Celi, the Most High God. Among the principal localities bearing Arthur's name are the following: Arthur's Round Table, at Caerlleon, on Usk; Arthington, Yorkshire; Arthur's Seat, Edinburgh; Great and Little Arthur, on the islets of Scilly Islands; Arthuret, Cumberland; Arthur's Chair, Breconshire; Arthur's Palace and Arthur's Well, South Cadbury, Somerset; Arthur's Round Table, South of Penrith, Westmoreland; Arthur's Round Table, Llansannan, Denbighshire; Arthur's Stone (a Cromleâch), on the northern slope of Cefn y Bryn, west of Swansea; Arthur's Stone (a Cromleâch), Moccas, Hereford; Arthur's Quoit, Newport, Pembrokeshire; Arthur's Table, on Berwyn Mountain; the Stone of the Hoof of Arthur's Horse, near Mold, &c. It should be mentioned also the constellation, the Great Bear, is called, by the Welsh, Arthur's Plough. The circle around the Polar Star is called Arthur's Table, and Lyra is called Arthur's Harp.

The reader is reminded the whole of the Island of Britain is the symbolical Island of Apples or *Insula Pomorum*; in the first place because three apples in it, among the Druids, symbolised the Sun at three annual stages, viz., the Vernal Equinox (Alban Eilir), the Summer Solstice (Alban Havin), and the Winter Solstice (Alban Arthan, that is, Arthur's prominent stations or precincts). In the second place, it was the earthly emblem of the Isle of the Blessed, the Druidic Paradise, which name is Persian for a circular garden. Like the land of Canaan to the Hebrews, Britain, and especially Wales, in the eyes of the Druids, was the land of rest to the people of God. Like the

Greek Delos, which, by a poetic fiction, was said to float on the surface of the ocean—Delos was sacred to Apollo—the Island of Britain was called by the Druids, Yr Ynys Wen, or the Holy Island. Literally, Yr Ynys Wen, we repeat, signifies White Island, but "White" is the vernacular word for "Holy."

It was the opinion of the Ancient Greeks, in conformity with the notions of the Hindoos, that Jupiter came from the Islands of the Blessed, which, according to Homer, were near the White or Holy Stones (Leuco Petrae), at the western extremity of the (old) world.[1]

Crishna, who is the Cretan Jupiter, was not, properly speaking, a native of India, but of the White Island, or Creta[2]—the *Ultima Greta* alluded to by the Roman writers. *Sweta Dwipa* the (White Island) in the west of the world, is the Holy Land of the Brahmins.

The *Asiatic Researches* state the Hindoos believe to this day the gods and goddesses dwell in the White Island, in the west of the world, in human shape. It is highly probable, were we to get at the inner life of the teeming millions of Hindostan, we would discover that these legends of the Vedas, the Indian Bible, about Britain as the White Island in the west of Europe, greatly assist to govern India from Britain, and that thus the British Druids rule India from their urns!

Because the sun rises in the Zodiacal sign of the he-goat (Capri), on the morning of the solar new year's day (December 22nd in Druidism, on Christmas day, 25th, according to the Julian Calendar), he is regarded by Greeks, Romans, &c., as a Kid, and the sun's mother, Ced of the Druids, as Minerva (Divine Wisdom) she-goat breasted. His father is Pan (half old man and half he-goat) meaning the old sun of the preceding old year.

---

[1] *Asiatic Researches*, v. xi. p. 36.   [2] *Ibid.* p. 84.

Spenser, in his *Faerie Queen* (Book vii., Canto 7th), refers to the sun in December as—

> " Upon a shaggy-bearded goat, he rode,
> The same wherewith Dan Jove, *in tender years*,
> They say, was nourished by the Idæan Maid."

Æsculapius, the sun as a healer and as the source of intelligence, is symbolised by a serpent. He is also represented as having been found a babe by Aresthanus, and having his head surrounded with resplendent rays of light. He was nourished by a stray goat of the flock of Aresthanus, which gave him her milk ; and a dog, which kept the flock, stood by him to shelter him from injury. In the same way Myses or Moses, otherwise Bacchus, was attended by Caleb, which is Hebrew for dog. The reader will recollect the story of Moses among the flocks of Jethro, and also what we state elsewhere, as to the Severn being called Havryn or Gavren (Goat of the Birth), and that the direction of the birth place is where the sun rises over the Severn on December 22nd ; which would be between Gloucester and Worcester, and in England over Dunwich, in the county of Suffolk. The numerous Druidic remains in the shape of circles of stones, &c., near St. David's Head, south-west of Wales, were places of solemn assemblies of Druids. On each December 20th, watching what they thought as being the struggle, on that afternoon, between Avagddu (Typhon) and Arthur, in the air, the Sun as Arthur, gelded Saturn—having lost Excalibur—under also the names Saturnus, Osiris, Adonis, Taliesin, Arawn, Aaron, and called by as many names as there were nations who had adopted the solar rites of the Druids, sinking, physically defeated, into the South Western Ocean at four o'clock that awful afternoon (Dec. 20th); but the sun's divinity— symbolised, as already often stated, by a wren, &c.,—being caught in the ocean by his mother Cêd (Cetus or Der

Ketos), and restored *in* a new glorified sun, regarded a new creation as to his body, after the lapse of forty hours. It would appear, by the many circles of stones at St. David's, the Druids observed there the ceremony of escorting the sun to the utmost limit of Wales at the period of his setting on the afternoon of the last day of the solar year (Dec. 20th) into the Atlantic. No doubt they likewise performed the ceremony of celebrating meeting him at his rising, or new birth, at Dunwich, and between Gloucester and Worcester, on the morning of Dec. 22, and that they named him their Cyvrangon, or mediator between light and darkness, and between destruction and themselves. It is worthy of great attention, that Caerlleon-on-Usk in the South East, and St. David's in the South West, of Wales—the former, the direction of the rising, and the other the setting, of the sun at the winter solstice—are the two sites of the Archbishopric of Great Britain in the olden time. St. David's was called Menepia by the Romans, and Menevia by the later Ecclesiastics. The names are each derived from the Druidic Menw, Menu, Minos (Menydd—Brains), from which the name Man is derived. A church a mile from the sea, and five miles from St. David's, is called Llanrian— correctly Llan-yr-Huan—or the sanctuary of the sun, Huan being one of the Druidic titles of the sun, and signifying the abode of Divinity. "Near the church of Llan-yr-Huan," states the *Topographical Dictionary of Wales,* "are some Druidical remains, consisting of many large stones, most of which are now (1823) broken. They were formerly erect, and in their arrangement and general appearance, formed in miniature a tolerably correct representation of Stonehenge." All, except one, had disappeared in March, 1892.

Since writing the foregoing we have ascertained the neighbourhood of St. David's contains the following

Druidical traces :—The hamlets there are called Cylchau,
or circles. A place called Barrows (Beddrodau in Welsh) is
covered with tumuli, or beehive-shaped graves. the
southern base of a rocky height, on the promont, we see
enormous rocking-stone. "There are, also on birth of
montory, divers square and circular areas, encle er 22nd.
stones, and there is also a remarkable *cromlech*, ruidism,
stone of which is twelve feet long, eight broad, Adonis,
feet thick, and which is supported by *a single us). Isis
stone*." Unless two have fallen, the Druids here r man
to the original Avebury sect, whose symbol was the as
as already explained. If so, the table stone is the s ool of
the whole earth above the rational horizon, sustained by the
virile power of Celi. There is also an extensive enclosure,
about one hundred yards long, and sixty yards broad, "and
is intersected by a natural perpendicular trench of great
depth and width." It is situate on a place which faces the
sea, called Carn Ochain, or the Hill of Lamentation. The
reader will bear in mind the weeping for Tammuz at
Jerusalem. Likewise at Borth, Cardigan Bay, is Bryn
Wylva, or the Hill of Weeping, which is above the edge of
the sea. In both places the Druids would lament and weep
for Arthur, as Arawn, setting into the sea on the shortest
day ; in the first-named, on the afternoon of March 20th,
and in the last-named, at 4 o'clock p.m., on December
20th. About a mile from the mainland is Ramsey Island,
which is about one mile in length, and one in breadth.
"The whole of Ramsey Island is elevated, and at each end
rises a lofty hill, imparting to it a grand and romantic
appearance. * * On the summit of these hills, which
command prospects of great extent and magnificence,
there are divers remains of antiquity, including entrench-
ments, *carneddau* (stone tumuli), &c. At the eastern end
of Ramsey Island," and therefore between the island and

inal .
the n₅5th nd, " are two small rocky islands." One is called
Ynys-y th n (e sound to the u—the Matrix Island), and the
oth ruidism -y-Cantwr (the Island of the Singer). Those who
at the lly read the preceding pages will understand
Morwyn ame of the first-named island signifies. As for
we have of the Singer, it is, doubtless, the spot where
B.C. to of the great Druidic choirs, stationed on the
sun, on f the mainland and on the Island of Ramsey,
Elgàn), ed the singing of the funeral dirges of Arthur at
the f his setting, into the Atlantic beyond, at four
o'clo. the close of the Druidic solar year, Dec. 20th.
With so an.ing eyes and cries of woe, they beheld the sun
sinking into the ocean that afternoon, the time he had
reached his utmost southern declination. Bell's *Pantheon*,
describing the Adonia, the solemnities observed at the loss of
the sun—observed in the East, as at Borth, Aberdovey, at
the vernal equinox, instead of at the winter solstice, the old
Druidic time—states " The Adonia was observed with great
solemnity by most nations. Greeks, Phœnicians, Lycians,
Syrians, Egyptians, &c." From Syria they are supposed to
have passed into India. Let the reader recollect what the
Indians say of Britain—Yr Ynys Wen in the West, or the
Holy White Island. " The Adonia lasted two days." On
the first day " all the pomp and ceremonies practised at
funerals" were observed. " The women wept, rent their
hair, beat their breasts, imitating the cries of Venus for
the death of Adonis." The reader will remember the
wailing and shrieking of the women when Arthur came to
the barge, and that one of them—Morwyn, the Druidic
Venus, called also Enid—was particularly attentive to him,
and sympathetic, resting his wounded head in her lap.
The flutes used that day, Bell's *Pantheon* goes on to state,
which were called after the Phœnician name of Adonis,
emitted the most melancholy sounds. The following day

was spent in every expression of mirth and joy, because Adonis had returned to life again. The most astounding thing of all is that, according to some, the name of the mother of Adonis was Myrrha, or Mary! Here we see an error arising from the mistake of observing the birth of Adonis (Sun) on March 21st, instead of on December 22nd. On March 21st the earth is Morwyn (Virgin), in Druidism, and she is erroneously stated to be the mother of Adonis, being mistaken for Cêd—the Black Virgin (Cehs), Isis the First, &c., being all the same character under many names. Cêd is the mother of the Archdruid's official representative character, as representing the Divinity in the Sun—symbolised by Taliesin, as a babe in the skin coracle, arriving at Borth, Cardigan Bay, from Ireland; Osiris, as a murdered god thrown into the Nile, by Typhon his brother, in a " box " or boat, and returning again as a babe ; Moses, as a babe in an " Ark of Bulrushes," in the flags by the side of the Nile ; Bacchus, called also Myses or Moses, Son of Father Iu or Hu (the Almighty, under the name of Jupiter,) and Luna, as a babe in a boat-shaped box (emblem of Cêd, the Sun's Mother, as a crescent Luna) by water to Oreatae, Laconia ; Adonis, as a babe in a boat of bulrushes, wafted across the Mediterranean from Alexandria to Phœnicia, in Palestine. By each of the above " babes " the ancients, in their allegorical religious systems, implied the new-born Sun of the new year, whose " birth " was celebrated among Eastern nations on March 21st, and by the Druids of Britain at sunrise on each Dec. 22nd. We repeat, the " boat," or coracle, was one of the emblems of Cêd, the sun's Mother. He was represented returning into her as a murdered old man--Osiris, Arawn, Adonis, Tammuz, &c.,—and after forty hours restored to the world as a brilliant infant son. Venus, or Myrrah, is the wife of the

Seminal Logos or Word, who is married to her on March 21st-25th (Lady Day). The sun is now personified as Tegid, the Seminal Logos, as a young man in correct Druidism on March 21st, and the Earth is personified at the same time as Morewyn, of which the name Morwyn (Maid-Venus) is an abbreviated form. As we have stated elsewhere, during the epoch (from 4619 B.C. to 2505 B.C.), the Druids exhibited the incarnate sun, on March 21st, by the figure of a White Bull (Tarw Elgàn), and the fecundity of the Earth, at the same time, by the figure of a White Cow (Buwch Laethwen Levrith—Cream White Cow). But, afterwards, the symbols of the sun in the Sanctuary on Earth was changed by the Druids, and the human form was adopted instead of the White Bull, and that incarnate representative of the Sun, in the Sanctuary—the Gilgal of Britannia—was the white-robed Archdruid called Taliesin, Gwyddon or Odin, Arthur, &c. No doubt there would be also a corresponding adoption of the female figure instead of the White Cow, and she would be a priestess robed in white, and she would be the quint-essence of the circular "Church," or the whole Earth. In the Aries (Ram) epoch she would be the Bride of the Lamb or Jupiter Amon, who would be the sun in the constella-tion Aries, and, like the Archdruid, would be represented by his High-Priest in the Church. The Greeks humanised the Jupiter-Sun in the heavens, but left the horns on his head. There is something enigmatical in the expression of the Lord Jesus—"I am the Son of Man which is in Heaven." Does he allude to himself as the son of Jupiter? He himself was on earth at the time he was speaking. We are referring to religious rites observed countless ages before the Christian Era. Were they literal types of the great Christian mysteries? It is interesting to observe the two separate localities, one on

the western, and the other on the south-western coast of
Wales, where these solemnities were observed, viz., at
Borth, or Cors Vochno, on the eastern side of Cardigan
Bay, and the other at St. David's promontory, which
correspond with the sun setting on March 20th and
December 20th respectively.   It is clear that in the
locality between the Dovey and Aberystwyth was observed
the Phœnician or Eastern time, and the St. David's Head
party the time of the ancient Druidic school of Britain.

CHAPTER XVI.

THE HEBREW TABERNACLE.

NYONE who has endeavoured to understand the arrangements of the Jewish tabernacle in the wilderness, as described in Exodus, Leviticus, Josephus, &c., must have risen from the study of the subject perplexed. We have consulted many authorities on the subject, and among them Calmet and Dr. Kitto, and we find they all contradict one another in their attempted description of the said arrangements. The following is the plan of the whole tabernacle, as given in the Jewish books mentioned above. First of all, there was a great enclosure or yard. This enclosure was 100 cubits (about 60 yards) long, from east to west, and 50 cubits, or about 30 yards in breadth. The top end of the great enclosure faced the east, and there was the only opening into it from outside. The bottom end faced the west, and it had no opening. Thus the east and west indicated the rising and the setting of the sun on March 21st, the time of the Passover. The south side of this outer court of 100 cubits in length was fenced in by network of linen, 5 cubits in height, or 9 feet 9 inches. The side facing north was exactly the same. Twenty ornamented pillars, held up the network fence on each side. On the western end was a similar network fence, held up by ten ornamented pillars or props. On the eastern end was a similar network fence, but leaving a wide gap in the centre for the only entrance into the enclosure. On each side of this entrance space were three pillars holding up the network fence. This left for the entrance the space which the four absent

pillars added to the six, to correspond with the ten pillars
at the western end, would have occupied. The ten pillars
at the western end occupied a space of fifty cubits. The
ten pillars would afford nine separate spaces between the ten
pillars. Allowing a little less than five cubits between each
pair of pillars, we find that each space was about eight feet
and nine inches. The four absent pillars at the east end
would afford three of those spaces of eight feet and nine
inches each. This gives to the entrance a space of twenty-
six feet and three inches wide, taking the cubit to measure
twenty-one inches.

We now come to describe the entrance or " gate " as it
is called in the English translation. " And the gate of
the court shall be an hanging twenty cubits." That
means that its height should be twenty cubits, or eleven
yards and twenty-four inches, filling a space of twenty-six
feet and three inches wide. King Solomon, when he built
the temple, naturally made the porch on the eastern
entrance into the temple, of the same height as that of the
entrance into the tabernacle enclosure in the wilderness.
" And the porch before the temple of the house twenty
cubits was the length thereof, according to the breadth of
the house ; and ten cubits was the breadth thereof before
the house " (i. Kings, v. 3), making it of the same breadth
as the sanctuary or the tent in the wilderness. It is clear,
we think, that for " length " in the above, we are to understand height. The hangings filling the entrance into the
great or yard enclosure, were of blue, purple and scarlet,
and it appears that over the hangings was fine linen network
wrought with needles. The gorgeous hangings were held
up by four pillars, which towered on the east end fifteen
cubits above the top level of the network fence of the
enclosure.

We now proceed to describe the contents of the great yard enclosure, called "Court." In the middle of the enclosure stood a building constructed of upright boards and cross bars, all richly decorated with gold and various draperies and skins. This building had two entrances—one facing east and the other west. The entire building measured, from east to west, thirty cubits. The interior was divided into two rooms. The room with its entrance facing the east, was ten cubits long and ten cubits wide. The other room, with the entrance facing west, was twenty cubits long and ten cubits wide. At the junction between the two rooms, the western end of one being against the eastern end of the other, was a great veil, forming the division between the two rooms. The larger room, facing the west, was called the Holy Place; the room facing the east was called the Holy of Holies. The veil between the two rooms is described by Josephus as follows: "At a distance of ten cubits from the most *secret* end" eastern "Moses placed four pillars and the veil was held up by them. Now the room within those pillars was the Most Holy Place, or Holy of Holies, but the rest of the room, westward of the veil, was the tabernacle, or the Holy Place, which was open to the priests." No human being except the High Priest, and he only once a year, on the great Day of Atonement, which occurred annually near the Autumnal Equinox, entered the Holy of Holies, which he did from the western room and not *through* the eastern entrance. No one but Jehovah Himself, by his Shechinah, *entered* through the eastern entrance into the Holy of Holies, and for that reason that entrance is called by Josephus, "*the most secret end.*" The expression that the High Priest entered the Holy of Holies only "once a year" has puzzled many, inasmuch as it is stated elsewhere he entered it, as is supposed, many times on the Day of Atonement. We will explain the apparent contradiction presently. N

In addition to the aforesaid four pillars, which in addition to holding up the veil to prevent it from being bulged by the western wind into the Holy of Holies, were seven other pillars on the other, or western side of the veil, and ranged along at regular intervals; and the effect of the four pillars on one side, and seven on the other, prevented the wind from the two entrances swaying the veil to and fro.

Let us, with reverent minds, follow the Shechinah through the most secret entrance at the eastern end into the Holy of Holies. The room is little more than twenty-five feet square. It is windowless, and the curtains of the hair of goats at the eastern entrance, are so arranged that no light comes that way. But in front of us an extraordinary radiating light shines, revealing under it a small coffer, dazzling with gold, and on each side, and standing on the golden lid of the coffer, is a figure with wings, the two figures facing each other and gazing down at the golden lid of the coffer. Their wings are raised towards each other. They are standing on a gold lid lying on the face of the ark; it is 53 inches long and 33 inches broad. This is the Mercy-Seat, or, more correctly, Seat of Reconciliation, and the Shechinah is between the faces of the two winged figures.

Let us now retrace our footsteps, eastward, into the open air. From the outside of "the most secret" entrance we pass along, outside, one of the sides of the whole building, which is ten cubits in height, and the boards composing it are all uprights. Across them are five bars inserted through gold rings. The third bar from the bottom runs the entire length of the structure, thus affording strength to the side where strength is most needed. We ascertain the other side of the building is constructed exactly like this side, and all richly adorned with gold.

We now arrive at the western entrance, and we find that opposite to us, that is to say, between us and the entrance, is a wide boarding, consisting of six boards in the centre and one at each corner, or eight in all. They all fit into the sides of each other.

Bars and decorations are on both sides of this boarding, exactly like those on the sides of the building itself. On the other or inner side of this boarding is a passage, and on its opposite side rise five pillars or props, reaching to the roof of the building. These five props afford four separate openings, into the Holy Place, facing us.

Fastened to hooks on the outside of the tops of the five pillars, is a gorgeous curtain or veil. This veil, according to Josephus, does not always descend to the ground, but leaves a space between its lower end and the ground, and through the opening the priests creep in and out of the Holy Place. We follow the priests on hands and knees into the Holy Place. The curtain we have crept under is the *first* veil, referred to in Heb. ix., 3. The *second* veil is that opposite, inside, dividing this room from the Holy of Holies, beyond. It will be borne in mind, we entered this room with our backs due west, and the first place we visited we had our backs due east.

Directly before us, in front of the second veil facing us, we behold the seven pillars cased in gold, with the veil beyond them resting against them, and against four others stationed in the Holy of Holies. Then opposite the middle of the veil is a golden altar, ornamented with a golden crown, the altar being one yard and six inches in height and twenty-one inches wide. It is elaborately decorated with gold, hence its name. It bears also the name Altar of Incense, because perfume for the Divinity on the other side of the veil is burnt morning and evening upon it.

A Rabbi states the sweet aroma, doubtless symbolising prayer and praise, burnt here was sometimes smelt so far as Jericho. ascending from the temple on Mount Zion, and carried by the breeze. Therefore, Jerusalem itself must have been full of it during the morning and evening Sacrifices.

To resume our description. The sweet perfume from this altar fills the tents in the wilderness. On the southern side of the room, on our right hand, is a golden candlestick, with three branches on each side holding lamps, and one lamp on the top of the pillar of the candlestick or seven lamps in all—emblems of the seven planets.

On the northern side of the golden altar in the middle, and on our left hand, is the table of shew bread. This table is thirty-one inches and a half in height, or three spans; half a cubit is each span. Its length is forty-two inches, and its breadth twenty-one inches. The whole is richly adorned with gold. On this table are two rows of loaves, each row consisting of six loaves—emblems of the twelve signs of the Zodiac. There are also upon it various small vessels containing wine. Behind all, and filling the space, is the gorgeous veil, ten cubits in height and ten cubits in breadth, woven of a carpet-like texture, and, therefore, is very strong. This veil, as well as the first one which we crept under, is made of three colours, viz. :— Sky Blue, Purple, Scarlet, and the figures of Cherubim are woven into the fabric.

The following is what Josephus states as to its appearance :—" This veil was very ornamental, and embroidered with all sorts of flowers which the earth produces, and there were interwoven into it all sorts of variety that might be an ornament, excepting the forms of animals." Respecting the first veil the same author states as follows :—" It was like the other in its magnitude and texture, and colours. Over this " the first " was a veil of linen of the same largeness with the former, and it was to be drawn this way or that way by cords, the rings of which, fixed to the texture of the veil, and to the cords also, were subservient to the drawing and undrawing of the veil, and to the fastening it at the corner, that then it might be no hindrance to the view of the sanctuary " Holy Place meant " especially on solemn days." In Exodus the linen is described as " twined linen wrought with needlework." Therefore, the covering of the outer veil was a net-work. It is interesting to mention that the second veil, or the one behind the seven pillars, and east of us where we stand in the Holy Place, was the one which, the moment the Lord Jesus yielded up the spirit on the summit of Mount Calvary beyond the walls of Jerusalem, " rent in twain from the top to the bottom, and the earth did quake, and the rocks rent, and the graves opened—he was passing into Hades or Annwn, whose entrance was supposed in the east to be westward, where the sun sets at the time of the Passover—and many bodies of the saints which slept arose, and came out of their graves *after His resurrection*, and went into the Holy City, and appeared unto many." It is implied they, after awakening, stayed in their graves until after He Himself came to life again forty hours later.

Now, it will be borne in mind that the entire length of the building, containing the Holy Place and the Holy of Holies, was thirty cubits, or eighteen yards and twelve inches. It will have been noticed we have hitherto said nothing about a roof of the building. The material for the roof is made of " ten curtains of fine twined linen,"

coloured "blue, purple, and scarlet, and cherubims" no
doubt winged bulls "of cunning work." Each curtain is
twenty-eight cubits in length. The breadth of the roof is
ten cubits. These gorgeous curtains are placed across the
roof, affording a splendid-looking ceiling to both the Holy
Place and the Holy of Holies. The width they cover
being ten cubits, and their length being twenty-eight
cubits, there remain eighteen cubits, or nine cubits to hang
down on each side of the building. On each side, therefore, the two ends reach within a cubit, or twenty-one
inches, of the ground outside the sides of the structure.
The weight of the two ends of the curtain would stretch
the middle, which acted as a ceiling to the interior. Each
of the ten curtains is four cubits wide, affording altogether
a breadth of forty cubits for a space of thirty cubits.
Thus, it seems, the ten curtains, in some degree, lap over
one another.

We now come to another set of curtains to be placed
over the ten curtains lying as already described. These are
eleven in number. There is a sacred meaning attached to
the limitation to the number " eleven" here, as we shall
show presently. These eleven curtains are of the hair of
goats, long and silky. It is usual to shear goats in Asia
Minor, Syria, Cilicia, and Phrygia, according to the statement of Ainsworth. Each of these curtains is thirty
cubits in length, and when lying across the roof of the
building covers both sides of it to the ground. The
breadth of these eleven, collectively, is forty-four cubits,
being four cubits each in breadth. This leaves the breadth
of the curtains of goats' hair fourteen cubits, or eight
yards and six inches wider than the entire length of the
building. " Thou shalt couple five curtains by themselves,
and six curtains by themselves, and shalt double the sixth

curtain in the fore-front" the eastern front "of the tabernacle." It will be recollected the two ends of these curtains reach to the ground, one on each side of the building, and the result of doubling the sixth of the eleven curtains in the fore-front—that is to say, the eastern front, is to form a great hairy framework, with a rounded edge to it, around the sides of the entrance into the Holy of Holies from the east. This entrance is the symbol of the *membrum virginalis* of the Virgin goddess of Israel, and the ark inside is her matrix. "And it shall be at that day, saith the Lord, that thou shalt call me Husband (Ishi), and shalt call me no more My Baal (Baali)."—Hosea, ii., 16.

According to Exodus xxvi., 10, 11, 12, the eastern opening was hooked together inside at the junction of the two last curtains, and in verse 12 we are told, "And the remnant that remaineth of the curtains of the tent, the half curtain that remaineth shall hang over the back of the tabernacle." The eastern front is referred to here as the "back," because the entrance of the priests was at the opposite or western end of the building. "And a cubit on the one side, and a cubit on the other side of that which remaineth in the length of the curtains of the tent, it shall hang over the sides of the tabernacle on this side and that side to cover it," really forming the hairy lips of the vulva. "To cover it" cannot refer to the northern, western, and southern sides of the building, for they were already amply covered over.

We now come to other coverings lying horizontally over the roof. "And thou shalt make a covering for the tent of rams' skins *dyed red*, and a covering above of" the skins of Tachash, or, unpointed, Tchsh, which, states Calmet's (*vide* "Badger"), is the Arabic for Dolphin. Therefore, it is clear the outer or upper covering was made of the skins of Dolphins (Delphus–Womb), otherwise of those of Cetus, or Der Ketos, or whale, the Oriental symbol of the Consort of the Creator.

The reason why the curtains of goats' hair number eleven only is that the goddess Minerva (Divine Wisdom) herself, whose hirsute appendages the said hair symbolises, is the twelfth figure to be understood.

It will be noticed the opening in the east end indicates the eastern heavens, where the sun on the morrow reappears; after having traversed Hades, below the earth, and when the High Priest is born through that end it is implied his new birth takes place there in September—that is to say, at the autumnal equinox, or near it, nine months from the previous December 22nd, when his Divinity leaped into separate existence by the joint action of Celi and Ced. Now, when the sun rose in spring due east the earth in the west opposite to it was then personified as Venus (Morwyn, Maid), Virgin, otherwise Enid (Soul) in Druidism. The priesthood of the Archdruid, called Gwyddon, the same as Odin and Woden, identical with Mercury, was regarded as the symbol of the outcome of the influence of the spring sun and the earth upon each other, and was regarded, therefore, as the incarnate son of both Jupiter and Venus, or, in Druidic language, of Hu Dad Eilir and Morwyn o Elved (Hu Father of the Renovation, and the Maid of the Autumnal Equinox), so called because when the sun rises due east the earth is in the constellation Virgo, in the west, opposite. But the Hebrews, by observing the spring rites at the close of their civil year (September), and the commencement of the new civil year, mixed the ceremony having reference to the death of Saturn (Dec. 20th), and the birth of Apollo, the new sun (Dec. 22-25), in Druidism, Hu Gadarn, Taliesin, Arthur, Gwyion Bâch, (Bacchus), &c., with the ceremonies having reference to the symbolical incarnation of the priest of the sun in spring. Indeed, the skin of the ram (Aries) and the hair of the goat (the female goat here), and the upper covering made of the skin of Cetus, Ketos, or Dolphin (Delphus—Womb), the eastern emblem of Cêd, the mother of the sun, to the sanctuary, imply the mixed character of the emblems of Venus and Cetus (Cêd) or daughter and mother, in the ceremony symbols of the Period of Atonement. We shall presently give the reason for it.

This Mother of the High Priest or Priesthood is the Virgin alluded to by the prophet Jeremiah. He is referring to the ark in the Babylonic captivity, and says, " Set thee up way marks; make thee high heaps; Set thine heart toward the highway, even *the way thou wentest* ; turn again, O Virgin of Israel, turn again to these thy cities."—Jer. xxxi., 21. " The Virgin of Israel is fallen ; she shall no more rise; she is forsaken upon her land; there is none to rise her up."—Amos, ch. v., v. 2.

" This is the word which the Lord hath spoken concerning him " (Sennacherib). " The Virgin, the daughter of Zion, hath despised thee, and laughed thee to scorn; the daughter of Jerusalem hath shaken her head at thee."— —Isaiah, ch. xxxvii., v. 22.

" Therefore, the Lord himself shall give you a sign ; Behold, a Virgin shall conceive, and bear a son (the High Priest " renewed "), and shall call his name Immanuel. Butter and honey shall he eat, that he may know to refuse the evil and choose the good."—Isaiah, ch. v., v. 14, 15. " For unto us a child is born, unto us a son is given ; and the government shall be upon his shoulder ; and his name shall be called Wonderful, Counsellor, The Mighty God, The Everlasting Father, The Prince of Peace."—Isaiah, ch. ix., v. 6. It is very remarkable to find Dr. Kitto, in his *Biblical Cyclopædia*, under the word "Festivals," stating—but he does not give his authority for the statement—that the Lord Jesus was born between the 15th and 23rd of Tisri (September O.S.) during the Feast of Tabernacles. The Day of Atonement was the tenth of that month. The High Priest, the incarnate Shechinah, was born, as regarded his priesthood of "the Virgin of Israel," every "Day" of Atonement, as will be shown farther on. It does not appear Dr. Kitto dreamed of the symbolical birth of the High Priest on the Day of Atonement. Either the information, as to the real period of the Nativity, was obtained by Dr. Kitto from some source where the symbolical birth of the High Priest was known, and regarded as typical of the birth of the promised Messiah, or that some writer of antiquity sought to make it typical of that event, as was afterwards done by the Gentile world, by making the Nativity, and calling it Christmas Day, coincident with the birth of the young sun of the New Year. The young sun of Dec. 22nd was regarded by the whole Gentile world as a newly born babe, and the Day of Atonement and the Feast of Tabernacles were celebrations of the end and the beginning of the Civil year of Israel, and of the official death and birth of the High Priest. The sun is in the sign of the He-Goat on Dec. 22nd. He is the son of Cēd, not of the Virgin Venus of spring-time. On the Day of Atonement Israel had *two* goats in their ritual. One—the scape-goat—was allowed to escape; the other was sacrificed. At the Passover, the end and beginning of the sacred year of Israel, Jesus and Barabbas are dealt with in a similar manner (*vide* "Azazel"). It is intimated by Dr. Kitto (*Biblical Cyclopædia*. "Bethlehem") that it is

stated the Emperor Adrian erected statues over the Holy
Sepulchre and on Calvary, and placed one of "Adonis"—
their child (sun of the new year)—over the spot of the
Nativity at Bethlehem.

THE GREAT ALTAR AND THE LAVER.

To the west of the western entrance into the Holy Place
was a Laver, or a vessel for the priests to wash themselves
with the water it contained. Beyond the Laver, and
farther westward, was the great Altar of Sacrifice. This
altar is called the Altar of Burnt Offering and Meat
Offering, and in Exodus xl., v. 29, we are told it was near
the door of the Holy Place, and looking westward. This
altar was square. Rising from each of the four corners
was what is called a "Horn," and each was encased in
brass. The length and the width of the altar was nine
feet and nine inches every way—that is to say, five cubits
square. Its height from the ground was three cubits, or
six feet and three inches. No steps were used to ascend to
the top, but a slant ascending to the *southern side of the
altar* was used to reach the summit. This approach to the
place of sacrifice, rising from the southern direction—the
direction of the dominion of Hades—will be found to be extremely significant when we come to deal with the Typhonic
character of the third person of the Oriental trinities,
especially the Egyptian one. The altar was constructed of
the same kind of wood as the rest of the tabernacle, using
the term for the whole tabernacle, including the Holy
of Holies, but here the wood-work was all encased with
brass. There was a place for the sacred fire in the centre
of the altar, and there the meats of the sacrifices were
roasted. A space ran round the surface of the altar,
along which the officiating priests moved during the
performance of their duty. We beg the reader to carefully

observe that the creative function of the Sun and Nature
was symbolised by the Shechinah and the hairy entrance
into the Holy of Holies from the East; and near the
western entrance into the Holy Place, the altar, with the
ascent from the direction of the Dominion of Hades, symbolised the destructive function of the Evil Principle.

THE PASSOVER AND THE DAY OF ATONEMENT—THEIR ROBES, RITES, CEREMONIES, AND YEARLY ARRANGEMENTS.

It is truly remarkable that it does not appear to have
occurred to any commentator's mind that the High Priest,
as representing what his priesthood symbolised, died on
the Day of Atonement. The High Priest had two sets of
official robes—namely, his pontifical, gorgeous robes, and
the simple suit of white linen. The learned Maimonides,
referring to the priests, states truly: "When their
garments" priestly "are upon them their priesthood
is upon them; if their garments be not upon them their
priesthood is not upon them; but lo! they are as strangers,
and it is written, 'The stranger that cometh nigh shall be
put to death. As he that wanteth his garment is guilty of
death, so is he that hath more garments'" than are
directed by Divine command.

The following is a description of the pontifical robe and
ornaments of the High Priest. An upmost coat called
Ephod, made of golden, blue, purple, scarlet, and fine
twined linen blended cunningly together.

This coat had two shoulder pieces joined at the two
edges. Then came a girdle made to match the colours of
the Ephod itself. There were two onyx stones with the
names of the twelve tribes, six on each stone, engraved
thereon, the name of the tribe of Levi being omitted, that
tribe being represented by the High Priest himself. The

names were engraved in the order of the birth of the sons
of Jacob. Those two stones were mounted in gold, and
one was placed on each shoulder of the Ephod, and from
the mounts of the two gems were two chains of wreathed
gold. Then came the breastplate of judgment, of cunning
work, like that of the Ephod, of gold, blue, purple, scarlet,
and fine twined linen. It was four-squared; they made
the breastplate double, and a span was the length thereof,
and a span the breadth thereof—being doubled. And they
set in it four rows of stones. The first row was a sardius,
a topaz, and a carbuncle. The second row was an emerald,
a sapphire, and a diamond. The third row was a ligure,
an agate, and an amethyst. The fourth row was a beryl,
an onyx, and a jasper. They were fixed in sockets of gold.
On the twelve stones were engraved the names of the
twelve tribes, the name of the tribe of Levi being again
omitted. The breastplate was fastened upon the Ephod
by rings of gold at the four corners, the two upper rings
being attached to the wreathed chains of gold from the
two gems on the shoulder, and the two rings at the
bottom corners being fastened with blue ribbons to the
girdle round the waist of the High Priest. The fabric of
the coat, or Ephod, was of blue colour, and the other
colours seem to have been embroidered upon it. At the
top of the coat, or Ephod, was a hole for the neck, and a
band round it. The whole of the lower hem of the
coat, or Ephod, which reached far down, was ornamented
with pomegranates of blue, purple, scarlet, and twined
linen. "And they made bells of pure gold, and placed
the bells between the pomegranates upon the hem of the
robe, round about between the pomegranates; a bell and
a pomegranate, a bell and a pomegranate, round about
the hem of the robe to *minister* in, as the Lord commanded Moses."—Exodus, ch. xxxix. and ch. xxviii.

" And it shall be upon Aaron to *minister*, and his sound
shall be heard when he goeth in unto the Holy Place" not
the Holy of Holies; the priestly robes to ' minister in '
were never worn there " unto the Holy Place before the
Lord, and when he cometh out that he die not."—Exodus,
ch. xxviii., v. 35. " And thou shalt make a plate of pure
gold, and grave upon it, like the engravings of a signet,
HOLINESS TO THE LORD. And thou shalt put it on
a blue lace that it may be upon the mitre; upon the fore-
front of the mitre it shall be." Such were the robe and
the ornaments of the High Priest as a *living and officiating priest*.

THE SHROUD OF THE HIGH PRIEST.

As we have already stated the High Priest's office came
to a close on the Day of Atonement, and he died, so far as
his office was concerned, on that day; and as symbolical of
that official death he divested himself of his priestly robes.
To still further symbolise his official death he washed his
whole body in the Holy Place, in accordance with a most
ancient custom of washing the body of the dead immediately
after death. It seems he did that himself, for, though the
priesthood was dead, the High Priest's human nature was
alive still. The washing having been performed, the High
Priest now donned his grave garments, or snowy shroud,
symbolising the death of his priesthood. We will follow
the description given by Josephus (page 73) of the grave
clothes of the defunct priesthood of the High Priest. He
wore a white linen robe fitted close to the body, and it
reached to the feet. The sleeves were tied to the arms.
An embroidered cord, otherwise girdle, was passed many
times round the arms above the elbows enclosing the body,
which, though physically " old," contained within him the
ever young Divine principle, symbolised by a Dove, Wren,

&c. This complete entwinement formed a band four fingers broad, but was placed loosely to enable the High Priest to push it up to his left shoulder when he needed his arms loose. The girdle was embroidered with flowers of scarlet, purple, and blue, and fine twined linen; it was tied on the breast, the ends hanging down to the ankles, and was called *Abaneth* by Moses. We have not seen it explained what Abaneth signifies, but we will venture upon the conjecture that it is the Druidic Abanedd, signifying, the Abode of the Son, implying old sun, Saturn, represented by the High Priest, as being the Father of the young sun, Aaron, otherwise Arawn, and in Phœnicia, Adonis, and in Wales, Taliesin, or Hu Gadarn (Mighty Jesus or Joshua), of the new year, to be born presently through the eastern front of the Holy of Holies, when the High Priest, robed in his shroud, would emerge as being born a babe son, through that outlet of "the Virgin of Israel." When Myses (Moses or Old Silenus) died, Bacchus, his foster-son (Joshua) took his place at the head of the nation. This is precisely similar, but rendered ritually, to the death of the old sun, Saturn (Elijah), and the birth of Apollo (Elishah—Hebrew for the Lamb of God!), his son, implying the re-incarnation of Saturn; the death of Silenus, and the birth of Bacchus, his foster-son; and in Druidism, the death of Arawn (old Saturn, the sun under another name), and the birth of Hu (Hea) Gadarn (Hesus the Mighty), Havgan, Adonis, Arthur, Osiris, and Tammuz, according to the divers names given, indiscriminately, to the old sun and the new sun by various nations. In reference to Abanedd, in Welsh, Ab (Mab) signifies Son; in Hebrew, now, it signifies Father. "Abram" is very much like Ab (Son) and Ram (High). The name suggests also Brahma. In Druidism, Arawn or Aaron was frequently a name given to both the old sun

and the new, and it appears the same custom prevailed
amongst the Jews. But we have not completed the
description of the death garments of the defunct priesthood.
The legs of the High Priest were encased in white breeches,
with a girdle at the upper part of them, for the purpose,
Josephus states, of tying the *privy parts*. In the margin
to Exodus, chap. XXVIII., v. 42, the words "flesh of his
nakedness"—as in reference to King David "uncovering"
himself—are used instead of the words "privy parts," used
by Josephus. This tying the "flesh of his nakedness,"
like the rite of circumcision, refers to the gelded condition
of old Saturn, or the old sun, bereft of his virile power,
which, in Britain, was on December 20th, the end of the
Druidic solar year. In Israel, the symbol was used,
incorrectly, at the end of the Hebrew civil year (September
O.S.), but it refers to the time of the sun setting in
the west at the time of the Passover (March). On his
head the High Priest now wore a white cap, and a piece
of white linen came from the top of the cap down the
forehead. This piece of white linen implied the white
napkin usually placed over the face of the dead. The
coloured flowers on the girdle, suspended from the breast
down to the feet in front, implied the ancient Druidic
custom, still popular in Wales, of decorating the prostrate
dead with beautiful flowers, as symbols of God and Anian's
(Anima of Nature's) powers of renovation. The customs
of using flower wreaths, and adorning graves with flowers
on Palm Sunday, are derived from this most venerable
mode of teaching the doctrine of the resurrection of the
dead by the Druids.

CHAPTER XVII.

THE Hebrew high priest, having divested himself of his priesthood, by taking off his pontifical robes, donned white grave garments in their stead. He now, with sanguinary offerings, passed *westwardly* into the Holy of Holies and was lost to view. The Holy of Holies was windowless and doorless. It was the symbolical Hades, Erebus, or Sheol, of Israel, and Aaron was the old sun—sometimes as an old goat, and named Pan, identical with Saturn—the Arawn of the Druids. He emerged presently through the *eastern* end, and the act, implying his having passed under the earth, symbolised his new birth in the eastern sky through Virgo. He immediately reinvested himself with his pontifical robes, and the sound of the golden bells, round the hem of his priestly robes, were the musical cries of the newly-born baby priesthood. But who was the Mother? The Holy of Holies was encased in the skin of Cetus, Der Ketos (Whale), or Dolphin (Delphus—Womb), and those who have read preceding pages are aware that, in the East, the Côd of the Druids, consort of Celi Almighty, was symbolised by a Whale or Dolphin. She was " the ancient but ever-young parent" of the old and young sun, whom the high priest, by his official death, and by his official new birth, represented.

It will be noticed that although the Day of Atonement is held at the autumnal equinox (September 23rd), the western *descent* and the eastern *ascent* of the sun at the vernal equinox (March 21-25), were observed by the high priest. At the *autumnal equinox* the Zodiacal sign of the

o

Virgin is in the *eastern heavens*, and the sun rises in it, but the sun leaves it on September 23rd, whereas, in the west, at the same time, is the Zodiacal sign of the Ram. So that the high priest, by descending into the *west*, passed through the sign of the Ram, there, and was born in the *eastern* heavens from " the Virgin of Israel." [1]

The Hebrews made their Virgin Venus (Ark of the Covenant) to be a development of Cêd ; this is shown by their placing the ark within the encasement of the skin of the Dolphin or Whale (Der Ketos or Tchsh) covering the tabernacle, and thus the sun (Adonis) was represented as passing from Cêd through Venus, his sister-spouse ! This absurdity was the inevitable consequence of adopting, as the end and beginning of the Sacred and Civil years, the vernal equinox (March 21st) and the autumnal equinox (Sept. 23rd) respectively, instead of continuing the correct solar one, having its end and beginning at the winter solstice. The same error which made the Hebrews refer to the ark as "the Virgin of Israel," representing Virgo of the Zodiac, with the sun passing from her into the eastern heavens on the Day of Atonement—the period of the autumnal equinox (Tishri 10th, with eleven days added to bring up the lunar year to correspond with the solar on September 21st, o.s.)—led the Orientals to describe the Virgin Myrrah, or Mary, as the *mother* of the sun, under his name of Adonis, instead of describing her, correctly, as his *sister-spouse.*

Be it particularly observed that the Virgin of the Zodiac is the earth in the *west* in March, when the sun rises in the first point, *east*, in that month. In September the sun rises in the eastern heavens, in Virgo, and the earth is then in the sign of the Ram (Aries), in the west. It will be observed that the points of the Colure of the Equinox (east and west) touch both signs.

Isaiah VII., 14.   Jeremiah XIV., 17, XXXI., 21.

As we mention elsewhere in this work, Dr. Kitto states, in his *Bible Cyclopædia*, that Jesus was really born of the Virgin Mary at the autumnal equinox. This would correspond with the priestly birth of the high priest from "the Virgin of Israel," on the Day of Atonement, through the goat-hair fringed "secret end" of the eastern end of the Holy of Holies. Both births agree with the eastern solar point of the birth of Adonis from the ark of bulrushes, after crossing the Mediterranean from Alexandria, Egypt, to Biblos, Phœnicia, and the birth of Taliesin from a skin coracle, after crossing from Arkle (corruptly "Arklow"), on the coast of Ireland, to Borth, Cardigan Bay. These considerations, no doubt, were what induced the Emperor Adrian— A.D. 134 to 179—to erect a statue of Adonis at Bethlehem, to place the figure of a Hog (Mars, of Mount Libanus, of the solar fable which states that the Hog stabbed Adonis in the groin), over that gate of Jerusalem leading towards Bethlehem.[1] Moreover, he erected a temple to Jupiter Capitolinus (In Father of the Skull or Head) on the site of the Hebrew temple. And on a medal of Jerusalem, as Ælia Capitolina of Adrian, is shown Easter—the Astarte, otherwise Ashtaroth, really identical with Myrrah, otherwise Venus—holding a "skull" in her right hand, and crushing under foot the Power of Darkness, who is seen crouching under her foot.[2] Astarte, likewise, is here misplaced; the figure should be that of Cèd, rescuing the old sun's skull after his fall into the sea, still symbolised in Wales, in a popular custom, by an apple in a tub of water.

With reference to the absence, from the tabernacle, of the *two* other daughter-goddesses of Cèd—we *do* find Venus there—it is possible that the flowers, &c., of the ceiling of the tabernacle symbolised Flora, and the golden crock of

[1] Calmet's *Dictionary* "Jerusalem."
[2] "Ælia Capitolina of Adrian." Calmet's, vol. i. p. 57.

manna, and the rod of Aaron which budded, symbolised
Ceres, the Druidic Tynghedwen-Dyrraith, the Spotted Cow
of the earlier Creeds. There were *four* sets of coverings to
the tabernacle.

As we have seen, the jewelled ephod and the other sym-
bols of the high priesthood, were left by the high priest in
the western room, called the Holy Place, before he ventured,
in his white shroud, to go beyond the Veil into the Holy of
Holies (Hades or Erebus). It is quite evident that the
Hebrews confounded the Shechinah with the Most High
God, who is the Celi of the Druids, and the Amen Ra of
Egypt; and confounded the Ark of the Covenant with the
Womb (Delphus) of Cêd, the mother of the sun and the
virgin earth, and thereby made Venus, or Myrrah, or
Morwyn, to be the mother of the young sun. It is clear
that the high priest, symbolising the sun, the old and young
alternately, was mistakenly supposed to undergo rejuvenation by the joint influence of the Ark and the Shechinah in
the Holy of Holies, whereas the rejuvenating powers should
have been Cêd and Celi, the parents of the sun and earth
personified. The Jews, and all Orientals, ignored Celi and
Cêd altogether.

The following is one form of the cosmic teaching which
the Druids have left us, touching the first birth of the sun
with the dawn of creation :

" God pronounced His Name, and with the Word all the
world and its appurtenances, and all the universe, leaped
together into existence and life, with the triumph of the
Song of Joy. The same song was the first melody ever
heard, and its music travelled as far as God and His existences are, and the way in which every other existence,
springing in unity with Him, has travelled for ever and ever.

And it sprung from inopportune Nothing; that is to say: so sweetly and melodiously did God declare His Name, that life vibrated through all existing materiality.

"And the blessed in Heaven shall hear it for ever and ever.

"And where it is heard there cannot be other than the might of being and life for ever and ever.

"It was from the hearing, and him who heard it, that science, and knowledge, and understanding, and Awen (Holy Spirit) from God, were obtained.

"The symbol of God's Name from the beginning was \I/; afterwards ◊ I V ; and now D I W ."[1]

The joy of the old Gentile world at the reappearance of the sun, after the shortest day, or end of the solar year, and immediately after the Saturnalia, which was, originally, a very solemn holiday, held by the Druids on Dec. 20th, had reference to the death of the old sun, under his title of Saidwrn (Saturn), otherwise Old Pan-Goat, Tammuz, Arawn, &c. The joyful holy-day for the re-appearance of the sun (Dec. 22nd), was called Adonia by the Phœnicians (but wrongly placed,) in reference to the young sun, under his title of Adonis ; by other races the name of the holy-day was Bacchanalia, in allusion to the young sun, under his title Bacchus, with the head of a Kid Goat. He seems to have been named Hu Gadarn, Gwy Iôn Bach (God's Humidity the Little), and Taliesin, by the Druids.

On the solemn first day of Adonia, really the Saturnalia, the emblems of the sexual organs of Adonis (Saturn) and Venus (Dyrraith—old and barren earth) were carried with all the pomp and ceremony practised at funerals. The women wept, tore their hair (symbol of the sun's lost rays,

[1] *Bardism.* p. 39.

or power of generation), beat their breasts, and imitating
the cries of Venus when she thought Adonis was dying, on
Mount Libanus, a solar Golgotha, after having been
wounded in the "groin," by the boar (Mars, called, also,
Typhon, Pluto, &c.).

In Egypt, the Queen, herself, piously carried the sexual
symbol of Adonis (Osiris). No doubt the King carried that
of Venus, represented as old and withered, but we have
seen no record of the last-mentioned. The ceremony reminds us of the lost sword of Arthur, and the Phallus of
Osiris lost in the Nile and Isis II. in search of it.

The second day of the Adonia was spent in every
expression of joy and mirth, owing to the return of Adonis
alive. Let not the reader forget that in Phœnicia and
Egypt these rites were observed at the vernal equinox, the
period of the Hebrew Passover, instead of, correctly, at the
winter solstice; for it is then the old sun "dies" and the
young sun "returns" in his stead.

St. Cyril mentions an extraordinary ceremony practised
by the Alexandrians, that is to say, Egyptians. A letter
was annually written to the women of Byblus, Phœnicia.
Alexandria was to the south-west of Byblus, and, therefore,
indicated the direction of the setting sun at the winter
solstice, or Christmas time. The letter was enclosed in a
kind of cradle made of bulrushes, and some say the image
of the babe Adonis, renewed, was also enclosed. The letter
was to the effect that the lost Adonis had been discovered.
Mark that one of the titles of Bacchus is Myses or Moüses
(a person rescued out of the water), and, when correctly
described, that both Adonis and Bacchus are titles of the
sun in the early stages of his yearly progress.

After the Alexandrians, we are told, had performed certain rites and ceremonies, the ark, or cradle, or coracle, with its enclosures, was committed to the Mediterranean sea, and it is stated it failed not to reach Byblus, Phœnicia, that is to say, Palestine, in seven days. These "seven days" are suggestive. The Hebrew Passover lasted "seven days," that is to say, from sunset on Nisan 13th, to sunset of the 20th.

On the arrival of the ark of bulrushes at Byblus, at the mouth, as it appears, of the river Adonis, issuing from Mount Libanus, the women ceased their mourning and became joyful.

During the day of mourning and lamentations, when Adonis was supposed to suffer, he was described as uttering wailing cries. To represent those cries, the Greeks, Phœnicians, Lycians, Syrians, and Egyptians, played, in the funeral procession of the Adonia (Saturnalia), flutes called Giggras by the Phœnicians, that being the name of Adonis in their language. They were short flutes and they emitted remarkably melancholy sounds.

In Calmet's *Fragments*, is the following: "Adonis, or Tammuz, was a deity well known in Egypt, and the story of his *yearly death* was there commemorated." In the book *The Syrian Goddess*, attributed to Lucan, is given the following account of it: "The Syrians affirm that what the boar is reported to have done against Adonis was transacted in their country, and in memory of that event, they, every year, beat themselves, lament, and celebrate frantic rites, and great wailings are appointed throughout the country." Another account is as follows: "After they have beaten themselves and lamented, they perform funeral

obsequies to Adonis, as one dead. Afterwards, on a following day, they feign that he is dead, and they *shave their
heads,* as the Egyptians do at the death of Apis," their
sacred bull, and emblem of the sun in spring from 4619 B.C.
till 2505 B.C. We remind the reader that the sun's disc
was often compared to a head or skull, and that the Syrian
and Egyptian symbol of shaving the head, in March, had
really reference to the rayless condition of the sun in Britain
in December, and the act of shaving away the hair of the
head was a token of sympathy with the sun in his apparent
rayless condition, as it appears in Britain at the winter
solstice. This is the meaning of Place of a Skull under
the names Golgotha, Capitolinus, Calvary, Temple, &c.,
throughout the world.

The Welsh name given to a Jew is Iuddew, which is an
abbreviation of Iu Ddewin or Hu's (*e* sound to *u*) Prophet,
or, Prophet of Hu. Lewis Glyn Cothi—time of the Wars
of the Roses—describes the Lord Jesus as " the Dewin of
Nazareth." At present the word Dewin is used in the same
sense as the word Magician is used in English.

EDINBURGH.

In the earliest Welsh poem extant—the *Gododin*—describing the terrible battle between the Anglo-British and
pure British, on the Solway Firth, and named Cadtraeth,
about A.D. 570, Edinburgh is referred to under the name
Idin. Din, in Welsh, means Hill standing apart. The I
in Idin appears to be a mistake for Hu—Hu Din. I and U
have each the sound of E in Welsh. That " Hu " (the sun)
is meant seems to be confirmed by the fact that a celebrated
hill, close to Edinburgh, bears still one of the names of the
sun, viz., *Arthur*—Arthur's Seat. This seems to indicate
that, in very remote times, Arthur's Seat; or Hill of the

Sun, was often the scene of Druidic religious solar rites. Certain columnar geological formations of that hill are called Samson's Ribs. "Samson" is a Shemitic title of the sun. Salisbury Crags, close by, also suggest solar associations, for "Salisbury" signifies Sol Barrow, or Grave of the Sun, and appears to imply that the solar drama of the sun's annual death, and his burial in the symbol of his mother Cêd's body, was wont to be annually performed on the summit of that Golgotha of Scotland.

We cannot too often remind the reader that, in Druidism, every cromleach and every tumulus was, symbolically, the Delphus and belly of Cêd, the birthplace, and the grave, of the sun. A coffin is still called Arch (Ark) in Welsh, a name borrowed from the appellation given to Cêd, as the refuge of the sun after escaping into the sea from the pursuing power of Darkness. The earth, as the Delphus and belly of Cêd, and as the source of all produce, as well as of the sun, was also regarded as a garden. As a garden she was a Maid in spring, hence Morwyn or Morewyn. The sun, as the cultivator of the garden, was Arddir (Arthur — a Gardener); and as the Husband of the Maid he was Tegid (All Beautiful), in spring and summer. Jerusalem, because the Ark, representing the earth's fecundity, was in its centre, representing Cêd's womb, or Delphus, like Delphi, in Greece, and the personified earth's fecundity, was described as a garden: "I am come into my garden my sister-spouse." "A garden enclosed is my sister-spouse." "He hath violently taken away his tabernacle-garden." "The daughter of Zion is left as a cottage in a vineyard, as a lodge in a garden." "My beloved" the Shechinah, as the Deity's virility "is gone down to his garden" Venus "to the bed of spices." Isaiah compares Jerusalem to a vineyard: "Now will I sing to my well-beloved" Shecinah

" touching his vineyard.   My well-beloved hath a vineyard
in a very fruitful hill."   In the margin of the text is the
following : " The Horn of the Son of Oil."   This gives the
reading as follows : " My well-beloved hath the Horn of
the Son of Oil."   " The vineyard of the Lord of Hosts is
the House of Israel."   This implies the " Bethel " of Israel.
Here, no doubt, the temple, with the Ark of the Covenant
in it, is meant.

Those who worshipped the devil, or destroyer, made use
of fruitful gardens for the destructive rites of their religion,
hence the prophet states, in the name of the Creator, " A
people who provoke me to anger continually to my face ;
that *sacrificeth* in gardens, and burn incense upon alters of
brick" (instead of unhewn stones of Divine worship) ; " who
remain among graves, and lodge in monuments ; which eat
swine's flesh, and broth of abominable things in their
vessels."   By eating swine's flesh the devil worshippers
here seem to be doing honour to the devil, typified by the
wild boar (Pluto) which stabbed Adonis in the groin on
Mount Libanus.   The same idea, in a contrary sense, is
still to be noticed in eating fish in the period of Lent, the
time of year the sun is in the Zodiacal sign of the Fishes.
But that is Sun worship, while the other is Satan worship.

The Roman Catholics describe the Virgin Mary as a
" fruitful garden "—Venus again.   As a symbol of the
fecundity of the earth, but the belly of Cêd, the Virgin
Mary is the garden of the sun in March.   Now comes the
most wonderful co-incidence.

The Saviour was interred in a stone grave (kist ?) in a
garden, near, if not within, Jerusalem, whereas the sun,
after his death at the winter solstice, was, symbolically,

buried in a stone kist, in the middle of a tumulus, symbolising the belly and womb of Cêd, the sun's birthplace each Dec. 22nd, and the garden-wife of the sun in spring and summer. Adonis is a name of the sun. Myrrah, or Mary, is said to be the mother of Adonis. Myrrah is the Druidic Morwyn, a title of the earth in spring; but the Phœnicians, as we have seen, having shunted the end of the year from the end of the solar year (Dec. 20th) to March 20th, they came to represent Myrrah, Morwyn, or Mary, to be the *mother* of Adonis (sun), instead of being his *sister-spouse*. Thus they represented Myrrah instead of Cêd, as being the mother of Adonis. Mount Zion was also named Mount Moriah. A tumulus, as the symbolised garden-grave of the sun, is Mynydd y Marw (Mount of the Dead), hence Mount Meru and Mount Moriah, of the Eastern Gentiles and Jews, all of whom corrupted the original pure Druidism.

To revert again to Myrrah; those who gave to Christianity its scientific aspect seem to have detected the Phœnician error, for they made the "church" to be the "bride" of the Aries (Ram-Lamb) sun, instead of being his mother. Still, the Roman Catholics confound Mary with both the "garden" earth, and with Cêd, wrongly placed, the mother of the sun or Adonis. The reader will still bear in mind that in the solar allegory the old sun of every dying year is the father of the young sun of the following year. That among other titles of the old sun, towards the close of his career, is Arawn, from which name it appears as if the name Aaron is derived. Arôn, too, is the Hebrew name of the Ark of the Covenant, and the three names resemble each other so much as to lead one to suspect that they have a common origin.

We know that the Druidic Ark was sometimes called Gwrn (Goorn), and we have it in the termination of the name Said-wrn (Saturn); Said is the Welsh Druidic for

the Linga, and Wrn, from Gwrn, is the symbo⌐ ⌐l Y⌐d
The Shechinah is the Linga, or Seminal Logo⌐   ⌐ the
Ark of the Covenant, is the Yoni, called, by th⌐   ⌐s the
"the Virgin of Israel." It is probable the Hel   orn of
is derived from Yr Wrn, pronounced "Yr Oorı ⌐osts is
Druids.   ⌐srael.
                                               ⌐uant

ARAWN, AARON, OURANOS, AND URANUS

Among the Hebrews the name Aaron, or ⌐ ⌐
applied throughout the year to the new year's sun ⌐. ⌐use
in Druidism, the old sun at the end of the solar y⌐ ⌐ ⌐on,
is called by that title. The young sun of the new   A
named Hu Gadarn (Hesous, or Hesus, the Mighty),   ⌐⌐;
(Lofty Hesous), Gwy Iôn Bach (Young Bacchus) ⌐⌐ ⌐
"kingdom" is the earth, as his consort, during the ⌐ar.
During the year he receives titles descriptive of his manifested attributes during his progress through the sı ⌐s of
the Zodiac, viz., Tegid, Tegid Voel, Dyvnwawl Mo ⌐nud,
Saidwrn, and Arawn.

In the East, owing to the error of mis-applying the title
of Aaron, or Arawn, the earth is said to be the "kingdom"
of Ouranos. In the English New Testament the Greek
name, Ouranos, which is the same as Aaron, Arawn, and
Uranus, is translated "Heaven." It is an act tampering
with the text. "Repent ye for the kingdom of *Ouranos* is
at hand" is translated "Repent ye for the kingdom of
Heaven is at hand." Ouranos is, also, identical with
Uranus, and both with Aaron, or Arawn, the old sun.

Uranus, meaning the old sun, in Druidism, is said to be
the son of Terra. This is precisely like saying the young
sun is the son of Semele and the "thigh" of the Almighty
confounded with Jupiter. Mythologists confounded, also,
Cœlus (Celi—Almighty) and Uranus with each other. The

bu.
ising ı ⁿ l is the Almighty, and the last-named is the old
Dec. 2:   old god, identical with Saturn, Pan, &c.
summer.
is said tᵒ , ın his *Greek Testament*, states, "It has been
Morwyⁿ   by recent critics that Ouranos signifies, not the
as we ʰ   or the Christian religion, but strictly the Messiah."[1]
the eᵃ   a preceding paragraph, states, " From the use of
came   ıs) here by St. Matthew, and also in c. iv. 17, and
moth   e may conclude that it was used by the Jews and
Thus ᵃ   d to mean the Messiah."
mot)
Morⁿ   t himself designates Ouranos the Kingdom of God.[2]
ᵉ   ᵉ, it is clearly implied that Ouranos, Uranus,
Aᵒ wıⁿ, or Aaron, is God, and that the Messiah, or the
Chrısᵗ, is that God.

S. choniathon, the Phœnician, states that Ouranos con-
trivea Bactulia stones, which *moved* as having life.[3] Those
stones can be no other than Logans, or Rocking-stones, of
the Druids.   In ancient times it was a common practice to
give the poetical names of the sun to his priests, the representations on earth of the emanatious passing through
it from the Creator.   Sanchoniathon's statement, therefore,
seems to imply that an old priest of the old sun contrived
to erect stones which "moved as having life."

MOREWYN, MARY, MIRIAM AND MYRRAH.

The Adonis (Sun), of the Phœnicians, is said to be the
son of Myrrah, the same as Marios, Mary, and, in Druidism, Morwyn (Maid).   This is like the absurdity of saying
he is the son of his own sister-spouse, and that Miriam

---

[1] St. Matthew vii., 3–4.
[2] St. Mark xii., 34.
[3] Stukely's *Abri Wits*, p. 97

was the mother of Moses.   The error is due to dating the
birth of the new sun in spring, instead of December 22nd,
thereby implying the sun's sister-spouse, otherwise Venus,
is his mother. To be correct, Cêd, called Cetus, Der Ketos,
Delphus (Womb), is Adonis's mother on December 22nd,
and Myrrah is his sister-spouse on March 21st.

CHAPTER XVIII.

COCK AND HEN SYMBOL.

THERE is remarkable agreement between the rites, ceremonies and symbols of the Druids and the Hebrews. When the Druids used the Corwgl Gwydrin (Glass Coracle), which was an egg-like symbol, and is now called "Mundane Egg," to symbolise the anarchial condition of the elements with which, afterwards, the earth was constructed in an orderly or scientific manner, the Druids employed also the figure of a hen, which they called y Iâr Ceridwen, the Hen of Holy Love, to symbolise the heat of the feminine principles, but none active unless the masculine bird had imparted into the contents of the egg his fertilising attribute. To symbolise the masculine principle, the Druids employed, to correspond with the said hen, a cock, to set forth the expression of the masculine principle of the Creator through the sun, while the hen symbolised the expression of the feminine principle of Cêd through the earth. In Payne Knight's *Worship of Priapus* an illustration is given of an ancient bust of a cock, standing on a pedestal, with the Linga for a beak. Underneath the beak is given, in Greek letters, *Zeus Soter*, or, Jupiter the Saviour. The two wings of the cock complete the trinity in unity. In Druidism, the "beak" implies Hu Dâd Eilir Hu Father of the Vernal Equinox, otherwise, Iu-Pater of the Spring Time. He is personified under the title Tegid, Alawn (Hermes), &c. It implies the sun's fertilising emanation on March 21st, as the Seminal Logos, when, jointly with the earth's emanation from Cêd, it fertilises the seeds in it. The modern Jews now—Jerusalem being

no longer available there can be no sacrifice—take a
white cock, on the Day of Atonement (Sept. 10th, lunar—
21st, solar, O.S.) ; and the women, a white hen. The
cock they swing *three times* about the head of the priest,
saying, "This cock shall be a propitiation for me." After
the Jews swing the cock three times they acknowledge
themselves worthy of death.

The swinging of the cock three times appears to refer to
the Gentile trinity symbolised by the beak and two wings
of the cock. The said trinity, in the eyes of the Druids,
symbolised the life-giving, perfecting and defending attributes of the Eternal acting through the sun.

The above ceremony of killing the cock corresponds with
the sacrifice of the Paschal Lamb, symbol of Jupiter ; the
sacrifice of the bull (Apis, of Egypt) ; the sacrifice of the
goat (infant Bacchus and Pan) ; and the sending of another
goat to Azazel, translated, "scape-goat," but really sent to
the devil. Recollect, the Passover is the time of the end
and the beginning of the sacred year, and the Day of
Atonement the time of the end and the beginning of the
civil year, of Israel. The Passover Aries, and the winter
solstice Capricornus, but the latter shunted to the begin-
ing of the civil year of the Jews.

DEATH OF THE OLD SUN. BIRTH OF THE YOUNG SUN.

There is nothing more clearly established than that the
old sun at the winter solstice, or the end of the solar year,
was, as regards its body, represented by the entire ancient
Gentile world as being at that season of the year put to
death annually by the Father of Darkness, whose evil
emanations the Druids symbolised by the evil trinity already
described (see page 19). To be exact, we must state

particularly, that from the beginning of the solar year (Dec. 22nd,) to the vernal equinox (March 21st,) he was named Hu Gadarn (Hesus, or Hesous, the Mighty), and Taliesin. From thence to the summer solstice (June 21st,) he was named Tegid (All Beautiful) ; from the autumnal equinox (Sept. 23rd,) forward he was called Tegid Voel (Bald, All Beautiful) and Arthur. Then followed the name Dyfynwawl (Sombre Light) Nearer, still, to December 20th, he was named Dyfynwawl-Moel-Mud (Sombre Light, Bald and Dumb) ; this had reference to his almost rayless condition, to his being no longer able to impart joyousness to the earth, and to the stillness of the birds, &c. Later on he received the title of Saidwrn (Saturn) ; and, last of all, Arawn, or Ouranos, on Dec. 20th. Arawn signifies, literally, " to wait," hence the old proverb, " Hir yw aros Arawn " (Long the waiting for Arawn). But, idiomatically, Arawn signifies, inertness, bordering on death—the condition, also, of Adonis, after being stabbed in the *groin* by Mars, the devil, in the shape of a wild boar on Mount Libanus—and implying the condition of the old sun at the end of the solar year, no longer able to perform his function in the work of fertilising the seeds of the earth.

In the East, on Dec. 20th every year, the sun was, among other names, called Baal-Peor, which name is derived from Peorus or Osiris, but the name was misplaced, for Osiris is the sun in summer. In the Psalms it is said of his worshippers at this particular season of the year, " They join themselves also to Baal-Peor, and eat the sacrifice of the dead. At this season it was customary, with some people, to offer sacrifice to the Destroyer, as a kind of blandishment to him, like sending the goat to Azazel, and Barabbas, likewise, in the devil's hour of apparent triumph over the sun of God, the dying old regent of the Creator in the visible universe.

P

The old sun devotees would now inflict physical injuries on themselves, so as to join the old sun in his supposed physical sufferings at the hands of the Father of Darkness. But Moses told the Hebrews, "Ye shall not make any cuttings in your flesh for the dead" (sun) "nor permit any marks upon you : I am the Lord." This injunction implies the worship by Moses of the Destroyer who had "killed" the sun.

It is curious to find that some of those nations of the East, including the Hebrews, who symbolised the Author of Darkness, or the devil, by the figure of a boar, abstained from pig's meat, whereas the Druids, owing, apparently, to the strong liking of swine for the fruit of the sacred oak, held swine in honour as having been fattened with the sacred fruit.

It is to this abstinence of the Hebrews from pork the Latin satirist, Juvenal, alludes in the following satire on the Hebrews :—

> " Quidam sortiti metuentem sabbata patrem
> Nil præter nubes et cœli numen adorant :
> Nec distare putant humana carne suillam,
> Qua pater abstinuit.   Mox et præputia ponunt.
> Romanas autem soliti contemnere leges
> Judaicum ediscunt et servant ac metuunt jus,
>
> Sed pater in causa, cui septima quæque fuit lux
> Ignava, et partem vitæ non attigit ullam."

> " Some men, who had a Sabbath-fearing father,
> Worship no god except the clouds and sky ;
> And deem swine's flesh as sacred as a man's
> *Because their father did* : then clip their foreskins,
> And, holding in contempt the Roman laws,
> They learn and keep and fear the Jewish code,
>
> Their father is to blame, who passed in sloth
> The seventh day, and therein would do no work."

The Druids of Anglesea were called, and the inhabitants are still nicknamed, Môch Môn," or, " the Swine of Môn," that is to say, the Swine of the Sacred Cow, meaning, the Priests of the Oaks. The same epithet is applied, to this day, to the inhabitants of Pembrokeshire, a district of the Principality containing numerous notable Druidic remains. It is the farthest point of Wales in the direction of the setting sun. We know, by Druidic songs which have come down to us, that the Druids called themselves " Perchill," or Young Swine. Faber informs us that the priests of the Cabiri, the seven gods—the sun passing through the seven planetary spheres—of the Phœnicians, were called swine as an honourable distinction. That the Hebrews supposed the devil and his angels were partial to swine, we see exemplified by the readiness with which, in the country of the Gadarenes, a legion—about 6,000—of devils entered into a herd of swine—about 2,000—three, or a trinity, of devils into each pig.

There were innumerable places in the ancient world where the death of the old sun, at the end of the solar year, was observed with woe and mourning. It will be borne in mind that Golgotha, near Jerusalem, bore that name *before* the crucifixion of the Lord Jesus, and therefore it is evident it was not given to it in consequence of that event. We repeat, much confusion has been caused through writers being ignorant of the fact that Adonis and Tammuz, otherwise Bacchus and Old Silenus, otherwise Apollo and Old Saturn, are, in each case, two pairs of names given to the sun ; one, the sun by day ; the other, the sun by night, that is to say, the nocturnal heat of the atmosphere, each old and then young again perpetually. Singular to say, in Ezekiel viii., 14, we find that certain Hebrews at Jerusalem, supposed the sun at the longest day, when in the tropic of Cancer (June 21), was Tammuz; tor they are charged with looking toward the north, and weeping for Tammuz: a rite observed in other countries when the sun was in the south, in the tropic of Capricornus. It is curious that in the unpointed form of the name, "Bethlehem," it signifies Beth-el-cham (objective case), and compounded of Bwth (Booth) or Bedd (Grave) El (Sun) and Cham (Black): the Booth or Grave of the Black Sun. In the place where the death of the old sun, as Tammuz, was ritually observed, would be also ritually observed, after the lapse of forty hours, his renewal, as a babe. It appears, judging by the name, that Bethlehem had been, in some ages before the birth of Jesus, the scene of the rites of the solar religion, where the death of the old sun and the birth of the young sun had been dramatically set forth annually. Bethlehem is six miles to the south-east from Jerusalem, a city where we find a name signifying solar associations, namely, the Place of a Skull, as explained elsewhere in this work.

HOW THE TEMPLE CAME TO BE BUILT AT JERUSALEM.

The story as to how the temple came to be erected on Mount Moriah—Mount Meru of the Hindoos, and Mynydd y Marw (Hill of the Dead) of Druidism—is very significant. In I. Chron. xxi., and II. Samuel xxiv., 16, &c., we find the circumstances related. In verse 19 of the first chapter here mentioned we are told that the tabernacle of the Lord, which Moses made in the Wilderness, and the altar of burnt offerings, were, at that time, in the High Place, at Gibeon. In I. Kings iii., 4, the locality is called the Great High Place. In verse 30 of the same chapter we are told, "the people sacrificed in High Places because there was no House built unto the Name of the Lord." In verse 5 it is said, "In Gibeon the Lord appeared to Solomon." But the Ark was not then in Gibeon, for King David had had it, years before, conveyed from there into Jerusalem, and lodged it in a tent on the site of the threshing floor of Araunah, or Aruna (Ark), states Calmet. In ii. Samuel xx., 8, we are told there was a great stone in Gibeon, which, no doubt, formed a part of the Great High Place, as the Stones of Gilgal, Bethel, and the Stone called Ebenezer, formed sanctuaries, before a " House " had been " built unto the Name of the Lord."

A similar stone—no doubt the identical stone—still remains on the site of the temple at Jerusalem, and is now covered by the dome of " the Sakrah." " It is," states Dean Stanley, " the most curious monument of Old Jerusalem." The same author states, " It is sixty feet in length, in one direction, and fifty feet in another. It projects about five feet above the marble pavement, and the pavement of the mosque (of Omar) is twelve feet above the general level of the enclosure, making the height of the stone seventeen feet above the ground."[1] The temple stood on that spot, and must have enclosed that stone. It is a natural fixture, and has been treated with reverence by Jebusites, Hebrews, Romans, and Mahomedans.

THE STONE OF THE FOUNDATION (LAPIS FUNDATIONIS).

There was a stone in lieu of the Ark of the Covenant in the second temple, and it was called Lapis Fundationis (Foundation Stone). " Foundation Stone " of what? The Ark of the Covenant was the " foundation " of Judaism, and can there be any doubt that the " Stone of Foundation," as a substitute, implied this very stone, sixty feet one way, fifty feet the other, an seventeen feet in height?

We have, associated with the selection of the site of the temple, an interesting legend. The Hebrew word translated

---

[1] Dean Stanley's *Sinai and Palestine*, p. 178.

"threshing floor," is Geren. It is very much like the Druidic Welsh, Y Garn (Stone Heap). No doubt a threshing floor was called *Geren* in Hebrew, but why? It is well known the threshing floors in the East are circular and in the open air, and that the straw, after being threshed, is thrown into a great heap in the centre of the ring. Is it not, therefore, very probable " Geren," in the first place, signifies any heap, and, in the second, a threshing floor?

Such a stone as that which still stands on the Holy of Holies is still called Ark Stone by the Druids of Wales, and is stationed in the centre of their Eisteddfodic Gorsedd of a Circle of twelve stones.

Marvellous to state, the name of the Jebusite who is said to have been owner of the said *Geren* purchased by King David, was Aruna (Ark), otherwise Araunah and Ornan. Dr. Morgan, afterwards Bishop of Llandaff, and subsequently of St. Asaph, in his translation of the Old Testament into Welsh, erroneously rendered Araunah, or, in Hebrew, Aruna, " Arafnah."

We remind the reader one of the titles of the sun, as an old god at the winter solstice, is Arawn, and he is then represented as a dying Head or Skull, and his temple is called, also, the Place of a Skull, Temple, or Golgotha.

Reverting again to the " Foundation Stone " (Lapis Fundationis), as the foundation of the Jewish religion, Jesus seems to have had this Lapis Fundationis in his mind when he uttered the words in reference to another " rock," viz: " upon *this* rock I will build *my* church." He seems to allude to some *other* church, built upon some other rock. Did he allude, as a contrast, to the Lapis Fundationis as the Ark, and the basis of the creed of the Hebrews? Or did he convey that he was going to restore

the creed of which the said Stone of the Foundation was
the emblem? Was that the re-building of the Tabernacle
of David (God) which had fallen, and referred to in
Acts xv., and the last chapter of Amos?

"Oaks and Groves of Oaks" states Calmet, "were"
(among the Hebrews) "esteemed proper places for religious
services; altars were set up under them."   "And Joshua
wrote these words in the Book of the Law of God, and took
a Great Stone, and set it up there under an oak that was
by the sanctuary of the Lord." This was at Shechem.
"And Joshua said unto the people, Behold this stone shall
be a witness unto us, for it hath *heard* all the words of the
Lord, which he spake unto us." See Genesis xxi., 23;
Judges vi., 2; i. Kings xiii., 14; Genesis xxxv., 4 and 8;
i. Chron. x., 12; Judges ix., 6; Isaiah i., 29, lvii., 5;
Hosea xiv., 13; Isaiah xliv., 14.   It was into an oak grove
on the Plain of Mamre, Adonai, in three persons, and one
of whom Abraham addressed by the name Jehovah, entered
to visit Abraham.   It was He who *spoke* to Abraham, and
who is addressed as Jehovah, is alluded to thus as the Word
of God. Taking all the above circumstances into consideration, we ask, with the learned author of the "Fragments"
(vol. iv., p. 502) to Calmet's *Dictionary*, "Was Abraham a
Druid? He was as fond of the oak as a Druid could be.
Was Joshua a Druid?   He certainly conformed to that
character when he raised a great stone under an oak, at
which stood the tabernacle of Shechem:[1] and when he
observed that the stone had *heard* the words of the Lord.
Was Samuel a Druid? When he erected his Ebenezer, his
"stone of help," he did that which a Druid would have
done." "The famous oracle of Dodona stood among oaks;
the oak was sacred to Iupater (Jupiter) Amon" (Hidden

---

[1] Principal Edwards sees reasons to believe Melchisedec was stationed at
Shechem. Vide *Epistle to the Hebrews*, v. 1, *Genesis* xxxix., 18.

Father Iu). *Sacta Jovis Quercus*, the asylum of Romulus
at Rome, stood between two sacred groves of oaks.[1]
Everything tends to prove that among the British Druids,
whose language was Cymraeg, or Welsh, are the earliest
religious tenets of mankind, and that the Gorsedd was the
earliest tabernacle erected to the Almighty on earth.

THE ARCHDRUID.

The Archdruid, himself, standing in the middle of the
said Gorsedd Circle, where the three symbols \|/ met in a
point, implied that three Divine emanations focussed themselves in him. He, therefore, symbolised the Divine
Word incarnate. Such was our Druidic High Priest! It is
clear there were three poetesses, or priestesses, to represent
the three feminine emanations of Cêd through the earth.
They would be represented, collectively, by the Druidic
"Church," the Archdruidess, who would be the sister-
spouse of the Archdruid. So early as the time of Homer,
the real signification of the three in one in the Druidic
"Church," had been lost in Greece. For, in reference to
the old sun, under his title of Saturn, and the three personified emanations coming through the new sun during the
year, after the old sun had been "renewed," Homer states :

"Three brother deities from old Saturn came."

DEIFICATION OF THE DEVIL.

In Volney's *Ruins of Empires* is a remarkable quotation
from Plutarch's. It shows clearly the Orientals' deification
of the devil. In Persia the devil is given the name of
Ahriman, and the monstrous error of placing the devil as
the third personified emanation of the Almighty is clearly
shown in the quotation: "Many suppose," writes Plutarch,
"there be two gods of opposite inclinations, one delighting
in Good, the other in Evil. Zoroaster has denominated

[1] *Dion. Halic.* lib. ii., cap. 15.

them Ormuzd and Ahriman, and has said that whatever
falls under the cognizance of our senses Light is the best
representation of the one (Ormuzd), and Darkness and
ignorance of the other (Ahriman)." He adds that "*Mithras*
(the second person of the Persian trinity,) *is an intermediate
being, and is, for that reason, called by the Persians
Mediator or Intermediator*." The reader will observe
carefully, in a succeeding table, that the devil is the *third*
person in many other trinities. In Druidism, however, the
third person of their personified three emanations of the
Deity, is Gwron (Hero) resisting evil; and Gwron, or the
Divinity in the sun, is symbolised by a Wren, &c.

Mithras corresponds with the sun as the Druidic Alawn
(Hermes—Harmony or Mercury). As the Archdruid on
earth with his face towards the east, and standing on the
Mound Cromleâch, or the Logan Stone, he is Marchogydd,
or Rider, in the sense of performing a certain function.
From Marchogydd is derived the name Mercurius. He is
the chief minister of the emanations, and, therefore, of the
"gods," on earth. He is the sun incarnate personified on
March 21st, when the earth, by her seeds, under the virile
influence of the sun, begins to develope offspring. The
sun, then, standing between winter and summer, Light and
Darkness, is a Mediator, and was called Mithras by the
ancient Persians. The Persian Ormuzd is the Druidic
Plenydd, or the sun on June 21st. The sun is then at the
highest point of his strength, and is compared to man in his
virile prime. Ahriman, the third person of the Persian
trinity, between whom and Ormuzd, Mithras stands as
Mediator, is, same as Pluto, the third person of the Latin
trinity; Hades, or Dis, the third of the Greek trinity;
Typhon, the third of the Egyptian trinity; Siva, the third
of the Indian trinity; &c. The third of the Druidic trinity

is Gwron (Hero, or Heroic), while Avagddu, the character corresponding with the *third* of the other trinities, is the first of the three devils in the trinity of evil in the Druidic system. We believe that the error of Orientals in substituting the devil for Gwron (Hero) as the *third* person of the Divine emanations of the Creator, is responsible for all the sanguinary sacrifices of the East, and for the horrible impiety of supposing that *blood or life* is an offering not only acceptable, but demanded, by the Eternal Father !

The subjoined table shows at a glance what we have stated above, namely, that every nation, except the Druidic, has either made three gods, or three eminent men, of the three personified emanations of the Deity, as revealed through the sun, in spring time, in summer time, and in winter time ; in other words, when, in spring he rises over the equator ; he rises in summer in the tropic of the Crab : and in winter in the tropic of the Goat ; March 21st, June 21st, and December 20th (in Druidism), respectively.

MASONIC SIGN. The Bee as symbol of the Sun in Spring Fertilising Nature. Botanists know Bees convey masculine Pollen from male flowers to fertilise the seeds of female flowers. The Second character in each Trinity is the symbol of the Seminal principle of the Logos.

TABLE OF GODS AND HUMANISED DEITIES OF THE OLD WORLD.

ADAM (Ad Hama—Persian Sun)
Cain   Seth   Abel
Eden Garden.

NOAH, or NINTH
Japheth   Shem   Ham
Ark.

HEBREWS
Adonai, or Elohim (Three Gods)
Abraham   Isaac   Jacob
Palestine.

ROMAN
Saturn (the Old Sun)
Neptune   Jupiter   Pluto
Earth.

GREEK
Sun
Poseidon   Zeus   Dis
Earth.

PERSIAN
Sun (Ad Hama)
Ormuzd   Mithras   Ahriman
Earth.

We have placed the Greek Zeus and the Roman Jupiter in their correct position in their relation to the earth in spring, and not in the incorrect order in which they are usually given.

INDIAN
Sun
Brahma   Vishnu   Siva
Earth.

INDIA (of the Vedas)
Sun
Surya   Varuna   Agni
Earth.

BABYLON
Sun
Shadrach   Mesach   Abednego
Earth

EGYPT
Sun
Osiris   Horus   Typhon
Earth.

DRUIDIC
Sun (Hesous the Mighty)
Plenydd   Alawn   Gwron
Earth as a Circle.

CHRISTIAN
Jesus (Sun of Righteousness)
Peter   James   John
The Church.

Jehovah is not the Almighty, Himself, but His Name; and, in Druidism, is represented by the three letters I A O rendered, hieroglyphically, thus \|/

THE COUNCIL OF NICE A.D. 325.

Dr. Rowland Williams has a very remarkable passage (*vide* Biography, p. 322) on the subject of the Trinity. He states "when the Nicene Fathers made the Word co-eternal, they did not mean to introduce plurality of substance; but our vulgar and carnal notion of *Person would have seemed to them to do so.*"

> "One Substance—Three Forms.
> One Person—Three Manifestations.
> One Being—Three Outshinings.
> One Essence—Three Agencies."

The above are precisely the Druidic teachings. One Eternal Father—Three Agencies through the Sun; and hieroglyphically illustrated by the sign \|/, and by the letter shin (ש) on the forehead of the Hebrew when engaged in prayer.

TYPHON OR DEVIL WORSHIP.

Josephus quotes the following from the writings of the Egyptian historian, Manetho (300 B.C.), touching the residence of the Jews in Egypt:—Amen Ophir, a king of Egypt, "having been asked to apportion, as a resting place for them, and as a covering, the city which was left empty by the Shepherds, granted to them Avaris. *This City is Typhonian, from ancient times, according to the theology.*"

Ἔστι δ' ἡ πόλις κατὰ τὴν θεολογίαν ἄνωθεν Τυφώνιος.

In the English translation of the above passage from Josephus' Greek version, the word Typhonian, that is to say, set apart for *devilish* worship, is rendered "Trypho."[1]

Observe Manetho employs the present tense in reference to the Typhonian character of Avaris, which implies that it continued down to his time, 300 B.C., to be a city devoted

[1] See Josephus' *Answer to Apion.* p. 618.

to the Typhonian worship. Manetho proceeds: "But they (the Jews) having entered into it, and holding this in revolt, they set up as their leader Osarsippus, who was said to be one of the priests of Heliopolis; and they took an oath to obey him in all things. But he first made a law for them neither to worship the gods nor to abstain from eating of sacred animals" (Bull, sacred to Apis; Ram, sacred to Jupiter Amon; Cow, sacred to Isis II.; Goat, sacred to Myses, or Bacchus).—*See* Exodus viii., 25-26. The said verses corroborate Manetho's statement respecting the manner in which the Jews conducted themselves towards the *sacred animal symbols* of Egypt. He further states that Osarsippus (from Osiris, the god in the city of the Sun,) had his name changed when he went over to this nation, and was called Moyses.[1]

Josephus is, naturally, furious with Manetho, and goes on to state the name Moses is derived from the Egyptian Moüses, and signified, a person who is preserved out of the water; for the Egyptians call water Moü. So was Adonis and Bacchus called Myses, Taliesin, from the coracle, &c.

In reference to Abraham, we find the following remarkable narrative in Genesis: "And Jehovah" (so it is in Hebrew) "appeared unto him in the plains of Mamre, and Abraham sat" (among oaks) "in the door of his tent in the heat of the day. And he lifted up his eyes and looked, and lo, *three men* stood by him; and when he saw them, he ran to meet them from the tent door, and bowed himself toward the ground, and said, ' Adonai, if now I have found favour in thine eyes,'" (so it is in Hebrew) "' pass not away from thy servant.'" He speaks of the three as being one individual, or one Jehovah (Name of the Creator, and not He Himself).

[1] Rev. Dr. J. A. Giles Translation *Heathen Records*, pp. 64-5. Ed. 1856.

It will be recollected that one of the titles of the sun, in both east and west, is Adonis, the one source of the three emanations, which are personified as one in the person of the Archdruid in the sacred Circle on earth, as representing the whole of it. Therefore the three persons before whom Abraham stood would be, in essence, one Adonai, or Lord, and Abraham addressed the three as one Memra, or Logos, accordingly.

In the beginning of chapter xv., we have reference to a previous visit of the same three "men" to Abraham, among the oaks of Mamre, intimating to him the forthcoming birth of Isaac. *Two* of the three appeared to Lot afterwards. Where had the *third* gone to? He had lingered behind on the road with Abraham, where the Patriarch pleaded with him on behalf of the inhabitants of Sodom and Gomorrah. The *third* person, when alone with Abraham, is addressed by the Name Jehovah by the Patriarch, and He is bent on *destroying* the Cities of the Plain. But, in this narrative, the *third* person is an avenger in consequence of sin, which is a departure from the satanic character of Typhon, the *third* god of Egypt. On the other hand, the fact that the Hebrews represent the sanguinary Abel as more acceptable to Heaven than Cain, gives to their Creed a Typhonic and sanguinary character. But the important point is that it was the *third* person of the three visitors to the Patriarch, among the oaks, was the one who is said to have actually *destroyed*. The two other persons—called "angels" in the next chapter of the Authorised Version—went to exercise mercy by warning Lot. We find Jehovah actually declared, by Isaiah, to be the author of evil or destruction : " I form the light and *create* darkness ; I make peace and *create evil* ; I, Jehovah, do all these things "—xlv., 7. And in Amos iii., 6 : " Shall there be evil in the city, and

Jehovah hath *not done it?*" (*vide* "Azazel," in this work).
The entire Hebrew worship seems to be based on this supposition, hence the worship of the creating attribute, symbolised by the Ark and the Shechinah, and the Rod of
Aaron which *budded*; and the destructive principle symbolised by the reeking altar with Typhonian horns! also,
by sending a goat to Azazel on the Day of Atonement.[1]

The Druids regarded evil as caused by the absence of
goodness, as darkness is caused by the absence of light.
Goodness purifies; evil causes moral putrefaction. And
the good, they thought, gradually becomes godlike, and fit
for Gwynva or Heaven.

---

[1] See Isaiah xxx., 27-33.

CHAPTER XIX.

INCARNATIONS.

T is necessary in this place to describe why it was the second person of the Druidic and Hindoo and other trinities was said to become, from time to time, incarnate. It will be recollected that the second person, Alawn or Hermes, Mercury on earth, of the Druidic trinity, is the emanation of the sun in the spring, or March 21st. Woden's, or Mercury's Day, is the middle day of the week. The sun then, as the ancient's believed, transmits into the seeds of the earth, from the Creator, a fertilising attribute by rays to propagate the said seeds. This is the reason why Alawn or Hermes is styled Father: Tâd, Tot, Ted, Taut, Tau, Taat, Thoth, each being a corruption of the original name Tâd of the Druids speaking the Cymric language. The sun in spring, from 2,505 B.C. until 389 B.C., was in Aries, at which period it entered in spring the sign Fishes instead. It will continue to rise in spring in that sign until the year 2,494; after that date, or the year 2,115 of the Christian era, when, in spring— March 21st—it will commence to rise in the sign of the Waterer. We are here giving M. Dupui's calculation of the precession of the equinoxes, which cause the change from one sign of the zodiac to the other.

We must point out here, parenthetically, the fact the sun is in the sign of the Goat from December 22nd till January 20th. Therefore, the tenth month, Tebeth, of the Jews, during which Noah's Deluge commenced, has next to it " Water," personified as Waterer ; and immediately after it come *Fishes*. Spenser noticed the striking fact that Fishes follows the **Waterer**, and wrote as follows:—

> " And lastly came cold February, sitting
> In an old waggon, for he could not ride :
> Drawn of two Fishes, for the season fitting,
> *Which, through the Flood before, did softly glide.*"
>
> Spenser's *Faerie Queen.* Book VII.

Now, during the long period of 2,115 years, when the sun rose in spring in the sign of Aries or the Ram-Lamb, Iu-Pater, or Iu Father, was represented as a Ram; and, eventually, as a man in his prime, with ram's horns on his head, one on each side of his temples. The earth's fecundating power was then called, in spring, the Bride of the Lamb, or of the Ram, Sun. These figures were afterwards borrowed to set forth Christ and his Church. An evergreen tree, within the sacred enclosure of churches, is still called yew; in the time of Chaucer it was spelt *ewe*, a female sheep, and the Phœnicians had a sheep as the consort of Jupiter.

This sheep is identical with the sacred cow, and with Venus Aphrodite, or Sea Foam, by the Greeks, which is also the exact meaning of the Druidic Mörewyn, usually now used to designate a Maid, by the Welsh of the present day. She is identical as said before, with Myrrah, or Mary, " Mother "—that is to say, Miriam (Venus Marina) —correctly, Consort of Adonis (Sun). As we have stated elsewhere, this is an error due to the Phœnicians shifting the beginning of the year from the winter solstice to the vernal equinox or spring. Myrrah, or Mary, is really the sister-spouse of Adonis, otherwise Iu Pater, while Cêd, wife of the Almighty Celi, was his real mother, when he rose from the sea on Dec. 22nd. The importance of this point can not be over estimated.

Q

In the Welsh almanacs, down to the present day, Lady Day, or March 25th, first day of spring of the erroneous Julian Calendar, is called "the day of the impregnation of *Mary of the Equinoctial line*"—Dydd beichiogiad Mair y Cylydedd. This expression is a Druidic survival and it refers to the Virgin Earth—called, by the Romans, Mother of the Gods—being now impregnated by the Alawn sun, otherwise Tegid, her young husband.

We remind the readers that, in Druidism, it is the time of the year when the sun and the earth are married. The bride is robed in her wedding garments, decorated with budding flowers, and her diamonds are brilliant rivers, glittering seas, and dancing mountain rivulets, and their wedding bells are the songs of birds. Thus the Divine emanation, as rays from the sun, awakening the seeds of the earth in spring, induced the Druids to represent the second person of their trinity as becoming, himself, incarnate; and the circular Church of the Druids, symbolising the round earth above the rational horizon, was the sister-spouse of the Archdruid, who represented the sun on earth. Thus is explained the incarnations also of Mithras, Vishnu, Horus, Hermes, &c.

Let the reader note particularly the error of representing Myrrah as the *Mother*, instead of the Wife, of Adonis, for it is found in all the Eastern and Western creeds, in their corrupt forms of Druidism.

THE MUNDANE EGG OF THE DRUIDS.

One of the symbols of the earth, in later epochs of the Druidic system, was an egg. This must have come into use after the Druids had discovered the earth was spherical in shape, and not shaped like a beehive with its base flat. The Archdruid wore, as the insignia of his representative character, the egg as the emblem of Cêd, the sun's mother, as a coracle-ark. It was called " Corwgl Gwydrin," or, the Glass Coracle, implying the source of all things. The chaotic contents of the egg symbolised the earth's elements before they were reduced to order, to be animated by the feminine principle of Cêd, as the "natural body"—unborn babe—is animated by the physical life within it.

It seems the earth's inertness in winter and the inertness of the sun at the same season, were supposed to be due to the principle of Evil, personified poetically as described elsewhere, and that the feebleness of both was due to the ascendancy of the destructive principle beginning to disintegrate both the physical body of the earth and the physical body of the sun. The poets gave now the name Ovum Typhonis, or Egg of Satan, to the inert earth. The Druids introduce the spirit of Cêd as coming to the rescue of the egg, and they gave to that spirit the figure of the Hen Ceridwen—Hen of Holy Love—and by brooding over the egg reintroduced into it the vital force, and the Destroyer lost it in his apparent moment of victory, and it is quickened by the masculine heat in conjunction with her own.

Because, as already stated, the moon six days old, being crescent-shaped, resembled in shape a boat—an older symbol than the egg—upon which the Divinity's masculine principle descended, and which was symbolised by a cock, consort of the said hen—at other times a white dove, and at other times a wren is the symbol employed for it—to fertilise the earth into which the feminine heat of the Ceridwen hen has entered already, the moon came to be designated Meen, or Mind (\|/), the said masculine fertilising influence being described as the Mind of the Creator. The English name, Man, is derived from the Greek Meen (Mind), the Greek name of the moon. We have shown that, in Welsh, the brain is called *Men*-ydd, or Mind, and the name of the Straits between Aronia and Anglesea, a place strikingly associated with Druidism, is called *Menau*—not "Menai"—and signifies Minds, doubtless in reference to the many learned Minds, or Druidic philosophers, who once dwelt in the celebrated oak groves on its Anglesea shore. It is possible, also, that on the said straits often rode the sacred boat, symbolising Cêd, the depository of the Divinity of the Sun, or Mind, after his escape, according to the solar allegory, from the ruins of the old sun on the afternoon of every December 20th.

There is no doubt that the popular old legend of "The Man in the Moon" is derived from the above association of the moon with the crescent-shaped ark or boat of the mysteries, which symbolised Cêd as the refuge of the Divine Meen, or Mind, of the Creator, as he descended into the Atlantic at sunset, on every December 20th.

As stated elsewhere, a coffin is still called ark in Welsh. It is, unquestionably, a name used in the same sense as the name boat or ark given to Cêd. It is a striking fact the side of a Welsh bed is named Erchwyn. We are inclined to believe the correct form of the compound is Archewyn, or Ark of the Foam, that is to say, of the Sea, given to a bed in the same sense as the name ark is given to a coffin. Moreover, the Druids were very fond of Triads.

In the ancient laws of Wales (Howell the Good's,) is the following:—"Lodging of a Guest: The host and two of his household men of the abode where he (the guest) slept, should swear, they were his guardians from the dusk of the evening (Gorch y Varwy) until the dawn; and the hand should be passed over him *thrice*," symbol of Divine protection. Also we find the following manner of enumerating days: Heddyw (to-day), Forn (to-morrow), Drenydd (thirdly). Backwards, as follows: Heddyw (to-day), Ddoe (yesterday), Echddoe is the name given to the third day backwards. We believe *Echddoe* is a corrupt form of Archddydd, or Ark Day, in reference to the entry of the sun's soul into his Arkite refuge or Mother Cêd's Delphus, on the first of the three days (Decr. 20th, 21st and 22nd,) of the solar allegory.

In reference to the crescent-shaped boat, Faber, in his *Mysteries of the Cabiri*, remarks, "The Chaldean astronomers, having observed the resemblance of the crescent moon to a boat, thought the waning moon was no unapt symbol of the ark, hence they (the moon and ark) were reverenced jointly; consequently, we find that the very same goddess" (Cêd) "was sometimes the personification of one, and sometimes of the other." "The mythologists," he goes on to state, "sometimes represent the moon, sometimes the ark, and sometimes the globe of the earth, emerging from the waters. This I apprehend to be the only key that can unlock the hidden meaning of the mysterious polytheism of the ancients." We cannot understand why Faber supposed the figure was that of the *waning* moon. Strange that Faber did not think of Cetus, or Der Ketos, or Delphus (Whale or Dolphin), to be also used to symbolise the same thing as the moon, ark and globe, namely Cêd of the Druids, Mother of the Sun and Nature, or Venus; Cêd rising in the sea to receive the fleeing Divinity of the sun.

At other times a serpent was represented encircling the egg. The Creator's and Cêd's combined wisdom was symbolised by the said serpent fertilising the egg, or inert earth, in the spring time. The sun is referred to by the title of Aeon—

"Aeon hath seen age after age in long succession roll:
But, like a serpent which has cast his skin,
Rose to *new life, in youthful vigour strong.*"

The expression "cast his skin" alluded to the idea that the sun of the old year had his body destroyed in the heavens at noon on each December 20th, by the Power of Darkness.

THE EARTH IN AUTUMN AND WINTER.

The earth in Autumn was also personified under the name Beroe (to bear)—carrying the seeds. She was said to be in labour in autumn, and to her delivery, Hermes or Alawn, otherwise Tegid (sun), was said to contribute. In September the sun is in the eastern heavens, in the sign of the Virgin, and the earth in the western heavens, in Aries. But, doubtless, what is meant by assisting at her delivery, the sunshiny days of harvest is implied so contributing. "Upon Beroe being delivered," states Bryant, "there was immediate joy through the creation, every animal testified its gladness." The meaning is obvious. Beroe, (Sanscrit Brhi ; Greek, Phero ; Cambro-British, Bru (Bre)—womb or belly. There are two hills at St. David's Head, in the direction of the setting sun at the time of the winter solstice, called Bru (e sound to u), corrupted into "Burry" in that locality.

Beroe is described by several characters—(1) Daughter of Oceanus. Oceanus is Heat in Humidity, as a masculine principle, *descending* from above; Beroe's mother is Terra (Cêd), or the heat *arising* from the earth in moisture, as a feminine principle ; the two principles by contact with each other, by the said agencies, giving activity to the seeds of the vegetable kingdom. Oceanus and Neptune are the same personage, and are names of the nocturnal sun, or Bacchus in his prime on June 21st, when in his full strength. Gwyion Bâch is the Druidic name of Bacchus, as a child. Indeed, it seems to us the Greek name is derived from the Druidic Bâch (Little), the first name being dropped, and the adjective Bâch being used as a full name. Professor Max Müller adopts a Sanscrit etymology in his *Hibbert Lectures* (Lond., 1878, p. 278, Note). He reads Dionysis (Bacchus) Dyu-Nis-ya, that is to say, the Child of Day and Night, or, of Heaven and Earth. The reason which made Bacchus receive, later in the year, the names Oceanus and Neptune, made Gwyion—Gwy and Iôn (Humidity of the Leader Lord)—receive the title of Nevydd-Nav-Neivion (Leader Lord Constructor). It should be distinctly remembered that each of the mythological characters is old and young alternately—old at the end of the solar year and again young with the beginning of the next Forgetting this fact, each nation giving a different name to the same personification, and then mixing up all the different names, are the causes which made mythology appear an inextricable confusion. (2) Beroe as an old woman and nurse of Semele. By Semele is meant the following year's sap, or unctuousness, of the earth's substance, which is the agent in the growth of vegetation. This, in Draidism, is called Saim (Grease), but when fertilised is called Nav, commonly Nôv. It signifies Constructor, hence Nevydd-Nâv-Neivion as a Druidic title of God. The said Nevydd-Nav-Neivion is the Druidic Oceanus. Beroe is to Semele what Silenus—said to be silent, because the dew, containing the fertilising warmth, falls silently—what Silenus is to Bacchus, who is said to be the foster-son of Silenus; precisely the same as Old Beroe is said to be the old Nurse of the young Semele. At first sight it would seem that, to be correct, old Silenus and old Beroe should be husband and wife. The reason why they are not so represented is that they are aged foster

parents of Bacchus and Semele, not their natural parents.
Too old to be fruitful, old Silenus is the old Nocturnal Sun,
which is the personified slight heat in the winter atmosphere
left there by old Saturn, the weakened Lord of Day. But
as the old foster-father of Bacchus it is the Nocturnal Sun
towards the close of the solar year who is meant by Silenus.

Young Apollo, otherwise Adonis, &c., becomes old
Saturn or Arawn, Tammuz, and known by other titles
towards the close of the solar year; Myses-Bacchus, of the
early part of the year becomes old Silenus, the foster-father
of the ensuing year's young Bacchus, towards the close of
the solar year. Thus there are two old men gods, side by
side, in December, one being the personified daily sun under
the title of Saturn, &c., and the other the personified
nocturnal sun under the title of Silenus. In another part
of this work we call attention to the similarity of the said
two old men gods to Elijah and Moses, and Jesus to the
young sun, Adonis in the East, and Hesus the Mighty and
Taliesin in Britain.

THE ALLEGORY OF THE NURSE BEROE AND THE MAIDEN SEMELE.

Now follows a poetical story which made mythology
unintelligible, except to the initiated in the greater
mysteries. Juno is the earth blooming in the height of
summer. She is developed Isis II., Easter, Venus, Morewyn,
Ashtaroth of the Phœnicians, and, as to each of them, the
cow was sacred to her. Juno, states the allegory, grew
jealous of Semele, and, disguised as the elder Beroe, the aged
nurse of Semele, visited the unsuspecting young Semele,
and, being bent upon her destruction, persuaded her to solicit
Jupiter in all his vigour and majesty. This innocent
Semele did; but Semele's mortal frame being unable to
sustain the energy of the god, she perished in his embrace,
and was reduced to ashes.

All this simply means that the sap in vegetation becomes exhausted under the draining intense heat of the sun in summer. Becoming exhausted in autumn vegetation begins to wither, becomes dry, and is, finally, reduced to ashes.

It is further stated that Semele was at the time pregnant with young Bacchus, or the substance for the body of the next year's nocturnal heat of the sun personified; that he was taken out of Semele's body alive, and then placed in the "thigh" of Jupiter, where he remained two months, and was then born. It is represented, therefore, that Semele was gone seven months with the babe Bacchus when she perished, that is to say, when the fermentation of the earth's sap ceased. The time of the autumnal equinox is meant, which, according to Jewish and other eastern calendars, is in the month Tishri and corresponding with our September or October O.S. When Easter falls in April, October is the Seventh month of the Hebrew and Phœnician sacred year. October then would be the date of the death of Semele (Saim—Grease). *Two months* later would be the date of the winter solstice, which is *nine* months from the vernal equinox. Bacchus's birth then would be at Christmastime, or the date of the winter solstice according to the Julian Calendar.

By Jupiter's "thigh" is meant the Creator's Almightiness. The nations confounded the old sun, as Father, with the Eternal himself. Bacchus being thus the Son of Semele, or the fertilised juiciness of the earth, an emanation of Cêd, and of the "thigh" of Jupiter, or of God's omnipotence, was said to be two mothered. Here Jupiter is confounded with the Almighty. Moses, whose name in a correct form, is Moüses or Myses, a title of Bacchus, is also said to have had *two* mothers, viz., Jocabed, the Jewess, and Thermutis, states Calmet, but Thermuthis states Josephus, daughter of Pharaoh.

It is a curious coincidence that Moses is said to have been hid for *three months*—until he was three months old—by Jocabed (meaning I A O is Glorious) his Jewish mother, and Moüses, Myses-Bacchus was hid *two months* in the "thigh" of Jupiter, and seven months in the body of Semele. Now, mark the following : Semele, as we have said, is the personified warm sap of the earth. Thermuthis, or Thermutis, the name of Pharaoh's daughter, is marvellously like the Greek Thermos (heat), and Thermeo (I heat).

Had the narrative stated Moses had been hid six months by Thermutis, and three months by Jocabed, why, it would have been sufficient to induce one to suppose both the histories of Moses and the history of Myses-Bacchus were identical. But the above marvellous coincidences are not all. Moses was found on the Nile, in a boat, constructed of bulrushes; Adonis, the name of the sun in Phœnicia, &c , was yearly sent as a babe in a boat, or ark, made of bulrushes, across the Mediterranean from Alexandria, Egypt, to Phœnicia, Palestine ; and the Taliesin sun was, it appears, sent annually as a babe in a coracle from Arkle (Ark Place) or Arklow, Ireland, across the channel to Borth, Cardigan Bay!—Myses-Bacchus was two horned— his *membrum virilis* made a third; Moses is represented with two horns of light, radiating from his forehead (\|/) and his " rod " makes a third. Dr. Adam Clarke, in his *Commentary on the Bible*, has the following :—" Bacchus is expressly said to have been exposed on the river Nile, hence he is also called Nilus, both by Diodorus and Macrobius; and in the hymns of Orpheus, he is named Mysus, because he was drawn out of the water. Mysus is said also by Orpheus to be a law-giver." The Druidic Dyvn Wawl Moel Mud (Dunwallo Molmutus), one of the titles of the sun when he is approaching the winter solstice, is said to be the original law-giver of the Ancient Britons, and it was those laws which were revised by King Howell the Good and his Council of Wales in A.D. 930.

Mysus-Bacchus is described as being accompanied by a dog. Moses was accompanied by Caleb, which is the Hebrew for dog. Snakes were sacrificed to Bacchus. Bacchus killed the serpent Python. Moses also experienced troubled with the fiery serpents in the wilderness, and erected on a pole, generally represented in the form of a cross, a brazen one, to counteract the venom of the fiery ones. It came down to the time of Hezekiah, who, because the people had made an idol of it, called it in derision, Nehushtan (a Trifle of Brass). "A triple serpent of brass, formerly in the temple of Apollo at Delphi, is still extant at Constantinople"—Calmet. St. George killing the dragon implies the same thing as Apollo slaying the serpent, viz., the sun destroying the power of winter. Like the two serpents, one on each side of the sun's disc on the temples of Egypt, the Druids had two serpents in their symbolical religious system. Those two are still to be seen opposing each other on the caduceus, or cross, of Mercury. Mercury stands on the terrestial equator facing the east, as the minister of the Gods, and the serpent which is opposite his left hand is a golden serpent (St. George) and represents the power of summer; the serpent opposite his right hand is a Red Dragon (Mars) representing the power of winter or destruction. They accord with the penitent and the impenitent thieves, one on each side of the cross of the Lord Jesus. The penitent one must have been on his right hand and the impenitent on his left hand.

Bacchus is represented as having been attacked, whilst asleep, by a *two-headed serpent*. In Welsh, the name of

Avagddu is really compounded of Y (the) Vagu—from Magu (to nurse)—and Du (darkness). It actually seems as if the V, the initial letter of "Vagu."—a mutated form of the verb to nurse—has been used heiroglyphically to set forth symbolically a two headed serpent. *Two-headed* because the evil spirit has no generative function to perform as has the middle rod of \V/, and therefore, he is represented minus the *membrum virilis* implied by the middle stroke of the symbol \V/. The middle stroke of the sign has been explained. The wings of the dove and wren, in each case, describe the span of the eastern heavens from the tropic of Capricornus to the tropic of Cancer, as the empire of spiritual influence, apart from the virile attribute, passing through the sun in the spring time.

CHAPTER XX.

MOSES, JOSHUA, AND JESUS.

THE Druids believed that Annwn (Egypt of the Hebrew allegory,) is the source of all incorporeal existences, as it was originally of the sun and the earth, and that the sun—Mysus, whose government was afterwards transferred to Young Joshua (Jesus)—was born of Cêd (Nun—a Fish) by the power of his Father Iôn, that is to say, the Almighty Himself. Afterwards Iôn and Cêd (Latona), otherwise Cetus, Der Ketos, Nun (Dolphin?), continued to propagate lives, and those lives by the influence of warmth everywhere derived from the sun, were raised into within the sphere of the operation of natural laws, to be there clothed with bodies. Bodies were referred to by the Druids as if they were cages for souls. Enclosing the life in the body of the sun and of human beings, each in a body, is the first act of the Creator and His Consort Cêd, called, also, the Black Virgin. The second act is the dissolution of that human body by death, and the liberation of the imprisoned vital spark—hence the Welsh name for death is *anghau* (unshutting)—to occupy in another body, in another state of purely spiritual existence, to which, by his actions during his corporeal life, he had qualified himself during his existence as a man on earth, which was deemed a state of probation, as a free agent, and with perfect liberty of will.

The following lines of Pope as to the state of the human will, according to Druidism is correctly stated: The Creator

" Binding nature fast in fate, left free the human will."

The Latin poet, Lucan, must have thoroughly understood what the Druids taught regarding death, for he states :—

> But forth they fly immortal in their kind,
> And other bodies in new worlds they find,
> Thus life for ever runs its endless race,
> And like a *line*, death but divides the space :
> A stop which can but for a moment last,
> A point between the future and the past.

In Druidism, the "wilderness" is this life ; the *line* between the present and the future life eternal is compared to the terrestial equinoctial *line*, dividing winter and summer.—This "line" is the River of Life, along which the Eternal Father, through the sun in spring, pours forth his fertilising wealth into the material earth, revivifying the seeds in it along its banks. But the Druidic river of *spiritual lives*, apart from the river of animal lives (the Equator) which they regarded as identical with the anima in the material substances, was the solstitial colure, running north and south like the Jordan river, wherein the Hebrews practised baptism of *re*-generation. "Jesus answered and said unto him, Verily, Verily, I say unto thee, except a man be born again, he cannot see the Kingdom of God. Nicodemus saith unto him, How can a man be born again when he is old? Jesus answered, Except a man be born of water and of the spirit, he cannot enter into the Kingdom of God." By the "water" is to be understood Cêd, Cetus, Dolphin (Delphus—womb)—the Font of the Church—Der Ketos, in the sea; by the "Spirit" is to be understood the Creator Celi, under his title of Iôn (Leader). The Jordan is used to prefigure the sea and the two rivers of life—the natural and the spiritual ones.

We would direct the attention of the reader to the fact, that although the Jews, on entering under the leadership of Joshua or Jesus, stood to the east of Jericho, and used a ram's horn—that of the Ram of the Zodiac—as a symbol of the Almighty's power, yet their aid is represented not as a Ram (Aries), but as a *Divine Man*, who called himself the "Captain of the Host of the Lord."—Joshua v., 13 & 14. This implies the Lamb-Ram as humanised, as the Greeks also did with the Ram, and called him Jupiter, leaving the horns on his head.

It will be observed that all of Bacchus' victories are said to be in the "East." It is when the sun is rising in spring due east (in the sign of the Ram) in Britain, he is a conqueror over all the powers of winter and decay.

The multitudes following in Moses', that is to say, Bacchus' train, through the Red Sea—"Red" because in the local Solar drama it was into it he, the old goat Pan, otherwise, old Silenus (Moses of the year before) had bled from the wounds he had received from Typhon, in the heavens, as already described—following in his train, are souls and the abundances springing from the earth after him, or succeeding his fostering influence, at night. He is described as the earliest of law-givers, because he is the causitor of the union of life with matter, and law and order, or a truce in spring, between light and darkness, and between life and death in the vegetable kingdom.

> " And lastly came cold February, sitting
> In an old waggon, for he could not ride,
> Drawn by two fishes (Pisces) for the season fitting,
> *Which through the flood* before did softly glide,
> And swim away.
> After these there came day and night,
> Riding together both with equal pace—(March 21)
> Th' one on a palfrey black the other white,
> But night had cover'd her uncomely face
> With a Black Veil, and held in hand a mace (sceptre)
> On top whereof the moon and stars were pight (fixed),
> And sleep and darkness round about did trace (move).
> But Day did bear upon his sceptre's height
> The goodly Sun encompassed all with beamès bright."
>
> *The Faerie Queen*, Canto vii., p. 552

THE FLIGHT OF THE JEWS FROM EGYPT.

According to Druidism, the Exodus of the Hebrews from Egypt is simply an old solar allegory, dressed up. Egypt is Hades or Erebus, the Annwn of the Druids. Pharaoh is Satan.   Aaron and Moses are Arawn (the diurnal old sun), and Mysus-Bacchus (Silenus) — the nocturnal sun grown old.   The Children of Israel are the progeny or children of the sun and earth.   Pharaoh's Egyptian army are the myrmidons of black Hades. Miriam—Mary—Mother—is the Myrrah of the Phœniceans, here correctly given as the *sister* of the sun under his dual title of Arawn' (Elijah—Shabbetha, or Jah is Saturn,[1] and Saturn is Arawn) and Mysus-Bacchus, or Aaron and Moses.

We explain elsewhere the cause of confounding Myrrah (Venus, Mor'wyn, &c.,) with Cèd.   The Red Sea is the Sea of Annwn or Hades, out of which the young sun and his sister ascend on every December 22nd.   The song of Moses and the sweet sopranoïmic vocal reply of Miriam, are the young Sun and Venus-Maid, or the young Earth's Anima, replying to each other, as explained elsewhere in this book.

The "Wilderness" is the journey of the sun upwards from the winter solstice to the celestial equinoctial line. That line is symbolised by the Jordan, and the land flowing with milk and honey—symbolised by Palestine—is the whole earth, above the rational horizon, when the sun is to the north of the equator during the summer months.   It symbolises also crossing the river into Heaven.

The music of the golden bells around the skirt of the high priest symbolise the same thing as the song of the newly born Moses, echoed back by newly born Miriam, his " sister." both having just ascended from the sea.

[1] Dr. Inman's, vol. II., p. 504.

Observe the following very remarkable facts :—

The Hebrew sacred year begins really at the time of the year when the sun entered the first point of the sign of the Ram (east) ;

The last thing the Hebrews are said to have done before leaving Egypt was killing the Ram of the Passover ;

When they crossed the Jordan into Palestine, their first act was erecting a stone circle of twelve stones, after the Druidic model (Joshua iv.) :

On 14th Nisan—but adding 11 days to be solar,—our March 25th, o.s., they slew the Ram of the Passover (Joshua v. 10) ;

Then came the Jericho horrors, dwelt upon elsewhere.

As stated above, the Jordan river is used also as a figure for the equator, with the Ram sign at its eastern point, which the sun crosses on the first day of spring—March 21-25, the time of the Passover—on his journey northward to the summer region. It will be remembered that the Jordan flows into the "Dead" Sea, and, in the allegory, two ideas are conveyed by that, namely, the sun setting on the shortest day of winter in the south-west, and the sun setting in the exact west on March 21st—25th ; both west and south were supposed in the ancient creeds to be the directions of the regions into which the dying depart, and where follows a period of "rest" for the people of God.

Jericho signifies the *end* of winter, and its walls falling at the blast of the Ram's (Aries) horn—not Rams'—is winter coming to an end, when the sun in those distant days entered the zodiacal sign of the Ram (first point of Aries) on March 21-25, the season when the Jews held their Passover, and killed the Paschal lamb—the Egyptian Jupiter Amon, or Hu Father Amen (Hidden).

R

It is interesting to note that, according to the book of
Joshua—son of Fish (Nun), Hesus, Hesous, or Jesus—
the first act the Jews are recorded as performing after
crossing the Jordan, the river where regeneration was
symbolised, was, as pointed out above, erecting a great
stone circle of twelve stones, after the Druidic model, and
that they named it Gilgal, or Stone Circle, "on the east
border of Jericho," and, therefore, *opposite the sign of the
Ram or Lamb of the Zodiac.*   Joshua, their leader into
the land flowing with milk and honey, signifies, and is
actually called, Hesus, or Jesus, exactly as the Druids
described the sun as Hu (Hea) Gadarn or Hesus the Mighty,
or Taliesin—son of the skin-covered coracle (Cêd, Cetus,
or Great Fish in the East)—leading from winter across
the equinoctial line into the upper region of spring and
summer.

The "crossing of the Jordan" took place on the 10th
day of Nisan (March O.S.).   The lunar year being eleven
days shorter than the solar one, Nisan 10th is made to
mean March 21st (O.S.), the date the sun was in Aries,
the very time of the year the sun "crosses" the equinoctial
line northwards, and Nisan 14th corresponds with March
25th, the time of the Roman vernal equinox.

It is very remarkable to find that the Druids believed all
incorporeal lives, or existences, were drawn from Gwenydva
of Annwn, or of Hades, by the sun, on his re-appearance
ascending from low down in the south-east on Dec. 22nd,
when, each year, he enters the Zodiacal sign of the Goat or
Pan, and of Bacchus-Moäses.   He, as the old sun of
the year before, is known also as old Pan, whose lower
extremities is a he-goat.—In spring he is identical
too, with Zeus, Jove, Jupiter, Tegid, Hermes, Thoth, Tal-

Father, Alawn, Mercury, &c. In allusion to the exercise of the sun's virile power in spring, that was the season of the year when each Roman child was permitted, for the first time, to don the Toga Virilis, as a sign that he also had attained puberty, or the state of manhood.

Minerva (Divine Mind or Wisdom) is identical with Cêd consort of the Almighty Celi, with whom (Celi) Jupiter and Zeus are frequently confounded in the literature of Greece and Rome. As the mother of the goat-headed babe sun Mysus-Bacchus, on December 22nd, Minerva is represented with a she-goat's breast (Ægus). We repeat, the crescent boat, often confounded with the crescent moon, was one of her symbols. As a roamer of the sea, under the titles of Cêd, Delphus or Dolphin, &c., Minerva is represented with fishes in her hair. As reflecting Divine Wisdom she is also Medusa, with a dignified countenance, and with serpents in her hair.

The Greeks, in their mythological confusion, having misrepresented Zeus, Jupiter, or Jove as the Almighty, represent the Ægus, or goat-skin of Minerva's breast, as "having been taken from the goat which suckled the infant Jupiter," instead of stating the infant Mysus-Bacchus, thus they imply the Almighty Celi of the Druids, or Amen Ra of Egypt, was suckled by a goat in his infancy.

The apparent mistake of stating Jupiter in his infancy was suckled by a she-goat, is due to the practice of representing the infant sun as Jupiter instead of as kid goat-headed Bacchus-Moüses on December 22nd, and calling him Jupiter, in spring only.

"THE GREAT PAN IS DEAD!"

It is stated by Plutarch (A.D. 66—106) that in the reign of Tiberius Cæsar (42 B.C. to A.D. 37) a voice was heard in the Ionian Sea, saying the words—"The Great Pan is Dead!" And Eusebius states the said voice was a supernatural one, and that God was pleased by that means to announce to the world the death of the Messiah, which happened in the reign of Tiberius Cæsar.

Thus Eusebius, who flourished in the reign of the Emperor Constantine, will have it that Pan, otherwise Arawn, Saturn, Silenus, Jupiter (wrongly placed), and the Messiah, were different names of the same person! Pan was the old sun personified, and if the Messiah in his death was that old sun, Eusebius is right (*See* Romans vi., 6).

Pan, we are told, assumed the guise of a Ram, this simply implies the sun going from the sign of the Goat to that of a Ram (Decr. 22nd and March 21st respectively). As a Ram he is Jupiter. In that guise he charmed Luna, or the Moon. Here the crescent moon as symbol of Cêd as the Llong Voel—Boat of the Sun, as his refuge when he falls into the sea, December 20th in Druidism, and March 24th in the East—is meant. But the Llong Voel (Crescent Boat) is a symbol of Cêd (Der Ketos, otherwise Delphus—Womb) Consort of the Celi. Thus Pan, when it is said he charmed Luna or Latona, is substituted for the Creator, instead of stating he is his son, but an old man in each December. "Pan," states Mythologist, "was of a very amorous disposition." Cupid was his rival, but Cupid was the author of the sentiment of love apart from sensuality. Pan, *as Jupiter*, was the Seminal Logos.

NEPTUNE CONFOUNDED WITH SATURN OR OLD PAN.

>   ⁕   ⁕   ⁕   "To win Deucalion's daughter⁕ bright,
> He turned himself into a Dolphin† fair :
> And like a winged horse ("Archer") he took to flight,

⁕ Morwyn, Isis H., Venus, Myrrah, Mary, the Church.

† Delphus (Womb) confounding Cêd with Saturn or Pan, the same as in the case of Dagon—Oannes the Man-Fish.

To snaky-lock Medusa to repair,
Of whom he got fair Pegasus that flitteth in the air (Apollo).
Next Saturn was (but who would ween
That sullen Saturn ever ween'd to love ?
Yet love is sullen, and Saturn-like seen,
As he did for Philyra it prove),
That to a Centaur did himself transform.
When, for to compass Philyra's hard love,
He turned himself into a fruitful vine (Myses-Bacchus)
And into her fair bosom made his grapes decline."

Faerie Queen, Canto xi., p. 439.   Nimmo's Ed.

" I am the true Vine, and my Father is the husbandman."

The old sun is in Sagittarius, otherwise Archer and
Centaur, from November 22nd to December 22nd.

    *   *   " Next chill December,
Yet he, through merry feasting which he made,
And great bonfires, did not the cold remember :
His Saviour's birth his mind so much did glad.
Upon a Shaggy-Bearded Goat he rode—
The same wherewith Dan Jove* in tender years,
They say, was nourished by th' Idaean Maid :
And in his hand a broad deep bowl he bears,‡
Of which he freely drinks a health to all his Peers.

Ibid. p. 552.

The "Idaean Maid" is goat-breasted Minerva (Divine
Wisdom,) she and Dolphin (Delphus—Womb) are identical
with Ced.

" THE VIRGIN OF ISRAEL."

We must here mention certain things of importance,
which we omitted in the proper place.

The Ox, by which is meant the Sacred Bull Apis of
Egypt (Taurus Sun in spring), and the Ram-Lamb—Jupiter

---

* Jupiter.
† Silenus, Old Myses-Bacchus or Noah, or sun in the ninth Sign of the
Zodiac.

Amon of Egypt (Aries Sun in spring), both referred to as the sacred things of the Egyptians, but which were "abominations" in the eyes of the Hebrews themselves, were ordered as sacrifices, to be eaten by them.

Things regarded by the Jews themselves as *abominable* were offered in sacrifice to the God of Israel! And to further show their contempt for the Apis and Jupiter Amon, holy symbols of the Egyptians, they are eaten by the Jews, and so defiled. But it was not lawful for the children of Israel to eat the flesh of swine. Swine were in Egypt sacred to Typhon or the Devil. "Among the Egyptians, those who could not afford to sacrifice real pigs had images of them in paste served up at the feasts of Bacchus or Osiris.[1]" He further states, it seems to have been done "to honour and conciliate the productive power of the sun by the symbolical destruction" of the porcine symbol of his (sun's) enemy. If eating the flesh of the Ram-Lamb and the Bull was done in derision of the symbols of the Egyptian mediatorial character of the sun, refraining from eating the flesh of swine by the Jews was the reverse.

In Exodus xiii and Numbers xxviii, it is seen that the Ram-Lamb, the Bull (called "Ox"), and two Goats are to be offered in sacrifice. *See also* Lev. xvi. The sun in spring is the masculine cause of the earth's *fermentation.* The Jews killed now that sun's symbol, and strictly ordered that no *leavened bread*, that is to say, *bread made from fermented dough, should be touched.* Only Mazzoth or unfermented, called "unleavened" bread, was lawful to be eaten. Can it be doubted all this meant, conciliating the *destroying power*, the foe of the creating Deity, who created by means of the productive principle of fermentation?

---

[1] Payne Knight. *Sym. Language.* s. 123.   Quoted from Plutarch's *De Carne Orat.* 1.

Now, observe, on the 14th Nisan, which commences at sunset on our March 13th (O.S.), two bulls and a ram, and seven other ram-lambs—eight in all—are ordered to be sacrificed. Add eleven days to bring up the lunar year of Israel to the solar year of the Egyptians, &c., and we have March 24th, the eve of the vernal equinox of the Julian Calendar, when the Jewish day following commences. But add seven days of the feast, regulated by the lunar year, and we arrive at March 20th, or the eve of March 21st, the astronomical vernal equinox. The eighth lamb appears to be added for both the 21st and 25th. Let the reader refer to the signs of the zodiac, and he will find that the signs of the Ram-Lamb (Aries), and that of the Bull (Taurus), are side by side in the eastern heavens at the time of the Passover of the Hebrews. It is the beginning of their *sacred year.*—Numbers xxviii., 19.

Let the reader now refer to Leviticus xvi., and he will find the sacrifices to be made are offered at the beginning of the Hebrew *civil year*, which is in the month Tisri (September), signalled by the Day of Atonement. In verse 3 we are told the sacrifices here, also, are a bull, a ram, and he-goats. It is the period of the autumnal equinox. Let the reader again refer to the signs of the zodiac, and he will see that the signs of the Ram (Aries) and the Bull (Taurus) —in September and October—are side by side in the *western heavens*, and the sign Virgo, or Virgin, is in the *eastern heavens*. But that is not all. On Dec. 22nd, the beginning of the solar year, the sun enters the sign of the He-Goat—the reader will recollect the old sun as old Pan Goat and the young sun re-appearing, afterwards, as the babe Bacchus, with the head of a goat. In addition to the bull and the ram, the Hebrews also sacrificed two he-goats (father and son) on the Day of Atonement.—Lev. xvi., 15.

Having thus killed the bull (Apis), the ram (Jupiter Amon), and the two he-goats (Pan and young Bacchus), the high priest, as Aaron (Arawn—sun), entered the west entrance of the Holy Place, symbolising the descent of the old sun through the sign of the Ram on the western horizon, as an old man. He then, with the blood of the "gods" of the Gentiles in his hand, passed, symbolically, below the earth, through the symbolical Hades—the Holy of Holies —and re-appeared in the east, passing there from Virgo of the Zodiac—the Virgin of Israel.

THE GARDEN OF THE SUN.

The Garden of Hesperus, like the Garden of Adonis, Phœbus, &c., signified the whole earth above the horizon, the symbol in the west being Britain itself, then each Druidic Circular Sanctuary, the principal ones in Britain being Avebury (Bryn Gwyddon or Odin's Hill), and Stonehenge (Côr Gawr—the Giant's Choir), Wilts. What did Hercules discover in the Garden of Hesperus? Three daughters of Hesperus. (*See* page 14.)

THREE HU'S.

This is the proper place to state there are three Hu's in Druidism, viz., Hu Cylch y Ceugant (Circle of Infinitude); Hu Cylch y Sidydd (Hu of the Circle of the Zodiac); and Hu yn Nghnawd (Hu Incarnate), signifying the Archdruid in his Circular Sanctuary on Earth, or, on the Mount, otherwise Garden of the Sun or Hesperus.

The next object Hercules discovered in the British Garden of the Sun, was, that it was guarded by an enormous serpent. This was another symbol of Cêd, as Divine Wisdom, known also as Anima of the Earth, and signifying Anian, that is to say, life pervading matter ascending from below through the earth, and symbolised in many ways, chiefly by the serpent, 2½ miles long, at Avebury, Wilts.

APPLES OF PARADISE OR ENCLOSED GARDEN.

The next things Hercules found in this celebrated Garden of the Sun, were, a tree, a serpent entwined around it, and three golden apples on the said tree. Here we have similar objects to those described as being in the Garden of Eden, namely, a tree, a serpent and apples! Not only did the serpent of the Garden of Hesperus guard the garden, but also the particular tree on which were the three Golden Apples.[1]

THE BLESSED ISLES OF THE WEST.

Efforts are being made by some authors to prove that some lost islands in the Atlantic Ocean are meant by the Atlantis, Fortunate Isles, Blessed Isles of the West, Islands of the Blessed, Garden of the Hesperides, &c. In the XI. Book of the *Odyssey* Homer designates the western-most part of the British Isles—Kymmri (Cymri), Wales—by the name Kimmeria (Cambri) to localise " old ocean's *utmost bound*," clearly showing that, in his time, no land in the west beyond Kymmeria (Wales) was known. Referring to Kimmeria as being in the direction of the setting sun, from Greece, he makes the high priest, whom he (Homer) names the Mighty Theban, or Mighty Arkite, ask Ulysses, who had landed there—

> " Why, mortal, wanderest thou from cheerful day,
>   To tread the downward, melancholy, way ? "

—the way of the setting sun.

It is very strange, and illustrating how very ignorant respecting the annals of their own country, many otherwise learned Englishmen are, that English authors suppose Kimmeria—Cimbri and Cimmerii—are not where all antiquity, including Homer's writings, point they are, but will have it they are in Germany.

---

[1] Bell's *Pantheon*, "Twelve labours of Hercules."

Plutarch, in his *Lives* v i., p. 454, announces the Cimbri were Celts. It is well known the Celts were divided into many tribes or clans, and Plutarch states that they, the Celts, were distinguished by different, or a variety of, names, according to their tribes ; that their whole body is comprehended under the general name Celto—Scythae. He also further refers to them under the name Kimmerians, and states what he had heard, namely, that "The greater and more warlike part of them dwelt *in the extremities of the earth*, near the northern sea." Afterwards he describes the natural characteristics of the Cimmerii or Cimbri (Welsh) as follows :—"As to their courage, their spirit, and the force and vivacity with which they make an impression, we may compare them to a devouring flame. Nothing could resist their impetuosity ; all that came in their way were trodden down, and driven before them like cattle" (p. 455). How nobly the united British nation, animated by the ancient Cimbric (Welsh) blood, still sustain the unconquerable characteristics of their remote ancestors !

All who are familiar with the physical and mental characteristics of the genuine Celts, will recognise in the words of Plutarch a correct description of them.

Like the ancient Greeks, who ruined history by their fables, so the English people, in our day, ruin history by wrongly interpretating ancient names. For instance, they pronounce Cimrii "Simrii," Cimbri "Simbri," and Celt "Selt"! "Salt" would be a more appropriate name than "Selts" for them. The C in ancient languages, and in Welsh among the rest, is sounded hard, as in the English word "come."

All common nouns in Welsh are remarkable for the poetical ideas which they are intended to convey, and those who are guilty of the gross barbarity of shattering these picturesque ancient names, are precisely on the same low level, as regards intelligence, as those " unspeakable Turks " who, at Athens, shot away with their guns splinters from the marble sculptures of Phidias !

As already intimated, Celi (Hidden) was the supreme title which the Druids gave to the Creator, and, doubtless, it represents the same idea, as to the incomprehensibleness of the nature of the Creator Himself, as the *Agnosto Theo* of the Athenians, the *Ignoto Deo* of the Latins, and the *Amen Ra* of the Egyptians; for, it is to be understood, all the other gods and the goddesses of Paganism were simply poetical personifications of the emanations of the Most High, but unknown, God, and his consort Ced, who, however are revealed, by their attributes, through the sun and earth, and made manifest to humanity by the operations of nature, under the influence of the sun and earth, hence the Druidic proverb, " The voice of God is heard in the voice of Nature or Anima."

The Cimbri were called Celts because the name of their God was Celi, as the Brahmins are so called because they worshipped Brahma.

A nation, calling the country which they inhabit Cymmry (pronounced Kymre), and the entire inhabitants calling themselves Cymmry (Cymmru—First from the Womb), in spelling simply changing the last letter from *u* to *y* (i) to distinguish between the name of the country and the name of their race, still inhabit a country which *is* in the extreme west of the old world, as it was known to the ancients, and down till the time of the discovery of the western continent of America by Columbus, towards the close of the fifteenth century. That country is Wales.

The inhabitants of Wales (Cambria) have an unbroken, or continuous, history of that country for upwards of eighteen centuries. Scholars know, by linguistic evidence, that the same language is spoken in Wales at the present day as was spoken there in 52 A.D., when the Roman commander, Ostorius, and his legions, landed there on the shores of Monmouthshire. A Roman historian, Tacitus, names South Wales "Siluria," which is the Welsh, or Cymric, name Ysyllwg Latinised. The Romans referred to the inhabitants of South Wales as Silurii; the inhabitants refer to themselves still by the appellation Ysyllwr (plural) and Ysyllwr (singular). In Welsh alone Siluria (Ysyllwg) is etymologically understood. The name signifies Green Prospects, or Views, and it is a correct description of the green plains of South Wales. The Romans referred to West Wales by the name Demetia, which is the name Dyved, Latinised. Dyvid is a Welsh abbreviation of Deiviad, which signifies, the Dwellers on the Teivi River. North Wales is named Ordovia by the Latin historians; it is the Welsh name Ardyvi, which signifies "On the Dovey" river, Latinised.

The great Cambro-British commander against the Roman advance into England is named Caractacus by Tacitus. We know that that form of the name is a corrupt one for Caradawg, which signifies Full of Love. In the original form of that name there is an *i* to be after the *r*. The Welsh, themselves, state that their tribal name, Cymry, signifies First-Born, and that the correct form of the name is Cyn-mru; Cyn (First) and Bru—*e* sound to *u*—(Womb) signifying, the earliest of the nations of the earth.

The Welsh name of Britain as a whole is Brydain, and is a compound of two words: Bryd (feature) and Cain (fair), the C dropped in the compound, for the sake of euphony, a common practice with the bards. Cain, a title of the sun, signifies fair; and he is called, in Druidism, Prydain, but the island as his Consort and is called Brydain, which the Romans Latinised into the form Britannia, and both the masculine and feminine names— that of the sun and that of the island—signify Fair Featured. England, standing by herself, was, and is still, known to the Welsh people by the name Lloegr—from Lloer, the Welsh name for the Moon; and has undoubtedly reference to the Arkite rites once practised there by the Druids— doubtless at Avebury and Stonehenge, Wiltshire, and on the Severn principally. We think it is Whittaker, in his most valuable and learned work, entitled "The History of Manchester," but which is really much more than that, who states, the inhabitants of Britain, at the time of the Roman invasions, were divided into many tribes. To this day the throne of imperial authority is named in Welsh, Gorsedd, which name signifies Great Throne or Sedd, and implying greatest or principal Throne. A subordinate state is called Talaeth, and a diadem, frontlet or head-band, is named Talaith; while a crown is named Coron, which seems to be a name closely allied with Corn (Welsh for Horn), used, in ancient time, to symbolise royal power, authority, or strength.—*See* Psalm 148, v. 14, Daniel viii., v. 5. In the last referred to, we have an allusion to the Infant Bacchus as a Kid Goat on December 22nd. Doubtless some will be inclined to state Coron is derived from Greek Corone, Latin Corona (Garland), but the Celtic tongue is now admitted to be older than all other European languages, and, there- fore, the probability is the Greek and the Latin names are derived from the ancient British one. The above two names prove the existence in Britain, in ancient times, of both imperial and tribal, provincial or state authorities, and that the tribal was subordinate to a throne of thrones.

It is a singular fact, however, that, so far as we are
aware, in none of the Roman historical annals, relating to
the Roman occupation of Britain, does the native name of
Wales, namely, Cymmru (e), occur in reference to Wales
itself.   It appears that the Roman writers, when referring
to Wales as a whole, designated it Britannia Secunda or
second Britain, and "the utmost bounds of the west."
When the earliest ecclesiastical writers, immediately
succeeding the apostolic age, such as Clemens Romanus,
the friend and fellow-worker of St. Paul, refer to Wales'
geographical position, in relation to the rest of Britannia,
they define it as being in "the utmost bounds of the west,"
which is perfectly accurate as the world was known at that
period; but we may probably have a further explanation
as to the reason why the Roman historians made no
mention of Cymmru (Wales,) by that name in the fact that
they had designated the inhabitants of Wales, Silurians,
Demetians, and Ordovians, and felt that, by employing an
additional collective name, to distinguish the inhabitants of
Wales apart from other Britons, they would encumber
British nomenclature to such a degree as to cause confusion.   Therefore, to convey that Wales was a distinct
country, and still connected with Britannia Prima, they
gave to it the appellation of Britannia Secunda, and also
" the utmost bounds of the west."

Another reason which may have influenced the Roman
writers to abstain from employing the name Cymmru to
distinguish Wales is that they found in the north of
Britannia Prima a powerful tribe who named themselves,
like the inhabitants of Wales, Cymmry or Cymmru, a
certain sign the inhabitants of both districts of Great
Britain gave their names to their respective localities, and
not the localities to them.   The locality in the north of

England, to which we refer, is now named Cumberland and Northumberland now counties of England, whose place names are still pure Welsh, very slightly mis-spelt.

Camden states that Marinus names Cumberland, Cumbrorum Terra, the land of the Cumbri. It is a striking fact that the British tribe bearing the name of Cymmry, the Cimbri of Plutarch, called also Cimmerians, "dwelling in the extremities of the earth," and whose march is compared to "a devouring flame," were the last to yield, even conditionally, to Saxon and Norman aggressions. In fact the Cymry of Wales did not yield until a Prince of Wales was appointed, and until afterwards one of their own race, Henry the Seventh (Henry Tudor) ascended the throne of Great Britain. Towards the close of the sixth century, while all the rest of England, in the face of native rebellion in England, assisted by Saxon aggression, most of England had succumbed to the foreign enemy, Cumberland and Northumberland (North Cumberland) held out until the great national engagement of Cattraeth (Cad--Traeth), near the Solway Firth, which is the subject of the great poem of Prince Poet Aneurin, viz., Gododin (Cad—Odin)—Battle of Odin, from Gwyddon, one of the titles of the Archdruid—which is the oldest poem extant in the Welsh language. In that battle most of the Welsh Britons of the east and middle of England appear to have united their forces with those of the Saxons against the Cymmry of both provinces, viz.: those of the north of England and Wales. The furious battle lasted seven days, and those of the Welsh Britons who escaped, like the princely bard, Aneurin, retired into Wales, where he found an asylum at the monastery of Cattwg, Llancarvan, near Cowbridge, Glamorgan, and where it is probable the poem was composed.

The leading tribe of the heroic British, Cymmric, or Cambrian, nation, once the terror of Europe, has always held its own and still dwells in Wales, maintaining there its ancient language, ancient literature, old customs, and national institutions; and in the valleys of Wales are still often heard the charming ancient melodies of the minstrels of the ancient Britons.

Homer flourished at least 800 years before the Christian era, and, as we have shown, he refers to the Cimbri, or Cimmrii, dwelling in Cimmeria, or Wales, even then, and he describes it as—

> " In old Ocean's utmost bounds,
> Where rocks control his waves with ever-during mounds."

How people have been so misled as to suppose that country is in Germany, or in Little Tartary, we are at a loss to conceive.

Hecataeus, of Miletus, writing 600 B.C., states: " In the regions over against Celtica (France) there is in the ocean an island not smaller than Sicilly; this island is situated below the constellation of the Bear (Ipsi Ursae Subjectam) —it is above our habitation now—and is inhabited by men called Hyperboreans, because they are placed beyond the blast of Boreas (North Wind). The land, being fertile, produces everything necessary, and, enjoying a fine temperature, produces two crops a year." " Now they " mythologists " state Latona " Ced, as Lleuad (Crescent Moon) " was born there, and that on that account Apollo " her son " is honoured by them above all other gods. That among them " Hyperboreans " there are some men, priests, as it were, of Apollo, and that consequently he is daily and continuously hymned by them with lyric songs, and exceedingly honoured.

There is also in the island, both a consecrated precinct of great magnificence (Avebury ?), and a temple of corresponding beauty (Stonehenge ?), adorned with numerous dedicated gifts, and in shapes spherical. That there is also a city (old Sarum ?) sacred to to the god, and they greatly magnify his deeds. They also state the Hyperboreans have a peculiar dialect, and are very kindly disposed to the Hellenes, and especially to the Athenians and Delians, and that they have inherited this friendly feeling from ancient times. They also state that some of the Hellenes have passed over to the Hyperboreans, and have left precious dedicated gifts there, bearing Hellenic inscriptions; that in the same manner Abaris, in a former age, had passed into Helles, and renewed, with the Delians, the bond of friendship and consanguinity. They also say the moon from this island appears to be not far distant from the earth, and clearly shows certain earthly eminences. It is also said that every nineteenth year the god descends into this island. Now every nineteenth year certain returns of the stars to fixed positions takes place, and on this account a period of nineteen years is called, by the Hellenes, the Great Year. That when the god (Apollo) makes his periodical appearances, he both plays the harp and dances during the night, from the vernal equinox " March 21st, " to the rising of the Pleiades " Taurus, on April 20th, 1891, " taking great delight in his own successful efforts."

Payne Knight, referring to the above passage, states: " This island can be no other than Britain." Knight also quotes Hecatæus as follows : " The Hyperboreans inhabit an island beyond Gaul (France) in which Apollo is worshipped in a circular temple considerable for its size and riches." Diodorus Siculus, who quotes the above from the writings of Hecatæus, flourished in 44 B.C.

S

It will be recollected that the name of England in Welsh, to this day, signifies the Land of the Moon, and the Archdruid was, symbolically, a personification of the sun, or Apollo; his circular church, with an oval symbol in its centre like the moon six days old, was the symbol of Cêd, as an ancient-shaped boat riding the Sea of Chaos.

CHAPTER XXI.

HERODOTUS in his *Melpomene* (Sec. 8), describing Hercules (Sun) driving away the Cows of Geryon (Gwron), or the name of the last of the three personifications of the sun, given to the sun collectively among the British Druids, and located at the winter solstice, states, "Hercules came to the region now inhabited by the Scythians, but which then was a desert."

Abaris, priest of the sun, is called by Suidas, a Scythian, and that he came from the Hyperborean *Island* to the north of Gaul (France).

Higgins states, Colonel Vallencey has proved as clear as the sun at noon, that the ancient gods of the Greeks came from the Hyperboreans (Druidic Britons).

We now proceed with the quotation of Herodotus: "This Geryon (Gwron—Hero, like Arthur and St. George) lived beyond Pontus" (Black Sea), "in an *island*, which the Greeks called Erytha, near Gades" (Cadiz—Spain), "which is situate in the ocean, and beyond the Columns of Hercules" (Gibraltar).

Here we have it stated, "Erythia is an island in the ocean near Cadiz, and to the west of Gibraltar." It is remarkable that no writer has ever noticed the resemblance between Erythia and Brythia, that is to say, Britain. The Welsh, to this day, frequently style themselves Brythians or Brythoniad, "Tra mor, tra Brython, oes y byd i'r iaith Gymraeg," which signifies, "While there is a sea, and

s 2

while there is a Brythian, the age of the world to the Welsh language?" It seems certain that some translator of Herodotus into English, or some other transcriber of the original Greek text, mistook the Greek initial B for the Greek E, and mistakenly placed E instead of B as the initial letter of Brythia, and therefore misled the world.

We are further told by the Father of History, that Hercules, going *westward*, arrived at this country, " now," he states, " called Scythia," where, finding himself over-taken by a severe storm, and being exceedingly cold, he wrapped himself in his lion skin, and went to sleep. They add that his mares, which he had detached from his chariot to feed, by some divine interposition disappeared during his sleep. The sun as a chariot drawn by fiery steeds, with Hercules or Apollo standing in the chariot of the sun, guiding the reins of the steeds, is familiar to everybody. " As soon as he (Hercules) awoke he wandered all over the country in search of his mares, till at length he came to a district called Hylaea." The Atlantic is called Heli, or Haul—le, by the Welsh. The name signifies the Place of the Sun, and alludes to the direction he sets into the ocean in the evening. " There," the story goes on, " in a cave." (See p. 27) " he discovered a female of a most unnatural appearance, resembling a woman as far as the thighs, but the lower parts were like a serpent. Hercules beheld her with astonishment, but he was not deterred from asking her whether she had seen his mares. She answered, they were in her custody. She, however, refused to restore them but on condition of his cohabiting with her."

It seems that Hercules was equal to the occasion, and the result of the cohabitation was that the dragon woman gave birth to *three sons* (\|/) who were named Agathyrsus, Gelonus, and *Scythia*. Hercules gave instructions that the one of his sons who could bend his father's bow, which he left behind for the trial of strength, should be honoured. Scythia, the *third* son—Gwron (Hero) identical with Arthur and St. George, the third person of the Druidic trinity—was the one of the three who had sufficient strength to bend the bow of his father, Hercules. The lower draconic half of the goddess is symbolical of Ced, as Divine Wisdom ; the human female upper half is symbolical of Venus (Mor'wyn) as a propagator. We have shown elsewhere who were the Atlantides, the seven daughters of Atlas, and also who was Hesper, and also who were his daughters, and what was meant by the garden, and the three apples, &c., of the garden.

We have shown in the preceding pages, the Druids in their Buarth Beirdd (Bovine Enclosure of Bards), meaning the holy circle, had, in the Taurine Sun period, three sacred cows, corresponding with the three bulls, which symbolised the sun on March 21st, June 21st, and December 20th. (*See* page 42). The said three sacred cows are, apparently, the cows of Geyron (Gwron), which Hercules, in the allegory, is said to have driven away. This, like Hercules robbing the three apples from the Garden (Britain) of Hesperides, may be intended to imply that at a certain remote period Greek influence had dominated in Britain or Brythia. In *Religion De Gaulois*, ch. ii., 85, we are informed the God Cernunnos was the heroic protector of the Gauls. Doubtless, Cernunnos is another form of the name Geyron or Gwron (Hero) of the year before.

As regards the serpentine lower extremities of the goddess, we are told by Eusebius the Egyptians worshipped the female Creator as a serpent under the name of Kneph. Nev is another name of Heaven in Druidism. Doubtless Gwenydva (Elysium) is meant.

This serpent encompassing the earth's circle of the rational horizon with tail in its mouth, signifies, states Eusebius, " the good genius," the female Creator.

Then follow certain traditions from the pen of Herodotus, and among them the name Cimmeria occurs repeatedly. We are there told that Scythians settled in Cimmeria (Wales), which statement seems to explain why Abaris, priest of the Sun, and whose learning astonished the Athenians, is described as a Scythian, and yet that he came from the Hyperborean Island, or Britain, within which Cimmeria, or Cambria, is situate.

It is unnecessary, because well known, to point out that the Twelve Labours of Hercules, and the Twelve Battles of Arthur, signify the apparent movement of the sun through the twelve signs of the zodiac annually. It will be observed that Hercules was represented as a destroyer. He is identical with Apollo, who is represented with bow and arrow and quiver, and in the act of shooting, which symbolises the sun shooting his scorching heat during the day. The sun is a nourisher of vegetation by the influence left behind at night by the day sun producing humidity, and that heat operating on the earth's vegetation is called Bacchus.

Now all antiquity refer to the west as the region where the sun, as Hercules or Apollo, ends his daily work. In Druidism the west is designated by two names, namely, " Gorllewin " (great region of the reflection of light), and Gorwel (great bed). It was, therefore, correct, allegorically, to describe Hercules falling asleep therein. As already pointed out, Wales and Ireland were to the ancients the remotest land known to them in the west of Europe, until the discovery of America by Columbus.

AN ANCIENT EISTEDDVOD IN THE ISLES OF THE BLEST.

Homer, three thousand years ago, describes the then known earth, instead of as a mount or as a garden, by the figure of the shield of Achilles,

> "Its utmost verge a threefold circle bound."

Referring to the surface of the shield as a mirror—the face of the earth—Homer writes :—

> "There shone the Image of the Master Mind :"
> There earth, there heaven, there ocean he designed."

He describes the Polar Star as

> "The axle of the sky,
> The Bear revolving points his golden eye."

It will be recollected Diodorus Siculus states the Hyperboreans dwell under the Bear (Ipse Ursae Subjectam). Homer, with a view to indicate land beneath the constellation of the Bear, refers to Ursæ Major as follows—

> "Nor bathes his blazing forehead in the main."

Then the great bard of Greece proceeds to describe the shield itself. Under the figures of two cities he implies that both peace and war were known in the region under the Bear. Referring to peace, Homer actually seems to refer to a Cambro-British Eisteddvod in remote ancient times—

> "The appointed heralds still the noisy bands,
> And form a ring with sceptres in their hands."

Then he describes the Druids acting as judges or adjudicators—

> "On Seats of Stone, within the sacred place,
> The reverend Elders nodded o'er the case.
> Alternate, each the attesting sceptre took,
> And, rising, solemn each his sentence spoke.
> Two golden talents amidst in sight,
> The prize of him who best adjudged the right."[1]

[1] Pope's *Homer's Iliad*, Book XVIII.

The chapter concludes by describing the final completion of the shield, or the earth, by the Creator—

> "Thus the broad shield complete, the Artist crown'd
> With his last hand, and *poured the ocean round* :
> In living silver seem'd the waves to roll."

This is what the encircling moat full of water of the great Druidical circle of Avebury, Wilts, implies, and such a moat is around every sacred mound.   It was anciently believed the ocean formed a border running around the edge of the earth's circle and the Lord's footstool.

Hesiod describes the shield of Hercules, "when," states Coleridge, "we are hurried back to Persus, the Gorgons, and other images of war, over *an arm of the sea*, in which the sporting dolphins, the fugitive fishes, and the fisherman, are minutely represented."   Is that "arm of the sea" the channel between the Continent and Britain?   In the maps of the Homeric geography, the country of Cimmeria is given in the extreme west of Europe, and a little beyond the fabulous entrance into the "infernal regions."   The Greek expression, "Cimmerian gloom," is clearly an ancient poetical one referring to Cimmeria, Cambria, or Wales, as being situate in the remote west of Europe, near the region of the setting sun, and, therefore, near the kingdom of night, according to ancient notions of geography.

Somehow, certain silly writers have sought to prove that Cimmeria is Little Tartary !   But Ovid refers to Cimmeria as the properest place for the Palace of the God of Sleep, because, as it appears according to the Druids, there was the great Bed of the Sun (Gorwely), and there, as we have seen in a preceding page, Hercules did actually fall asleep, and lost his mares, which he had unharnessed, his day's labours being at an end.

Taking the above facts into consideration, we understand why the twelfth " labour " of Hercules is in the west, and why the mythologists describe him in the West of Europe robbing the Garden of Hesperides. The proper name of the west in Latin is *Occidens*, and in Greek Hesperos, and the evening is called in Greek *Hesperos*, and *Vesper* in Latin, and the evening star is named both Hesperus and Vesperus. It appears to be the root of the word *Hes* (Hu or Iu ; U has the sound of E in Welsh), from which Hesus and Hesous (Jesus) are derived. Now, the name of one of the gods of Gaul was *Hesus*, sometimes spelt *Esus*. We are not to suppose that the said two names are derived from the word evening. Besides, we are told Hesperus was a son of Japetus (Japheth), brother to Atlas (Adlais—Echo), which is quite enough to show that, in the opinion of the ancients, Hesperus was an individual, and that by Hesperus was originally meant the direction of the Country of Hesperus, and the inhabitants of that country were called Hesperides ; and Hercules is said to have stolen their cows and the three golden apples from their garden.

Can there be any doubt Hesperus is identical with the Hesus of the ancient Gauls ? [1] The supreme name of the personified sun among the Druids was Hu, and he is called " He " Gadarn, or Hu the Mighty ; and the Druids of Gaul were the disciples of the Druids of Britain. But the Gaulish God is called *Hesus* by Roman writers.

The Archdruid, as high priest of the sun, was call Hu yn Nghnawd, or He, the Incarnate Sun ; for Hu (He) signified both the Creator and the sun. The Roman writers

made a mistake when they supposed the Druidic Eesus
was Mars, the God of War; and the error arose, doubtless,
from the fact that the permission or sanction of the Archdruid, as the supreme pontiff of the throne of thrones
(Gorsedd) of Great Britain, was necessary before engaging
in war, and in that sense alone was he the " God of War."

CHAPTER XXII.

BEYOND THE RIVER.   THE GARDEN OF SANCTIFIED SOULS.

HE Druids thought the dormant condition of the seeds of the earth in winter time illustrates what we call "death" in the spiritual system of God.

The introduction in spring time into the earth's seeds of the impulse of inoculation, causing their growth and development as the result of the said masculine propagating influence of the sun's rays, the Druids compared to what the soul undergoes in the spiritual sense at "death," on the threshold of eternity, under the influence of God's spiritual Word, as that of the sun of the spiritual world (*See* James I., 21). But the soul—a Divine emanation, and compared to a spiritual seed—must be free from the corruption or rust, or dross, of sin, otherwise it will not be admitted, because it cannot grow and bloom in the spiritual garden of God, beyond the northern heavens. In the spring-time of the year, the Druids held their Festival of the Dead—the Sul-y-Bloden (" Flowering Sunday ")—the Palm Sunday of Wales, when, in Glamorgan and Monmouth, the ancient country of the heroic Esyllwyr, the Silurians of Roman historians, and where the tenets of the Druids have been preserved by its bards, the graves are still decked on the said Sunday, every year, with beautiful flowers and floral wreaths. The floral emblems imply that the souls of the departed friends are blooming on high beyond the northern skies, in the spiritual Garden of God.

In Druidism, there are two "rivers." In astronomy, those two "rivers" are named respectively, the Equinoctial Colure and the Solstitial Colure. The former runs east and west, and the latter from where the sun appears at noon on the longest day to where he appears at noon on the shortest day. Those two lines cross the equator at right angles, and the line of the Solstitial Colure crosses both the Tropic of Cancer and the Tropic of Capricornus (see p. 95).

The river Jordan runs from north to south, and thus it describes the Solstitial Colure, and at its southern end, very appropriately, it has the Dead Sea or Sea of the Dead. The South was regarded by the Druids as the entrance into Annwn (Hades), because there the sun descended, according to the Druidic allegory, in his helplessness, on each December 20th. It is from the south-west they supposed his Divinity passes below the earth through Annwn, and rises 40 hours later, rejuvenated, born again on the morning of December 22nd–25th. In Druidism, he brings with him from Annwn, "lives," as explained where we deal with the Druidic system of transmigration of souls. The emblematical character of the Jordan river is the reason why it was used to denote the regeneration in baptism, for not only were new souls supposed to ascend in, or drawn by the sun when he himself returns on December 22nd–25th, but souls who have lived human lives, but had been relegated back to the circles of Abrèd (spiritual parallels of latitude) on account of impurity or dross, now cleansed of the dross or impurity which had gathered around them during a former existence. In the Druidic system, the Equinoctial Colure (east to west) is the "river" of the material essence, to renovate the seeds in the earth, which essence streams vigorously

from the sun. when in spring he traverses it from east to
west.   But the Jews having the end and beginning of
their sacred year in spring, that is to say at the vernal
equinox, instead of at the time of the end and the beginning of the solar year, that is to say at the winter solstice,
came to use the River Jordan to symbolise both " rivers."
In Druidism the Solstitial Colure is the "river" along which,
by the agency of the sun, souls *ascend* from Annwn, to
the " City of God " in the northern heavens.   On the
other hand, the Equinoctial Colure is the " river " along
which the material essence from the sun *descends* to im-
pregnate the seeds of the earth.

It is to the Solstitial Colure and heaven the Psalmist
refers so beautifully in the words :—" There is a river, the
streams whereof shall make glad the City of God.   The
holy place of the tabernacle of the Most High God is in
the midst of her.   She (the city) shall not be moved : God
shall help her and that right early."

In addition to the " river," the Druids employed also
figure of circles—parallels of latitude—to describe the
ascending staircase from Annwn in the south, by which
the Druids meant the apparent circular daily journey of
the sun across the meridian, or, across the heavens (while
ascending the ecliptic) from his rising to his setting in
the evening.   It will be borne in mind the Druidic
theory is based on the supposition that the earth is flat
bottomed, and that its limit is the rational horizon of
the old world, but the sun, they saw, went round.   The
word Abréd is compounded of Ab and Rhéd.   The sun
is here referred to by Ab, as the Son-Father ; that is
to say, Son of the Almighty, the sun being himself a
parent, and called Hu Dad Eilir (Hu Father of Spring-

time). Rhêd, the word completing the compound,
signifies "run," and the full name signifies, the circles
of the Son-Father of all things that run, meaning of all
corporeal beings. The conceiving attribute of the earth's
anima is their mother.

The lower rung of the circles is in Annwn, down in the
south region of the shortest day; its highest rung in
this life is on the Equinoctial Line of free will of earthly
existence. A sinner at his death is relegated back to that
depth in the circles of the terrestrial latitude to which he
himself by the weight of dross on his soul, has adapted
himself for during his life here below. But no one, the
Druids thought, was so devoid of goodness as to weigh
him back all the way to the lower rung end to Annwn,
whence his life had ascended, step after step, by transmigration, with the sun's assistance as a father, and then
left to shift for himself on the equator of human
existence. Therefore, it was said by the Druids "Nid
cir i Annwn ond unwaith " (there is but one visit to
Annwn) The pure and holy at his death, passes beyond
the Line of the probation state of this life, to heaven,
called by the Druids Gwynfa, literally, the White Place,
meaning Holy Place. It should be remembered, the life
imparted in spring signifies, physical life only; the life
coming in the sun journeying up the ecliptic from
Annwn (Hades)—alluded to as the birth-place of Souls
—starting on December 22nd each year, is spiritual or
intellectual life.

It will be observed also, the sun on the meridian on the
longest day of summer (June 21st) is symbolised by Sun-
Day, and the sun on the meridian on the shortest day of
winter is indicated (Dec. 20th) as Saturn's Day (the
shortest), and refers to the sun being in the sphere of

Saturn, the last of the list of the seven planets at the
end of the line—north to south—of the said seven.[1]
It should be recollected that Mercury (due east) is identical
with Woden or Odin, and the middle day of the week is
named Woden's day or Wednesday in consequence.
Gwyddon is one of the titles of the Archdruid, who is Mercury's representative in the Druidic church on earth as the
Minister of the Divine Emanations. Literally Odin signifies
Woodman, in reference to the ancient British mode of
writing or carving literature on wood, which is still done
on the Tallis of the British Exchequer. But the name
Gwyddon (Odin) signifies, secondarily, scientist; and
science is still called in Welsh, Gwyddoniaeth, or the
philosophy on wood ("Woden") of the scientist. Gwyddon,
as the sun's representative, when the sun formerly rose in
spring in the constellation of the Bull, symbolised a Bull,
and afterwards Aries or Lamb. He was also Gwy lôn
Bach, otherwise incarnate Bacchus, who is represented as
bovine-footed.

Plutarch affirms that the women of Elis were accustomed
to invoke Bacchus in the words of the following hymn :—
" Come, hero Dionusus, to thy holy temple on the sea-
shore ; come cow-footed God to thy sacrifice, and bring the
graces in thy train ! Hear us, O Bull, worthy of our
veneration ; hear us, O illustrious Bull!" In the Orphic
hymns Bacchus, or Bull-sun's, emanation fertilising, is

[1] The Planet Saturn. "The Planets, in their orbits, were known very
early to the Chaldeans. The evidence of this is to be found in Bis Nimrod,
of which Sir Henry Rawlinson has given a description in the 18th vol. of
the Journal of the Royal Asiatic Society, from which the following account
is condensed:—'The Tower (Bis Nimrod) consisted of seven stages, built
upon a raised platform of crude brick. The first, or lowest, stage, was
about 272 feet square and 26 feet high, and was covered with bitumen,
to represent the sable hue of the Planet Saturn.'"—Inman.

styled the god with two horns, and, like Adonis, is the lover of both Venus and Proserpine, that is to say, of summer and winter. The animal symbols seem to have haunted religion long after the humanised symbols were adopted in their stead.

Returning to the legend of Hercules' visit to Brythia or Britain.

In reference to the cows which Hercules is said to have drove away, we refer the reader to the Welsh triads mentioned in page 50, which refers to the three cows, consorts of the bulls ; and when regarded as emblems of the three emanations of God (\|/) through the sun as three white bulls ; and the three white cows as emblems of the emanations of Cêd through the earth, the last of the three spotted (*See* page 52 note). The six cattle would be assembled on the great religious gatherings, or Cymmanvas, in the Buarth Beirdd, or the Bardic Bovine Enclosure. It will be re-collected that, afterwards, three priests came to be employed instead of the three bulls, and *three priestesses* instead of the three cows. When the Archdruid stood on the Holy Mound, Cromleach, or Logan Stone—each symbol signifying the whole earth—in the centre of the Holy Circle he and his " Church " symbolised the incarnation of the Divine attributes of God, and the circular " Church " the Divine attributes of Cêd, the Almighty's consort.

A mixture of good and evil was anciently called Grey (Llwyd) in Welsh, hence the title of " spotted " given to the third cow, but the " spots " have been added to the natural mother for a useful purpose, viz., defence of her offspring ; notwithstanding the infernal origin of the ferocious quality which the spots symbolised.

White, used both in a masculine and feminine sense, is the Welsh for Sanctus. One of the said three cows is described as bellowing in May (Meinddydd), when the sun was in the constellation Taurus (Bull), and the sun-bull is said to be blowing in his horn. This fact of the cow being said to "call" in May upon the bull—sun, is extremely interesting, for it indicates the Druids had observed the sun no longer rose in Taurus on March 21st. We have no evidence they, like the Egyptians, adopted the Ram-Lamb (Aries) in lieu of the Bull as the symbol of the Mediatorial sun in Spring. The windpipe is called horn (Corn Gwynt) in Welsh. It is still common to hear Welsh agriculturalists stating in reference to the sun's rays spreading (tes), " Y mae y Tarw Elgan yn chwythu yn ei gorn " (the White Bull is blowing in his horn). See *Rites, &c., of the British Druids*, pages 121, 177, 567.

At Memphis, Egypt, a sacred cow was the symbol of Venus (Isis II.), and the sacred bull, Apis or Menevis, was the male personification of the sun (in spring) there and at Heliopolis, or City of the Sun.

The Phœnicians employed the same emblems, hence the Cadmians (people of Thebes, Egypt) are said to have been conducted by a cow to the place of their settlement in Bœtia (Thebes again). The diphthong (œ) seems to be the Druidic " u " in *Bu* (Bull), pronounced " ee " in Welsh. The name of the temple there, constructed of a circle of stones, was the Serpent's Head (Pausanias, Bœtia xix., 2). " The Thebians call a certain little spot of ground, surrounded by stones selected for the purpose, the Serpent's Head." See in page 72 what we state of the Serpent's Head (Ogben) at Avebury (Wilts). See also page 15 Wilder's edition of Knight's *Symbolical Language*, note. In page

T

35 of that work is the following, quoted from Scholia in *Lycophror*, v. 1206:—"Theba, among the Syrians, signifies a cow." It is also the name translated "Ark" of Noah's Deluge. In the foregoing we perceive the origin of the fable of Bacchus ("night heat as nocturnal sun") as having been born at Thebes. His body, as the son of Semele (Sap), was born of that personification set forth as a cow, and afterward as Mor'wyn, and also as Isis ii. or Venus. His Divinity \I/, or Dove, is the joint offspring of Celi and Cêd, or Amen Ra and Isis i. But it appears it was inferred Isis i. was the agent who annually also clothed the Divinity \I/ with the radiant material body; for Semele herself had been reduced to autumnal "ashes." Yet it seems to be inferred that, though dead herself, it is the material she imparted which is used by Cêd in constructing a glorious new body for him.

Here we discover the origin of the error of stating that Myrrah, or Mary (Morewyn), was the mother of Adonis (sun). As the earth's emanation in spring, she is his sister spouse. The error has caused the "Church," the symbolical consort of Celi and the Virgin Mary, to be often confounded one with the other, and likewise Isis i. and Isis ii.

A cow is still revered as the sacred symbol of the great Mother Nature, daughter of Cêd or Isis i., by the inhabitants of India, "among whom," we are told, "there is scarcely a temple to-day without the figure of a cow." In the Scandinavian mythology, we are further told by Knight, the sun was fabled to recruit his strength during winter by sucking the cow Adumbla, the symbol of the productive power like Semele till September. When Semele dies, he is placed in the "thigh" of the Almighty.

On the Greek coins the cow is most commonly represented suckling a calf, the young sun's body, thereby nourished and strengthened from his birth on December 22nd, till he attains full maturity on March 21st. At other times, instead of a calf, he is symbolised by a kid goat, son of Pan. In the *Asiatic Researches* we are told the Hindoos believe they are descended from a cow (Nature).

Diana is named Tor Iona, or Dove of the Belly or Ark. Tor is the Welsh name of belly to this day. Baal and Baaltis are identical with the sun and nature. The bull Moloch was either black or red, and symbolised the Destroyer, and had seven hollows within, "to receive seven degrees of victims," the said seven being antagonistic to the seven emanations of Adhais (Atlas), creative functions of the echo of the Divine voice as the Word through the sun during his yearly passage through the seven planetary spheres.

In reference to the last named, Shakespeare, in his "Man's Seven Ages" or stages, must have had an insight into some of the Druidic teachings, for his description is modelled on the Druidic seven stages of the personified sun, beginning with the infant Taliesin, or Hu Gadarn, and ending in the seventh stage with old Saturn, Silenus, or Arawn, known also by other titles.

"NO MAN SHALL SEE ME AND LIVE."

On the Day of Atonement the high priest passed into the Holy Place (not the Holy of Holies) in his gorgeous robe, flashing with gems, and the golden bells suspended from the lower hem of his robe, called Ephod, sounded musically as he walked. But he returned outside from the Holy Place, as it were into the world to sacrifice, on the Day of Atonement, *in his shroud only*, having divested himself of his gorgeous robes, and with them his office in

T 2

the Holy Place. Dr. Kitto, in his *Cyclopædia of Biblical Literature*, under the words " Atonement, Day of," states, " Every Jew, on the Day of Atonement, wears a white gown, the same *shroud* in which he hopes to be buried." It is evident the white robe which the high priest returned dressed in, a minute description of which we give elsewhere, symbolised he was no longer alive as a priest. His priesthood had been left behind in the Holy Place with the symbols of the priesthood in the veiled presence of the Word, that is to say, Jehovah. He had returned back to the Almighty the office with which he had been entrusted on the previous Day of Atonement twelve months before, and he now, after reigning a year like the sun, came *back* into the world through the west entrance *dead*, as a *priest.* " Thou canst not see my face, for there shall no *man* see Me and live." Exodus xxxiii., v. 19 and 20. The high priest now, as a dead priest, proceeded to prepare the sacrifice, and with the blood of that sacrifice in his hand, he, a man, was enabled to do what no " man " without it dared to do, namely, enter into the Holy of Holies, and look at the Shechinah, the *face*, as it were, of Jehovah! That Shechinah, however, was not the Most High Himself, but His emblematic Word, the Seminal Logos, His propagating attribute.

OTHER SYMBOLS OF THE OLD SUN, YOUNG SUN, AND THE SUN'S MOTHER.

The Egyptians and other nations of antiquity symbolised the new sun on December 22nd as a kid he-goat, that symbol being selected because the sun rose then in the sign of the he-goat (Capricornus). That young he-goat at the end of the solar year following, was represented as an aged he-goat, and was named by the Greeks, Pan, and which, as they did with the Ram they called Jupiter, they humanised. They humanised the upper half of the he-goat Pan. It will be remembered the old sun of one year was said to be the father of the young sun of the next, and thus we have at the end and the beginning of the solar year, the old sun and young sun symbolised by the old he-goat Pan and the young kid he-goat Bacchus respectively. The sun was poetically said to be amphibious, because every evening he is seen decending into the waters of the Atlantic. Sophocles (*Ajax*, 694—700), therefore, addresses Pan, the old sun, in the words following :—

> "Io! Io! Pan! Pan!
> Oh Pan, *thou Ocean Wanderer*."

The Choral odes sung in honour of Bacchus were called Tragodiai, or Goat Songs. Herodotus (ii., 46), states, " the artists in Egypt delineated and sculptured the symbol of Pan, like the Greeks, as having the countenance and limbs of a goat." It will be recollected the Day of Atonement marked the end and the beginning of the Jewish *Civil Year* (September), and they practically offered in sacrifice *two* goats on the tenth of Tishri, otherwise Ethanim. " And he shall take the *two goats* and present them " (on the Day of Atonement), " before the Lord at the door of the Tabernacle of the Congregation." (*See* page 42; corrected in page 49 note).

The blood of *three* kinds of animals, and all *three* sacred living symbols in Egypt, namely, that of the Bull, the Ram, and the Goat, are offered that day to Jehovah. It seems as if the Jews believed that nothing less than the blood of other " gods " would satisfy Jehovah, and induce him to renew for another year their high priesthood. It appears, when we think of the horrors which befell the Hebrews, that they suffered from Divine vengeance for the awful blasphemy which their horrible bloodshed implied. Their own blood was poured forth in crimson rivers at Jerusalem and Cæsarea by the Romans.

ROMAN AND HEBREW RELIGIOUS RITES SIMILAR.

But the Romans themselves sacrificed a Ram on every January 13th, and on March they observed their Matronalia in honour of the earth as a young mother (spring), when husbands made presents to their wives.

Afterwards, they honoured the *devil*, by the Salii carrying the shields of Mars (Pluto) through Rome. On March 18th—eve of the vernal equinox—was observed the Liberalia in honour of Bacchus, when the Roman youths put on the Toga Virilis, the significance of which is obvious. After that, a festival was held in honour of Minerva (Cêd, as Divine Wisdom). On March 23rd and 24th, a Lamb was again sacrificed. The last corresponds with the Jewish Paschal Sacrifice; for the Jewish year being lunar, and the Roman one solar, the Jewish Nisan 13th (March, O.S.), in the evening of which the Passover commenced, corresponded with the Roman 24th. On March 25th (our Lady Day), the Hilaria was held in honour of the mother of the gods. The above facts prove the Romans also had mixed the worship of the Creator with that of the destroyer or devil. This might have been expected, for did they not worship Jupiter, Neptune, and *Pluto*, the last named being the Power of Darkness, and identical with Typhon, the third person of the Egyptian trinity. By thus alluding to Venus as the "mother of the gods," we see the Romans, like the Phœnicians, who confounded Myrrah (Morewyn) of the vernal equinox, with Cêd, Delphus—Womb, (Cetus, &c.)

of the winter solstice, confounded Venus with Cêd or Delphus. This fact proves they had imbibed the error from the east, probably through Greece.

St. Augustine, of Africa, who was born A.D. 354, states Jesus Christ was born on the 8th day before the calends of January (December 25th) in the ninth month (March being the Julian first month) ; was conceived surely about the 8th day before the calends of April (March 25th) in the first month, which was also the time (March 25th) of His Passion. *Questiones in Exodus*, lib. ii., *Opera*, tom iii., p. 337, *D. Quest* xc. Eleven days added to the lunar Nisan 14th (Day of the Passover) we arrive at the solar March 25th, the date of the Roman Hilaria, the great Roman annual festival in honour of the Mother of the Gods. Thus, according to St. Augustine, the Most High observed the dates of the erroneous calendar of Julius Cæsar.

In another place St. Augustine argues against the statement of some Gentiles that the reign of the Christian religion would be only during 365 years. For " years," no doubt "days" was originally meant, that being the number of days in the solar year, and the poets and mythologists had taught the world the lifetime of each sun was that number of days. The allegation of the Gentiles prove that those who made it identified the Christ with the sun Ouranos, Aaron, the Arawn of the Druids. Strange St. Augustine did not observe this.

Cêd, the sun's mother, is now represented as a she-goat and named Minerva. Thus we find Cêd represented by the symbols, Cetus, Der Ketos, Tebah, Tub or Ark, Delphus (Womb), Dolphin, Minerva or Divine Wisdom, and Medusa.

Medusa is said to be one of the Three Gorgons[1]. Really, she is Cêd, confounded with one of the Three Graces (*see* p. 14). To this day in the British language, Gorcân or Gorchân, is the name given to the canon or fundamental part of Music. It will be recollected what we state in pages 68 and 69 in reference to Mali, or Mary—Mother (Miriam), echoing back the melodious voice of the Almighty Celi in sopranoimic cadences. The voice is that of Cêd, but heard by mortals though the instrumentality of the anima of the material universe, as Venus or Morwyn, of Druidism; hence, it will be recollected, the saying, "the voice of God is *heard* in the *voice* of nature," hence, too, the Bath Kol of the Hebrews, meaning "the daughter's voice." Gorcân signifies now also, incantation or enchantment. It is a word compounded of Côr (Sanctuary), and Cân (Song). No doubt the name came to imply it from the practice of the Druids of performing dramatically their story of the creation. "Corcan" is used, too, to denote a pert woman. The luxuriant fancy of the Greeks nearly smothered the simple poetical characters of the Stone Age! By stating Medusa is one of the Three Gorgons, the Greeks confounded Cêd with Mor'wyn, one of her own three daughters.

THE HU GADARN AND TALIESIN SYMBOLS OF THE YOUNG SUN.

The orthodox Druids of Britain celebrated, as we have already stated, the birth of the young sun on December 22nd, the beginning of the solar year, and called him Hu Gadarn, or Iu, as in "Iu" (Hee) Pater, Iu the Mighty

---

[1] "Gorgo is supposed to have been a foreign title of Athene Minerva as Bendeia and Dictynna were of Diana."— Knight's *Symbolical Language*, sec. 179 foot note.

otherwise Hesus, or Hesous the Mighty, and by others by the title of Taliesin.

But, as stated elsewhere, a school of Druids who seem to have separated themselves from the older order of Druids, and to have enrolled themselves under the Taliesin title of the young sun, observed the death of the old sun, and, forty hours later, the birth of the young sun, calling him Taliesin in both instances, at the vernal equinox, March 21st or 25th, at Borth, Cardigan Bay. At the date of the end and commencement of the Hebrew sacred year, Nisan. March, O.S., the Phœnicians, the next-door neighbours, as it were, of the Jews, and also the Syrians, Greeks, Lycians, Egyptians, &c., symbolised young Adonis as a young ram, and they called him also Jupiter Amon, and, since writing the foregoing, we find it stated by Rev. George Rawlinson that a sheep (ewe) was their symbol of his consort Venus. At that period the sun entered the sign of Ram on March 21st, and was therefore, in their religious solar allegories, described as a ram, and the earth as a sheep.

THE SACRIFICE OF THE PASCHAL RAM LAMB.

Now on the tenth day of the moon of the month Nisan, which, solarly, would be March 21st, O.S., it was ordered that the Hebrews should take a lamb for a house or family, "a male of the first year." It had to be over seven days old, "without blemish," and it had to be kept alive until after mid-day of the 14th day of the moon, which, solarly, would be the afternoon of the 25th March, O.S., the lunar year, as often stated, being eleven days shorter than the solar one. The evening of our thirteenth day of the moon of March, O.S., the Jews counting the evening *before* the day, was the date of their "preparation of the Passover." On the afternoon of the fourteenth, equal to the solar twenty-fifth, each lamb had to be conveyed to the great brazen altar within the sacred enclosure of the temple, "between the two evenings," that is to say, between the time of the sun's beginning to decline after the noon hour and his setting. At noon, on March 21st-25th (Nisan 10th and 14th), the sun would be exactly in the middle of the vault of the heavens.

What an awful scene the precincts of the temple and the streets of Jerusalem must have presented during the slaughtering time of hundreds, if not thousands, of male lambs, "between the two evenings," when the lamb-sun was hastening towards the west !

From sunset on the evening of the 14th were observed seven days of unleavened bread, which bring us to the evening before Nisan 21st. Thus from the capture of the male lamb on the 10th of Nisan to the 21st, would be eleven days, and from his slaughter on the 14th to the 25th, would be likewise eleven days.

It appears the sacrifice of the Paschal Lamb was regarded as only the principal *incident* of the Passover, but that the sacrifice of other animals was included in the general name "Passover" (see Deut. xvi., 2). This is what St. John alludes to in c. xviii., 28, and not to the Paschal Lamb. Jesus was then in custody, and he had partaken of the Last Supper the evening before, and we are, therefore, irresistibly forced to the conclusion that, as is held by the Greek church, he and his disciples either transgressed the law by eating the Paschal Lamb on the evening of the 13th, instead of that of the 14th, or that he himself did *not* partake at all of the Paschal Lamb that year. There is one small, but very interesting, incident confirming this conclusion. Not only the male lamb (Aries,) but a cock was used by the entire Gentile world to symbolise the sun's fertilising influence at the vernal equinox, that is to say, the time of the Passover. Doddridge points out that the Jews state all cocks were removed out of Jerusalem at the time of the Passover, but a cock crew thrice near the house of the high priest, apparently before daybreak, on the morning of the day of the crucifixion. This proves the removal of the cocks had *not* then taken place, and, no doubt, the cock symbolising the same thing as did the Paschal Lamb, the removal of the said birds could be delayed until "between the two evenings" of the 14th. It will be seen in another page of this work, the Jews, after the destruction of Jerusalem, where alone the Paschal Lamb could be slain, fell back on slaying the cock symbol instead.

THE CIVIL YEAR AND THE "DAY" OF ATONEMENT.

At the appearance of the seventh new moon of the sacred year the civil year commences, and the name of that month is Tishri or Ethanim. This corresponds with our September O.S.

Let the reader refer to Numbers xxix., and he will see the character of the preparations which were made from the first day of the civil year for the Day of Atonement, which is on the tenth day of that month or moon. Moreover, in Lev. xxiii., 27, we find the following :—" On the tenth day of the seventh month," September 10th, O.S., and solarly the 21st, " there shall be a Day of Atonement."

Then the next was the feast, commencing on the *evening* of the 14th, and called the Feast of Tabernacles. That continued seven days—eight days in all—thus terminating in the evening of September 22nd, O.S., nearly the exact date when in springtime the earth leaves the sign of Virgo in the west, according to the ancient astronomy, and the sun entered, on March 21st, the first point of the ram, Aries, in the east. But on Sept. 21st (the lunar 10th of Tishri), the sun was in the sign of the Virgin in the east, and the earth was in the sign of Aries or lamb in the west. The earth, like the sacred island of Delos, was supposed to be loose on the surface of the ocean and floating into the various positions. Now, the Ark of the Covenant is named "Virgin of Israel" by both Jeremiah and Isaiah; and then, on the Day of Atonement, took place the symbolical death down west, and, passing through Hades or Sheol, below the earth, afterwards the high priest is "born again" from the "Virgin of Israel," through the eastern front of the Holy of Holies.

Then followed the merry-making of the Feast of Tabernacles, in celebration of the *new birth* of the high priest, symbolising the new sun.

The tenth day was one of awful solemnity, for the high priest died then, symbolically, and was shrouded; but on the *evening* of the 14th, the entire assembled nation danced by torchlights, made of the cast-off linen garments—the old shrouds, as it were—of the priests; and young Pan played his pipes, and the high priest rang the bells of the ephod. This merrymaking was extremely popular, as readers of the writings of Josephus are aware.

We know not how the Jews occupied themselves from the tenth to the evening before our fifteenth, when the revelry commenced. It maybe that period of time was allowed them to erect their leafy tabernacles on the slopes of the adjacent hills surrounding Jerusalem. But the probability is that the erecting of the tabernacles was the first thing the people did on reaching Jerusalem, preparatory to the Atonement and feast which followed; for, otherwise, where were they to find lodgings in such vast numbers? Anyone reading the xvi. chapter of Leviticus, where the whole of the solemnities to be performed on the so-called " Day " of Atonement are described, will conclude the " day " is over-crowded with incidents. Calmet, in his *Dictionary of the Bible*, points out that in ancient times the expression, " year," "month," &c., were uncertain, because varied in meaning. Thus the Egyptian year was solar, which Calmet thinks was the original year of the Hebrews, following the Egyptian example. " But," states the same high authority, " after the time of Alexander the Great, and of the Grecians in Asia, the Jews reckoned by lunar months, chiefly in what related to religion, and to the festivals." Again, " Originally, the Egyptians allowed but one month to their year, then two, then four months, and lastly, twelve months. They varied *   * in their months and *days*." It is extremely likely, therefore, that, originally, by the " Day " of Atonement was understood, not *one* day, but the *period* of Atonement, and that it began on the evening before the tenth and continued until the *evening before* the fifteenth, and that the incidents crowded into the " tenth day " of Tishri, as the word "day" came afterwards to be understood, were really spread over five days, and that immediately after the new " birth " of the high priest, the festivities of the tabernacles began.

The reader will bear in mind, Nisan (March) was the first month of the Jewish *sacred* year, and Tishri (September) the first of the *civil* year. He will have observed the Passover Lamb was " housed " on the tenth of Nisan, and that the High Priest was, so to speak, " housed " on the tenth of Tishri. The Passover Lamb was slain between two evenings, as already explained, on the day *before* the festival (15th of Nisan), and on the evening, at sunset,

before the fifteenth, commenced the festival of unleavened
bread, which corresponded with the beginning of the Feast
of Tabernacles, commencing on the evening before the
fifteenth of Tishri (September). As hinted before, among
the Druids, Greeks, &c., a white cock was one of the
symbols of the sun, and a hen was a symbol of the earth's
anima, and the material earth was symbolised by the mundane egg. In Welsh mythology the Anima or Anian is
called the Hen Ceridwen, or Holy–Beloved Hen. The
following is by the Rev. Thomas Godwin, B.D., *Moses and
Aaron*, page 132 :—"The modern Jews now, on the Day
of Atonement, the men take a white cock and the women a
hen. The cock they swing three times about the priest's
head, saying, ' This cock shall be a propitiation for me.'
After that they kill the cock, acknowledging *themselves*
worthy of death. * * The word Gebher in Hebrew
signifies a Man, but in the Talmud it signifies a cock." Like
the Ram–Lamb of the Passover, the cock is made to
signify " Man." Be sure, reader, to refer here to pages
176 and 177.

Killing the white cock on the period of the Atonement,
at the autumnal equinox, corresponds with killing the
Passover lamb at the vernal equinox, or in other
words, in Tishri and Nisan respectively. But who is
Gebher, or the Man whom the white cock symbolises?
The high priest, as representing the old sun, called by the
Druids Arawn, Saidwrn (Saturn), Arthur, Dyvnwawl
Moelmud ; and by the Orientals, Tammuz, Adonis (old),
Osiris, &c., and being put to death by the Power of Darkness, victorious at the winter solstice, and the Divinity
being rescued at sea by his mother Cêd, and by some Druids
by a shrine containing an Avanc (Beaver), and also, it will
be remembered, by a wren in a small arkite box, when that

Divinity (the Logos or Word as a Divine emanation) after his physical body had been wrecked in the heavens on the afternoon of December 20th, is falling into the South-Western Sea, or the Gwyllionwy of the Druids, beyond St. David's Head, Pembroke, but "born again" from the South-Eastern Sea on the morning of the 22nd, after an absence of forty hours, and the Phœnicians welcomed him, but at the wrong time of the year (spring), with the joyful greeting of "Hail to the dove, the giver of light!" As already stated, Cêd, the mother of the dove, or the young sun, was often symbolised by a boat, or ark, or mastless ship. Often the young sun was symbolised as a newly-born babe, and called the Crowned Babe. He was Adonis in Phœnicia; Horus and also Osiris in Egypt; Hu Gadarn, also Taliesin, in Britain and Gaul (France), where also he was called Hesus (*Lucan* i., v. 445) or Jesus. We have shown clearly that the Passover and the period of the Atonement and Tabernacles, with the rites and the ceremonies of each, refer to the same wonderful subject and that the death and birth of the High Priest, first as an old man, and then as a new creature, refer to the allegorical "death" of the old sun at the close of the old solar year, and the "birth" of the new sun at the beginning of the solar new year. Were the two events given at the dawn of creation to the British Druids by the Almighty to be types of the death and the resurrection of the Lord Jesus Christ? We cannot answer. There is this difficulty to reconcile that with the Druidic doctrine, namely that the old sun (the old Adam) was viciously put to death by the Power of Darkness, and that therefore, like the "scape goat," he was a sacrifice offered to Azazel, or the devil, and not given voluntarily as a ransom to the violated law of God. But the Christian father Tertullian believed all these were rehearsals of the incarnation and death of the human nature of the Word of God.

THE TWO GOATS OF THE DAY OF ATONEMENT.

"And he (Aaron,) shall take of the Congregation of the children of Israel two kids of the goats, for a sin offering, and one ram for a burnt offering" on the Day of Atonement, Tishri 10th (September 21st, O.S.). "And he shall take the two goats, and present them before the Lord at the door of the tabernacle of the congregation" western entrance. "And Aaron shall cast lots upon the two goats; one lot for Jehovah, and the other for the scape goat" ("For Azazel" in the margin). "And Aaron shall bring the goat upon which Jehovah's lot fell, and offer him for a sin offering. But the goat on which the lot fell to be the scape goat" (correctly "for Azazel") "shall be presented alive before the Lord," like the other at the western entrance, to make an atonement with him, and afterwards was sent "for Azazel" into the wilderness. Lev. xvi., 7—10.

The following is copied from the "Fragments" to Calmet's *Dictionary of the Bible, vide* "Azazel":—"Spencer affirms Azazel signifies some demon, and that the goat sent to Azazel was given to the devil. Mark, the head of the Marcosian heretics, called the devil Azazel Epiphan, whose name he used in his juggling tricks. Hacres, 84. But we prefer the Greek interpreters (i. lxx.), who derive Azazel from the Hebrew, Haz or Hez, a goat, and Azal, he went away." The note in the Hebrew Bible used by modern Jews, states that "Azazel" signifies a mountain. "The following ceremonies," writes the author of the "Fragments," "the Hebrews tell us were observed relating to the scape goat (Mishna in Joma, Maimon, Jom, Haccipurim)." "Two goats were led into the inner court of the temple, and presented to the High Priest on the north side of the altar of burnt offerings; they were placed one on his right, the other on his left hand. Therefore, we notice he himself (the Man—but implying Saturn —Sun) in the middle between the two goats, like Jesus between the two malefactors. " An urn was then brought and placed between them, and two lots were cast into it. * * On one lot was engraved, " For the Lord," on the other, " For Azazel." After the urn had been well shaken, the High Priest placed both his hands into it, and each hand drew out a lot; that in his right hand decided the fate of the goat placed opposite that hand —that in his left, of the goat on his left hand. " After drawing these lots, the High Priest fastened a narrow piece of scarlet to the head of the goat 'For Azazel.'" * * * The other goat was then sacrificed "For Jehovah " on the altar. The Goat " for Azazel " was then brought to the High Priest, and he placed both his hands on its head "and confessed his own sins, and those of the people ; then it was taken into the wilderness by some fit person." If the above, in reference to the inscription on the two lots, be correct, it would be as true to say that one goat " was Jehovah," as to say the other was " Azazel." Both were " for" two distinct objects of worship ; and if Azazel was the devil, it was to him, therefore, the High Priest " confessed his own sins, and those of the people." The above re-opens the great question as " to whom the ransom for sinners was paid." " For this purpose the Son of God was manifested that He might *destroy* the work of the devil."— 1. St. John, iii., 8. Dean Alford explains the Greek word, translated " destroy" to mean " do away, break up, pull down of a building, or a law, or an organized whole," Was that done to open the way to " preach " or proclaim " deliverance to the captives " ? Whose captives ? Isaiah (c. xlix.) compares the captivity of the Jews in Babylon

to the captivity of souls by Satan, and he announces a
Deliverer; and the bard crying with ecstacy describes Him
saying—"Listen, O Isles unto Me, and hearken ye nations
afar off." It is interesting to speculate as to the "Isles"
meant by the Deliverer. In St. Luke iv., 18-21, we find
the Lord Jesus asserting in the Synagogue at Nazareth,
he was that Deliverer of the captives of Satan. In Druidism the "captives" would be souls in the circles of transmigration.

THE SUN'S DIVINITY DESCENDING TO ANNWN (HADES).
THE DIVINE SPIRIT PREACHING TO "THE SPIRITS IN PRISON."

It is intimated by St. Peter that Christ immediately
after his death, "went and preached unto the spirits in
prison." The words are:—"For Christ also hath once
suffered for sins, the just for the unjust, that he might
bring us to God, being put to death in the flesh, but
quickened by the spirit, by which also he went and
preached unto the spirits in prison." 1. St. Peter iii., 18
and 19. In the above it is clearly intimated it was the
disembodied Spirit of Christ who "preached unto the
spirits in prison." He clearly stated to the penitent thief
that he—that is to say, His Divinity—was going that
day (Friday) to Paradise, which was the name of a
district of the Greek Hades, the entrance into which was
described by the setting sun, and where, since then, the
American continent and the Antipodes have been discovered.

Then St. Peter goes on to compare the deluge to baptism. Noah and his family, eight in number, " were saved
by water." "The like figure," he goes on to state,
" whereunto baptism doth also now save us *   *   *   *
by the resurrection of Jesus Christ." Dean Alford,
after stating that the literature in ancient and modern

times on the above verses, " constitute almost a library in itself," adds himself, " The course of thought is unusual, is startling, is mysterious." The simple explanation as to St. Peter's meaning is the following. At the time he wrote, the legend was well known describing the divinity of the sun, when, on December 20th, the body of the sun was *annually destroyed in the heavens at noon*, on the cross, described by the line of the tropic of Capricornus crossing the line of the meridian, escaping out of it as a white dove, into Hades ; then after the interval of forty hours, reappearing in the S.E., clothed with a luminous and radiant new body, and named " The Crowned Babe " by the Druids. It is implied by the apostle that the divinity, the Christ of the Lord Jesus, likewise returned, ascending from Hades *through the sea*, and the act is described as a baptism and a resurrection. And that, as the result of his return (he, Arawn or Ouranos), we also shall be saved, and our salvation is prefigured by baptism. The ascension of Noah, too, is, in December, like that of the young sun of the new year ; for the month Tebeth is December. But the Hebrews, having the end and the beginning of their sacred year at the vernal equinox (March 20th-21st), instead of at the winter solstice (December 20th-22nd), the allegory of the latter is transferred to the former, with a still further confusion caused by the appointing of several of the leading incidents of the allegory as described elsewhere in this work, to the period of the Atonement and the Feast of the Tabernacles (the autumnal equinox—September O.S.)

Taylor, in the " Fragments to Calmet's," states that the goat sent to the wilderness as an offering to Azazel was sometimes caught and eaten by the Arabs.

It should be borne in mind here that the goat (Capricornus) is the zodiacal sign of the end and the beginning of the *solar* year, but in current astronomy, the sun does not enter the sign of the goat until December 22nd, or December 25th, in the incorrect Roman calendar.

It appears the sending away the goat to Azazel brought to a close the preparatory sacrifices, before the high priest ventured into the Holy of Holies, which he did with the blood of gods in the vessel in his hand *for the first and only time.* This is the " once " referred to in the Epistle to the Hebrews and elsewhere in the Bible. All the other rites, like taking the two goats to the threshold of the western entrance of the holy place, which was distinct from the Holy of Holies, had to be performed some outside the threshold and others in the holy place. Now the large outer court even of the tabernacle as a whole was *cleared,* everybody, except the high priest himself, going outside to see the scape goat departing, with the scarlet streamer fastened, as it appears, to his horns. Assistance was necessary to perform the sacrifices, but now, they being over, the high priest was left alone, and with blood and smoking incense, entered the Holiest of All.

While doing all this, he was dead as a priest, and, to additionally signify that, his *membrum virilis* as gelded was confined by means of ligatures. Did circumcision imply the same thing?

He also, as the old sun (Saturn), divested of his crown and government, was without his royal vestments, to be restored, however, to him after his " new birth " through the hairy eastern outlet of the Virgin of Israel.

CHAPTER XXIII.

WAS THE LORD JESUS CHRIST A DRUID?

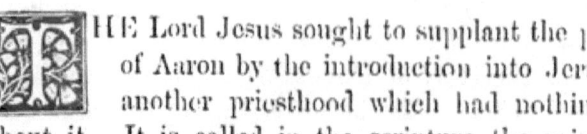

THE Lord Jesus sought to supplant the priesthood of Aaron by the introduction into Jerusalem of another priesthood which had nothing Jewish about it. It is called in the scripture, the priesthood of Melchizedec. Melchizedec was a priest of the Most High God; was not a son of Abraham, and that patriarch, according to the Epistle to the Hebrews, acknowledged the superiority of the priesthood of Melchizedec over that of the tribe of Levi, which was a purely Jewish priesthood. Melchizedec, a contemporary of Abraham, not being a son of Abraham, and existing before the priesthood of Levi came practically into existence, was a Gentile, exercising the duties of a Gentile priesthood, which, unquestionably, was Druidic, and was represented on the east station of the circle, the position occupied by Judah. *Numbers* ii., 30.

In the Council of Apostles at Jerusalem, reported in Acts xv., a question relating exclusively to the Levitical priesthood, namely, circumcision was the great question to consider which the Council had gathered together. Now, James the Just, the brother of the Lord Jesus, and, therefore, likely to be familiar with the inner springs of action in the career of the Lord Jesus, after he had listened to the speech of the learned and eloquent Paul, the impulsive utterances of Peter, and to Barnabas, relating their experiences, unrolled the sacred scroll, and directed the attention of all assembled to Amos ix., 11 and 12, and the words, " In that day will I raise the Tabernacle of Dovid " the Almighty, and not of King " David," as is taught by divines " that is fallen, and close up the breaches thereof; and I will raise up its ruins, and I will build it *as in the days of old.* That they may possess the remnant of Edom, and all the heathen *upon whom my Name is called*, saith the Lord who doeth this." It is implied the Gentiles were named after His Name. We have adopted the words in the margin instead of the ambiguous words, "which are called by my name," in the body of the text. Depend upon it, that was not the first time James the Just had read the above sentences, and that his immortal Brother and he had often discussed them together at their humble home in Galilee. The result of the disclosure of James was that the apostles and the elders unanimously agreed that circumcision was abrogated by Christianity. No wonder! Circumcision referred to the personified old sun as a Saturnine symbol. The Lord Jesus was the "new sun," and bore the title of "the Sun"—the young sun—"of Righteousness."

Theologians have confounded the name *Dovid* with *David*, and have, in consequence, inferred the reference is to the kingship of Jesus as being of the royal family of David. But what had the *kingship* to do with circumcision? To discuss whether or not the observance of that rite was to be continued by Christians the Council had met. What "tabernacle," too, had King David ever had? "Tabernacle" here is used as a figure contrasted with the tabernacle or tent of the Levitical priesthood. Dovydd is one of the titles of the Almighty in Druidism, and the name signifies, literally, Tamer, and implies, Ruler of the World and of the Elements in Spring. The royal tribe of Judah was, as stated, stationed *east* of the Tabernacle of Israel, while that of Levi was indicated by the position to the west of that tabernacle, into which position, on the withdrawal of Levi, Ephraim, the second son of Joseph, was thrust, while Manasseh, Joseph's first-born, represented Joseph himself in the circle. The new-born priesthood of the sun, as the husband of the vernal earth, appeared every spring (March 21st) in the eastern heavens.

The Welsh names of the cardinal points indicate to this day, that the eastern point of the heavens was sacred in the ritual of the Druidic religion. The Welsh for east is Dwyrain (two parents), the fatherhood emanation in spring coming through the sun; Mor'wyn (Virgo—Venus—the anima of the earth in spring) the mother, symbolised by the top slab of the Cromleach in the middle of the Druidic Circular "Church" as symbol of the belly of Ced. The sun is then called Hu—Dâd—Eilir, or Tegid, also Alawn, Iu Pater (Jupiter), or the masculine cause of the renovation of the earth in spring.

The Welsh for north is Gogledd, or sword side—the left side of the presiding Druidic priest, who is Tegid's representative as Mor'wyn's husband. For south, the name is De, or right-hand side; and for west, Gorllewin, or region of the reflection of light. The first name indicates the position of the Druids, in the springtime, during worship. Now, Jesus is said to be a priest after the order of Melchizedec, and that he (Jesus) was of the Tribe of Judah, which indicated the sun rising due east (Numbers ii., v. 3). We are thus irresistibly convinced the Lord Jesus Christ was a Druid, and a priest after a most ancient order, whose headquarters was Britain!—the "Isles" of Isaiah. Jesus came from the border of Phœnicia.

It is not surprising in this view the ancient Druids of Wales, and the rest of the isles, accepted Christianity readily; for they must have recognised the priesthood of Christ *as being their own most ancient one.* But they continued to state " the Pillar is necessary with the Gospel." In Hebrews i., 3, we have a very remarkable Druidic passage, as if St. Paul had penned it immediately after returning to Rome from a visit to the Druids of Wales, to the

family of Caractacus. In that passage he refers to the Word
of God (/ʌ) "upholding" the earth. St. Peter represented
oriental ideas, and supposed the heavens were certainly
constructed by the Word of God, but that the earth was a
sort of large island—Flat Holms like —which, to employ
his own words, the Prince of the Apostles states : " Stands
in the water and out of the water," and, therefore, is
surrounded by water. II. Peter, iii., 5. St. Peter's description corresponds with the description of the earth and
the sea around it, given by Homer in his description of the
Shield of Achilles. But St. Paul, while, no doubt, thinking
like the most learned men in that age, and the Druids
among them, that the bottom of the earth was flat, believed it was sustained in its firm position by the echo or
Adlais (Atlas) of the Word of God. The Slab of the
Cromleach symbolised the earth, and the three stone props
"upholding" it, symbolised, it will be recollected, the
reverberation of the Word of God, and hence we find St.
Paul wrote the passage referred to, viz , the Word of God
is "*upholding* all things by its power."   In the same
verse the apostle compares Jesus to the sun, as being " the
brightness of the glory " of the Creator.

THE ALLEGED VISIT OF ST. PAUL TO SOUTH WALES.

Stillingfleet, in his *Origines Britannicæ*, page 40, states,
ancient authorities generally say St. Paul was in the west
of Europe—in the utmost bounds of the west—and one
ancient writer states, during *eight years*. St. Paul was
set at liberty with other prisoners in A.D. 59, as a token of
Nero's joy at the murder of Agrippina, his own mother.
That would give from A.D. 59 to A.D. 67, during which time
St. Paul was, to use the usual expression in reference to
the event, in " the utmost bounds of the west," which, in
those ancient days would be the correct description of
Wales and Ireland, and would be used instead of Britain,

then extremely well known, to distinguish the particular locality of Britain, honoured by the sojourn in it of St. Paul.

Now Stillingfleet, and the ancient writer quoted by him, in reference to the eight years spent by the Apostle in the utmost bounds of the west of Europe, could have had no knowledge of the ancient records preserved in the Welsh language. Rees, in his *History of the Welsh Saints*, p. 77, quoting from ancient records of the Welsh nation, states that Brân the Blessed, father of Caractacus, who was a member of a distinguised South Wales family, was during *seven years* at Rome, as hostage for his son. This implies that Brân gave himself up *voluntarily* to the Roman authority, to remain as a substitute there for another during that other one's absence from the control of that authority; that his son, Caractacus, was absent *seven years*, and that at the termination of the seven years, Caractacus returned into captivity, and Brân returned to his own country, and according to the Welsh records, taking with him to Wales Ilid, Cyndav, Arwystli Hen, and Mawan. It is believed Arwystli was Aristobulus. It is most interesting to observe that "Arwystl" signifies in Welsh "as Hostage," and it appears as if the Latin name Aristobulus, had suggested to Brân the Welsh name of the position he himself had occupied at Rome during the seven years of his detention there, and that he now playfully applied it to one of his companions during the voyage home.

A Church on the Dunraven Estate, near Bridgend, Glamorganshire, is called Llan Ilid, or the Sanctuary of Ilid; and according to local tradition, that estate was the patrimony of the Brân family, and a house a few hundred yards to the west of the church, is still called Brân's House. Close to the Llan Ilid Church, is a great Druidic Knoll, called Gwyddva, and is named after Ceri, the grandfather of Brân the Blessed.   Singular to state, cherry trees still grow among the oaks on that knoll or mound, and that that fruit was first brought to Rome at the period of Brân's detention there.

The above historical facts strongly confirm the local tradition that St. Paul visited Glamorgan ; and also the supposition that he and Caractacus returned together to the Imperial City in A.D. 67.   St. Paul was beheaded early in the year A.D. 68, by the command of Nero, who himself was murdered about June that year.   We think there is no question St. Paul wrote the *Epistles to the Hebrews.*   It mentions Timothy, and the Temple at Jerusalem as then standing.   The Temple was destroyed in A.D. 70.   We infer, therefore, it was written in A.D. 67, or during the Apostle's stay in Glamorgan, and the word " prophets " alluded to were, doubtless, the Druids among whom he was at the time.   His contact with the Druidic priests of Wales, would naturally suggest to his mind the priests of Israel ; and the Epistle is devoted to *two* priesthoods, namely, that of Aaron, the priesthood of the Hebrews: and that of Melchizedec, the priesthood of the British Druids,   In Calmet's, Vol. iv., 502, it is asked, were Abraham, Joshua, and Samuel Druids ? It is answered, they were as fond of oaks and stones as the Druids were.

" THE MOST SECRET END."

In reference to the eastward station in religion, Josephus states, p. 72, par. 4, that the hair at " the most secret end," that is to say the eastern one of the Holy of Holies, was arranged to appear like a triangle **V.**   The reader will recollect what we state elsewhere, in reference to the nether limbs of the goddess Venus, the Mor'wyn of Druidism.   Also Taliesin, speaking as the personified virility of the sun, says :—

" Cysgais yn mhorphor,
Gan ddy lan, ail môr :
Yn nghylchedd yn mhervedd,
Rhwng denlin Teyrnedd."

" I slept in scarlet (fire),
The birthplace of humidity : a second sea :
In the circle of the belly (and)
Between the two knees of the king."

The sceptre shall not depart from Judah, nor a lawgiver from between his feet until Shiloh come. Dr. Inman gives the translation of the passage thus: " The sceptre shall not depart from Judah nor the ruler's *staff* from between his feet, even when they come to Shiloh ; and to him shall be submission of nations." Then he states, " the words are supposed to refer to the secession of Jeroboam, in whose kingdom Shiloh was situated. (Dr. Kalisch's *Genesis*, pp. 727-747). *Inman's* Vol. ii., p. 726, alleges the words are fraudulently put into the mouth of Jacob. The whole passage is understood by the Christian world to refer to the advent of the Messiah. The other view is that it refers to the masculine vigour or strength of Judah against his enemies to culminate at Shiloh.

The King in the above Welsh verse, is the Creator, and the sun's collective rays in spring is Priapus, that is to say his virile power. The " knees of the King " are the masculine triangle ∧. The Jews have a double triangle in every synagogue to this day, and they call it " The Shield of Dovid," not " David."

" Duw, Ior y Duwian eraill,
Dovydd, a Llywydd y eraill." [1]

Iolo Goch, A.D. 1100

---

[1] God, Leader God, and Ruler of the other gods

THE TRAGEDY OF MOUNT CALVARY.

We now reverently invite the reader to return in thought
to the Jewish Day of Atonement. and also to the occasion of
the Passover. The High Priest, on the Day of Atonement,
stood between the two goats, one "For the Lord" and
the other "For Azazel," or the devil. The Lord Jesus at
the Passover was, on the cross, between the penitent and
the impenitent thieves. The latter represented Barabbas,
and perhaps was he. Both men were thieves, and Jesus
was "*made* to be sin for us" (2 Cor., v. 21.) See page
108, "Abomination." See also our list of Trinities. The
high priest, on the "Day" of Atonement, entered the Holy
Place, facing west, in his pontifical robes, and there un-
robed himself, and after washing his whole body with water,
put on in their stead the white linen garment or shroud.

At the Passover the Lord Jesus was dealt with as
follows: "And the soldiers platted a crown of thorns, and
put it on his head, and they put on him a purple robe, and
said, "Hail, King of the Jews!" * * * Then came
Jesus forth," in sight of the Hebrew ecclesiastical authorities and Romans, "wearing the crown of thorns and the
purple robe." The soldiers meant derision of the august
sufferer, but it appears as if St. John, whose description
of the scene we quote, saw, or thought he saw in the figure
of the crown of thorns that which he supposed had been
prefigured by the golden *crown* of the altar of incense;
and in the purple robe the purple cloth with which that
altar was clothed during each march in the wilderness.[1]
M. Renan would have said St. John had adapted the description to suit a fulfilment of the typical emblems.

---

[1] *Exodus*, ch. 30, v. 3. Numbers, ch. 4, v. 13.

At the period of the Atonement the high priest's two arms were tied or bound with a cord or girdle called Abaneth by Moses, and Emia after the Babylonian captivity.

At the Passover, the Lord Jesus was sent by Annas, bound to Caiaphas, the high priest.[1] And care is taken to state he had been bound by Jewish soldiers of Herod, and not by Roman ones.[2] The high priest stripped naked in the Holy Place, and then washed; and it is still customary in Wales to wash the dead all over immediately after death. At the Passover, Jesus was stripped naked on Calvary. We infer this, because "the party who suffered this kind of death was first stripped of all his clothes, for he suffered naked,"[3] And we have it on the authority of St. John that the soldiers—they were *four*—divided his clothes in four lots among themselves. Even the number of soldiers, like the four Evangelists, seem to be intended to symbolise the four cardinal points.

The high priest, after his official death, and the washing of his whole body, put on the white linen dress and white linen mitre. After the death of Jesus, he was clothed in white linen.[4] Jesus referred to the preparation for his crucifixion as a baptism. "I have a baptism to be baptised with."[5] The sun, it will be remembered, descended to Côd, in the sea, at the end of the Druidic solar year. But there are other equally remarkable coincidences which agree equally with the Gentile incidents of the death of the old sun, under the names of Arawn, Saturn, Silenus, Pan, Tammuz, &c.; and the birth of the young sun as Apollo, Adonis, Hu,

[1] *St. John's Gospel*, ch. xviii. v. 12 and 24.

[2] *St. Luke*, ch. 23, v. 11.

[3] *Moses and Aaron*, p. 125, ed. 1658.

[4] *St. John's Gospel*, ch. 19, v. 40.

[5] *St. Luke*, ch. 12, v. 20.

Gadarn, Hesus the Mighty, Crowned Babe, Taliesin, &c., as with the official death and afterwards with the official birth of the high priest from "the most secret end" of the Holy of Holies. We must again call attention to the following verses wherein Jesus is represented old and young alternately. "Know this, that our Old Man is crucified *with him*, that the body of sin might be destroyed." Romans vi., 6. "That ye put off, concerning the former conversation, the Old Man, which is corrupt according to deceitful lusts (Saturn or old sun as Silenus). And be renewed in the spirit of your mind; and that ye put on the New Man, which, after God, is created in righteousness and true holiness. Ephesians iv., 22, 23, and 24. The first verse quoted has a direct reference to Jesus; the others are important as illustrating that St. Paul employs solar figures, familiar at the time to the Gentiles, to whom he was writing, quite apart from the death and resurrection of Jesus. We believe the figures are borrowed from the allegory of the death of the old sun under the title of Silenus, and the birth of the new sun as Bacchus, otherwise Myses. "Lie not one to another, seeing that ye have put off the Old Man with his deed, and have put on the New Man, which is renewed in knowledge"— the Old Man *renewed*—"after the image of him that created him." Col. iii., 9 and 10. "For ye know the grace of our Lord Jesus Christ, that, though he was rich, yet for your sake he became poor" (as a wren) "that ye, through his poverty might be rich." ii. Cor., viii., 9.

HUMILITY OF CHRIST.

The following lines are by Rhys Brydydd, or Bard, who resided at Blaen Cynllan, Llanharan, Glamorgan, between A.D., 1450 and 1490 :—

Bychanav or bychenid
Yw Hu Gadarn, vel barn byd,
Ar mwyav a Nàv i ni,
Da coeliwn a'n Duw Celi,
Ysgawn ei daith ac esgud—
Mymryn tês, gloewyn ei glud :
A mawr ar dir a moraedd,
A mwyav a gar ar G'oedd :
Mwy na'r bydoedd ! Ymarbedwn
Anmharch gwael ir mawr hael hwn.

The above have never been translated correctly; the
following can be relied upon as being correct :—

The least of the little ones[1] is Hu Gadarn, as the world judges.
But, to us, he is the greatest Nav (Constructing Lord)—
Thoroughly we believe he is our Hidden God !
    A small ray is his Car :
    Light his course and active,
    And great on *land* and *sea*—
    The greatest that I manifestly can have —
    Greater than the worlds !"

Iolo Goch, Prince Owain Glyndwr's Poet Laureate,[1]
describes Hu Gadarn (the divinity of the young sun) as
follows :—

Hu Gadarn is the sovereign : the Lord Protector ;
The King : the giver of the wine and the song of praise :
The Emperor of the *land* and the *sea*,
And the life of the whole is he :
And he held after the Anarchy [2] the strong beamed plough— [3]
A cutting plough—a most excellent plough. [4]
Our leader Lord (Iôr), the polished genius, did this, to show to the
    proud and the humble-wise alike,
That it is best in the eyes of God not to regard (any) calling
    as useless. [5]

---

[1] The Wren symbol of the Druids.   [2] "Dilyw" (Deluge), the word used in
the original signifies, literally, Rudderless.   [3] End of January and the
beginning of February—the ploughing season.   [4] "Arnawdd Gadr
aradr Gwiw."   [5] It is clear by the context, "Gair," is used in the same
sense as Calling or Craft.

In the above, the reader will notice the sun is represented as alternately great and small. The expression "least of the little ones," will remind him of what we state else-where about the wren—the "cutty" wren, that is to say, the Wren of Côd or Cetus, and in the east, Cetus, Der Ketos, that is to say, of the Dolphin (Delphus—Womb), whale or ark, being, like the dove, symbol of Adonis, sacred to the sun, like the wren was in Britain at the winter solstice, and the dove in Phœnicia at the vernal equinox.

CHAPTER XXIV.

THE PLACE OF A SKULL.

MUCH has been written on the subject as to why the place where Jesus and the two malefactors were crucified, bore the singular name of " Place of a Skull." Thousands of times it has been asked, " Why skull and not skulls?" Whose skull? Some learned men had glimpses of the truth, as the result of their studies of the ancient Gentile mythology, and have replied that it is to the skull of Adam the name refers. Others, without the slightest knowledge, have supposed the name was given to the spot because it was the common place of executions, and have inferred " skulls " were there lying about. Some others have supposed the hill of Golgotha resembled a skull in shape. " The Mahomedans have a book wherein is a dialogue between Jesus Christ and the " skull " of Adam "—Calmet. The reference is to the skull of Ad Hama (old sun), the sun, being globular in shape, was among the Druids in their personification of the luminary, regarded as a skull or visible head, and his rays were sometimes said to be his hair, and also his strength. At the

v

Adonia, the Phœnician women, who lived within a few score of miles from Jerusalem, when—like the women whom Ezekiel saw in the porch of the temple at Jerusalem, "weeping for Tammuz," another name for Adonis—were wont, when, at the time of the Passover, they mourned for the " loss of Adonis" (the old sun) *to shave their heads.*[1]   We have dealt with this subject in another part of this work, and shall only add here a quotation we could not then find in reference to Jupiter Capitolinus, or of the head : " At Rome, when the foundation of a certain temple, in honour of Jupiter, was laid, a man's head, full, fresh, and lively, as if it had been lately buried, yea, hot blood issuing out of it, was found there."[2]   Then, we are told, the temple came to be called Jupiter of the Head.   That " explanation " is pure nonsense ; the old sun or Jupiter (Iu Father) was the head, under the title of Saturn, and the most ancient religious rites, simular to those of the Saturnalia, otherwise Adonia, had been practised where the Roman temple stood.   It will be observed the " head " is described as being in a condition of dead-alive ; the Logos in it.   Such was the condition which the old sun was supposed to be in on Dec. 20th at sunset, that the Logos escaped, and that he returned in a " renewed " body every December 22nd.   His divinity could not be killed.

Now, " the Place of a Skull," no doubt, bore that name in reference to similar religious rites, relating to the allegorical death of the sun every year, at the time of the Passover in Palestine, and at the time of the winter solstice in Britain, and which had been observed on Calvary in preceding ages.

---

[1] Bell's *Pantheon.*
[2] Godwin's *Roman Antiquities*, p. 1   " De Monte Capitolino.

Strange that the death of the Sun of Righteousness should have taken place on one of the *very spots* where, in ancient times, the crucifixion of the sun of the heavens had been annually and dramatically observed, and that the evangelists should have taken particular care to mention the name of the hill so called, outside the walls of Jerusalem. And quite as strange is the fact, that no one has since satisfactorily identified the spot. In concluding the foregoing list of remarkable coincidences or agreements between the incidents of the period of the atonement and the incidents of the last scenes in the life of Jesus on earth, may be mentioned wounding his august head also by means of a crown of thorns. This was in accord with the Druidic and Phœnician, &c., myths, respecting the wounded head of King Arthur, Adonis, &c., in reference to which, and in sympathy with the sufferings the wound in the "head" entailed, the three ladies of Arthur's Court shrieked forth their lamentations, as did likewise the Phœnician women in sympathy with the sufferings of Adonis. "And there followed him (Jesus) a great company of people, and of *women* who also bewailed and lamented him. But Jesus turning unto them, said *Daughters* of Jerusalem, weep not for me, but weep for yourselves and for your children,'" &c.

There are still other striking coincidences between the acts of the High Priest, on the period of the Atonement, and the acts of Jesus when dying, and again appearing at the period of the Passover.

THE TRANSFIGURATON OF JESUS TO BE HIGH PRIEST AND KING ON A MOUNTAIN.

The purpose of the transfiguration of the Lord Jesus, according to the opinion of the early Christian Fathers, was to convey to Peter, James, and John, a convincing

v 2

proof that he was the Messiah. He himself describes the
event as "the Son of Man coming in his kingdom."
(Matt xxi., 28). The transfiguration, therefore, is to be
understood as his coronation as King of the Kingdom of
Ouranos (Arawn). He was to be High Priest and King.
The Sanctuaries of the Druids were on high mountains,
hence the terms "High Place" and Llans (Ir Lan), and
the expression "going up to the House of God." The
Archdruid as the Word (Logos or Speech) of the gods,
or the personified Divine Emanations, was Mercury :—

> " His "station" was that of the Herald Mercury,
> New lighted on a heaven-kissing hill."

Like a Druidic High Priest and King, "after the order
of Melchisedec," the Messiah, "the Son of Man," came
to his kingdom on " a high mountain apart," that is to
say, isolated as a Sanctuary.

In Druidism were three priests, symbolizing the three
distinct emanations of the Logos or the Divine Word,
which were set forth as "the fulness of the Godhead,"
(Col. ii., 9), incarnated in the Archdruid. The said three
Druidic Priests, in every age, bore the titles Plennydd,
Alawn, and Gwron, and were represented as Divine
Emanations thus \|/.

Peter, James, and John bore precisely the same
symbolical relation to the Messiah on the Mount of Trans-
figuration, as Plennydd, Alawn, and Gwron did to the
Archdruid in the Sanctuary of Druidism! Elijah and
Moses symbolising Saturn (Arawn), and Silenus (Gwydd
Naw, otherwise Seithynun Veddw, otherwise Noah, or
Bacchus as an Old Man), attended the coronation of their
successor, "the Son of Man" as Ruler "of the Kingdom"!

St. Matthew describes the coronation of the Messiah as follows: " His face did shine as the Sun, and his raiment was white as light. And behold there appeared unto them Moses and Elias talking with him. Then answered Peter and said unto Jesus, ' Lord, it is good for us to be here: if thou wilt, let us make here three tabernacles, one for Thee, and one for Moses, and one for Elias.' While yet he spoke, behold a bright cloud overshadowed them ; and behold a voice out of the cloud, which said, ' This is my beloved son in whom I am well pleased. HEAR YE HIM." (c. xvii). The " voice " is the Bath Kol of Israel. The reader will carefully observe the above extraordinary event took place just before the crucifixion of the Messiah, on the place of a skull, near Jerusalem. St. Luke tells us the subject of the conversation between Jesus, Moses, and Elias on the mountain was his own approaching death at Jerusalem (ix., 30-31). In v. 32 we are told, significantly, Peter, James, and John, " were heavy with sleep." It is implied it was when they suddenly awoke they beheld the brilliant scene of the transfiguration. Then we have the extremely pathetic scene in the Garden of Gethsemane. Jesus had just told the disciples—we believe he exclusively referred to Peter, James, and John, as symbolising the three elements of the triune Word (\|/)—" *I am in my Father, and ye in me, and I in you.*" (St. John xiv., 20). Jesus ordered the rest of the disciples to sit down, and accompanied only by Peter, James, and John, He himself went farther alone, leaving the said three disciples behind at a spot between the place where he had ordered the other disciples to sit, and where he stationed Himself. Here again Peter, James, and John, as they did on the high mountain, fell into a sleep. The three disciples, in their symbolical relation to Jesus, implied the same thing as the body and two wings of the dove or wren did to the incarnate Logos or Word. It seems to be conveyed by the narratives that both on the high mountain and in the Garden of Gethsemane the presence of heavenly spiritual beings overpowered their nature, and that then they were three agents transmitting the Word to Jesus from the old Father (whose Divinity was being transferred to the new sun). Observe the darkness, and Jesus crying " Eli ! Eli !" and not Jehovah, Elohim, nor Adonai. The by-standers supposed he was calling Elijah, and, as we have seen, Elijah was Saturn (the old sun), whose " day " is the Sabbath of Israel. Eli is the Greek Ilos and the Welsh Haul. Luke, in c. xxii., v. 43, states that in the garden was an " angel from heaven strengthen-ing him." In the Druidic religion, the central position, occupied by James, is that of the generating or begetting principle of the Seminal Logos, with Peter on the right and John on the left. Dr. Inman (vol. i., p. 599) states, the Hebrew meaning of Iacab, or James, is " to make hollow," and " to be deep as in a pit." In reference to Sarah, her matrix is called " pit " by the prophet Isaiah : Thus in the original, " Listen to me ye pursuers of righteousness, ye seekers of Jehovah. Look unto the stone with which ye were hewn, and to the hollow of the *pit* ye were dug. Look unto Abraham your father and unto Sarah that bear you.--Isaiah li., v. 1 and 2. Abraham's virile organ is compared to an ancient stone obelisk, or one of the round towers of Ireland, and Sarah's womb to a " hollow pit." The figures refer to the ancient Linga and Yoni symbols. Abraham's Linga and Sarah's Yoni being old, the result is referred to as a Divine miracle.

In Acts ii., 1-2, we learn that the above James was put to death by Herod Agrippa, and his martyrdom is said to have taken place in either A.D. 42 or 44 ; and in Acts xv., we find that another James, son of Cleopas, otherwise Alphæns, called the brother of the Lord, had been placed in authority instead of the martyred James, son of Zebedee and Salome, and in v. 9, c. ii. of the Epistle to the Galatians, he, called James the Just by Josephus, acts, in conjunction with Peter and John, on behalf of the infant church at Jerusalem, in giving to Paul and Barnabas the right hand of fellowship. In the transaction of the *business* acts of the church, James, and not Peter, is named first, viz., "James, Cephas, and John." But in the narratives describing the spiritual scenes of the transfiguration and that of Gethsemane, Peter is mentioned first. The last-mentioned James the Just was also put to death by order of the high priest Ananius, son of Annas, father-in-law of Caiaphas. For the murder of James the Just King Agrippa took the high priesthood away from Ananius after he had enjoyed the dignity three months, and for the same offence he was threatened with punishment by Albinus, the Roman governor of the province.

The High Priest's priesthood having died, and that death being symbolised by the divesting himself of his pontifical robes, he passed as officially dead, and wearing his grave garments or shroud, and napkin of linen on his forehead, and with both arms bound with the girdle, into the room called the Holy of Holies within the second veil. He was then absolutely alone, no one else being permitted to be, not only in the lesser Sanctuary or Holy Place, but even in the great outer court, wherein were the laver and great brazen altar. But the High Priest had his priesthood renewed in the secrecy of the dark chamber of the *Sanctum Sanctorum*, and he emerged forth with the priestly life "renewed" as a babe as regards his priesthood through the eastern outlet, "the

most secret end." Only the Seminal Logos, passed
in that way. St. John (c. xx.), states Mary Magdalene
travelled through *darkness* to the Sepulchre of the
Lord Jesus, and she being associated with Hades,
from whence the Lord's soul was returning into his
glorified body,[1] was appropriately the first to see him
in the garden on his return. In verses 6 and 7, we see
that the shroud and the napkin of the head and face had
been carefully folded and laid aside. This implies the
same thing as the High Priest, carefully laying aside the
linen robe, the abaneth, and the mitre and napkin of the
head and face, after *his* return into the Holy Place from
the Holy of Holies, and donning in their stead, the
garments of the High Priesthood, "renewed" through
the eastern outlet from the vulva of the Virgin of Israel.
But in the case of the Christ, his grave and second birth-
place, or "cave" of the garden, is the stone kist of the
older Druidic system.

Referring to the last act of the High Priest going
eastward, it is said, "And he" as old Saturn under the
name Arawn "shall take of the blood of the bullock, and
sprinkle it with his finger upon the mercy seat *eastward*,
and *before* the mercy seat shall he sprinkle of the blood
with his finger *seven times* (Lev. xvi., 14.) It will be
recollected the Holy of Holies was only about twenty-five
feet square, and that the expression "before the mercy
seat" signifies that part of it facing the east. Pool, in the
Rev. John Eadie, D.D., LL.D's *Illustrated Bible*, com-
menting on this verse, states, "EASTWARD, with his face
eastward, or upon the eastern part of it towards the
people." He came eastward from the west, underneath
the earth. The people were on the outside of the curtains

---

[1] St. John's Gospel, xii., 16.

of the outer court beyond the *eastern* side of it, clearly waiting for the high priest to emerge through the hairy eastern end of the Holy of Holies, implying the sun appearing on the eastern horizon, travelling from Hades beneath the earth. The following is clearly intended to imply that the divinity of Jesus also, the moment his body died on Calvary (Place of the Head), passed into the Holy of Holies *westwardly*. And Jesus cried out with a loud voice, and gave up the spirit. *And the veil of the temple* was rent in twain from the top to the bottom," "from the top to the bottom," as indicating it was not done by human hands, for "the top" was ten cubits in height. The expression may be intended to imply the spirit of Jesus—the spiritual white dove or the Word—descended with great electrical force from the heights of Golgotha from the west, into the Holy of Holies containing the Delphus (womb) of Cêd.

The *force* is implied by St. Matthew's additional particulars. He states, " And behold the veil of the temple was rent in twain from the top to the bottom ; and the earth did quake and the rocks rent." The expression implies the divinity passing into Hades or Annwn, beneath the earth.

It will be remembered that at the winter solstice, December 20th, in Druidism, the old sun descended in the south-west into Cêd or Delphus, otherwise Cetus, &c., in the sea of Annwn or Hades, or, according to another Druidic name, Gwyllionwy (the dark waters of Iôn).

Among Eastern nations, as we have often stated, the old sun's divinity was said to descend at the end of the sacred year, into the womb of Cetus or Der Ketos, Dolphin (Delphus) or whale, as symbolising Cêd's womb, the

consort of the Almighty and the mother of the sun in the
south-western sea.   It is startlingly remarkable to find
that the Holy of Holies was enveloped in the skins of a
great fish species.   The "badger's skin," translation of
the Hebrew name for the said skins (Tachash) is now given
up, and it is now known Tachash is Arabic for the Dolphin
(*Delphus*—womb).   In Numbers iv., 6, we find that the
skin of the Tachash or Dolphin, was used also to cover the
Ark of the Covenant when the Israelites were on the march
in the wilderness.   Again, the Lord Jesus and his twelve
disciples agree with the British Arthur and his twelve
Knights of the Round Table.   Peter, James, and John,
the Lord Jesus's inner Cabinet, correspond with Plennydd,
Alawn, and Gwron, the Druidic personification of the three
elements of the Word or Divine emanations of the Creator
passing through the sun, as frequently explained in this
work.   The three Marys, too, correspond with the Three
Maids of Druidism, and the Three Graces of the Greeks.
(*See* page 14.)   Further, as if the system of the Christian
religion was modelled upon the erroneous frame-work
of the Druidism of the East, instead of on the pure
original Druidism of the West, that is to say, of Britannia,
one of the twelve zodiacal representative characters, Judas,
is like Typhon, the Druidic Avagddu, set forth as causing
the death of the sun of righteousness, or Jesus, referred to
by St. Paul as being, before his murder, an " old man."
The Christian Alexandrian school must have detected the
error or heresy in the Egyptian trinity, otherwise the place
occupied by St. John the Evangelist, the *third person* of the
inner Cabinet of the Lord Jesus would have been occupied
by the Typhonic Judas.   But, on the contrary, in the
Christian system, St. John is represented as being in
loveableness almost the counterpart of the Lord Jesus
himself.   The third Mary (the Magdalene) corresponds

with the Satanic consort of the evil third person of the Eastern trinity, viz., Typhon. As we point out elsewhere, his nephew Mordred is the Judas of King Arthur. (*See* page 178.) That one of the Knights of the Round Table occupies this position, proves one of two things, viz., either Druidism had become corrupted by the Orientalism of the Phœnicians, as in the case of the legend of the death and recovery of Taliesin at Borth, Aberdovey; or that the Christian monkish writer of *Morte de Arthur*, framed the legend on the framework of the apostolic church of Jerusalem.

T has frequently been pointed out by students of the Bible as being curious that a garden was the scene of mankind's fall, and that a garden was likewise the scene of mankind's redemption or uprise, namely, the Garden of Eden, and the Garden of Joseph of Arimathea, respectively. It appears, by the teachings of the schoolmen, as if the first Adam was far more successful in pulling down than the second Adam was in uplifting. It is said *all* mankind fell with the first Adam, but all mankind did not rise with the second Adam. No theological fineness can get over this; but we are not engaged upon the task of attempting to unriddle theological conundrums, but we may state that the pith of the doctrine is this: Mankind had no choice but to fall with the first Adam, but they can rise or not, as they please, with the second Adam. Thus the old Morienic or Pelagian doctrine of free will stands good, and the justice of holding mankind responsible for remaining down is obvious. We know Pelagius, whose Welsh name was Morien, was a Glamorganshire man, and flourishing towards the close of the fourth century, and during the existence of the British Church as a distinct branch of the Christian Church, which naturally was strongly imbued with the Ancient Druidic philosophic doctrines, which taught that, while the animal creation was tied and regulated by instinct, man was entrusted with freewill, illustrated by the fact that he alone of earthly creatures was entrusted with the capacity to light such a dangerous thing as fire. Fire was regarded as sacred by

the old Gentile religionists, not only for the service it
renders mankind, by causing heat and giving light, but as
a token of the confidence or trust it implied the Creator
placed in man. The Druids, at certain seasons of the
year, lit great fires, often repeated, and named each a
Coelgerth, which signifes Manifest Great Faith, that
is to say, the Creator's "faith" in every man ultimately
attaining perfection made evident by Him entrusting
man with fire. The Baal-Tan, or Fire of Baal, called
commonly "Beltane," is clearly of Phœnician origin, as the
name Baal implies, introduced into Britain by those who
came here principally for tin, and which was made to rival
the old Druidic Coelgerth. The Welsh termination *tân*
(fire), implies that, like the shifting from the winter solstice
to the vernal equinox, as the period for observing the death
of the old sun and the birth of the new sun, the Phœnicians
had succeeded in introducing this innovation also among
some of the Cymric-speaking Druids.

We shall show in another portion of this work that the
garden which the Lord Himself planted—the Eden or
Paradise of the Hebrews—is (1) the whole round earth
above the rational horizon; (2) the Druidic Circular
" Church " as the symbol of the former ; (3) each tumulus ;
(4) each Gwyddva, or the Place of Presence, surrounded by
a trench full of water, and on the summit of which a Druid
priest stood—and standing on a Cromleach cr rocking
stone, signified the same thing—offering up his prayers,
and from which also, as from a pulpit, he preached to the
people ; (5) the round shield of every British warrior. The
mound is the original mount of the congregation or assembly
of gods ; the Druid priests, as officially representing the
Divine attributes on earth, were regarded, by virtue of the
offices they held in the representations, as " gods " incarnate

The Druidic Circular "Church" is the Garden of Arthur, or the sun as the Almighty's gardener; the Garden of Adonis, and its floral representations, were called "the Garden of Adonis." As a mound of the dead it is simply Mount Meru (Marw—dead) or Moriah, and the Lotos flower, another of its emblems which floats in the water, as the bee-hive-shaped earth of the ancients was supposed to do, and carrying, as the earth does, its seeds to plant in the water new creations like itself. Doubtless, some of the ancients, not knowing the earth was regarded by the Druids as Cêd's belly, believed the stars were new worlds, which had derived their origin from the seeds of this earth; like the seeds of the Lotos, scattering new creations, like it-elf, in the waters of the Nile and elsewhere.

Thus the Druidic tumulus symbolised several meanings.—

1.   The beehive shaped earth above the rational horizon.

2.   The Garden of the Sun.

3.   Mount Meru, that is to say, Mynydd y Marw (Hill of the Dead).

4.   Place of a skull; Calvary, otherwise Golgotha.

Mount Meru and Mount Moriah are identical in meaning; Gwyddva or Druidic pulpit.

5.   As the belly of Cêd, the stone kist in the centre of the mound, symbolised the matrix of Cêd, the consort of the Creator. To this day a coffin is called "ark" by the Welsh, and as such the matrix of Cêd was considered to be, and in the symbol of it the Druids deposited their dead. As a garden, it implied the fecundity of the earth as the source of everything, and personified as Venus.

6.   As a grave, it signified that into which everything returns, and as a womb the birth-place of all things. The

personified sun was the husbandman or cultivator, of the whole earth's surface considered as a round garden. Paradise is a Persian word denoting an enclosed garden, and both Palestine and Eden were called Paradise, because both symbolised the whole earth as the garden which the Lord himself planted.

EASTERN ERROR.

In the East the sun, as Tammuz, Osiris, Adonis, &c., was represented as being killed in the heavens at the vernal equinox, the attack beginning at noon, instead of at the winter solstice, by Mars, Pluto, Typhon, each name implying the Power of Darkness, and immediately afterwards his divinity being received into the Delphus, that is to say, another symbol of the matrix of his mother Cèd, in the ocean. The solar drama was enacted in innumerable number of places, but the localities of the Red Sea and the Indian Ocean are sites most familiar to the world. The sea called " Red," was so named because it was allegorically taught the old sun, mortally wounded, as Tammuz or Adonis, had *bled into it*, after being mortally wounded by Mars, Typhon, or Pluto. Each stone kist in a tumulus was, symbolically, the matrix-grave of the sun. And inasmuch as the sun itself rose again into life, it gave to our ancestors reason, as they thought, to believe the souls of the dead, in radiant new bodies, like the new body with which the new sun was clothed, would also return from the dead. In Britain, Silbury Hill, Wilts, was the principal symbol of belly or cave, that is to say, matrix of the great mother of the sun. The name is Sol-Parrow, or grave of the old sun.

The reader will bear in mind what we state elsewhere, viz., the equator is called in the old language of the Druids Cyhydedd (Cydhidbedd) or equal length of a grave.

The whole earth being considered as a garden grave, and Silbury Hill its principal symbol in the British Isles.

On the other hand, in the East it was taught that Venus was born from a ship or ark, Llong Voel, (naked ship of Druidism). That ship or ark was one of the symbols of Cêd, and the personified fecundity of the earth was Venus. Therefore it is probable the floating Lotos was another symbol of Cêd, and that the Orientals believed the stars were, like Venus, her offspring, and that the seeds of the Lotos were used as symbols to illustrate that beautiful supposition. By the way, it is curious to find "Silbury" near Avebury, and "Salisbury" near Stonehenge.

THE TEMPLE OF AVEBURY, WILTS.

As intimated already, in Druidism, and in all the ancient creeds of the world, the whole earth above the rational horizon was regarded as the garden of the Creator, and the sun was regarded as his gardener. Hence the poetically personified sun, under the titles or names Adam, Noah, Adonis, Arthur, St. George, &c., are referred to as husbandmen, or land cultivators. In Druidism, the sacred circular temple of the bards, be it small or large, was, symbolically, the circular earth as a garden.

Take, for example, the vast Druidic circle of Abiri or Avebury, Wilts, the largest of the kind in the world. The circular space within the circular moat, is, according to the measurement of Sir R. Colt Hoare, Bart., twenty-eight acres and twenty-seven perches. Its diameter in one direction is 1,260 feet, and in another 1,170 feet. Encircling the entire green arena is what remains of a broad and deep moat, evidently formerly holding water as a canal. Rising backwards from the outside of this canal or

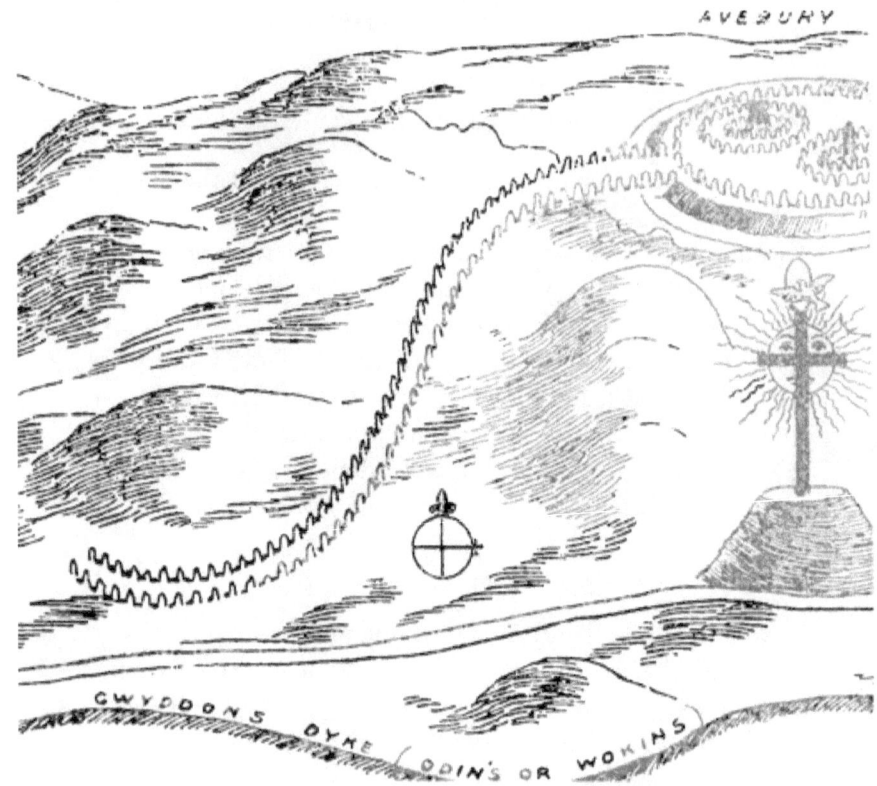

AVEBURY

GWYDDON'S DYKE (ODIN'S OR WOKINS)

THE GOLGOTHA OF BRITAIN

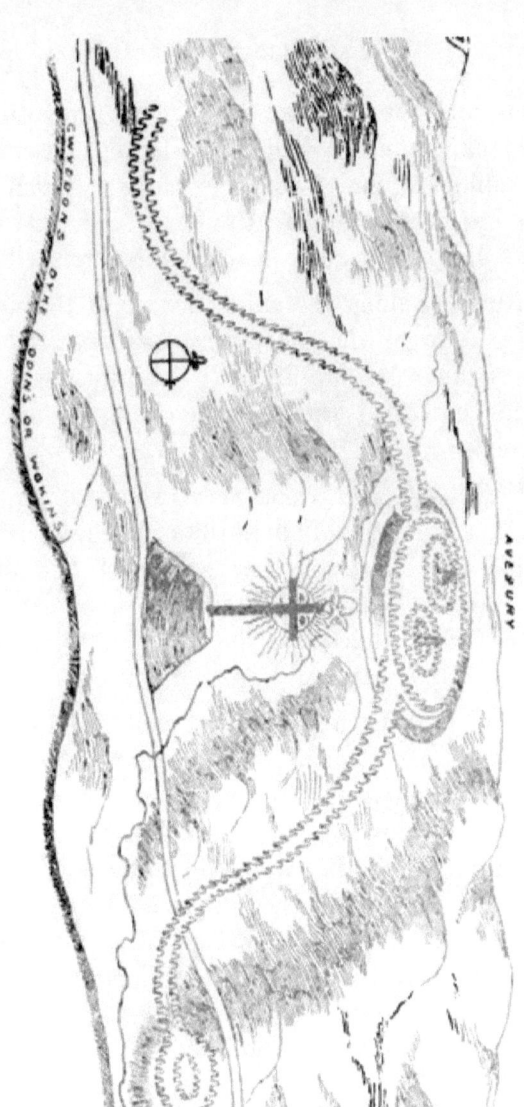

AVEBURY is spelt Abri by the Rev. W. Stukeley, M.D., Rector of All Saints in Stamford, A.D. 1720. Abri seems to be the correct form of the name, and it signifies Ab-Ri, or Son of God. Ri or Rhi is one of the Druidic titles of the Most High (vide Giraldus). It will be observed that solitary Hill is due south from the temple. The monotone Calvary, with a cross on the summit, on the south side of very old Druidic churches, was, it seems, an imitation of this mound of Ab-Ri, &c.

AVEBURY

OGBEN

moat, and running like it all round the entire circle, is a lofty embankment. On the sloping ascent of the said embankment, and facing the vast flat green arena within the space enclosed by the moat, are distinct traces of rows of seats, all, of course, now covered with verdure.

Running along the entire border of the circle above the inner edge of the moat were *one hundred great stones*, placed endways in the earth, and forming a magnificent circle, enclosing within it the arena of 28 acres and 27 perches.

Within the said arena were two great circles, and each circle consisting of two rows of circles of stones, one inside the other. In the centre of one of the double circles were three immense upright stones, each 21 feet high, and arranged like the three legs of an old-fashioned Cymric chair or stool.

Lying flat on the top of the said three uprights, was an immense flat stone. Each outward circle of upright stones consisted of 30 stones, and each of the inner ones consisted of twelve stones. The space or cove formed by the three uprights, was open towards the east and the spring day sun. The other set of double circles were like the one described, but instead of a vast chair-like cromleach as the other had, was an immense round single pillar of stone, its lower part imbedded in the earth, signifying its point, stood in the centre of this double circle. It was twenty-one feet in height, and eight feet nine inches in diameter.

SILBURY HILL—CYVRYNGOM.

A short distance from and to the exact south of the circular temple of Avebury, or Abiri, is the enormous artificial beehive-like mound called Silbury Hill. There

w

is no doubt the Druids called it "Pych Cyvryngom" (the Hill of Mediatorship). Dr. Owen Pughe has interpreted the word differently, but it is evident "Cyvryngom" is an old form of the word "Cyvryngydd (Mediator). In the fourteenth of the Welsh Bardic Triads, the name is rendered "Cyvrangom"—"a" instead of the middle "y." That is clearly another error. At the end of the word we have placed m instead of "n," the latter being a mistake of some old scribe.

Sir Richard Colt Hoare, Bart., gives the dimensions of this extraordinary artificial mound as follows :—

"The circumference of the hill, as near the base as possible is 2,027 feet. The diameter at the top is 120 feet; the sloping height is 316 feet, and the perpendicular height 170 feet. The entire mound covers the space of five acres and thirty-four perches of land" It is important to observe that *the meridian line of the temple*, or the line of the solstitial colure (see p. 95) runs through the centre of the mound. It is traditionally stated by the bards of Wales, that the Druids watched the sun on the afternoon of each shortest day (December 20th in Druidism), when, in his supposed agony, he was in the heavens level with the cross on the summit of Silbury Hill. That the assembled Druids stood, on each such occasions, either on the north or on the south-east of the said Silbury Hill, so as to witness the sun, either on the meridian or gradually descending into the south-west. We wrote to the Astronomer Royal, Greenwich, as to the period when the sun did appear at noon, when on the Tropic of Capricornus, at an altitude level with the said hill. In reply we received the following communication from Mr. H. H. Turner, M.A., the Assistant Astronomer Royal of Britain :—

" Sir,—With reference to your letter, the Astronomer Royal requests me to inform you that the period you refer to, when the latitude of the British Isles was very different, is not recognised by Astronomers, and, consequently, the meridian altitude of the sun on the shortest day is not considered to have varied from its present value—about 14° or 15° ; at which altitude it would appear 300 feet high at a distance of a quarter of a mile."

It will be observed the sloping height of Silbury Hill is 316 feet, and the perpendicular height is 170 feet.

That the entire locality was associated with Mercury (Odin) is implied by the name of a vast dyke bordering it, and called Odin's Dyke.

THE GREAT SERPENT OF AVEBURY AND CYVRYNGOM.

Running from the south-west towards the south-east, in wavy bends, was a figure of a vast serpent, its middle passing through the circle of 28 acres and 27 perches, and, therefore, it was intended to imply the serpent's head *had passed that way*. The entire length of the serpent was about two miles.

The entire figure of the serpent was constructed of *two* parallel sinuous lines of large upright stones, so arranged as to describe the entire distance a smooth surface to the beholder, and exactly showing the proportions of a serpent on the march. The head of the serpent rested on the summit of a gentle hill, called Overton. The head *faced the sun on its rising on every December 22nd*, described as a " Crowned Babe," coming to rule the world another year. The exact spot where the head rested is still called " Hackben." Now, " ben " in the name is the mutated Welsh Pen (Head), therefore, it is certain " Hack " is Welsh also.

w 2

But there is no such word in the Welsh language, and we, therefore, conclude " Hack" is a corrupt Welsh name. The serpent is a gigantic symbol. The temple itself is a symbol of the earth as a garden, rising all around from the rational horizon, with the sea around it. The serpent symbolises Cêd, otherwise Minerva, or feminine Divine wisdom, animating the whole earth or garden. She had just given birth to the Divine Son in that district of Annwn, otherwise Hades, called Gwenydva, in the dark regions below the earth, from her Delphus (Womb) into which the old sun's Divinity (\|/) had escaped at sunset on December 20th, and described by Homer as going like a sea-gull :—

> " *Down* he bent his way,
> In semblance like a *Sea Mew* (that)
> Dips her light pinions in the briny wave."

In another passage, Hermes, who is above described as a Sea Mew, is called Helius or the sun. On the morning of the solar new year he is returning clothed in a dazzling new body towards the very region of the heavens wherein, as an old man, his old body had been shattered by Avagddu (e), otherwise Pluto, Typhon, &c., forty hours before. And now Avagddu and his dusky forces, like Pharaoh and the Egyptian army pursuing Moüses and the Children of Israel into the Red Sea, are pursuing the young son-babe. Hesus the Mighty, and his train of redeemed souls from Gwenydva ! It appears as if Gwenydva was beyond Hades, in Druidic mythology, and that in the East souls of the blessed were supposed to be there in captivity ; but annually liberated by the Divinity of the sun. The immense serpent, symbolising feminine Divine wisdom, has just slipped up through the garden—Earth—swiftly to face the babe, like a mother doing so, to encourage him to advance and to terrify his pursuing enemies. Her awful countenance on Overton Hill is supposed to strike with quailing horror the pursuing foes, and they retire to again attack him in his next decline on the next December 20th.

"Hackben" is clearly a corruption of the name Ogben, which signifies Swift Head, rushing to meet her radiant off-spring, and to terrify his murderous pursuers!

In the Druidic symbolical system there were two other serpents : a golden dragon and a red dragon. The former symbolised the life in matter ; the latter destruction, and called "the Red Dragon," and is the Cymric or Welsh symbol of war to this day. It is sometimes called the Red Dragon of Cadwalader—Cad Chwalu Tir—and signifying, literally, the tumult of earth scattering.[1] The Prince Cadwalader is said to have flourished about A.D. 634, and we are told he was "the last of the Welsh princes who assumed the title of chief sovereign of Britain." But we refer to the etymology of the word, and not to any particular prince. The great serpent of Avebury signified the mother of the Golden Dragon or Venus and Sun.

The water of the moat encircling the Temple of Avebury symbolised the ocean encircling the earth at the horizon, according to the erronious geographical knowledge of the ancients, and described by Homer as being where the Divine artist, or architect, or carpenter (*See* page 101) "poured the ocean round." The Celi and the Word, the latter being an emanation of the former, are one in essence, but the last-named an abstraction from the Celi.

The three uprights, with the great slab lying athwart their summits, was a Cromleâch, and was another symbol of that of the ark of the sun and belly of Ced. The Egyptian city called Thebes signifies ark and also cow. It

---

[1] Referring, doubtless, to Raising Earthworks, &c.

will be remembered Homer states Thebes had a *hundred
gates*, the exact number of stones along the outward rim
of the arena of Avebury, and encircling the Druidic ark,
shown in Egypt as a shrine on the deck of the sacred barge
on the Nile. The barge was a symbol of the belly of Isis,
and the shrine Venus, or Isis II. In the Welsh language
to this day, a *circle* is called "a hundred," as "*cant
olwyn*" (the rim of a wheel) ; "*cant* gogr" (rim of a sieve),
&c. Bryant in his *Analysis* states, a hundred was,
anciently, a symbol for indefinable space. And the hundred stones encircling Avebury implied, like the "hundred
gates" of Thebes, the illimitable space beyond the border
of the circle of the earth, that is, beyond the circle of the
rational horizon, as symbolised by this most ancient temple,
erected for the purposes of Divine Worship.

In the foregoing particulars we find a garden and a
serpent; and outside the temple proper we have an
artificial mound, known now as "Silbury." When the
present English name was given to it there were, no doubt,
people alive who were able to explain what it really
signified. As we have seen, the Druids called it Pych
Cyvryngom (Hill of Mediatorship), also called Cluda'r
Cyvryngom. The name "Cyvryngom" would also imply
an intermediary, and it refers to the hill as being that of
the sun in the character of intermediary between the inhabitants of the earth and utter darkness. Silbury Hill is
the principal Golgotha, or Place of a Skull, of Britain.
The said "hill" is literally "without the gate," that is to
say, "without" the circle of the temple enclosure, and,
therefore, emblematically, beyond the world of government and order (Hebrews xiii., 12), and, therefore, in
"Sodom" and Egypt, each the allegorical Hades or Shoel
(Rev. xi., 8) of the Bible. It is almost certain that, in

ancient days, a cross, with a loop on the top of it
stood on the summit of Silbury Hill, the straight
beam, the colure of the solstices, and the
horizontal cross beam describing the line of the
Tropic of Capricornus, the loop being the
symbol of the Vulva of Cêd, to receive into it for safety
the flying Divinity inhabiting the sun, and symbolised
by the wren, &c. (*See* Galatians, c. iii., v. 1). During
the sun's supposed sufferings, the multitude here wept
and lamented, as likewise did the multitude at Carn
Ochain (Hill of Groans), St. David's ; and Bryn Wylfa
(Hill of Weeping), Borth ; and, doubtless, also on the
Meirionydd land projecting into the sea opposite Arklow,
Ireland, and called Pwllheli (Pwll-Haul-Le), the Chasm
Place of the Sun, meaning the adjacent channel to the west.
These rites agreed with the weeping for Tammuz mentioned
by Ezekiel (c. viii., v. 14., but when the sun is on the Tropic
of Cancer), and with the Adonia and the Saturnalia and
with the solemnities of the Day of Atonement when the
high Priest entered Sheol or Hades !

CHAPTER XXVI.

THE TEMPLE OF AVEBURY (AB RIII), BRITAIN, AND THE CIRCUS MAXIMUS, OR GREAT CIRCLE, ROME.

THE world appears not to have noticed the resemblance of Avebury and the Circle Maximus at Rome to each other. The legend referring to the vast Roman Circle, or Circus, is to the following effect. It was constructed by Tarquinius Priscus, a character as legendary as our own King Arthur. It is stated that while Tarquinius Priscus and his wife Tanaquil, were journeying with a large number of people from Etruria towards Rome, and when they were on Mount Janculum in full view of the city, an eagle came down with a gentle swoop, and took the cap off the head of Tarquinius Priscus, and then wheeling round him, replaced it. His wife Tanaquil, who was skilled in augury, like all the Etruscans, interpreted this to be an Omen of good. He eventually became King of Rome. The following is another bit of legend founded on the solar myth :—When King Tarquinius was in the regal office, two countrymen, who pretended to have quarrelled, appeared before him as if to seek judgement, and while one of them was speaking, the other smote the king on the head with an axe, so that he fell dead. We are here reminded of Mithras, between Ormuzd and Ahriman, and Horus between Osiris and Typhon, (and the latter killing the former), and of Jesus dying between two thieves on the Place of the Head. Now, the following is what is stated about the Circus Maximus. After stating Tarquinius Priscus constructed it, we are told, "it lay between the Palatine and Aventine hills, and was of an oblong circular form," (egg shaped), like Stonehenge.

The length of it was three stadia (or furlongs), and a half, *i. e.* 437 paces, or 2187½ feet ; the breadth, a little more than a stadium (606 feet and 6 inches). It had rows of seats all round called fori or spectacule, rising one above the other. The lowest row of seats was of stone and the highest of wood, where separate places were allotted to each class of the people, and also to the senators, and to the equites. It was said to have held at least 150,000 persons, or according to others, above double that number ; according to Pliny 250,000. Some moderns say 380,000. Its *circumference was a mile.* It was *surrounded with a ditch or canal* called Euripus, *ten feet broad,* and ten feet deep, and with porticoes three stories high, both the work of Julius Cæsar. Two statues of Mercury (Odin or Woden), stood there, holding chains to keep in the horses. A line called creta or calx (calch—lime), seems to have been drawn chiefly to mark the end of the course or limit of victory (Pliny xxxv., 17, s. 58 ; xviii., 37). It is to this " line " Horace alludes, "mors ultima *linea* rerum est," death is the line (end) of all human miseries.— Ep. i., 16, fin. Augustus placed here an obelisk 132 feet high, which he had brought from Egypt, and at a small distance from it, another obelisk 88 feet high. There were also *seven* other pillars, having oval figures, called ova (eggs), which were raised, to denote how many rounds the charioteers had completed. Above each of these ova (eggs), was the figure of a Dolphin (Delphus —Womb), from which the earth's Anima, symbolised as an egg, had originally come. Public games, like in the courses at Stonehenge, were then associated with religion, and before they began in the Circus Maximus, the images of the gods were led along in procession on carriages, in frames, or on men's shoulders, with a great train of attendants, part on horseback and part on foot.

Next followed the combatants, dancers, musicians, &c. When the procession was over, the consuls and priests performed sacred rites. Vide *Roman Antiquities* by Alexander Adam, LL.D. ; p.p. 274-276.

As at Avebury, there was a serpent associated with the Circus Maximus, and she was once seen as an awful omen, "issuing from the altar of the Royal Palace." Tarquinius erected close by an immense temple to Jupiter, on the Saturnine Hill. Saturn was Jupiter (sun) in each March, but represented as an old sun-god, Saturn, in December. This hill was sacred to Saturn, or old sun, as Silbury Hill, Avebury, was, and as we suppose Salisbury or Old Sarum was in relation to Stonehenge. Tarquinius obtained the Sybilline books of the Cumaean Sybil, identified by Aristotle with the Erythræan Sybil, who seems to have been identical with the Cimmerian Sybil. The reader will recollect what we state elsewhere about "Erythia" of Herodotus; that it is really Brythia or Britain. The "Cimmerian" name is undoubtedly Cymmru (Wales).

It is simply sheer lunacy, the allegation that the Romans erected either Avebury or Stonehenge. It may with equal nonsense be said they erected the Cromleâchs of Asia, including the many in Palestine which the Palestine Exploration Society's surveyors have recently discovered there. It appears highly probable that in pre-historic times, the Circus Maximus was constructed after the plan of Avebury, which in magnitude and deep canal encircling it, the Roman sanctuary so correctly imitates. One of the most conclusive proofs that Avebury was in existence when the Romans invaded this country, is the fact that the road from London to Bath, which they constructed, on its approach to Silbury Hill makes a sudden bend to *avoid* Silbury Hill. We have stood on the summit of that hill, and have seen with our own eyes that peculiarity in the course of the Via Badonica.

IMMORTALITY OF ADONIS.

In reference to the " death of Adonis at the vernal equinox, on the following day they feign that he is alive and ascended into heaven ('the heavens') and shave their heads as the Egyptians do at the death of the sacred bull Apis."[1] The name " Samson " signifies sun (from " shemesh " and " shemosh "—the sun).[2] It is said his strength lay in his " hair," and that, when Dalilah, said to be a bad character like the Druidic Anhras, the consort of Avagddu, the Druidic Pluto, had " cut off his hair as he lay asleep in her lap," he, after being deprived of his hair, became an easy prey to his enemies " In Hebrew," says Calmet, " it is stated literally, ' the hairs of his head began to put forth as they were shaved.' " Calmet says further that Samson continued in prison at Gaza about a year (this means one day, December 21st), and on the morrow—" a year and a day "—he re-asserted his powers as Hu Gadarn (Hesus the Mighty).—See p. 128. Philo, Tertullian, Origen, and others of the early fathers, were not mistaken when they supposed many things in the Old Testament were sacred allegories, and therefore were not to be understood literally. The Arabs, says Herodotus, shave their heads in a circle and about the temples, in honour of Bacchus (the sun), and the sun was painted by the Egyptians at the winter solstice as having but a single hair on his head. When the hair was cut off in honour of the dead it was done in a circular form. Allusion is made to this in the *Electra* of Sophocles, line 52. See also Ovid—

" Scisse cum veste capillos."

[1] Calmet's *Fragments*, vol. iii. pp. 576 a el 577.
[2] *Ibid. Dictionary of the Bible* under " Samson."

By way of humiliation to a captive woman, if a foreigner,
a Jew was directed to shave her head.[1] In page 198 of
Herodotus is the following: "In honour of the Hyperborean virgins (Britons), who died at Delos, the Delian
youth of both sexes celebrate certain rites, in which they
cut their hair." No doubt the sun at the winter solstice
being said to be rayless, was supposed to be in a condition
of profound humiliation, and afterwards cutting off the
human hair came in consequence to be a token of sorrow
and humiliation among his sympathisers.

Now, the meridian line—north and south—of the temple
of Avebury runs through the middle of Silbury Hill.[2] And
the sun is at noon on the shortest day (December 20th)
exactly above Silbury Hill, and south of the temple.
Renan, in his *Life of Jesus*, page 298, states, on the
authority of St. Jerome, Hakeldama[3] (translated the Field
of Blood) was *on the south of Mount Zion or Moriah*. This,
possibly, indicates the tragedy of the crucifixion itself was
associated in the popular mind with that direction from
Mount Zion. It will be recollected that in Druidism the
old sun, every year, was put to death on the meridian line
in the south, running through the Tropic of Capricornus.

We have read somewhere a statement, we think made by
Bishop Percy, that the ceremony of crucifying the sun (at

---

[1] *Deut.* xxi., 12.   [2] Higgins' *British Druids*, page 25, on the authority of
Dr. Stukely and confirmed by Sir. R. Colt Hoare, Bart.

[3] Hakeldama is rendered Aceldama in the A.V. Scholars, however, are not
agreed upon the meaning of the name. Is it Ach (Hebrew for brother, El
(sun), Dama (blood) Blood of the Brother (of) the Sun? There is exceeding
probability Judas Iscariot was intended to represent Typhon, who killed Osiris
his brother, and that Osiris, Horus, and Typhon were identical with Jupiter,
Neptune, and Pluto, who, in the corrupt mythology which concentrated at
Alexandria, were said to be "three suns of Saturn," or the old sun of each dying
year.

noon) on the shortest day is still observed by the Scandinavians. It is hardly necessary to state, because well known
to the learned, Mithras, the second person of the Persian
pagan trinity—instead of the third, as in Druidism—was
annually crucified at the winter solstice.   The same can
be said of Tammuz (the sun in Syriac); Chrishna, India;
altogether sixteen Divinities, but each implying the old sun
under various mythological titles, are said to have been
crucified.   As to whether the sun's crucifixion at the winter
solstice, that is, at the end of the solar year, was typical of
the crucifixion of the Lord Jesus Christ at the end of the
sacred year of the Jews—Nisan 14th or March 25th, O.S.,
each reader must determine in his own opinion.

St. Paul seems to have become cognisant of the ceremony
among the Celts or Galatians, of Asia Minor, and to
regard it as a typical rite; for he addresses them as
follows :—" O foolish Galatians, who hath bewitched you,
that *ye* should not obey the truth, before whose *eyes* Jesus
Christ hath been evidently " (" openly," says Arnold) " set
forth, *crucified among you.*" The remarkable expression
of the Apostle has puzzled all commentators, ignorant of
the wonderful fact the Druids—and no doubt, like all Celts,
the Galatians were Druids—performed annually at the
winter solstice the drama of the sun's crucifixion. Judging
by the mode the Druidic wren symbol of the sun's death is
set forth in the Isle of Man, it appears that the sun was
depicted as being crucified with arms stretched out, and
that those arms were symbolised by the Druids by the
stretched out wings of the wren on a pole. (*See* Psalm
xxii., 16.) This leads us to suppose that in ancient times
a great cross with an oval loop on top stood on the summit
of Silbury Hill, and that when the sun appeared to the south
from the temple and level with the middle of the cross, he

appeared to those standing in the temple on the northern
side of the hill, as if suspended on the tree, but his divinity
as a wren escaping through the loop the vulva of Cêd. But
now comes a tremendous difficulty as to how to reconcile
this allegorical crucifixion of the sun with the crucifixion
of the Lord Jesus. In Druidism it is the Power of Darkness
who puts the sun to death, as it was Mars or the Destroyer,
in the shape of a wild boar, who mortally wounded Adonis
on Mount Libanus, and Typhon killing Osiris.

THREE DEVILS PURSUING THE DIVINE LOGOS.

The Divine Logos in the sun, however escaped, symbolised by a white dove in Syria and by a wren in Britain,
and is received back into herself by Cetus—Cêd of the
Druids, or mother of the sun—symbolised also as Delphus
(womb), an ark, whale, and by the beaver in an ark.

The trinity of Hades, that is to say devils, are represented as pursuing the Divine Dove or Logos, which has
just escaped from the body of the sun, pursuing him in the
form of a three-headed dog called Cerberus; Montfaucon
shows it on the ark into which the sun has escaped from him.
The three heads of Cerberus are shown thus:—a human
head (intelligence), a dog's head (fidelity), a monkey's
head (filthiness). These, in Druidism, are Avagddu,
Cythraul, and Atrais. We have seen, in the foregoing,
the Druids not only had a garden, similar in every respect to
the Garden of Eden, but also their Mount Calvary, which
was also a garden, and signifying both the birth-place and
grave of the sun—the same womb and grave, or dual symbol,
being also symbolised as already stated by a crescent moon
shaped boat (Cêd).

We now return to the garden of the sun of the Druids.
There were, we are informed, two trees in the Garden of

Eden, namely, "the Tree of Knowledge of Good and Evil," growing in the midst of that garden, and also "the Tree of Life," likewise in the midst of the garden. Two trees in the middle of Eden. Adam and Eve "ate" of " the Tree of Knowledge of Good and Evil," and the result was that the Elohim (gods) became alarmed, and said to each other, " Behold the man is become one of *us* to know good and evil," and to prevent the man from attaining to the possession of a still higher god-like quality, namely, immortality, it is said by the Elohim (gods) "And now, lest he put forth his hand and take also of the Tree of Life, and eat and live for ever ;" therefore, the Lord God—Elohim, referred to collectively as one Archdruid—sent him forth from the Garden of Eden, to till the ground *from whence he was taken*. This signifies he was turned out of the Garden of Eden to that ground *from whence he had been originally taken into the garden*; for the earth or ground of the Garden of Eden was not different to any other mould, therefore, the reference here is not to the substance with which the body of Adam was made, but to his excommunication, and to his being sent back to the place from which he was taken into the Garden of Eden. The cherubim guarding it, to prevent their return into the " garden," were winged bulls, like those flanking the Shechinah, and were, like them, on the *east* side af the tabernacle, and what is translated, " a flaming sword turning every way," ought to have been translated, " an Irradiation of Glory."[1]

Abbe Pezron, in his *Antiquities of Nations*, page 89, makes the following important statement: " We find that the Phœnicians, by the testimony of Sanchoniathon, quoted by Eusebius, the companions of Saturn" (old sun and three

---

[1] Rev. Wm. Cooke, M.A.'s. *Enquiry into the Patriarchal and Druidical Religion. Temples, &c.*, page 12.

sons) "whom he calls Il" (Sun—Haul of the Druids,)
"signifying God, were called Elohim" (gods) "in the
Phœnician language ; wherefore it is certain the ancient
heathens looked upon the Titans as gods." The Titans
were Tydeiniaid, a sect of Druids. The name signifies the
vocal T, but correctly the symbol ⋀ emblem of Adlais
(Atlais) or the reverberation of the musical utterance of the
Creator (See page 68). Hence Tydain, as the Divine
voice, is said to be Tad Awen (Father of the Holy Muse).
But Nature is the instrument of the voice, as Miriam is
described echoing back the song of Moses, hence the Druidic
proverb "the voice of God is heard in the voice of Anian,"
or the earth's Anima, hence also the Bath Kol.

We must add the following here, having omitted it in the
proper place :—

PAN, HIS PIPES, AND THE MUSICAL REEDS.

When Virgil, in the third book of his *Georgics*, intimates
that Pan charmed the moon (Cêd as an Arkite boat) by
playing on his pipes or Syrynx, he also confounds the old
sun with the Almighty Celi of the British Druids. "The
writers of ancient fables report that Ouranos, whom the Latins
call Cœlus, *King of the Atlantic Islands*, was reputed father
of all the gods, and gave his name to the heavens, which from
him, were by the Greeks termed Ouranos, and by the Latins
Cœlum, because he invented astrology (astronomy), which
was unknown till his time."[1] Here again is confounded
the old sun (Arawn) with the Almighty Celi. "Others," Dr.
Potter continues, "ascribe the invention both of astrology
and the whole science of the celestial bodies to Atlas ; from
him these discoveries were communicated to Hercules, who

---

[1] *Diodorus Siculus*, lib., iii., p. 132. *Et Scriptores Mythologici*, quoted by
Dr. Potter in his *Religion of Greece*, vol. ii., p. 518.

first imparted them to the Greeks; whence the authors
of fables took occasion to report that both those heroes
support the heavens with their shoulders." The reader
will recollect what we state elsewhere about the reverberation—Adlais—of the musical vociferation of the Creator
Celi, echoed back by Ced, sustains the earth over the
Abyss, and that the reverberation, or echo, and the earth's
material body, are symbolised by the three stone props, and
the great flat stone lying upon them. In the foregoing
Atlas (Adlais) is the echo of the voice; Hercules is the
sun, here referred to as on the equator in spring.

The allegory of the sun and nature, otherwise Tegid and
Mor'wyn, answering each other vocally in spring after
crossing the river of life (the equator) northwards, is thus
described by Lucretius. After stating

> " Pan thought he had hugged his mistress, when indeed
>   He only hugged a truss of marshy reed,"

it is said of the god,

> " He sighs ; his sighs the tossing reeds return
>   In soft small notes, like one that seemed to mourn :
>   The new, but pleasant, notes the god surprise,
> ' Yet this shall make us friends at last,' he cries."
>
> *Lucretius.* i., 5.

Here also the sun carries the title of "Pan" (Pen,
meaning Chief,) through the solar year.

Virgil states :—

> " Pan loves the shepherds, and their flocks he feeds."[1]

That implies the sun in spring and summer.

The reader will carefully bear in mind that Pan, like
Silenus, is Bacchus as an old man, and that Bacchus is
also called Moses. Pan, and the vocal reeds answering
his musical sighs, "in soft small notes," are much like

---

[1] Psalm. xxiii., 1.

Moses and Miriam singing after ascending from the Red
Sea (Exodus xv.). Here it is the W (Seminal Logos) in
spring (March 21—25) that sings, and the echo is the
"sopranoimic cadences" of Mor'wyn (Virgo, Virgin, Myrrah
or Mary), referred to in page 68. The "voices" of spring
are meant. Thus the singing of Moses and Miriam
should have been placed after crossing the Jordan, instead
of after crossing the Red Sea. The error is due to the
Jews commencing the year at the vernal equinox, instead
of at the winter solstice. Pan's life lasted each year 365
days, minus 40 hours; the deficit being from December
4 o'clock p.m. on the 20th, to 8 o'clock a.m. on the 22nd
of that month.

Not only was the old sun called Saturn—Silenus, Pan,
Arawn, &c., but also Il (Haul—Sun) by the Phœnicians,
according to Sanchoniathon, and Il's three sons are called
Elohim (gods). Those three sons of Saturn or Il, were
symbolised by three Druidic Priests, as we have frequently
explained. This is the reason why the Druids regarded
their priests in their representative capacities as "gods" or
Elohim, and the Archdruid as Lord God, and no doubt
their priestesses were, for a similar reason, regarded as
goddesses.

To this day, at the Gorsedd (throne of thrones) of the
National Eisteddfod of Wales, it is customary, according
to habit, to announce the "gods" Plennydd, Alawn, and
Gwron are present, though invisible, in the Holy Circle.

Dr. Franz Delitzsch, the eminent Hebrew scholar,
translates the lxxxii. Psalm as follows:—"Elohim standeth
in the Congregation of God, among the Elohim doth He
judge. How long will ye" (Elohim), "judge unjustly,

and take the side of the wicked (Selah)." Verses 6 and 7 are given as follows :—" I have said ye are Elohim, and sons of the Most High are ye all. Yet as men shall ye die, and as one of the princes shall ye fall." Then the same name as given to the " men," no doubt the priests, is given to Jehovah (Jahve) himself in the eighth verse : — " Arise, Elohim, oh judge the earth, for thou hast a claim upon all nations." In the authorized version the name " God " is translated " mighty," and the first named " Elohim " (gods), is translated God, when it is evident that the priests (Elohim) are alluded to as " standing in the Congregation of God." The Lord Jesus alludes in St. John's Gospel, x , 34 and 35, to the use of the Elohim in this Psalm, and to the application of it to the priests.

THE CREATOR CELI AND HIS NAME OR WORD.

Referring to Jehovah as Elohim (gods), and to Elohim as Jehovah, prove that the Hebrews worshipped the Name or Word (Logos), and not the Creator Himself. This throws a flood of light on the following statement :—" And to Seth, to him also there was born a son, and he called his name Enos. *Then began men* to call upon the NAME of the Lord."[1]

The Druids evidently regarded as idolitary the adoration of the symbol of the NAME of the Lord, and therefore of its priestly representatives, instead of the Creator Himself. for it is said :—

" Einigan, the Great, beheld three columns of light, having in them demonstrable sciences that ever were or ever will be.

" And he took Three Rods (\|/) of the Quicken Tree, and placed on them the forms and signs of all sciences so as to be remembered ; and exhibited them.

---

[1] *Genesis* iv , 26th.

" But those who saw him misunderstood, and falsely apprehended them, and taught illusive sciences, regarding the Rods as a GOD, whereas they only bore his NAME.

" When Einigan saw this, he was much chagrined, and in the intensity of his grief, he broke the Three Rods, nor were others found that contained accurate sciences. He was so distressed on that account that his heart broke, and with his parting breath, he prayed God that there should be accurate science among men in the flesh, and there should be a correct understanding for the proper discernment thereof.

" At the end of a year and a day after the decease of Einigan, Menw, son of the Three Musical Vociferations, beheld Three Rods growing out of the mouth of Einigan, which exhibited the sciences of ten letters, and the mode in which all the sciences of language and speech were arranged by them, and in language and speech all distinguishing sciences—all except the NAME of God, which he made secret, lest the NAME should be falsely discerned ; and hence arose the secret of Bardism of the Isle of Britain.

" And God imparted His protection to this secret, and gave Menw a very discreet understanding of sciences under His protection which understanding is called Awen from God; and blessed for ever is he who shall obtain it. Amen, so be it.

From the mouth of Adda (Good A.), like blessed trees, three crosses, &c., Rods of fine growth were obtained, being trees from the mouth of Adda."

Apparently some old Christian Druid supposed the sign \|/ implied *three crosses*. (*Bardism*, p. 50.)

"Adda" is translated "Adam," but it is a borrowed Druidic name of the sun.

The quintessence of the church of the Druids is the great stone in the centre of the circle and top of the cromleâch. It is very remarkable that in the original apostolic church at Jerusalem, we find Jesus, with Peter, James, and John, corresponding with the British Archdruid, and with Plennydd, Alawn, and Gwron. In the Garden of Gethsemane, after leaving the rest of the apostles in the rear, the Lord Jesus said to them, "sit ye here while I shall pray yonder. And he taketh with him Peter, James, and John, and began to be sore amazed and to be very heavy."[1] On the mountain of the transfiguration a similar thing took place. As in Druidism, the three seemed to represent the three elements of the triune Word, which three met in Him as complete Logos, implying the fulness of the god-head centred in Him bodily. (Col. ii., 9.)

In the book of Revelation we are told something more about the Tree of Life than is given in Genesis. "And he showed me a pure river of water of life, clear as crystal, proceeding out of the throne of God *and the Lamb*, and in the midst of the street[2]—stream—of it, and on either side of the river, was there the Tree of Life, which bear twelve manner of fruits,[3] and yielded her fruit every month, and the leaves of the tree[4] were for the healing of the nation."

THE THRONE OF GOD AND THE LAMB.

It will be observed the River of the Water of Life proceeds or issues forth from the throne of God *and the*

---

[1] *St. Mark*, xiv., 32, 33. *St. Matthew*, xxvi., 36. [2] *Revelation*, xxii. 2.
[3] The tree itself standing in "the river." [4] Branches.

Lamb. It becomes now necessary to inquire where the ancients supposed the throne of God and Jupiter was located. The northern heavens being to the north of the eastern point of the equinoctial line, and the space traversed apparently upwards by the sun during spring and summer, the seasons when the influence of the sunbeams fertilise, and afterwards ripens, the fruit of the earth, the northern heavens were supposed by the ancients to be the locality of the throne of the Creator and the sun. The throne of the Destroyer is in the south, the region of darkness. To this day the Welsh refer to the northern heavens as the Bwrdd Arthur (Arthur's table), described as round. It is referred to also as Arthur's Garden, and the Great Bear is called Arthur's Plough (Arad'r Arthur). It is singular that *Arth*, the Welsh for Bear, the constellation in question is also named Bear, whereas the name in the Druidic language, refers to *Arthur*, one of the Druidic titles of the sun as a husbandman or gardener. It seems as if some astronomical student in very remote times, receiving his lessons from the Druids, and being himself imperfectly acquainted with their language, supposed Arthur, because of the similarity of *Arth*—the first syllable in the name of Arthur—to the Welsh name for a bear (Arth), gave the name of Bear to the constellation of the northern sky. As to where the ancient Hebrews supposed the throne of God to be situated, see pages 22 and 23 on this subject.

The River of Life is the equinoctial line, from the eastern apex of which the fertilising essence coming, according to the mistaken geography of the ancients, through the sun, streams into the earth in the spring time. That line is described by the Druids hieroglyphically by the letter I, which, in the Druidic alphabet, has no horizontal strokes. It is called Iwen or Holy I. The name Iwen or Holy I is now spelt "yew," and is usually supposed to refer to the evergreen sacred tree growing within ecclesiastical enclosures, but the name, without a doubt, was originally given to the sacred enclosure itself, when such enclosures belonged to the Druids. "Ewe" is English for a female sheep, and the Phœnicians, &c., adopted the sheep as the symbol of their "church," as the consort of Jupiter Amon, or the sun in the sign of the Ram in spring, in the same way as they had previously adopted the cow as the consort of the sun in the sign of the Bull in spring (see p. 37). We remind the reader that Mal I or Mali (like I), is to this day a Welsh pet name for Mary. It is identical with the name Iva or Eve, the reputed mother of all mankind in the Garden of Eden. In the writings of Chaucer, "yew" is spelt "ewe," which proves that the present mode of spelling the name is a late one. In reference to the ram and sheep symbols of the sun and earth, in a letter to us, the Astronomer Royal of England states, "the vernal equinox passed from the Bull to the Ram in 1845 B.C., and from the Ram to Fishes in 125 B.C., and will pass from Fishes to the Waterer in 2719 A.D. But if slightly different boundaries be adopted for the constellations, the above figures would be modified."

Thus the slaying the Paschal Lamb could not have taken place before 1845 B.C., neither could the exodus from Egypt have taken place before that date. But the Hebrews continued to annually slay the Paschal Lamb after the sun had ceased to rise in the sign of the Ram Lamb at the time of the Passover, and rose in the sign Fishes instead, as it does still on March 21st, or, lunarly, on Nisan 10th, when the Paschal Lamb was "housed" or imprisoned.

The Druids saw two rivers or streams of "life" in the universe of the creator Celi and Céd, his consort. The sun's meridian route from the south to the northern sky attaining the chief point in the last named region at twelve o'clock in the day on every June 21st, when the sun is crossing the Tropic of Cancer. It is the period of the sun's greatest strength. The period of his greatest weakness, the Druids thought, is at twelve o'clock in the day on December 20th, when he is crossing the Tropic of Capricornus in the southern heavens. That meridian line is the Druidic River of Life. Let the reader always recollect we are writing of astronomy according as the science was understood by the ancients. The parallels of terrestrial latitude were the Druidic circles called Abred (see p. 21), through which "lives" transmigrated by the agency of the animal kingdom. It should be borne in mind the Druids supposed animal lives were human ones in progress of development, to be delivered eventually to a human condition of free will, the station of which in the system of "lives" is compared to the line of the equator of geography. To the south of it is winter and death: to the north of it summer and life eternal in the heavens. The same idea is seen in comparing the "wilderness" to this life, the Jordan to the River of Death, the Dead Sea to Sheol or Hades, and Palestine to Paradise or Heaven.

It was anciently believed that the lives of the dead would return from Annwn or Hades, along the apparent meridian path of the sun and drawn by it, hence the most ancient way of burying the dead was with the feet, and therefore, the face southward. That is the Persian mode of interring the dead to this day; and on Pontypridd Common, South Wales, about one hundred yards to the north-west from a Druidic Rockingstone there, is seen to this day a stone cist grave, the stones pointing exactly north and south.

The other river of "life," the "natural" one, causing physical growth, is the equinoctial line. The sun rising in the sign of the lamb (Aries) on its eastern point, it then floods the earth along the equinoctial "river," with chemical "life" properties, re-animating, by its flood of rays, vegetation, that is to say, the seed germs in the earth. Thus the sun's position at the longest day or the summer solstice, and the sun's position at the vernal equinox—two positions—are referred to as "the throne of God *and the Lamb.*" This is what the Prophet Isaiah means by referring to the northern heavens as the "Mount Assembly of Gods," and "the corner of the north."

The Tree of Life, which bears twelve manner of fruit, is the sun's virile power—the Seminal Logos—exercised in spring along the line of the equator, here compared to a "river." The "Tree"—the sun's power—sustains the heavens with their twelve signs of the Zodiac, compared to branches, the sun in each exercising fruitful influence, varying in kind according to the season, and "the leaves of the tree are for the healing of the nations."

CHAPTER XXVII.

THE GARDEN OF THE SUN.

THE twelve loaves of shewbread, and the golden candelabra of seven lamps in the sanctuary of Israel, symbolised respectively the twelve signs of the Zodiac, and the seven planets. The last named referred to the apparent path that the sun traverses annually from the point of its lowest southern declination, to the highest point it reaches northward, which space is indicated by the sacred name symbol \\/ The whole space is divided into seven spaces, periods, or stages, of the sun's progress during the year, indicated by the seven planetary spheres, viz., Sun, Moon, Mars, Mercury, Jupiter, Venus, and Saturn, the sun's position being that he occupies in the Tropic of Cancer, or longest day. Completing the septentrio or seven included the three—\\/.

As mentioned elsewhere, the sign, when shown thus /\\ with the cromleach lying horizontally on its top, is the symbol of the Word of God as Adlais (Atlas) or reverberation, returning from Hades, otherwise Annwn (Great Deep) against the bottom of the earth, and thereby holding it up in space. The earth thus held up, is described by various poetical figures, viz., the garden of the sun, the source of flowers and fruit; the belly of Cêd (source and also grave of all things), Consort of Celi Almighty; as a tumulus, it is Mynydd y Marw—Mount Meru, otherwise Mount Moriah —Mount of the Dead—the kist in its centre is the symbol of the "Cave," Delphus—Womb of Cêd, mother of the sun, and into which he returns as Old on each December 20th as a blackened skull or head; it is then the Mount of the Skull or Golgotha.

This is the reason why both Delphi and Jerusalem were each said to be the middle of the earth's surface, with the " cave " in the centre of its circumference.

BAPTISM OF RE-GENERATION.

In the Christian Church, the Baptismal Font is the symbolical Delphus, otherwise " cave " or womb of Cêd, consort of Celi Almighty, from which the regeneration by water and "spirit" takes place. The idea is borrowed from the notion that the sun itself is regenerated on each December 22-25 from the womb of Cêd, who is said in mythology to be floating in the sea, the earth being her belly, and the stone kist or font being her symbolical womb. Here we have the tumulus or belly represented by the navis or Ark of the Church itself. In the act of spiritually regenerating the baby from the water of the font, the priest pronounces the triune Word, now represented by the Father, Son, and Holy Ghost, the priest at the time symbolising the Celi Almighty uttering His Word. This is the spirit which, in conjunction with the water, meaning mother Cêd, regenerates the child in a spiritual sense.

The first " child " similarly regenerated was the babe sun, or Son of God, on the morning of the first day of creation, and repeated on the morning of every December 22-25 ever since.

In the Christian Church, and continued in the Churches of Rome, England, and we believe in the Greek Church also, the priest, when the triune Word is pronounced by him over the head of the child that is being regenerated from the font, holds up his thumb and two fingers to symbolise the sacred \I/ ; the venerable emblem of the Word of God which animates.

To symbolise the echo of the music of the triune Word, which is supposed to ascend from below into the water of the font from Cêd, as the passive principle combined with the active, the Druids had what is called Tydain—lath, shaped thus ⋏ This is Titania's Wand. As a Welsh proverb this wand is called "Tydain, Tâd Awen." The name signifies T, the musical vociferation of the Father of the Holy Spirit (Awen). For the Roman T the Druidic ⋏ is to be understood. *Ydain* is compounded of *ud* (vociferation) and *cain* (beautiful or charming). In Welsh, *Cainc* is used to describe a strophe in music, and by the proverb is to be understood the reverberation of the music of the Sacred Word—three notes in one melody—echoing back from Annwn or Hades through the entire fabric of physical nature, and the Holy Spirit or Awen, as an emanation, thereby entering those minds qualified by the purity of their lives to receive it.

No wonder the ancient world believed the gods dwelt in the Isles of the Blest in Western Europe. The entire teachings of the Druids were incentives to virtue. It is traditionally stated the Druids, by way of lustration, sprinkled dewdrops on the head of each about to be admitted into their sacred order, and that it was performed at noon on the longest day, therefore when the sun was on the meridian on June 21st, which was called by them Sul-Gwyn, or "Holy Sun" day; literally, White Sun Day. It seems that to symbolise that holiness, each disciple was robed in white. The Sul-Gwyn was the Pentecost of the Britons. Each disciple to be sprinkled with dew drops, stood with his back to the sun, but the officiating Druid stood facing it, and he held a birch bough in his hand. and dipping it in the collected dew drops in a boat-shaped vessel, sprinkled the sacred water on the head of the disciple. The birch is still called Bedwen or Holy Bed in Welsh, and Baptism is called *Bedydd*. The Welsh Bed is another form of Bâd (boat), a symbol of Cêd, the mother of the sun (*vide* the boat in p. 66, with the infant sun rising out of it). The dew symbolised the masculine principle of God descending as heat in the dew ; the boat the feminine principle of Cêd. It is stated that owing to the position the disciple stood in relation to the sun, a small rainbow often appeared in the mist, as a brilliant arch of beautiful colours. A rainbow is called in old Welsh, " Envyg," corrupted to " Envys." It is a compound of Ein (our) and Mysg (midst), and implying the rainbow was an emblem of the Divine presence at the ceremony, as was the flashing of the diamonds on the shoulders of the high priest of the Jews. Dew is called in Welsh *gwylith*, or the lesson of the water. The Maypole of Wales was always a birch one, and was called y Vedwen Hâv, or the Holy Boat of the Summer. In what sense will be understood by the reader.

The Druidic high priest stood on the summit of the sacred mound, which was encircled by a trench full of water, symbolising the sea around the earth. His own person symbolised the sun on earth as the husband of the church representing Morewyn or Venus Marina or Aphrodite, the mother of the earth's progeny. It is to this Divine paternity and maternity, as two principles but one natural force, the poet Aratus alludes in the words " we are his offspring," quoted by St. Paul before the Athenian judges in the Areopagus.

The Archdruid as symbolising the incarnate winged sun of the vernal equinox, was called Father and Duw and Dâd—hence Lucan states the Druids worshipped Teu-Tates (Teutates). It will be recollected Father is called

Tâd and Dâd in the language of the Druids, and that name has been corrupted by other nations to Taute, Toute, Toot, Tud, Ted, Tet, Thoth; and Dew (God) as Tew, as in Tew-Kesbury, in various parts of England. The Arch-druid faced the eastern heavens during worship. He had three planetary spheres on each side of him, and he himself in the middle was the incarnate Mercury, the minister of the " gods," that is to say, of the Divine emanations passing through the sun to the earth during the annual journey of the sun through the seven planetary spheres. Mercury is identical with Odin and Woden, hence Woden's day (Woodman's day, that is to say, Man of Letters) is the middle day of the week, with three days on each side of it.

The wand of Titania symbolised the equinoctial line, and the /|\ on its summit the Adlais (Atlas) or the rever-beration of the Divine Word.

THE VOICE OF GOD.

In the Druidic cosmogony, the Eternal is said to have awakened the silence of eternity by suddenly delivering sweetest music over and into Chaos, and that his consort Cêd echoed back the enchanting melody of the WORD in the midst of the waters in the dark obscurity. The follow-ing is what was copied before A.D. 1600, in the Raglan Castle Library, also by the Bard Meyryg Davydd. That library was the resort of the bards for information its MSS. afforded on the subject of the ancient lore of the Druids:—" God in vocalising His Name, said \|/, and with the Word all worlds and animations sprang coinstan-taneously to being and life, from their non-existence ; shouting in esctacy of joy /|\, and thus ECHOING (Adle-varu) the Name or Word of the Creator." We find in Druidism that the Sun's Divinity came into existence here,

and that he also sang the song imparted to him by the
voice of Celi Almighty; for that is the meaning of the
following lines by Prince Aneurin:—

> "The Crowned Babe, on the first day (December 22nd)
> Sang a chant in GWENYDVA (Elysium)
> By Awen from the Highest :
> Calling worlds into existence, and the Good A. lived."

It is clear, we think, that by the "Good A." is meant
the luminous body of the sun, as the vehicle of the Awen.
See page 68, and *Iolo MSS.*, pages 45, 424, and 265. It
will be borne in mind that the sign /|\ is the symbol of
the echo of the Divine voice coming from Côd; and the
sign ⊤, with a longer vertical centre stroke, is the symbol
of the echo of the voice of Tegid, transmitted by his
sister-spouse Morwyn (Maid) through the material universe.
She is Titania, or Breasted, and is identical with Miriam, or
Mary Mother, only the latter is the earth in spring, and the
other is the earth, as a baby, on December 22nd. Moses
and Miriam, after ascending from the Red Sea, chanting
(Miriam answering the song of Moses), signify Tegid and
Morwyn on March 21st after crossing into spring; Red Sea
placed instead of the River of Life.

Be it particularly observed at this point, the departure
from Egypt is fixed as having taken place at the vernal
equinox, and that crossing the Jordan into the Holy Land
is likewise said to have occurred at the vernal equinox.
But there is this difference : The first event is said to have
occurred *before* crossing the Red Sea, and the second *after*
crossing the Jordan. The first is said to have been followed
by the destruction of Pharaoh and the Egyptian army; and
the second followed by the destruction of the City of Jericho
and its inhabitants, and Moses and Miriam sang *after*
crossing the Red Sea ; the priests sounded the trumpets,

and the people shouted, *before* the destruction of Jericho
and its inhabitants.   *See* Exodus xii. and xiii., also Joshua
iv. and vi. In the two narratives the Druidic solar allegories
of the winter solstice and the vernal equinox are mixed.
Joshua or Jesus is both Hesus the Mighty, of December
22-25, and Tegid, of March 21-25.

The cross of Egypt called Tau (Father)
with a loop on top, is a most striking illustration of the corruption introduced into Druidism
by the Egyptians at some remote epoch in the
history of religion. The loop on the top of the
said cross is the Delphus (Womb) of Cêd, and belongs to
the symbols of the winter solstice.   It is into it that
the Divinity of the Sun (\|/), symbolised by a white dove,
a wren, &c., escapes at sunset on December 20th, from the
cross of the Tropic of Capricornus.[1] But the name Tau
(Father), given to this cross itself, proves it to be the
incorrectly placed symbol of the Seminal Word — the
middle stroke of \|/ — at the vernal equinox, when the sun
is the agent of fatherhood, because he then fertilises the
seeds of the earth.   It is clear the cross here should not
be called Tau (Father), for it is the cross of the death of
the old sun, formed by the Solstitial Colure crossing the
middle of the Tropic of Capricornus (*see* page 95), as
shown in our illustration, with the open loop as the vulva of
Cêd, ready to receive from the cross of death the Divinity
of the Sun \|/ escaping from " the Prince of the Air." The

The Wren. We forgot to mention in p. 99, that Dryw, the Welsh name of
Wren, signifies Druid. We may as well mention the esoteric teaching that the
wren's nest is a Druidic symbol of the *membrum virginalis*, and the body of the
wren of the Seminal Logos. The wren's nest, too, is an emblem of the vulva of
the great goddess-mother Cêd as the "grave" into which the Divinity of the sun
escapes for refuge and also rehabilitation, December 20-22, and from which his
resurrection takes place annually.

serious mistake was made by those responsible for placing the death of Osiris, Adonis, Arawn, Silenus, Tammuz, Saturn, Pan, &c.—all meaning the same old sun—at the *vernal equinox* instead of at the *winter solstice.* They thus substituted the spot where the lines of the cardinal points cross each other at right angles on the equator for the place of the death of the old sun in the heavens, instead of the spot where the Solstitial Colure crosses the Tropic of Capricornus. Having thus blundered in one thing they did so in the other by substituting for the cross of the death of the old sun at the winter solstice, the vernal equinox cross, and gave it the name of Father, and describe it also as the spot of his physical destruction in the heavens at noon in March instead of December ! Thus they made the days of the personified sun's marriage to his sister-spouse the day also of his death at noon in the air at the hands of his " brother," Typhon, or Avagddu in Druidism.

The young sun, endowed with the Word (\|/) in all its attributes at his birth on December 22nd-25th, fights his way through his dusky enemies up to the equator. He is now in his prime ; is married to the earth (Miriam, Venus, Mary, Titania Morewyn, &c.), and transmits his pollen to the seeds of the earth's ovary. When now he is on the equator in spring, the points of his wings touch the Tropic of Cancer and the Tropic of Capricornus respectively. In short, the body and two wings of the sun symbolise \|/, and the exercise of the variety of attributes, entrusted to him by Celi and Cêd at his birth on December 22nd-25th.

THE ALMIGHTY MELODIOUSLY PRONOUNCING HIS
INEFFABLE NAME OR WORD.

    °   °   °   °   *   °   " God

Pronounced aloud His own eternal NAME—
Forth at that WORD, with vernal radiance bright.

Y

> Leapt new-born Nature into Life and Light.
> Oh! Heavenly utterance! O! melodious WORD!
> Thou grand creative music of the Lord!"
>
> Taliesin Ab Iolo's *Triads*.

But owing to either the Egyptians or the Phœnicians adopting the error of making the vernal equinox, instead of the winter solstice, the end and beginning of the year, Moüses, Myses or Moses, and Miriam; or Adonis and Myrrah, or Tegid and Morwyn alone, are made to perform the duties apertaining in the first place to Almighty Celi and his consort Cêd—Amen Ra and Isis ɪ.—and forgetting *them* altogether! The same music of the sun is set forth by the pipes of Pan, and the piping reeds.

In the light of what we have been stating the following is very remarkable :—

"It seems that when we sing, if we sing properly, it is perfectly easy for us to see as well as hear the notes we produce. Mrs. Watts Hughes has proved no less in her pamphlet on "Voice Figures," just published by Messrs. Hazell, Watson, and Viney. Mrs. Hughes sings into a tube of her own invention, which she calls the Eidophone, and the sound waves register their vibrations on an elastic membrane, in definite shapes. When the membrane is covered with sand, or other powder, the shapes are usually geometrical; when covered with a liquid they are in the form of leaves and flowers. Thus we have only to set to work in the right way to sing a pansy or a fern. Mrs. Watts Hughes reproduces some impressions obtained in this manner, and they might have been printed straight from the ferns themselves. The geometrical shapes are perhaps the most curious. Here are stars, and circles, and crosses, and a sort of letter "S" which looks like a double-headed serpent of Old Nile. Some of the figures obtained by the use of liquid plaster of Paris look like the most richly variegated patterns of crochet work. If you sing in the wrong way, with the wrong pitch, or the wrong intensity, you simply addle your egg of sound shape and get a more or less formless figure. Mrs. Watts Hughes does not claim to be the discoverer of this extraordinary process. More than a century since, as she tells us, Chladni showed that the vibrations of plates under the violin bow caused powder strewn upon them to form regular patterns. A few years ago Professor Sedley Taylor exhibited by his Phoneidoscope the crispations of a soap film set in vibration by a vocal sound. The Eidophone only carries these great discoveries to higher reaches of beauty and of wonder. When the vibrating disc is covered with the impalpably fine seeds of the puff ball, a skilful singer can make this exquisitely sensitive material do almost anything he pleases. The discovery opens up infinite possibilities. Music has long since been shown to be only a sort of mathematics; and now here is a demonstration that it may also be pictorial art."—*London Daily News*, July 23rd, 1891.

The signs \\/ and /\\ are shown in combination as a double triangle (*see* p. 250), by which is implied the union of the masculine and feminine principles as divine agents at work perpetuating creation. Both symbolical signs were made by the Druids with the wood of the sacred oak, and both, therefore, were " trees." Those two " trees " are the Druidic " Tree of Life," and the " Tree of Knowledge of Good and Evil " of the Druidic Garden of the sun. The sign \\/ was named the Tree of Life because it symbolised the " Word of God " or of the Celi Creator, uttering it most melodiously, and as the result " life vibrated through all existences, and through every existing materiality, and the blessed in heaven shall hear it for ever and ever."

The two wings of Tydain or Titania's "Tree" as a symbol of the voice echoed by Nature, point one south and the other north. The wand itself, as already stated, indicates the equinoctial line that was held in the middle of the sacred circle. Thus the southern wing indicates the route of the sun during the winter months southward of the line, and the northern wing the route of the sun during the summer months northward of the line. As already stated, winter with its darkness, coldness, and discomfort was regarded by the Druids as typical of physical and moral evil. Summer, with its light, warmth, and myriads of blessings, as typical of every physical and moral goodness. Therefore the Titania's Wand with vertical beam, and its two wings indicating summer and winter respectively, was said to be "the Tree of Knowledge of *Good* and *Evil*" by the Druids. This was the "tree" upon which the Druids placed three golden apples symbolising the sun in spring, summer, and winter, as already explained in preceding pages. It is very curious and remarkable to find the penitent and the impenitent thieves, one on either side of the dying Saviour, represented good and evil ; one on each side of the Sun of Righteousness.

We have seen in the foregoing the Druids had a cross, and they named it Tydain Tad Awen, or, Melodious Reverberation of the Voice of the Father of the Holy Spirit. It was not a cross of death, but one of knowledge of good and evil, and adorned with three apples as symbols of the sun's fertilising essence exercised throughout the year. In St. Paul's Epistle to the Druids of Galatia, he seems to allude in c. xiii. to a crucifixion as existing among them, and which he regarded as typifying the crucifixion of the Messiah.

As stated already, it is at noon on the shortest day in the southern heavens the Druids taught allegorically the old sun is put to death by the Power of Darkness, on the middle of the Tropic of Capricornus every December 20th ; and *it is a most curious coincidence that at the most ancient of our churches the cross is found fixed on the top of a miniature Calvary opposite the southern entrance into the church*, with, as said elsewhere, the porch for the *loop* of the cross.

It would seem these symbols are British, for had they been Egyptian or Phœnician, the cross and the loop would have been to the *east* of each church. Moreover, the great mound of Silbury Hill is to the *south* of the vast Druidic temple of Avebury. At Stonehenge there is no mound, but Salisbury seems to be a name really derived from Sol-Barrow, or Grave of the Sun, and it bears the same solar relation to Stonehenge as Silbury Hill does to Avebury, being, like the latter from Avebury, to the south of Stonehenge. Having names signifying sepulchres of the sun does not, however, imply they did more than sorrowfully witness what they supposed to be his death as a luminous body, but his divinity escaping into that part of Hades called Gwenydva.

It appears to us quite certain the cross was placed facing south or the middle of the Tropic of Capricornus and on the meridian line, running north and south, at the churches of Wales, by the Christianised Druids of Wales, in deference to the popular Druidic old custom of observing ritually the death of the old sun at noon each December 20th, in the heavens as typical of the crucifixion of the Saviour at Jerusalem at noon, on Nisan 14th, or solarly, March 25th, O.S., the end of the Hebrew sacred year.

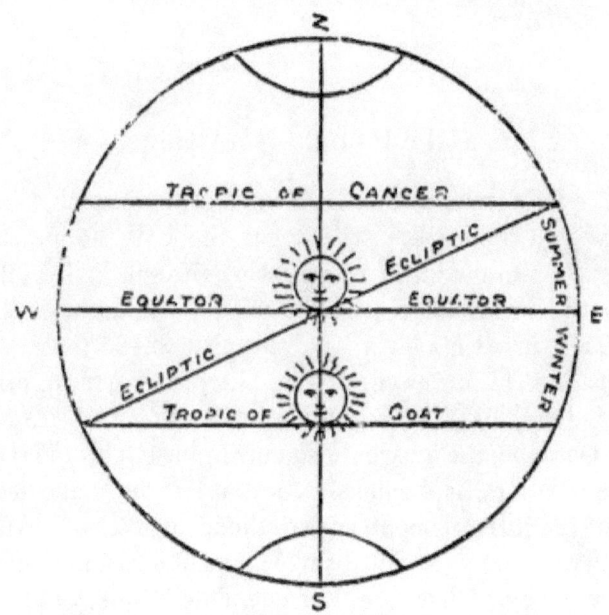

THE SEVEN PROFOUND MYSTERIES AND THE SEVEN
DAUGHTERS OF ATLAS.

In Druidism we are told of "y Saith Gyvrinach Orddovn"
(the Seven Profound Mysteries).   These refer to the operations of the sun by his influence on the earth, as the garden
of the sun, during his annual progress through the *seven
planetary spheres*.   There were seven corresponding ones
emanating from Cêd by the agency of Morwyn, assisted by
the Adlais (Atlas) which is the musical reverberation of the
voice of God, which musical voice gave the vocalising
impulse which Nature has been echoing ever since.   We
repeat again, those seven divisions of the reverberation,
masculine and feminine blended, are the seven daughters of
Atlas, usually named the Atlantides.   In Greek mythology
Atlas is said to be "one of the Titans, son of Japetus."   In
the Noahic division of the earth, Japheth, occupies the
west and north; Shem, the middle; and Ham, the south.
In other words, Japheth, Europe; Shem, Asia; and Ham,
Africa. North-western, eastern, and southern parts of earth.

CHAPTER XXVIII.

THE Archdruid on the centre of the Mound, Circle, Cromleach, or the Logan Stone, is the incarnate sun on earth, representing the sun by his office. He is the incarnate Word who is Hu the Mighty, otherwise Taliesin, at his birth, on December 22–25; Tegid at his marriage to Morewyn, March 21st; and Arawn, otherwise, Saturn, &c., at his physical "death" on Dec. 20th. He is Ouranos, the incarnate son of Cœlus (Celi) and Terra as Cêd's Anima as Semele. As a priest he embodies in himself the three elementary priesthoods of Plenydd, Alawn and Gwron, the personified three elementary emanations of God, and he is, therefore, the complete Word; and it is said, therefore, that in him dwell the fulness of the Godhead bodily. As mentioned before, when the Archdruid is engaged in Divine Worship he faces the east. His left side is towards the north, hence that cardinal point is called in Welsh, the sword side; his right hand side is towards the south, hence the south is called De (right hand side); the west is behind him, hence the west, in allusion to the setting sun, is called Gorllewin—Goror-y-Llewyrch—Region of the Reflection of Light.

THE GOLDEN DRAGON AND THE RED DRAGON.

Now to revert to Titania's wand ↔ . The two sloping arms indicate as stated before, respectively summer and winter; light and darkness; and knowledge of good and evil. Being stationed on the geographical equator opposite to where the sun rises when day and night are of equal length, it is regarded by the Druids as a period of truce between

the conflicting power of light, and the power of darkness,
and between life and death.   The Druids represent the
Red Dragon of blood as twirling up, on the southern arm of
the cross; and the Golden Dragon twirling on the right
arm, as if preparing for another fight for mastery ; the Red
Dragon is preparing to attack the sun as the cause of life;
the Golden one is there to defend the sun.   On the rod of
the wand—line of the equator—are a male and a female
serpent, dallying in loving embrace, symbolising the
wisdom of God and the wisdom of Cêd, engaged in propa-
gation.

THE EDEN GARDEN.

According to the Druids, the Garden of Eden is simply
the symbolical Druidic enclosure, as the emblem of the
whole earth as the garden of the sun.   Adam, the
gardener, is the personified sun in spring , and Eve is
Venus or Mor'wyn (Maid) of Druidism, called Mal 1
(Mali); and Myrrah of the Phœnicians, the I being the
same symbol as the upright wand of Titania, that is to say,
of the geographical Equinoctial Line.   If the reader will
revert to what we state about the Taurine period, he will
see that a white bull stood for Adam—A-dda—and a
white cow for Eve, or Mal I, and that the *four* " rivers"
of Eden are the *four* udders of the sacred cow.[1]   In the
period when the Druids abandoned the Taurine symbols,
three priests instead of three bulls, and three priestesses
instead of three cows, came to be employed as symbols, and
it appears the three priests, judging by what Sanchoniathon
states, were called gods, and that those three priests would
be called Elohim (gods), a plural name translated " Lord"
in Genesis.

[1] Observe the remarkable fact, there are three notable A's in Welsh or Druidic
mythology, viz, A Wen (Holy Spirit), A - Dda (Good A), but translated
"Adam," and A Ddu (Black A—the Evil Spirit).   Each of the three A's is
evidently a Druidic hieroglyphic.   There is also a notable I, as in Iwen (Holy I).

In the Hebrew narrative Adam and Eve had been *taken into the Garden from outside*, and the Elohim (gods) became annoyed with their precocity, especially in reference to the apple they had taken off " the Tree of Knowledge of Good and Evil," and lest they should also " take of the Tree of Life, and eat and live for ever," the Elohim (gods) had both Adam and Eve *turned out of the garden*, to till the ground *outside*, " from whence they were taken" into the garden. So they had had an existence in some lay sphere *before they were taken into the garden*. There cannot be any doubt, we think, that by the garden is meant an ecclesiastical enclosure. Paradise is the Persian name to this day for an enclosed garden. What can be more astonishingly absurd than the interpretation that it was the Almighty saying to Himself, " Behold the man is become one of *us* (!) to know good and evil; and now, lest he put forth his hand and take *also* of the Tree of Life, and live for ever," therefore, Jehovah— Elohim (observe it is Jehovah—gods, or gods of the Name or Word) sent him (*them* meant) forth to till the ground from *whence he* (they, as one) *was taken*, that is to say, where they had been before.

This implies they were turned out, meaning, we think. excommunicated, from the " garden," to till *other* ground than that of Eden. That *other* ground was the earth, in the sense we now call " the world," as distinguished from the " church," which, in Druidism, would be called Cylch or Circle (Paradiso—Circular Garden). It implies that Adam was returned into the place from whence he was originally taken into the garden, which it appears was simply a circular structure of stones emblematical of the circular earth above the rational horizon, as the garden which *the Lord Himself planted*. The allegory implies

Adam was a layman, who had made the priests jealous. It
is a medley throughout. Adam is Ad Hama (the Persian
name of Lord, the sun). Referring again to the wand of
Titania ♈, Higgins quotes the following from the work
of the learned Shedius:—" The Druids seek studiously for
an oak large and handsome, growing up with two principal
arms in the form of a cross, besides the main upright
stem. If the two horizontal arms are not sufficiently
adapted to the figure, they fasten a cross beam to it.
Upon the right branch they cut in the bark, in fair
characters, the name Hesus (Jesus) ; upon the upright
stem" above the junction of the two arms "the word
Taramis." The last name should have been Tarianydd
(shielder), meaning Côl, or the loop Delphus—the porch.
" Upon the left branch," Shedius goes on to state, "is
carved 'Belenus.'" Now Belenus is identical with the
Druidic Gwron (Hero), the third person of the Druidic
trinity, and we know, therefore, that the "left branch"
of the cross is that opposite the spectator's *right* hand,
when facing the eastern point of the heavens, and that by
the "right branch," is meant that opposite the spectator's
left when he is standing in that position; and that the
"right branch" points to the northern side of the equinoctial line, and the "left branch" to the southern space of
that line. Belenus, or Gwron, is conquering the Red
Dragon of winter. Hesus, or Jesus, is the conquering
sun of summer.

Shedius continues:—" In the space between the two
horizontal bars, they" the Druids, "cut the name of the
God—Thau " (Tâd—Father), "and under the same repeatedly Thau." [1] The upright or trunk of the tree symbolises the equinoctial line—east and west—where the

---

[1] Higgins' *British Druids*, p. 139.

sun in spring, Father Hermes, exercises, when then rising due east, his fertilising influence upon the seeds in the earth, hence he is Tâd (Thau, Thoth, Tat, Tot, Toot, &c., as the Welsh, or Druidic, name has been corrupted in various languages).

We believe it is quite evident that Shedius obtained his correct knowledge of the Druidic cross, and the names inscribed thereon, from the Druids themselves, with Latin translations of two of the names, namely, Hu (Hesus), and Gwron (Belenus).

BIRTH OF SOULS.—THE NAME " CLERGY " ASSOCIATED THEREWITH.

Faber mentions a remarkable fact, which bears on the curious theory of the ancients as to the birth of souls. " Bees," writes he, " were thought to be proper emblems of what the Opoptæ termed New-born Souls." [1] Faber further states, " those new-born souls were believed to have been produced from bull," Taurine Sun. " Hence," he proceeds, "Bees were named Bugenis." In Welsh *Bu* is the ancient name of bull, and the Welsh name is prounced " bee," and *Geni* is the Welsh verb to be born. A cow in Welsh is Bu-Hwch, and signifies Bull's Sow.

Virgil, after describing in an extremely interesting manner the habits of bees, remarks, " From these indications, and led by these examples, some have alleged that a portion of the Divine mind and a heavenly emanation, may be discovered in bees, for that the Divinity pervades the whole earth, the tracts of the sea, the depth of the heavens; that hence the flocks, the herds, men, and every species of animal, each at his birth, detaches from the Divinity its unsubstantial (incorporeal) existence." [2]

[1] *Mys. Cabiri*, vol. ii., p. 367. [2] Virgil's *Georgics*, Book iv.

Botanists are familiar with the fact that all flowers are either male or female, and that bees are the sun's messengers in carrying from the male flowers the fertilising pollen to the female flowers to make their seeds fruitful. That duty performed by the bees seems to have induced the Druids to regard bees as God's messengers on earth.

It is well known to all Celtic scholars that the Welsh Bards were called Clêr, and that their going on circuit was called Clêra (Beeing). All flies are called Clêr by the Welsh of the present day, and bees are, as a distinctive name called Gwenyn. In the *Ancient Laws of Wales* is the following :—" The extraction of nobility in bees is from Paradise, and on account of the sins of man did they come from thence : and God gave His blessing upon them." [1]

Using the name " Paradise " in the above passage, proves it was compiled, in its present form, during the Christian era. But obviously the allusion is to the emanations of heaven, which the bees symbolised in the Druidic creed, and that, by comparison, the Druidic bardic clergy, as Divine messengers to mankind, were called Clêr, and that Clêr signified bees only, among the Welsh, unless *all* flies symbolised among them the Divine emanations. We think not.

The etymology of the modern exclusive Welsh name for Bees, viz., " Gwenyn," which ought to be Gwynyn, affords us a key to the matter. It is a compound. *Gwyn* (white) signifies *Holy*; the termination " Yn," used in a plural sense, is evidently the word *Yni* (energy) with the " i " clipped off. Gwynyn, therefore, signifies Holy Energy.

The reader should consult Brand's *Popular Antiquities* (vol. ii., p. 300), touching the superstitious reverence for

---

[1] Dr. Owen Pughe's *Welsh and English Dictionary,* " Gwenyn."

bees still entertained in many parts of England. *See* also Bryant's *Analysis on Bees* (Melissæ or Melittae), and Faber's *Mys. Cabiri*, vol. ii., p. 365.

Hugh Miller, in his *My School and Schoolmasters,* mentions a Highland story, which doubtless, is a legend having its origin in the Druids associating human life, apart from corporeal existence, with bees. His cousin, George, communicated to him the following story :—" Two young men had been spending the early portion of a warm summer's day in exactly such a scene as that in which he communicated the anecdote. There was an ancient ruin beside them, separated however from the mossy bank on which they sat by a slender runnel, across which there lay, immediately over a miniature cascade, a few withered grass-stalks. Overcome by the heat of the day, one of the young men fell asleep; his companion watched drowsily beside him, when all at once the watcher was aroused to attention by seeing a little indistinct form, scarce larger than a humble-bee, issue from the mouth of the sleeping man, and leaping upon the moss, move downward to the runnel, which it crossed along the withered grass-stalks, and then disappeared in the ruin. Alarmed by what he saw, the watcher hastily shook his companion by the shoulder and awoke him; but with all his haste, the little cloudlike creature, still more rapid in its movements, issued from the interstice into which it had gone, and flying across the runnel, instead of creeping along the grass-stalks as before, it re-entered the mouth of the sleeper, just as he was in the act of awakening." The sleeper then told his companion, he was in the midst of a delightful dream when he was disturbed by him.

All Saints, or Hallows (November 1st), and All Souls (November 2nd), and the Beltân and Coelgerth firing at this season, are ancient celebrations associated with the supposed birth of souls passing from the sun into babes in wombs at that season of the year, that is to say, figuratively set down as, in each instance, taking place at the end of any six months after the fertilisation of the human ovum.   Wordsworth, in the following stanza, implies a belief in the former existence of souls :—

> " Our birth is but a sleep, and a forgetting
>   The soul that rises in us, our life's star,
> Has had elsewhere its setting,
>   And cometh from afar."

There is no doubt the custom of informing the bees of a death, comes from the ancient practice of making the event known to the Druidic Clergy called Bees or Clêr.   Some years ago, observe a correspondent of the *Athenæum*, a gentleman at a dinner-table happened to mention that he was surprised, on the death of a relative, by his servant inquiring whether his master would inform the *bees* of the event, or whether he should do so.   On asking the meaning of so strange a question, the servant assured him that bees ought always to be informed of a death in a family, or they would resent the neglect by deserting the hive. Afterwards it was ascertained the practice of informing the bees, and placing tokens of mourning on beehives, prevails in Cornwall, Devonshire, Isle of Ely, Gloucestershire, Yorkshire, Suffolk, &c.   Benefit societies still place out signs of mourning on the occasion of the death of a brother.[1]

In Leviticus xi., 23, Bees are described by the Mosaic Law as " unclean."

---

[1] Brand's *Popular Antiquities*, vol. III., p. 300.

BUTTERFLY.

"The celestial or ætherial soul was represented in symbolical writing by the butterfly, an insect which first appears from the egg in the shape of a grub crawling upon the earth, and feeding upon the leaves of plants. In this state it was aptly made an emblem of man in his earthly form, when the ætherial vigour and activity of the celestial soul, the *divinæ particula mentis* is clogged and encumbered with the material body. In its next state, the butterfly grub, becoming a chrysalis, appears by its stillness, torpor, and insensibility, a natural image of death, or the intermediate state between the cessation of the vital functions of the body, and the emancipation of the soul. * * And the butterfly breaking from this torpid chrysalis and mounting into the air, afforded a no less natural image of the celestial soul bursting from the restraints of matter and mixing again with its native æther."[1] "The soul was supposed to be part of the æthereal substance of the Deity, detached from the rest, and doomed for some unknown cause to remain during certain periods imprisoned in matter; all its impulses, not immediately derived from the material organs, were, of course, impulses of the Deity. * * According to the ancient system there were *two souls*, one the principle of thought and perception, the other the mere power of animal motion and sensation, both of which were allowed to remain entirely in the shades, in the person of Tiresias only."[2]—"Tirisia" would mean in Welsh "lowest earth."

The angry nymph in the *Odyssey*, p. 526, Pope's translation, states :—

> "Ungracious gods! with spite and envy cursed!
> Still to your *own ethereal race* the worst."

---

[1] Knight's *Symbolical Language*, sec. 163. [2] *Ibid*, sec. 163, 164.

The *Divinity* in the sun was supposed to be " a part of the ethereal substance of the Deity detached from the rest." This idea is, unquestionably, the primitive one respecting the Logos or Word, which, it is said, became incarnate in the Virgin Mary.

THE FLY.

" The common fly being, in its first stage of existence, a principal agent in dissolving and dissipating all putrescent bodies, was adopted as an emblem of the Diety."[1]—The Jupiter Fly is the Beelzebub of the Hebrews.

THE BOAR.

" In the poetical tales of the ancient Scandinavians, Frey, the Deity of the Sun, was fabled to have been killed by a boar, which was, therefore, annually *offered to him* at the great feast of Juul, celebrated during the winter solstice. *   * It was, it seems, an expiatory solemnity, meant to honour and conciliate the productive power of the sun by the symbolical destruction of the adverse power."[2]—Did the ancient Jews abstain originally from swine's flesh through fear of offending that " adverse power " ? The " Juul " of the Scandinavians seems to be identical with the Welsh *Gwyl* (Festival).

---

[1] Payne Knight's *Symbolical Language*. p. 37, sec. 125.   [2] Ibid. sec. 122.

CHAPTER XXIX.

SPIRITUAL AND NATURAL LIVES.

THIS seems to be the proper place to describe the notion of the Druids respecting the incorporeal priestly life, as symbolising the spiritual or intellectual human existence, apart from corporeal, physical or animal life, with both of which human and animal beings were believed to be endowed. This most ancient philosophic idea as to the dual nature of every human and animal life is taught both in Genesis and by St. Paul. In the Old Testament we are told that man, as a living *animal*, was created before the Creator " breathed into his nostrils the breath of life, and man became a living *soul*." In the New Testament it is stated, " That was not *first* which is spiritual, but that which is *natural* and afterwards that which is spiritual." In his official or ministerial character, wearing his white, that is to say, holy robe, the Druid priest symbolised the Divine, Spiritual, or Soul life, temporarily tenanting every physical body, in conjunction with the animal life, called by the Apostle, *natural* life. It seems the Druids considered that the combination of the dual lives constituted every earthly individuality. In every babe and animal, at his or its birth, both the spiritual and the animal lives were supposed to be in union and both perfect in their degrees of excellence, hence the classic proverb that " those whom the gods love die young," that is to say, they stop not in a world where their purity might become sullied. It is quite clear that the Druids supposed, and poetically taught, that the sun also is endowed with physical or corporeal life, as well as with the Divine

z.

spiritual life which the Creator had imparted into him like-
wise as \|/. Hence the sun is called Huan, or Abode of
Divinity. The human, or rather the natural, species are
propagated, bloom, and ripen into physical proportions by the
agencies of a masculine triad; likewise, the sun, as the Divine
agent, was represented as operating on Nature, triunally—
\|/. See what we state elsewhere about the sword of
Arthur, and the Phallus of Orisis. The body and two
wings of the sacred white dove, and the body and two
wings of the sacred wren of the Druids, and the body and
two wings of the cock, and the Shechinah (Seminal Logos)
and two winged cherubs, or bulls, of the Holy of Holies,
the same triune agent of the Creator's living principle
transmitted to the earth on March 21st, June 21st, and
December 20th, respectively. But it appears that the
middle stroke, on March 21-25, applied exclusively to the
vegetable life and human natural life. On March 21-25
the fulness of the sun's virile power was, it was thought,
exercised annually in the earth; during, likewise, the exercise
of the maximum human power, the human babe as the effect
of the climax of physical energy, exercised in the springtime
of our bodies, was conceived in the womb, but as the
noblest of animals only. It is the season of the year, too,
when birds seek their mates.

It appears that the Druids thought they beheld in the
functional capacity given to man, in the springtime of life,
to deliver into the ova the fertilising influence, at a period
when the parents are strong and well able to contribute
towards the bodily wants of their progeny, strong evidence
of the exercise of Divine Wisdom. In the springtime, too,
the earth receives a similar impulse from the sun, hence the
sun is called Father Hermes, and the earth's fecundating
force is called Maid or Virgin, and, in Druidism, Mor'wyn.
In Druidism she is each year a renewed virgin, in the
same sense as the sun of each year is a renewed one.

Now, the souls, or spiritual lives, each a ray of the Divine Nature itself, came into existence, as a "spiritual body," and like the Divinity in the sun itself, in Gwenydva, where is located the Great Mother Cêd, or Ceridwen, or Medusa, otherwise Minerva, Consort of the Almighty, on each Dec. 22nd. Regarded as the passive principle in the spiritual nature of the Creator, her co-operation, the Druids thought, was necessary even to the birth of souls. The Druids saw that grain only required six months—from March to September—to attain ripened perfection. The body of the human child in the womb, likewise attains full physical maturity in six months, viz., compared to the period from March 21-25, to September 23rd. They regarded his body as a tenement gradually built to receive the *spiritual life into it.* September 22nd is nine months from December 22nd, when the birth of the souls took place simultaneously in Gwenydva, with that of the babe sun. The child "leaping" in the womb of Elizabeth at the end of six months from the date it was conceived, the moment the Virgin Mary kissed her, implies the influence of the complete Word (Logos) in Elizabeth, using the body of John the Baptist, before he was born, as a carnal substratum, to operate therefrom upon the womb of the Royal Virgin of the House of David. This explains the additional curious legend about John the Baptist being Old Elijah, or the Old Sun, with the Logos in it, as explained elsewhere (see p. 133).

The human child, however, needs an additional three months (the period of time the Virgin Mary stayed with Elizabeth, when the human generation of John became complete[1]) to enable the natural life and the spiritual lives to attain a mysterious blending of the two lives (see p. 412, line 27). The child quickening in the womb, was regarded

[1] Luke i., 56 and 78.

z 2

by the Druids, as the process of shutting in the spiritual life in the human body. Death, the second act, is called Anghau, or Unshutting the Life. We found it necessary to repeat the foregoing to follow what immediately preceded it.

" The cherubim," states Dean Alford (Heb. ix., 5), " are referred to as *masculine agents*," and we add, so also is masculine the Shechinah, the symbol of the male agency of the sun in spring, and male consort of the Ark of the Covenant. St. Paul has the following : " Brethren, I would not that ye should be ignorant how that all our fathers were under the cloud, and all passed through the sea; and were all baptised unto Moses in the cloud and in the sea; and all did eat the same spiritual *food*; and did all drink the same spiritual *drink*; for they drank of that spiritual rock that followed them, and that rock was Christ."—1 Cor., x., 1, 2, 3, and 4. Observe Moses is here placed as the Shechinah !

But Moses, as the leader, was the first to pass through the Red Sea and under the *cloud*, and the others followed. Therefore, Moses himself was baptised, like the rest, " in the ' cloud ' and in the ' sea.' " Baptism is the symbol of regeneration by water and the spirit, and here is the " cloud " (the Shechinah) as the emblem substituted for that " spirit." And the Red Sea for the water containing Cêd. Here again the Eternal Celi is ignored !

Moreover, the Manna is made to symbolise the bread, and the water out of the Rock of Horeb is made to symbolise the wine.

Here we have the Eucharist of the Last Supper of the *spring* time, otherwise the time of the Passover of Israel. How singularly is the narrative like that relating to the new birth of Hesus the Mighty, otherwise Taliesin, from the coracle, and, according to another figure, from the egg, and of the babe Bacchus —Myses (Sun) born of Ced out of the sea—Moüses signifies Drawn out of the Water—and the souls following, or accompanying, him from Hades (Egypt) to commence a new life !

" Natural creations," remarks Dean Alford, " reflect passively the Creator ; the spiritual or soul life is an expression of the Divine Mind—lineaments of the Almighty." The natural creations exist, like Gwyion Bach did before he received into his physical body the three Divine drops or sprays out of the cauldron of Ceridwen (First Begotten Love). The spiritual life became united with the material life by Gwyion Bach taking into his body the three Divine sprays that leaped out of the cauldron, which illustrates Gwenydva.

The natural life, animating physical bodies, was symbolised by the Druids by the Mundane Egg, living passively and in an inert condition, but, on receiving the three drops, becoming fertilised spiritually by containing the spiritual emanations or Æons. Ceridwen, as the material source, is symbolised by a hen, while the sun is symbolised by a cock, the transmitter of the Æons (\I/). The hen yields the egg, and one, who, entering the egg or matter as Gwyion Bach with the three drops in him, comes out of it under the dignified title of Taliesin. Here, by Taliesin, is meant the Archdruid in his representative capacity, as representing the sun and also both mind and matter—natural and spiritual lives, and that the sun is similarly endowed, and the source of \I/.

Man's natural life is the substratum on which the Divine emanations are impressed. That is what is meant by the expression that the Elohim, or Divine emanations, under the title of Gods, made man after his (their) own image. Our Druidic Ancestors illustrated the natural and spiritual lives of man by the white robe over the ordinary garments symbolising natural life. Closely observing, they saw that,

as man grew older, the whiter he became. They regarded
this as evidencing that as the natural or physical life in man
weakened its hold the spiritual life in him became more and
more dominant. White is the Welsh for Sanctus.

"ELI, ELI, LAMA ASABATANI!" (A.V. *Sabacthani*).

It is well known that by the words, Eli, Eli, Lama
Asabatani. the Lord Jesus repeated the first words of Psalm
xxii. The inscription at the head of that Psalm is, "To the
Precentor. Upon the Hind of the *Morning Dawn*." The
Hind is a female deer, but in Genesis xlix., 21, we find the
following : "Naphtali is a Hind let loose." Therefore, it
is plain "Hind" is used also in a masculine sense. These
facts prove Hind is used for the genus of the deer, which
includes goats. Besides, in Hebrew, a stag is called *Ail*.
In Psalm xviii., 33, is said, " God *   * guided me with
strength, and made my way perfect, making my feet like
Hinds' feet, and who set me *upon my high places*." (Delitzsch's
translation.) The allusion is to the security of foot of the
goats among beetling crags, or "high places." A city in
the territory of Naphtali, near the source of the Jordan,
was called Paneas, and we know Pan is represented as having the lower half like the he-goat, and the upper half like
an old man. Thus it is conclusively proved the Hebrew
word translated *Hind* signifies a he-goat. Psalm xxii.
is, therefore, the song of the he-goat ; and the words
of it are put into the mouth of that symbolical character by
the Hebrew bard. It will be recollected that Pan and
Elijah are both symbols of Saturn, the old sun. It will
be recollected we state elsewhere the old sun was annually
crucified at noon in the heavens on the Tropic of Capricornus, or the He-Goat. In the Authorised Version the
sixteenth verse is as follows:—"For dogs" (the three-
headed dog Cerberus of Hell,) "have compassed me, the

assembly of the wicked have inclosed me, they pierced my hands and my feet." In the reign of Tiberius Cæsar, states Plutarch, a voice was heard in the Ionian Sea, crying, "The Great Pan is Dead!" And the eminent Christian father, Eusibius, states that God was pleased to intimate to the world in that way the death of the Messiah. (Romans vi., 6).

The Psalmist represents suffering Pan, or "Hind," as calling plaintively—and the pathos of this remarkable poem is wonderful—to Eli. It will have been observed that, throughout ancient mythology, the diurnal sun and the nocturnal sun, in their old age, towards the close of each solar year, are described as *two* old men, namely, Saturn and Silenus (Apollo and Bacchus respectively aged), Saidwrn and Scithynun Veddw (Hu Gadarn and Taliesin respectively aged), Adam and Noah, Aaron and Moses, and Elijah and Moses. Elijah and Aaron are one and the same individual, under different names. As we have shown in preceding pages, Pan is a title of Silenus, or Bacchus as an old man. In the sense that the old sun is the father of the young sun, that is to say, Saturn is the father of Apollo, Silenus or Pan, is the father—said to be his "foster"-father—of Bacchus. But in the sense that the diurnal sun is the cause, and, therefore, the "father," of the heat left behind in the atmosphere at night, and personified by the Druids as Bacchus (Gwy Ion—Taliesin), Saturn is the father of Pan, otherwise Silenus, and therefore Pan in his sufferings calls to Saturn, in the Psalm, "Eli, Eli, Lama Asabatani?" or, "Elijah, Elijah, why hast Thou forsaken me?" This is the meaning of the statement of the Koran that the skull of Adam (old sun) and Christ carried on a conversation with each other on Mount Calvary.[1]

---

[1] St. Matthew xxvii., 46-7; St. Mark xv., 34-5.

THE INCARNATION OF THE LORD JESUS.

It is remarkable that theological writers, so far as we know, have never inferred that there is a connection between the announcement made by the Angel Gabriel to the Virgin Mary to the effect that Elizabeth was pregnant and gone six months with child, and her own forthcoming pregnancy. During the Angel's interview with the Virgin Mary at Nazareth he simply foretells the incarnation, in the following words :—" The Holy Spirit shall come upon thee, and the Power of the Highest shall *overshadow* thee, therefore also that holy thing which shall be born of thee shall be called the Son of God." The event itself is simply promised. Observe the words, *overshadow thee.* The figure employed is a bird with spread wings *overshadowing* a hen. Most theologians are oblivious to the fact that by the Seminal Logos is meant the middle attribute transmitted in spring through the sun (March 21-25), and that the complete Word, in three elements, is implied by the body and wings of the symbolical wren, white dove, and the cock with a Priapian beak. Therefore, the expression *overshadow thee* was deliberately intended to convey the meaning that the Seminal Logos, Himself, would descend and fertilise the ovum in the womb of the Virgin Mary, and become, Himself, thereby incarnate.—*See* p. 161.

Now, be it carefully observed, Elijah, or Elias, was Saturn, the old sun, known by several other titles, and he contained the three principles in his decrepid aged body, and to bring his three attributes down to earth, into contact with the Virgin Mary, for the purpose of the incarnation, we find old Zacharias[1] and old Elizabeth the male and female agents to carry that out. The first act is generating the physical body of John in the womb of Elizabeth, whose name translated is " House of the Helper of the

---

[1] The name signifies : The Watchful Sun.—Dr. Inman.

Sun "—Eli (Sun) Za (Helper) Beth (House). When John is six months old he is a perfect or complete body, and is fit to receive the spiritual tenant.

Recollect the similar circumstances to those in the begetting of John, in the history of Abraham and Sarah in the begetting of Isaac, who is made the type of the Messiah. Isaac also is represented by the Ram or Lamb (Aries), Ram-horned Jupiter of the Equator—Gen. xxii., 13, Hebrews xi., 17—20.

The Jewish nation is represented as the descendants of the type, who, mark, is the *second* person (Jupiter) in the Jewish human trinity, namely, Abraham, *Isaac* and Jacob. Here "Ram" is placed instead of "Man," but in Joshua v., 13—14, "Man" is placed instead of "Ram." It will be recollected, also, what we state elsewhere about the "Man" and the High Priest. In the case of Jesus the "Man" is placed in the station occupied, elsewhere, by Ram-Lamb (Jupiter).

Recollect the expression of the Lord Jesus, alluding to himself as the Divine Word in these words : "Even the Son of Man which is in Ouranos"—Arawn or Aaron, the first named, the Old Sun, and the last named, the High Priest on the Day of Atonement (end of the civil year), representing the Old Sun with the Son of Jupiter (Word) within it, the Huan (Abode of Hu) of the Druids. The following is the verse in both languages :—

Καὶ οὐδεὶς ἀναβέβηκεν εἰς τὸν οὐρανὸν, εἰ μὴ ὁ ἐκ τοῦ οὐρανοῦ καταβάς, ὁ υἱὸς τοῦ ἀνθρώπου ὁ ὢν ἐν τῷ οὐρανῷ.

The verse is translated thus in the A. V.: "And no man hath ascended up to Heaven (Ouranon), but he that came down from Heaven (Ouranou), even the Son of Man which is *in* Heaven (Ouranô).—John iii., 13.

Let the reader at this point, refer carefully to pp. 236-7, and observe what Dean Alford states about the meaning of the name Ouranos ; also in page 422 what Archbishop Potter states, as to the identity of Ouranos with Cœlus. But they are not identical, Ouranos is the Old Sun in December, and Cœlus is the Druidic Most High Celi !—the Agnosto Theo of Athens.

It is a remarkable thing in the character of the Hebrew trimurti, viz., Abraham, Isaac and Jacob, that, genealogically, Abraham is reproduced in Isaac and Jacob, and Abraham, as old Saturn, to whom a Typhonic character is given, appears as *an old man circumcised*—Gen. xvii., 24. It seems, too, that by "the eighth day" is meant the Day of the Sun, that is to say, the morrow after the day of the week sacred to Saturn. Annually that would be on Dec. 22nd—the Old Sun's "Day of Rest" would be on the 21st (*see* pp. 121 and 360). On the 22nd the Young Sun of the solar new year would appear, and the Circumcision, on that day, implied the Jews clung to the worship of the Old one, impotent though he was, and sanguinary since Pluto came to be identified with him.

The old sun, at the winter solstice, was called Tammuz, in the East, and the day dedicated now to "St. Thomas" (Dec. 21st,) was given that Saint's name as a substitute for Tammuz. But we find, in Ez. viii., 14, that some of the Hebrews "wept for Tammuz" when the sun sets on the longest day, in the Tropic of Cancer (June 21st), instead of when he sets in the Tropic of Capricornus, on the shortest day (Dec. 21st).

Let the reader now refer to our table of Trinities, in p. 251, and carefully observe that the *third* person of the Egyptian trinity is Typhon, or, the Devil. Observe, also, what Manetho states, in pp. 252-3, respecting the character of the Hebrew worship.

Now "Abraham, *Isaac* and Jacob" are arranged according to the usual solar representations of the triune Word or Divine Name. But Tammuz being placed where the sun is on the *longest* day instead of where he is on the *shortest* day, the usual order is reversed, and Typhon is made to occupy the first position : that of Osiris; and Osiris the last position: that of Typhon; and Horus, the middle position, between the two. Abraham, then, is here placed first and still is identical with Typhon (the Oriental Saturn, or Tammuz, of Phœnicia); Isaac is identical with Horus (Jupiter—Iu-Father) ; and Jacob with Osiris—the sun on June 21, March 21 and Dec. 21, respectively; or, in other words, the sun on the Tropic of Cancer, on the Equator, and on the Tropic of the Goat ; but the Hebrews observe Saturn's Day—the last of the week—right enough.

The learned reader will recollect the Egyptian story about Typhon killing his brother Osiris (*see* pp. 191-2-3). Now Horus is the name of Osiris on March 21, when the sun is in the first point of Aries or Ram. Abraham, in the character of Typhon, offers to kill Isaac (Horus—Os'ris), but is given a Ram to kill in his stead! Can there be a doubt as to whom the sacrifice was made? That it was of a Typhonic character? No wonder the gentle Nazarene told the Jews, with indignant scorn, that the devil was their father (*see* St. John's Gospel viii., 37-44).

Sarah is Sarrat the Assyrian for Queen. Sarri, another form of the name, is Sar-Ri, or Queen is Ri. Saraph is Sar (Queen) and Oph (Ophis) a Serpent—Queen Serpent. This means Céd as Divine Wisdom, as at Ab-Ri or Avebury, Wilts, and six miles from Calne.

Circumcision implied that the worshipers placed themselves in the same condition as him whom they worshipped, namely, Saturn, who was said to be impotent at the end of the year.   That signification, too, is alluded to in the Gospel of St. Matthew, xix., 12, where it is stated by the Lord Jesus that "some make themselves eunuchs for the Kingdom of Heaven's sake"   Observe, it is not done for their *own* sake—"*Basileian tôn Ouranou*," that is to say, of Ouranos—Arawn or Saturn. See also p. 241, lines 4-8. "Ouranos," see pp. 236 and 237.

We follow the narrative in the first chapter of St. Luke's Gospel. The Angel Gabriel now descends into "a city of Galilee, named Nazareth," and, visiting the Virgin Mary, tells her that her cousin Elizabeth is six months gone with child. We are not to understand that the Angel Gabriel went about simply to tell one woman that another was *enciente*. Be it observed that what would happen to herself is mentioned by the angel before he informs her (Virgin Mary) as to the condition of Elizabeth, and in a mysterious manner the two events are associated with each other. The Virgin Mary "arose in those days, and went into the hill country with haste, and into a city of Juda, and entered into the house of Zacharias, and saluted Elizabeth. And it came to pass, that, when Elizabeth heard the salutation of Mary, the babe leaped in her womb, and Elizabeth was filled with the Holy Spirit,"—like Cêd receiving into her body the Awen, or the Melodious Vociferation of the Eternal Celi, and echoing it back (*See* pp. 30 and 68),— "And she" (Elizabeth) "spoke out with a loud voice, and said, Blessed art thou among women, and blessed is the fruit of thy womb."   *The leaping was that of the Divine Word*, about to "overshadow" the Virgin.[1]

[1] "The *Day-spring* from on High" a beam of the spring sun. Dean Alford translates it "light." This would be on March 21-25, when the sun is the Seminal Logos. St. Luke i., 78; see also Isaiah xi., 1, and Isaiah ix., 2. In the first chapter of the Epistle to the Colossians, St. Paul, from the 15th verse onwards, founding his argument on the doctrine that the Lord Jesus came into existence, as a Man, by the action of the Seminal Logos—the only man

It was *now*, when that act was performed, the promise of the Angel was fulfilled to the Virgin Mary. The narrative, associated with what took place at the baptism of *regeneration* of Jesus by John, seems to imply the Seminal Word impregnated the Virgin by the instrumentality of an emanation from his own essence; but at the baptism the "bird," the symbolical white dove (♉), in all his spiritual effulgence, descended on the august head of the young Nazarene, and entered it. Elijah was the agent in both generations: the natural one, and the symbolical one by water. "Elias," states Dr. Inman, "means Sun; and Elijah signifies El is Jah."[1] "Saturn's Day was made sacred to the God of the Jews, and the planet is called Cochab Shabbath (the Sabbath Star) and Shabbetha (Jah is Saturn)."[2]

We must here point out a most extraordinary agreement between the above narratives of St. Luke, and the particulars which have come down to us respecting the symbols and rites of the Oracle of the temple of Delphi, Greece. We remind the reader Delphi is from Delphus, the Greek

who came into existence in that way, and, therefore, "the only begotten Son,"—is himself an extraction of the Seminal Logos, and is, therefore, the Father incarnate. Then the Apostle goes on to state that "by him were all things created that are in heaven and that are in earth, and he is before all things, and by him all things consist." The Logos, or Word, is an emanation of the Creator, and personified as the triune Elohim or Adonai, also symbolised by the white dove, wren, &c. Accordingly, therefore, the Father of the Lord Jesus is the *second* person of the triune Elohim, and not the Creator, Himself; in other words, Alawn, of the Druidic system, and Hermes, of other systems, symbolised by the middle stroke of \|/, but, incarnate, thus /|\. Alawn is identical with Tegid, the All Beautiful of the Druids, and also with their Taliesin or Lofty Hesus, or Hesons, or Jesus! Taliesin is one of the Titles of the Archdruid, and he says of himself—

> "I am a Tower, I am a Wren;
> I am a Carpenter, I am Wise."

Buarth Beirdd, Myvyrian.
p. 28, Ed. 1870, lines 10, 11.

By "Carpenter" (Saer, in the above), is evidently meant the Sun as the Architect of the Universe.

[1] Dr. Inman's *Ancient Faiths*, vol. I., p. 51.　[2] *Ibid*, vol. II., p. 501.

name for Womb. That Womb was set forth, symbolically,
by an opening in the rocks, called *Cave*. As if ascending
from that cave was a tripod (/|\). *That tripod was a
symbol of the Divine Word ascending as an echo (Adlais—
Allas) of \|/, as explained elsewhere in this work, through
the " Cave," which implied the Vulva of Cêd who, like
Elizabeth, is styled aged—"aged parent " (See* page 91).
On the apex of /|\, as the echo of \|/, where a circular seat
was constructed, sat a naked virgin, who received into her
matrix the Divine Word, which, by the instrumentality of
the virgin's substance, made itself heard. speaking inside
the virgin's body as a Divine Oracle, whose utterances were
interpreted by the priests. See also (in page 79) what we
state about the " cave " of mythologists. It is now
established beyond question that by the name Hyperboreans
(Dwellers beyond the North Winds), the Greeks meant
the Britons, who were Druids. And Pausanias x., 5, states
the Delphian Oracle was founded by the Hyperboreans,
especially Olen (Alawn) one of the Druidic titles of the sun
in spring, and, therefore, of the priest of the sun. Pausanias
also quotes one of the hymns of Bœa, a Delphian lady, to
that effect. Cicero argues, " it is impossible the Delphian
Oracle should ever have gained such repute in the world, or
have been enriched with such vast presents from almost all
kings and nations, had not the truth of its predictions been
sufficiently attested by the experience of ages." [1]

In reference to the foregoing, and what appears to be the
Delphian aspect of St. Luke's narrative of the Incarnation
of the Lord Jesus as the Divine " Word made flesh," we
beg to refer the reader to the observations of Tertullian,
given in page 167 ante.

At the still older Oracle of Dodona in the oak forest, it
is stated, in Bell's *Pantheon*, that the oracles were pro-

---

* In laurel.   [1] "Oracle of Delphi". Bell's *Pantheon*.

nounced by *three women* (Strabo), and that the temple *was
inhabited by the seven daughters of Atlas*, who were called
Dodonides and Atlantides. (*See* pages 14, 17, 18 and 20.)

In page 25, the figure /|\ rising from a boat on the water,
, implies the same thing as the figure of a crowned
child in page 66, also rising from a boat, viz., the Word or
Logos \|/ echoing back from Cêd on the sea, upon which
the earth was supposed to float. Cêd is, in both figures,
represented as a crescent-shaped Ark. As an Echo, the
Word is Adlais (Atlas), and is also called Tydain or the
Father of the Holy Voice—T-udain, Father of the Awen or
of the Holy Λ. The Holy Voice or Speech, otherwise
Word or Logos, is an abstraction of the Celi, himself, and
is clothed by Cêd, his mother, with a radiant new body, and
called Haul or Hu (Hee) Ail, or Second Hu. Λ is represented also as a white dove, wren. &c., coming out of the
Ark! In pp. 259-60-61, the descent of the Mind of the
Creator to be, forty hours later, reverberated back as Adlais
(Atlas), is described.

In accordance with the eastern error, the ascent from the
Red Sea (typical sea of Hades), is made to appear to have
taken place at the vernal equinox, or time of the Passover,
instead of at the winter solstice. Owing to this error, the
Crucifixion of the Lord Jesus is said to have occurred on
the anniversary of his Conception in the Virgin's Womb,
viz., on Nisan 14—solarly, March 25, o s. (Lady Day).

We also find that, in consequence of the same eastern
mistake the spring rite of partaking of the Eucharist is
associated with the ascent from the Red Sea. This is why
St. Paul saw in the water from the rock at Horeb a type of
the wine of the Last Supper, and in the manna a type of the
bread of that supper (*See* i. Cor., x.). As will be recollected,
Abbot Dunawd, in the sixth century, ordered an army

of Wales to drink the sacred water of the Dee, in memory
of the blood of the Lord Jesus, and kiss the earth in
memory of his body !   The sacred Dee flows from the Lake
of Tegid, called Bala Lake.   Tegid is a title of the sun in
spring, or time of the Passover, and, no doubt, the lake
had been, during untold ages, associated with the worship
of the emanations of Celi passing through the sun,
poetically personified as Tegid, and, as we have seen, receiving also several other titles at various periods of each
year.   It appears as if Abbot Dunawd had learned to
regard Tegid as typical of Jesus and of Moses, and that
he founded his direction to the army of Wales upon what
St. Paul states in the said chapter of the Epistle to the
Corinthians as to the typical character of the water of
Horeb and the Manna.

It must be repeated here that the Druids supposed
there was a system of gradations in the system of lives —
from the animal to the human — similar to the degrees of
terrestrial longitude in geography.   Instinct is called
Greddv in Welsh ; it is the same as Gradd (Degree).
The v termination to Greddv seems to be an abbreviation
of Van (Place or Station).   In Druidism the lines of the
terrestrial longitude are " furrows " in the garden, or earth
considered as a garden, whose husbandman is the sun
under as many titles as there were ancient languages. The
Druidic system of transmigration of lives, starting from
Hades, down south, and ascending to the equator of lives—
the position occupied by man as a free agent — was the
spiritual garden where lives grow by the fostering influence of
Celi (Cœlus) through the Word inhabiting the sun.   Then
after occupying the " line " of the equator of " lives," at
death those " lives " either passed higher to the realm of
the just made perfect, otherwise Gwynvyd, beyond the

northern heavens, or were relegated back to the Circles of Abed—or the degrees of the spiritual longitude—to be purified of the dross which sin had produced on *their* souls during their existence on earth as human beings, and to be again restored to the spiritual equator of this life for another trial against evil. The dual character given to the earth's anima in spring, that is to say, when the sun is above the terrestrial equator at that season, is the reason why Venus is called in Druidism also Enid (Soul)—*See* p. 16. For as the expression of the feminine principle of the great goddess-mother Cêd, she acts both as a mother of composite bodies and of souls.

Thus we have fully revealed the marvellous lore of the ancient Druids, preserved, most of it orally, by the bards of Glamorgan, the direct descendants and representatives of the Druidic priests and philosophers of heroic ancient Siluria. Anciently Caerlleon-on-Usk was included in Siluria. At Caerlleon-on-Usk, Arthur and his Knights of the Round Table disappeared in the mist of ages. So we have been the instrument to dispel the clouds, and to reveal beyond the gloom of time, the entire Druidic system of religion, which, at some remote epoch in the history of the earth, spread from the Baltic to the Ganges, and, during its incorrupt condition, guided all mankind to adore the author of the universe, taught the children of men to love one another, to aspire to a higher life, and that the only way to reach it is by the exercise of virtue.

MAY GOD DEFEND THE RIGHT!

APPENDIX.

THE SACRED TREES AND PLANTS OF THE DRUIDS.

THE OAK.—The female oak is called Derwen in Welsh, and the male oak is called Darwen in that language. The "wen" termination, in both instances, signifies Holy, and therefore Derwen signifies Holy Der; and Darwen, Holy Dar. Der is an abbreviated form of Daear, the Welsh for Earth; the tree as the producer of the sacred symbols, cup and acorn, is sacred to the feminine principle pervading the earth—the Anima Mundi. Dar seems to be identical with Daronwy (Thunderer), a title of the Deity. Reading is called Dar-llen in Welsh from Dar and Llen (learning, scholarship, erudition). Dar-ogan from Og (swift), and Cân (chant); the compound is used in the sense to foretell or to prophesy, no doubt in allusion to the practice of the Druids of chanting their teachings among oaks. The female oak is also called y Dderwen Fendigaid, which signifies the Blessed Holy Earth.

THE MISTLETOE (Viscum Album). — This eminently sacred shrub of the Druidic religion bears several names in Welsh. viz., Uchel-lawr (high stationed), Uchel-wydd (high shrub), and Pren-awyr (the tree of the air). As is well known, this shrub was eminently sacred among our Druidic ancestors. The ancient custom of the sexes kissing under it at the festive season of Christmas proves two things, namely, that the shrub was associated in the olden time with the winter solstice, and with the relation of the two sexes to each other. Now in spring, summer, and autumn, the produce of the earth were associated in the Druidic system with the sun under his various poetical titles ; and with the earth under her various poetical titles. At the winter solstice the old sun was poetically said to be unable any longer to fertilise (in Britain) the seeds of the earth, and the surface of the earth herself, under the title of Dyr-raith, was regarded as old and withered. But the mistletoe, in the midst of the general decay and death of vegetation, manifests vigorous life, and that, too, between the aged earth and the aged sun. It attains blooming perfection at the winter solstice. For these reasons, the mistletoe was sacred to Celi (Cœlus), and Côd (Cetus), the Divine Father and Divine Mother of the sun and the earth. The kissing under the mistletoe at the winter solstice was performed as a loving symbolical act, perpetuating commemoratively the affec-tionate relationship eternally existing between Celi and Côd, the universal parents.

THE HOLLY.—This tree is one of the shrubs with which all Celts decorate their habitations with its branches and crimson berries at the winter solstice. In Welsh the tree is called Celyn : Côl (concealed) yn (yni—energy)—Con-cealed Energy. The allusion is to the source of perennial energy, viz., Celi, and Côd, though concealed in Britain at the winter solstice. The English word Holly signifies Holy.

THE IVY.—In Welsh ivy is called Iorwg, which name signifies the Green of the Leader Lord, implying the earliest creating attribute of Celi or Côd, directed to operate on the atomic particles of matter, and thereby commence the work of creation. The ivy, too, seems prone to clothe things inclined to fall into decay and ruin, and to support things tottering on their foundation. "The women" (of the British Isles), "crowned with Ivy, celebrated his (Bacchus) nocturnal rites upon the shore of the Northern Ocean."—*Dionysius the Geographer* 1., p. 170. *Kissos* or Ivy is a

Greek title of Bacchus. The extreme fondness of Goats for Ivy is well known. Doubtless, this is the reason why the Ivy became a sacred plant among the Druids. It is similar to the reason why acorn eating swine became sacred among them.

THE LEEK.—This is called *Ceninen* in Welsh. It is a symbol of verdure and the light of the sun. Its roots symbolise the sun's rays, and should be always worn with the root uppermost. We are inclined to believe the old Druidic name is a compound of *Cen*, as in *Cenad* (an Ambassador), and *yni* (Energy), with the " i " at the end omitted, and " yn," alone, standing for a plural sign. Cenynan is the name singular, the " an " termination being a diminutive sign. Some may suppose Cèn signifies the skin of anything ; but the terminations " yn " (plural) and " an " (singular) militate against that supposition.

BIRCH —This is called Bedwen or Holy Bed in Welsh. According to tradition it was with a bough of this tree the Druids lustrated their disciples with dew held in a boat-shaped vessel, hence bed, here meaning boat, symbol of Cêd as the Ark of the sun called the Llong Voel (Naked Ship). It is with a bough of this tree the Welsh mothers still chastise their children. Using the sacred bough implies the chastisement, though painful, is an act of love. The maypole was always one of these trees ; and the birch was invariably used in the construction of the gallows.

THE EMBLEMS OF THE DRUIDS.

At the Vernal Equinox	— The Shamrock.
At the Summer Solstice	— The Blessed Holy Oak.
At the Autumnal Equinox	— Ears of Wheat.
At the Winter Solstice	— The Mistletoe.

THE NAME "DUW CELI."

THE ANTIQUITY OF THE PEITHYNEN.

The following, by the author, appeared in the *Western Mail*, on February 20th, 1893 :—

In the deeply interesting leading article on Thursday on the Rev. Canon D. Silvan Evans' Dictionary of the Welsh language there are some points which, in the interest of pure history, should be noticed without a moment's delay.

The first of those points is the opinion of the learned Welsh scholar that the Welsh Celi, a title of the Most High, is a corruption of the Latin Cœlum (Heaven). The Rev. D. Silvan Evans may as well say that the Duw Dad (God the Father) of the ancient Britons is derived from the Teu—Tates (Teutates) of the Latins!

Now, Dr. Potter (a late Archbishop of Canterbury), states as follows in his *Religion of Greece*, vol. i., p. 518 :—

"Writers of ancient fables report that Ouranos, whom the Latins call Cœlus, King of the *Atlantic Islands*, was reputed the father of all the gods, and gave his name to the heavens, *which, from him*, were, by the Greeks, termed Ouranos, *and, by the Latins, Cœlum*, because he invented astronomy, which was unknown till his time" (Diodorus Siculus, *Lib*. iii., p. 132, et Scriptores Mythologici). There is no doubt Uranus, Ouranos, and Aaron are, likewise, each the British Arawn, a title of the Sun, compared at the end of the solar year to an old man. Arawn signifies the same thing as Aros (to wait, as an old man), hence the proverb, *Hir yw aros Arawn* (it is long waiting for Arawn). But Celi is not the Sun. He is the Creator Himself, and Cêd (*Cetus* of the Latins, and *Der Ketos* of the Greeks) is his consort. All the gods and goddesses of Paganism are their emanations personified, hence Diodorus Siculus (B.C. 44,) could truly state that Cœlus, "King of the Atlantic Islands," was "the father of all the gods."

The Druids compared the Sun's annual "life" to the "life" of man on earth. The Sun was a babe at the winter solstice, and in old Welsh poems he was called "Crowned Babe." At the vernal equinox he was Tegid, and called also Taliesin (or Lofty Hesus); at the autumnal equinox he was Tegid Voel or Bald Tegid, with but few hairs (rays) left. From that date (Sept. 23) to Dec. 20, he was known by the names Dyfnwawl Moelmud (sombre light, bald, and dumb), Saidwrn, Pan, and, finally, Arawn. Many nations, except the British, confounded the Old Sun, at the winter solstice, with the Almighty Celi, and Morwyn (the Virgin) with Cêd. The Old Sun was said to be the father of every next year's "Crowned Babe," who is represented as a trinity, symbolised, in Britain, by the *body and two wings* of the sacred wren, and, in the East, by the sacred white dove of the Phœnicians. Many other nations greeted the "Crowned Babe," or New Sun, with the cry, "Hail to the Dove—the giver of light!" Cœlus, "King of the Atlantic Islands," is the Celi of the Druids, that is to say, the Creator; and, as seen above, a learned scholar, 44 years before the Christian era, declares the Latin Cœlum and the Greek Ouranos are derived from the name of the "King of the Atlantic Islands." Those islands can be no other than the British Isles. In my *Light of Britannia* I prove the Greek Atlas, after whom the Atlantides, the root of the name "Atlantic," is no other than the British Adlais (the reverberation of the personified melodious voice of Celi of the Druidic system). Celi is identical with the *Agnosto Theo* of the Greeks, whom St. Paul told the Athenians on

Mars Hill he preached unto them. He is identical, too, with Amen-Ra of the Egyptians. The meaning of the names in each instance is the Hidden One !

The second point in the Welsh lexicographer's statements is the allegation that the Druidic alphabet, called "Coelbren of the Bards," is a system of letters " modified forms of the Roman alphabet." It is very difficult to write with patience any comments on such an absurd statement !

It is well known that the Roman alphabet, as distinguished from the older one of the Druidic bards, is called " Coelbren of the Monks." If there were not two systems of letters in existence in the British Isles, why two separate names for two such systems ?

Julius Cæsar (B.C. 99-44) states the inhabitants of France (Gaul) were the pupils of the inhabitants of Britain, and we are told by implication by Cæsar that the Gauls were literary men ; for he states (*Lib* v., cap. 48) that he had to write a letter to Cicero in the Greek language, lest, being intercepted, his (Cæsar's) designs might be known to the enemy. But that the Gauls could read both Greek and Latin writings is made clear by Cæsar, who states that the registers of the Helvetii (*Lib.* i., cap. 29) were written in the Greek language. The inference derived from the writing to Cicero in Greek instead of the Latin tongue is, that the last-named was better known than Greek by the pupils of the Britons. The Latin poet Lucan wrote as follows of the Ancient Britons : —

> " The bending willows into barks they twine,
> Then line the work with skins of slaughtered kine,
> Such are the floats Venetian fishers know
> Where in dull marshes stands the settling Po.
>
> On such to neighbouring Gaul, allured by gain,
> *The Nobler Britons* cross the swelling main.
> Like these, when fruitful Egypt lies afloat,
> The Memphian artist builds his reedy boat."

Can it be believed, for a moment, the diciples were better scholars than their masters, the Britons ? Further, can it be supposed by any man in his senses that a people who could read both Latin and Greek—a people who, according to all antiquity, had a literature of a wonderful description—had no alphabet of their own !

The following is one of the oldest statements extant in the old British language :—

" Einigain the Great was the first that made a letter to be a sign of the first vocalisation that was ever heard, namely /|\, the name of God. After that, Einigain the Great saw reason for other and different organs of voice and speech, and subjected the rays to other combinations, from which were made the signs I and R and S, whence they were sixteen signs or letters. After that, wise men were appointed to commit them to memory and knowledge, according to the art which he made ; and those men were called " Gwyddoniad."

The last name signifies, literally, Woodmen, but to this day scholarship is called " Gwyddoniaeth " in the Welsh language. The inference is, that the writing was carved on wooden "books," each of which we still call " Peithynen." In allusion to the old mode of carving literature on bars of wood, the Welshman says " cutting " my name instead of " writing " it. I am told some of the records of the British Exchequer are kept by notching bars of hard wood called Tally or Tallies. In Welsh the verb signifying to " pay " is called *talu* (pronounced tally).

In reference to the above statement that the first letter of the Druidic alphabet, viz., /|\ or Λ, was a symbol of the name of God, I find this confirmed in Hebrew writings, quoted by the Rev. Thomas Maurice in his *Indian Antiquities*, Vol. iv., p. 582, where it is stated that " all the letters of the Hebrew Alphabet depend upon the name Jehovah," and it is represented by the letter Shin, which is the sign /I\ rendered thus \I/. " The three branches arising out of the root of this letter are an emblem of the Heavenly Father, Jehovah, our Lord Jehovah." (*Zohar*, fol. 54, col. 2). Lifting the three fingers by the priest in giving the Benediction signifies the sacred Name. It is also stated the Name is described by the rays of the Sun.

Before the Rev. Canon D. Silvan Evans, B. D., can prove that the " Coelbren y Beirdd " (the Druidic alphabet) " are modified forms of the Roman alphabet," he must prove likewise that the Hebrew alphabet also is derived from the same source, and destroy the accepted doctrine of the whole learned world that the Hebrew alphabet is derived from the hieroglyphics or sacred symbols of the ancient Egyptians.

Thus we have it clearly established that carving literature on bars of wood is as old as the Welsh language, the ancient tongue of the British Isles; that, as in the Hebrew alphabet, the symbol of the name of God is the key to that alphabet. Then we have a poem bearing date 1450, composed by Gytto'r Glyn full of allusions to carving literature on bars of wood. *Vide* Iolo MSS., p. 694 :

> " Felling trees to form a song,
> Llawdden, with his axe,
> Will not leave wood materials
>   Wherever he comes ;
> Extensive is the work of his craft,
> The felling of trees for the keys of verse."

It is really a very great misfortune that in a work of so much learning as the Rev. Canon's great Welsh and English dictionary such things as I have pointed out disfigure it.

In reference to the above most sacred sign of the British Druids, which sign is identical with the celebrated Tripod of Apollo at Delphi, Archbishop Potter in his *Grecian Antiquities*, vol. i. p. 323, states as follows: " Phurnutus (Initio Pluti) will have the Tripod to have been sacred to Apollo, either because of the perfection of the Number Three, or in allusion to the THREE CELESTIAL CIRCLES, two of which ' (the two Tropics) "the Sun touches, and passes over the third" (the Equator) " in his annual circuit. And that Scholiast upon Aristophanes will have the three legs of the Tripod to signify the knowledge of God." The Tripod, as the white dove, wren, " Crowned Babe," each signifying the same thing, rising from the sea each December 22nd, from Côd, the Divine Mother of the Word, is thus fabled by the Greeks :—

" Certain fishermen at Miletus having sold their draught to some persons that stood by, cast their net into the water and drew up a golden Tripod. A quarrel ensued as to the right of ownership, and a visit to Delphi was the result. The Oracle there replied as follows :—

> " Give it him whose *wisdom* claims a right (to it)
> Above all others."   *Ibid*, p. 321.

It has been clearly established the Britons were called Hyperboreans, and, in the story of Abaris, also Scythians, by Ancient Greeks. Archbishop Potter, p. 325, has the following :—" Bœo, a Delphian lady, in one of her hymns, reports that Olen " (Alawn ?) " with the Hyperboreans, first instituted this " (Delphi) " Oracle, and returned answers in heroic verse, of which he was the first inventor." Her words we find in Pausanias (A.D. 200) to be thus :—

> " Where Hyperboreans, to thy lasting praise,
> Eternal Oracles did consecrate ;
> No Grecian yet, warm'd with poetic fire,
> Could fit th' unpolished language to the lyre,
> Till the first Priest of Apollo, Olen, rose
> And chang'd for smoother verse their stunning prose."

Archbishop Potter also further states :—" The Pytha " (Priestess) " being placed on the Tripod, received the Divine afflatus in her belly. She was no sooner inspired but she began immediately to swell, and foam at the mouth, tearing her hair, cutting her flesh, and in all her other behaviour appearing like one frantic and distracted.' Plutarch describes one of these priestesses as becoming so frantic that the priests themselves were so terrified that they ran away. This Pytha died. " Some say " states His Grace, " that under the Tripod " (where was the cave symbol of the Vulva of Cèd) " sometimes a serpent appeared that returned answers, and that the Pytha was once killed by it. *And Eusebius reports that a serpent rolled itself about the Tripod.* The Oracle gave its answers only in Spring.

" When Apollo forsook Delphi, he betook himself to the Hyperboreans—Scythians, as we learn from Claudian : —

> " The fair Apollo leaves his Delphic home,
> O'er distant Hyperborean climes to roam."
>
> Dr. Potter's *Grecian Antiquities*, vol i., p. 331.

DÂWEN, COWBRIDGE.

This is the name of the river running N.S. through the town of Cowbridge, Glamorganshire. In the native language, the town, from time immemorial, has borne the name of Pont-y-Von, *i.e.*, Bridge of the Cow (*see* foot-note p. 51). It appears the Romans gave the name Taberna

Amne (Tavern by the River,) to the country on the east
side of the Dâwen, and Bovium (Oxen or Cows,) to the
district on the west side of it, where the old town stood, and
still stands ; and that the name applied as far as Bovirton,
the name of an ancient mansion four miles beyond the town
of Cowbridge. Thus a "Cow" was associated with the
locality at least eighteen centuries ago.

Dâwen is a compound of two words, *Dâ* and *Wen*.
The *Dâ* is the Welsh legal name for goods or chattels.
It is applied to horned cattle generally, but with more
definiteness to cows in particular. " Cerdda i vovyn y
Dâ," would be understood by a Glamorgan peasant to
imply exclusively " Go and fetch the *Cows*."

'*Wen*, the second word of the compound, is an abbreviated form of Gwen, the *g* being dropped in the compound
for the sake of euphony. Gwen, in Dâwen, signifies Holy
(feminine), Gwyn being the masculine for Holy. Therefore,
Dâwen signifies Holy Dâ. But Dâ is plural for cows.
As applied to horned cattle, Dâ has no form singular, but
Wen is in the singular number. Therefore, we conclude
the Dâ, in Dâwen was used in the singular number for
the sacred White Cow of the Druids during the Taurine
period (4,619 B.C. to 2,505 B.C.) The bridge leading
into the old town, over the Dâwen river, is named after the
Vôn, mutated from Môn, which is another Welsh word
signifying Cow. At present *Buhwch*, or Sow of Bu (Bee)
i.e. Bull, is the name for Cow.

No doubt, in remote times, a vast Druidic circular
sanctuary, sacred to Nature, stood here on the bank of the
river, and that the river received its name from it.

BARRY ISLAND, GLAMORGAN.

It seems that Barry Island, like the Island of Delos, was, in Druidic times, sacred, and that, after the introduction of Christianity into South Wales, and its adoption in lieu of the former religion, it continued to be the resort of pilgrims. Leland, who visited Barry Island about A.D., 1540, writes as follows :—Right against Aber Barry " lies Barry Isle. The passage into it at full sea is a flight of a bow shot across ; as much as the Thames above the bridge. At low water there is a broken causeway to go over, or else over the shallow streamlet of Barry Brook on the sands. The island is about a mile in circumference, and has very good corn, grass, and some wood.   *   * There is no dwelling on the island, but there is in the *middle* of it a fair little chapel of St. Barrok,[1] *where much pilgrimage* was formerly (usid)." *See* " Cave," p. 27, and " belly of Ced," p. 28.

Giraldus Cambrensis (vol. I., ch. vi.), referring to the island, states :—" On a rock in the sea here, is a small cleft (cave), to which if you put your ear, you will hear a noise as of a forge. Sometimes the blast of the bellows, sometimes the stroke of the hammer, sometimes the loud gratings of the grindstone and the iron, the hissing of the steel, and the roaring of the fire. I could easily suppose these sounds to be occasioned by the sea, which enters these cavities unseen, were it not that the same noises are heard when the sea is out and the shore left bare, as well as when it is in." Camden in his *Britannia*, vol. ii., p. 494, has the following in reference to Giraldus' statement :—" Clemens Alexandrinus (*Stromata*, vii. Book),

---

[1] Camden gives this name as " Baruch." Doubtless this is a corruption of Bru (Bree) Âch Bruâch (Vulva, Source of Progeny).

states, ' historians say there is in the Island of Britain a *cavern* under a mountain, having a cleft at the top ; and when the wind blows into the cavern, and whistles in its recesses, the sound of a number of cymbals is heard.   For the repercussion of the wind makes a very great noise.' "

It is needless to remind the reader that each island, as symbol of the round earth as the belly of Côd, with the umbilicus, of course, communicating with the matrix in its centre, was, like each sacred tumulus, supposed to be a mound, which foreign writers would naturally suppose to be a " Mountain."   The superstitious exaggerations of Giraldus are probably due to his fancy being heated by the tales he heard during his visit respecting the associations of the supernatural with Barry Island, in popular legends. He wrote about A.D. 1187.

ERRATUM.—p. 428, line second: read "*Borium*, a name derived from Bos, the Latin for Ox or Cow."

* DANIEL OWEN AND CO., LIMITED, CARDIFF.

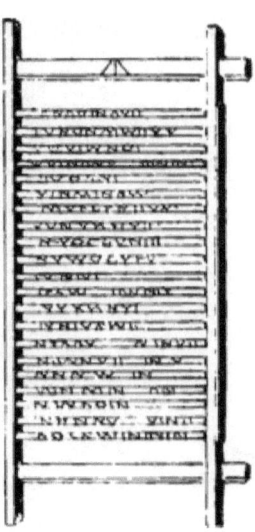

AN OLD DRUIDIC BOOK, CALLED "PEITHYNAN."

Each bar, which revolves, is four-sided and has a line of poetry carved on each — a stanza of four lines on each bar. In the reign of Henry IV., the English Parliament made it a criminal offence to keep Welsh children at learning, or to apprentice them to any trade or calling in any town or borough of the realm. See "Ordinances of Wales," January, 1401. The Welsh People then fell back on the ancient Druidic mode of imparting education on Bars of Wood.

www.ingramcontent.com/pod-product-compliance
Lightning Source LLC
Chambersburg PA
CBHW031055110726
47900CB00003B/941